Praise for *The Lives of Jewish Things*

"From the timeworn benches of ancient synagogues to a Bedouin hut repurposed as a Jewish sukkah within the complex Israeli-Palestinian milieu, this collection of essays unveils new dimensions of Jewish history and culture. While much of our understanding of Judaism's past is anchored in texts predominantly authored by men of the rabbinic elite, the contributors of this volume reveal how fleeting artifacts of material culture can shed fresh light on the daily, religious, and social lives of individuals often relegated to the margins of historical narratives—children, women, and the unknown figures who shaped Jewish societies across diverse eras and regions."

—Shalom Sabar, professor emeritus,
The Hebrew University of Jerusalem

"*The Lives of Jewish Things* speaks with rare and thoughtful eloquence to our own fraught historical moment, a time of heightened awareness of the power of performativity and keen sensitivity to topics such as appropriation, cultural ownership, and identity. While the essays in this volume address and interrogate the capacious nature of the concept of 'Jewish things,' their shared focus on specific items, lived experiences, and often overlooked corners of global Jewish history brings a curio cabinet of stories vividly to life. In doing so, the volume as a whole reframes and deepens key discussions taking place in Jewish studies and cultural history more broadly. A true gem!"

—Laura Lieber, professor for the transregional
history of religion, University of Regensburg

"As Jewish museums proliferate around the world, greater scholarly attention is being paid to what they display and, more generally, to what constitutes Jewish material culture. *The Lives of Jewish Things* offers an array of essays addressing these issues, including insightful contributions by some of the leading academics, artists, and curators on the subject."

—Jeffrey Shandler, author of *Homes of the Past:
A Lost Jewish Museum*

The Lives of Jewish Things

Raphael Patai Series in Jewish Folklore and Anthropology

A complete listing of the books in this series can be found online at wsupress.wayne.edu.

The Lives of Jewish Things

COLLECTING AND CURATING MATERIAL CULTURE

Edited by Gabrielle Anna Berlinger and
Ruth von Bernuth

Wayne State University Press
Detroit

© 2025 by Wayne State University Press, Detroit, Michigan 48201. All rights reserved. No part of this book may be reproduced without formal permission.

ISBN 9780814350454 (paperback)
ISBN 9780814350461 (hardcover)
ISBN 9780814350478 (ebook)

Library of Congress Control Number: 2024934557

On cover: Wimpel made for Asher Berlinger, born 11 Tishrei 5670 (September 26, 1909), by his father Naphtali Berlinger. Photo credit: Gerald Lynas and Aron Berlinger.

Cover design by Will Brown Design.

Published with support from the fund for the Raphael Patai Series in Jewish Folklore and Anthropology.

Wayne State University Press rests on Waawiyaataanong, also referred to as Detroit, the ancestral and contemporary homeland of the Three Fires Confederacy. These sovereign lands were granted by the Ojibwe, Odawa, Potawatomi, and Wyandot Nations, in 1807, through the Treaty of Detroit. Wayne State University Press affirms Indigenous sovereignty and honors all tribes with a connection to Detroit. With our Native neighbors, the press works to advance educational equity and promote a better future for the earth and all people.

Wayne State University Press
Leonard N. Simons Building
4809 Woodward Avenue
Detroit, Michigan 48201-1309

Visit us online at wsupress.wayne.edu.

CONTENTS

Introduction   1
   Gabrielle Anna Berlinger and Ruth von Bernuth

I. Jewish Things in Landscape and Soundscape

1. Canonizing the Ephemeral: A Bedouin Structure in an Ecotourism Ethno-Enterprise and a Jewish-Bedouin Sukkah in an Art Museum   17
   Diego Rotman

2. Sound Objects: Music, Material Culture, and the Sound Study of the Synagogue   49
   Francesco Spagnolo

3. Please Be Seated: Benches and the Infrastructure of Judaism   65
   Juliana Ochs Dweck

II. Jewish Things on Display

4. The Evidence Room: Contemporary Holocaust Reliquary   95
   Laura Levitt

5. Making Space for Jewish Culture in Polish Folk and Ethnographic Museums: Curating Social Diversity after Ethnic Cleansing   117
   Erica Lehrer and Monika Murzyn-Kupisz

6. Jewish Things at the Museum of Fine Arts Boston: A History   163
   Simona Di Nepi

7. Notes for a History of the Judaic Art Gallery of the
   North Carolina Museum of Art   199
   John Coffey

III. Jewish Things Up Close: Two Southern Studies

8. Sanctified by War: A Tale of Two Silver Bowls   219
   Dale Rosengarten

9. My Grandfather's West Texas Salvage Store:
   Prophetic Lessons for Twenty-First-Century Museums   231
   Suzanne Seriff

Afterword   273
Barbara Kirshenblatt-Gimblett

Acknowledgments   283

Appendix: Collectors' Roundtable: Gabriel Goldstein in Conversation with Max N. Berry, Jane Gershon Weitzman, and William L. Gross   285

Contributors   309

Index   313

INTRODUCTION

Gabrielle Anna Berlinger and Ruth von Bernuth

An "old golden ring" topped with a miniature Gothic tower and engraved with Hebrew lettering appeared in the cabinet of curiosities installed in the sixteenth-century court of Duke Albrecht V of Bavaria in Munich.[1] This cabinet, like others of its time, was a true "repository of artificial and marvelous things"—a cultural production that Flemish scholar Samuel Quiccheberg remarked should serve as a "theater" for viewers to "be able to acquire a unique knowledge and admirable understanding of things."[2] The old golden ring inside this cabinet of curiosity was a marvelous thing. It was displayed alongside other ornate rings variously decorated with zodiac signs, Hebrew, Arabic, and Latin scripts, coats of arms, Christian iconography, and even diminutive images of Roman emperors. By the start of the twentieth century, however, curators and scholars began to recognize this ring for its specifically Jewish history and significance, featuring it in collections of Jewish objects rather than among eclectic "other" marvels. From its sixteenth-century display in Duke Albrecht's cabinet to its inclusion in the opening exhibition of the Jewish Museum in Munich in 2007, this ring has evoked wonder and signaled cultural positioning through its collection and curation. The simultaneous Jewish and non-Jewish histories of this ring reveal its variable meanings and sustained relevance across cultural, spatial, and temporal contexts.

Like the example of this wedding ring, *The Lives of Jewish Things: Collecting and Curating Material Culture* provokes questions about how and when things might be considered Jewish, or decidedly not Jewish, as they move through shifting perceptions of purpose and use. As they explore the complex range of materials in the category "Jewish things,"

FIGURE I.1. Jewish wedding ring, ca. 1500. ResMüSch.III, Kat.52, DI002984, BSV–, Treasury, Munich Residence, Bayerische Verwaltung der staatlichen Schlösser, Gärten und Seen.

our contributors examine explicitly Jewish things used by Jews in their religious and cultural lives, everyday things turned Jewish things by virtue of their use, and things with imagined Jewish connections. All these things have the potential to become part of Jewish and non-Jewish collections. They move into and out of domestic spaces, synagogues, museums, and marketplaces, and meanings deepen as contexts multiply. Because religious and cultural objects can serve ceremonial or everyday functions depending on their contexts of use, the multiple identities of these things reveal shifting values. Each time these materials cross geographic, cultural, or social borders, they enter new dialogues about maker and user, buyer and seller, and insider and outsider, and their Jewishness is recreated.

The Lives of Jewish Things probes the multiple roles that Jewish material things play in individual and collective consciousness and in private and public experience. This book is thus soundly situated within the field of material culture studies. Bernie Herman describes material culture studies as based on an "ability to imagine, evoke, and question the myriad relationships among people and artifacts in whatever way they described them for their own purposes and on the basis of what we learn from surviving objects and their uses."[3] In this volume our contributors examine this accumulation of relations—intellectual, social, and emotional—that things acquire throughout their lives and the necessary negotiations of meaning that ensue. Within the subfield of religious material culture, scholars have mapped these webs of connection, tracking patterns of relationship between person and thing not only for their symbolic meaning but also for their social and cultural meanings.[4] They have recognized the range of values that these materials gain as they move through systems of exchange and individual encounter. Recent studies have also illuminated the significance of the affective experience of a religious material thing, its sensory, emotional, and felt characteristics that engage people in religious expression and belief.[5] From these perspectives, material culture scholars expand the study of religions through the lens of "vernacular religion"—the lived experience of encountering, interpreting, and practicing religion in everyday life.[6] As Herman notes, it is this lived experience of relating to a thing that upends the notion of any absolute meaning inherent in an object, instead making absolute the "possibility of a range of meanings—conflicted, situational, enduring, and ephemeral" in any material thing.[7] By centering people and things in the study of religion, material culture scholars foreground how and when religion is at work each day, recognizing new meanings that emerge in and across changing contexts.

The contributors to this volume importantly advance religious material culture study by contributing cases specifically drawn from Jewish religion and culture. The Jewish things in this book include ritual structures and retail spaces, ceremonial Judaica and dining room dishes, synagogue sounds and artifacts of atrocity. They are physical and spatial, explicit and implicit, remnants and projections.[8] These are things shaped out of nature and culture that transform unmarked spaces into intentional places. They are experience and expression made material.[9] By studying the layers of meaning within the master contexts of the creation, consumption, and communication of these Jewish things, our contributors identify distinctly Jewish expressions of attachment to place, displacement and exile, cultural custom and religious practice, community and belonging.[10]

However, a focus on the role that material culture plays in Jewish experience is not new. Seminal scholarship on the history and diversity of Jewish art by such scholars as Richard I. Cohen, Vivian Mann z"l, and Shalom Sabar laid the foundation for mid-twentieth-century attention to Jewish aesthetics and creative expression.[11] Expanding their focus to include material culture, more broadly, Barbara Kirshenblatt-Gimblett and Jeffrey Shandler introduced a 2007 special issue of *Material Religion* by stating, "The so-called 'People of the Book' have produced a rich inventory of items—ritual objects, articles of clothing, furniture, buildings, posters, souvenirs, utensils, games, toys, dolls, collectibles, greeting cards, postcards, stamps, coins, photographs, product packaging—that testifies to an extensive and complex engagement with material culture over the centuries and around the world."[12] That publication examined the great degree to which material culture figures in Jewish religious practice in the United States.[13] Further studies of Jewish material culture across the fields of religious studies, American studies, women and gender studies, anthropology, and folklore studies have continued to counter the misconception of aniconic Jewish histories and practices.[14] This growing research illuminates modes of subjective and affective engagement with Jewish experience through the creation, collection, and interpretation of material culture.[15] *The Lives of Jewish Things* attests to this fundamental and ongoing engagement with material things in Jewish life not only to express one's relationship with Jewish religion or culture but also to communicate one's orientation to *other* people, cultural conditions, and social landscapes—Jewish and not Jewish—throughout the world.

In previous studies of Jewish material culture, scholars have considered how particular things can signify Jewish belief and practice in more and less explicit ways (consider the menorah or the bagel), and they have illuminated the range of expression attached to each of these Jewish things. The designation of these things as more or less explicitly Jewish is rooted in the halachic (Jewish legal) determination of the level of holiness of a material thing and in the ritual or ordinary context of interpretation and use.[16] Such studies highlight the ability of Jewish things to change value and purpose as the social circumstances and cultural customs of Jewish populations change as well. The contributors to *The Lives of Jewish Things*, however, expand the study of Jewish things beyond the explicitly Jewish frame in an original way: They consider Jewish things that move between Jewish and non-Jewish realms. The things in this book can be described as both Jewish and not, as instruments of both religious and artistic practice, as objects that circulate in both public and private realms, as artifacts both familiar and strange. These are materials that move, things that reside in the interstitial spaces between absolute classifications. These Jewish things symbolize home and dislocation; they acknowledge community and isolation; they evoke trauma, memory, and dream. Through an embrace of their ambivalence and change in meaning across contexts, the contributors advance a future for Jewish material culture studies in recognizing the simultaneous histories of tradition and transformation across cultures that have sustained these things. Recall the opening example of the sixteenth-century golden wedding ring—a Jewish thing layered with distinct meanings and functions throughout its existence, challenging any single interpretation. Like that ring, this book maps the adaptations of material things of Jewish religious and cultural experience, communicating the alternating narratives of Jewish presence and absence around the world and over time.

The Jewish things presented in *The Lives of Jewish Things* could be considered individual pieces unto themselves, but they also might be considered parts of a greater whole. When they are a part of something greater, they belong to collections cared for by both public and private stewards and are housed in museums, sacred sanctuaries, and everyday spaces. Their value is renewed when they move into closed sets that lend them new meaning in order.[17] That transformative renewal is evident in the range of collections represented by the Jewish things in this book—from the Jewish ceremonial objects displayed in the Judaic Art Gallery of the North Carolina Museum of Art, to the Jewish artifacts exhibited in non-Jewish museums across Poland, to the Bedouin shelter turned Jewish sukkah installed at the Israel Museum, to the singular expressions stored in the homes of private collectors. These Jewish things reveal the varied conceptual goals—personal, practical, and existential—that are expressed through their collection in Jewish and non-Jewish museums and in public and private spaces.

Similarly, these Jewish pieces reflect the specific interpretations of their curators when displayed in art, historical, or cultural exhibitions. When curated, they are selected and arranged with aesthetic and intellectual rationale to convey a message. The process of curation is a process of knowledge production, as meaning is created through intentional association, close or distant, between the things on display. Whether the Jewish things in this book have been exhibited alongside other Jewish things or displayed among non-Jewish things, arguments about Jewish experiences of belonging run throughout. From early modern period cabinets of curiosity until today, Jewish things in collection, curated and concealed, reveal the conceptual and creative messages of their private and public guardians. They are gathered and arranged to address difference and similarity, social division and cohesion, removal and return.

As editors of this book, we are engaged with cultural institutions and local communities outside the academy in our own work, valuing public-facing and community-embedded perspectives in our research. As such, in the fall of 2018 we co-organized the three-day symposium "Wandering Objects: Collecting and Interpreting Jewish Things."[18] The North Carolina Museum of Art and the Carolina Center for Jewish Studies at the University of North Carolina, Chapel Hill, partnered to host an international slate of scholars, curators, and collectors whose work seeks to reveal the multiple lives of Jewish things in order to learn about the generations of people who have cared for and about them.[19] They hailed from diverse settings—museums, private collections, archives, and universities—to demonstrate how multilayered understandings of object collection, curation, and interpretation can create more nuanced understandings about the purpose and place of material things in Jewish life. These experts brought to the symposium, and now bring to this volume, particular intentions in their engagement with Jewish things, and, as such, this volume highlights the multiple voices and distinct narrative styles that represent their diverse backgrounds.

Uniformly, however, these essays illustrate how the bridging of scholarly and curatorial perspectives can deepen awareness of the multidimensional value of a thing. By placing these museum curators and private collectors, artists, archivists, and research scholars in dialogue through this varied set of case studies, *The Lives of Jewish Things* weaves together four approaches to understanding the layered meanings of Jewish things: (1) historical contextualization, (2) collection and interpretive display, (3) close material study of the object, and (4) ethnographic analysis. Although many scholars use several of these approaches in their work, most rely on and foreground one. Critically, this book laces together all four approaches to paint a complex picture of Jewish things that relates their temporal, aesthetic, and sociocultural significance on equal ground.

In this holistic approach to material culture study that crosses disciplines and bridges public-academic divides, our contributors examine object creation, use, and reuse over time to tell stories. Their stories are the unwritten narratives of Jewish experience that diversify the authors and actors of Jewish history and practice. Their studies reveal the different relationships that people form with these materials as modes of communication about Jewish pasts, customs, and communities. These relationships inform the collection, preservation, and presentation of these things—all processes of evaluation of the thing itself as well as of the cultural histories, practices, and beliefs that lend the object its broader contextual meaning. This book begins with the material thing and ends with multiple spheres of meaning embedded in new narratives of commitment to and divergence from Jewishness, across cultures and over time.[20]

The volume opens with three case studies of Jewish material things that have moved through lived spaces largely outside the museum to acquire different value. The first case centers on the transformation of a Bedouin hut built and used by the Jahalin tribe in the Judean Desert into a Jewish ritual sukkah built and used by Jews in Jerusalem (Chapter 1). Performance scholar and artist Diego Rotman examines how these same materials of shelter then transmuted a third time to become an art installation in the Israel Museum. Begun as a commissioned art project, the physical movement and critical transformation of the vernacular structure first owned by the Jahalin tribe, then by Israeli artists-activists, and finally by a national art institution highlight the poetics and politics of its charged presence across changing landscapes. Rotman studies the afterlife of the construction as well, raising questions about the lasting relationships between tourism, heritage, place, and material authenticity.

In the second chapter, curator Francesco Spagnolo suggests that considering the sounds of the synagogue space rather than the music of this house of prayer can open a rich new area of material culture study. Spagnolo illustrates how a "sound study" of the synagogue can frame music *as* material culture, allowing for analysis of sounds made by both people and ritual objects. By examining "modes of sound production that characterize synagogue rituals," he introduces a new methodology at the intersection of music and material culture with which to make meaning of individual engagement with synagogue space, performance, and community.

The ubiquitous bench in Chapter 3 is an embodied object that evokes personal memory and structures ritual experience in Jewish spatial histories, both ordinary and extraordinary. Examining benches of learning, benches of prayer, benches used for life-cycle events, and benches of exclusion, curator Juliana Ochs Dweck asserts that this humble piece of furniture is the quintessential object for a diasporic people. A piece of the everyday environment becomes an instrument of negotiation between the self and society, a material performance of the balance of will and circumstance.

The volume continues with four case studies of the complex meanings made through the display of Jewish material things on exhibition. In Chapter 4, on the Robert Jan van Pelt and University of Waterloo team's 2016 Architectural Biennale exhibition of Holocaust material, religious and gender studies scholar Laura Levitt analyzes objects of the past that are fixed in place yet still moving forward. She reflects on this exhibition as "a container of memory" that aids in the preservation of Holocaust memory. The newly constructed space to hold these pieces actively creates a memory process for the future as much as it memorializes the past.

Since the early 2000s, a series of new Jewish museums have been opened in Europe, among them the Jewish Museum in Berlin and, most important, POLIN Museum of the History of Polish Jews. Other Jewish museums have revamped their core exhibitions, including the Jewish Museum of Switzerland in Basel, the Jewish Museum in Frankfurt (Main, Germany), the Jewish Museum in Budapest, and the Jewish Museum in New York. Whereas these Jewish museums and new exhibitions have been highlighted in conferences and publications in recent years, various collections of Jewish things also exist within larger diverse collections in art and ethnography museums.[21] The histories of these collections and how Jewish material things are integrated into or separated from the museums to which they belong are often ignored. In Chapter 5 anthropologist and curator Erica Lehrer and Monika Murzyn-Kupisz offer a discussion of lesser known exhibitions of Jewish things in three non-Jewish museums in Poland and their shared commemorations of Polish Jewish history.

In her essay curator Simona Di Nepi notes that Jewish collections within non-Jewish collections can be "broadly characterized by the absence of purposeful collecting and, until recently, by an abandonment to chance" (Chapter 6). They are often connected to a personality—a collector, a donor, or a curator. Di Nepi explores the history of Jewish things at the Museum of Fine Arts in Boston, which shifted from collecting "accidental Judaica" to the establishment of a formal collection of Judaica at the beginning of the twenty-first century.

Whereas the Museum of Fine Arts in Boston displays Jewish things throughout the museum, the North Carolina Museum of Art chose a different approach, designing a single, separate gallery for its pieces. Established in 1983 when the original collector of its core collection, Abram Kanof, moved to North Carolina, the NCMA's Judaic Art Gallery has expanded four times over the years and developed international reach and material diversity. Under the stewardship of curator emeritus John Coffey, this collection grew to include both rare survivals restored to their former beauty and contemporary ceremonial artwork commissioned from modern artists. In Chapter 7 Coffey offers the storied history of the NCMA's Judaic Art Gallery and its connection to the broader mission of this state art museum.

The volume closes with two narratives that speak as much to the perspectives of curator-scholars as to the meanings of the Jewish objects themselves. First, curator emerita Dale Rosengarten examines the effect of diasporic conditions on people and things by contrasting the journeys of two silver bowls (Chapter 8). These parallel objects, both of the antebellum South, illustrate the depth of assimilation of elite Southern Jews. Transforming from ordinary domestic objects into potent symbols of survival, these silver bowls narrate Jewish Southern experiences of migration and belonging.

In Chapter 9 folklorist and curator Suzanne Seriff journeys back through her own family's Jewish Southern history, centered in her grandfather's retail store, to highlight how everyday things endure and transform to become markers of Jewish experience. Reflecting on her curatorial work, Seriff considers the Jewish take on the revolutionary potential of museums as fertile third spaces for radical storytelling and civic engagement in the twenty-first century. She concludes with five curatorial lessons about the materiality of Jewish things and the power of their political and historic contextualization.

The scholarly contributions to *The Lives of Jewish Things* close with an afterword by professor emerita of performance studies Barbara Kirshenblatt-Gimblett, the keynote speaker for the "Wandering Objects" symposium. Kirshenblatt-Gimblett offers a long view of the perception and performance of Jewish material culture on display and on the move in the recent past and near future.

Last, the volume concludes with an appendix that brings readers back to the original "Wandering Objects" symposium where it all began. This appendix presents the complete transcript of one of the symposium's collective discussions—the "Collectors' Roundtable: Collecting the Past for the Future" (November 12, 2018). During this session, curator Gabriel Goldstein moderated a conversation between three prominent contemporary collectors of Judaica: Max N. Berry, Jane Gershon Weitzman, and William L. Gross. Their discussion reveals how collectors' activities, outlooks, and priorities have been formative for an understanding of the significance and potential of Jewish material things across contexts.[22]

In this international, interdisciplinary study of Jewish things in context, scholars, curators, and collectors consider the diverse meanings cultivated through the acquisition and interpretation of Jewish material culture. *The Lives of Jewish Things* demonstrates the significance of the shifting presence of a Jewish thing as it transcends binaries through repeated transformations of use and value. One might begin with the thing itself, but the changing relationships between thing and person, thing and place, and thing and action will narrate stories of cultural shift and cultural stability, of inclusion and exclusion, of remembering and forgetting. *The Lives of Jewish Things* explores the relationships of meaning created not in one context but across many. The meaning revealed in these changing contexts of use and reuse address how the collection and curation of Jewish things communicates one's sense of self and other, cultural value, religious belief, and modes of social belonging. It exposes the social and cultural worlds in which these Jewish things have circulated and the moral structures in which they were made and out of which they have broken. The things in this volume demonstrate how movement between categories of classification contributes to their Jewish quality. By moving with these Jewish things across time, place, and culture, we trace complex stories of individual and collective struggles to survive.

Notes

1 See Fickler, *Das Inventar*, no. 953: "Ein Alter guldiner ring." Cabinets of curiosities, known as *Kunstkammer* or *Wunderkammer* in German, held collections of creative and curious things as a treasure—a common

practice in sixteenth- and seventeenth-century Europe, preceding the museum. See Daston and Park, *Wonders*, 74.

2 Quiccheberg, *First Treatise on Museums*, 61.
3 Herman, "Bricoleur Revisited," 56.
4 Key North American scholars of Christian religious material culture, such as Colleen McDannell, David Morgan, Leonard Primiano, Kay Turner, and Joseph Sciorra, exemplify this. For an international representation of such scholarship, see Houtman and Meyer, *Things*.
5 For example, Morgan, *Thing about Religion*. For a comprehensive list of scholarship on the material study of religions, see Morgan, *Thing about Religion*, 199–205.
6 Primiano, "Vernacular Religion," 44.
7 Herman, "Bricoleur Revisited," 40.
8 On explicit and implicit Jewish objects, see Ochs, "What Makes a Jewish Home Jewish."
9 "Material culture is culture made material" (Glassie, *Material Culture*, 41).
10 Glassie, *Material Culture*.
11 See Cohen, *Jewish Icons*; Mann, *Art and Ceremony*; and Sabar, *Ketubbah*. See also Shalom Sabar's presentation at the "Wandering Objects" symposium (2018): vimeo.com/374882236.
12 Kirshenblatt-Gimblett and Shandler, "Introduction," 309.
13 Also see Ochs, "What Makes a Jewish Home Jewish"; and Ochs, *Inventing Jewish Ritual*.
14 For a history and critical analysis of the notion of Jewish aniconism and an examination of the central role of art and aesthetics in Jewish experience, see Bland, *Artless Jew*.
15 See, for example, Bronner, *Jewishness*; Leibman, *Art of the Jewish Family*; Eichler-Levine, *Painted Pomegranates*; Joselit, *Wonders of America*; Levitt, *Objects That Remain*; Gross, *Beyond the Synagogue*; Salamon, *Israel in the Making*; and Sienna, "'Remarkable Objects.'"
16 See Ochs, "What Makes a Jewish Home Jewish"; and Heilman, "Jews and Judaica."
17 As Susan Stewart writes, in the bound conditions of a collection, history is replaced with classification, "with order beyond the realm of temporality" (Stewart, *On Longing*, 151).
18 The first of its kind in the southeast United States, this symposium was interdisciplinary and expansive in its inquiry, engaging the insights of

art historians, anthropologists, folklorists, religious studies scholars, philosophers, cultural critics, curators, and private collectors in conversations about the changing meanings of Jewish material culture today and, in particular, how these materials are displayed and interpreted in museums, used as instruments of inquiry, and drawn upon as archives of information. The participants in this symposium traced histories of the struggle to define the identity and purpose of the "Jewish" object and imagined futures of this effort as material things move with increasing ease across the globe today in physical, virtual, and imagined forms. See jewishstudies.unc.edu/events/wandering-objects/.

19 The "Wandering Objects" symposium featured presentations from the following scholars: Laura Arnold Leibman, Shalom Sabar, Erica Lehrer, Francesco Spagnolo, Diego Rotman, Laura Levitt, Juliana Ochs Dweck, Samantha Baskind, and Jenna Weissman Joselit. Also featured was a curators' roundtable with Simona Di Nepi, Juliana Ochs Dweck, Suzanne Seriff, and Barbara Kirshenblatt-Gimblett; a collectors' roundtable with Max N. Berry, Jane Gershon Weitzman, William L. Gross, and Gabriel Goldstein; and a keynote address delivered by Barbara Kirshenblatt-Gimblett. The symposium's co-organizers were Ruth von Bernuth (University of North Carolina), Gabrielle Berlinger (University of North Carolina), John Coffey (North Carolina Museum of Art), and Gabriel Goldstein (North Carolina Museum of Art). Video recordings of the symposium presentations and roundtables can be viewed on the UNC Carolina Center for Jewish Studies Vimeo website: vimeo.com/user4784851/videos/page:2/sort:date.

20 See Shandler, "Jewish Material Culture."

21 See, for example, Rosman, "Categorically Jewish"; Erica Lehrer's 2013 exhibit "Souvenir, Talisman, Toy" at the Kraków Ethnographic Museum (MEK) in Poland and, in 2014, her accompanying book, *Lucky Jews*, with online exhibit, available at www.luckyjews.com; and the Judaica collection at the Museum of Fine Arts, Boston (www.mfa.org/collections/judaica).

22 The video recording of the collectors' roundtable session can be viewed at vimeo.com/317256024 (accessed November 2023).

Bibliography

Bland, Kalman P. *The Artless Jew: Medieval and Modern Affirmations and Denials of the Visual*. Princeton, NJ: Princeton University Press, 2001.

Bronner, Simon J., ed. *Jewishness: Expression, Identity, and Representation*. Liverpool, UK: Littman Library of Jewish Civilization, 2008.

Cohen, Richard I. *Jewish Icons: Art and Society in Modern Europe*. Berkeley: University of California Press, 1998.

Daston, Lorraine, and Katharine Park. *Wonders and the Order of Nature, 1150–1750*. New York: Zone Books, 1998.

Eichler-Levine, Jodi. *Painted Pomegranates and Needlepoint Rabbis: How Jews Craft Resilience and Create Community*. Chapel Hill: University of North Carolina Press, 2020.

Fickler, Johann Baptist. *Das Inventar der Münchner herzoglichen Kunstkammer von 1598: Editionsband—Transkription der Inventarhandschrift cgm 2133*, ed. Peter Diemer. München: Bayerischen Akademie der Wissenschaften, 2004.

Glassie, Henry H. *Material Culture*. Bloomington: Indiana University Press, 1999.

Gross, Rachel B. *Beyond the Synagogue: Jewish Nostalgia as Religious Practice*. New York: New York University Press, 2021.

Heilman, Samuel. "Jews and Judaica: Who Owns and Buys What?" In *Persistence and Flexibility: Anthropological Perspectives on the American Jewish Experience*, ed. Walter P. Zenner, 260–80. Albany: SUNY Press, 1988.

Herman, Bernie. "The Bricoleur Revisited." In *American Material Culture: The Shape of the Field*, ed. Ann Smart Martin and J. Ritchie Garrison, 37–63. Winterthur, DE: Winterthur Museum, 1997.

Houtman, Dick, and Birgit Meyer, eds. *Things: Religion and the Question of Materiality*. New York: Fordham University Press, 2012.

Joselit, Jenna Weissman. *The Wonders of America: Reinventing Jewish Culture, 1880–1950*. New York: Macmillan, 2002.

Kirshenblatt-Gimblett, Barbara, and Jeffrey Shandler, eds. *Material Religion* 3, no. 3 (2007): 308–13.

Leibman, Laura Arnold. *The Art of the Jewish Family: A History of Women in Early New York in Five Objects*. New York: Bard Graduate Center, 2020.

Levitt, Laura S. *The Objects That Remain*. University Park: Penn State University Press, 2020.

Mann, Vivian B. *Art and Ceremony in Jewish Life: Essays on the History of Jewish Art.* London: Pindar Press, 2005.

Morgan, David. *The Thing about Religion: An Introduction to the Material Study of Religions.* Chapel Hill: University of North Carolina Press, 2021.

Ochs, Vanessa L. *Inventing Jewish Ritual.* Philadelphia: Jewish Publication Society, 2007.

———. "What Makes a Jewish Home Jewish?" *CrossCurrents* 49, no. 4 (1999): 491–510.

Primiano, Leonard. "Vernacular Religion and the Search for Method in Religious Folklife." *Western Folklore* 54, no. 1 (1995): 37–56.

Quiccheberg, Samuel. *The First Treatise on Museums: Samuel Quiccheberg's Inscriptiones 1565*, trans. and ed. Mark A. Meadow and Bruce Robertson. Los Angeles: Getty Research Institute, 2013.

Rosman, Moshe. "Categorically Jewish, Distinctly Polish: The Museum of the History of Polish Jews and the New Polish-Jewish Metahistory." *JSIJ Jewish Studies, an Internet Journal* 10 (2012): 361–87.

Sabar, Shalom. *Ketubbah: The Art of the Jewish Marriage Contract.* New York: Rizzoli, 2000.

Salamon, Hagar. *Israel in the Making: Stickers, Stitches, and Other Critical Practices.* Bloomington: Indiana University Press, 2017.

Shandler, Jeffrey. "Jewish Material Culture in the Modern Age." In *Routledge Handbook of Jewish Ritual and Practice*, ed. Oliver Leaman, 150–60. Abingdon, UK: Routledge.

Sienna, Noam. "'Remarkable Objects of the Three Religions': Judaica in Early Modern European Collections." *Journal of the History of Collections* 31 (2019): 17–29.

Stewart, Susan. *On Longing: Narratives of the Miniature, the Gigantic, the Souvenir, the Collection.* Durham, NC: Duke University Press, 1993.

Part I

JEWISH THINGS IN LANDSCAPE AND SOUNDSCAPE

1

CANONIZING THE EPHEMERAL

A Bedouin Structure in an Ecotourism Ethno-Enterprise and a Jewish-Bedouin Sukkah in an Art Museum

Diego Rotman

The Sukkah as a Refugee Home

The Jewish holiday of Sukkot commemorates the Exodus from Egypt through the commandment to build sukkot (pl. of sukkah), the temporary shelters that the Israelites erected in the desert during their wanderings (Exodus 33:6). Accordingly, during the festival Jews build a sukkah—a temporary hut topped by palm fronds or other foliage so that the roof is partly open to the sky—to observe the commandment "live in booths for seven days: All native-born Israelites are to live in booths, so your descendants will know that I had the Israelites live in booths when I brought them out of Egypt" (Leviticus 23:42).

The construction of the sukkah varies according to tradition, economic situation, and available materials. Its architecture and traditional interior decorations often reflect popular crafts and local tastes as well as the political or religious ideologies of the sukkah builders.[1]

In 2014 the director of Hansen House for Art, Design, and Technology (which is housed in the former Jerusalem Leprosarium in West Jerusalem) invited the Sala-Manca Artists Group (of which I am a member) to create a public sukkah for Sukkot. The Sala-Manca Group discussed the project with the Underground Academy, a research study and artists-in-residency program at the Mamuta Art and Research Center, which the Sala-Manca Group founded and directs. They decided to frame this project as part of their current research program, which concerns the connections between Jewish and Israeli ethnography and contemporary art.[2] After a long process of research and discussion, the Sala-Manca Group, along with artists Itamar Mendes-Flohr, Yeshaiau Rabinowitz, Hagar Goren, Chen Cohen, and Ktura Manor, decided against constructing an innovatively designed sukkah in the style of projects such as the successful and creative Sukkah City (New York, 2010).[3] Instead, they resolved to delve into the charged meaning of the sukkah in the Israeli-Palestinian context. The artists sought to highlight the temporary nature of the structure and its associations with exile, thus evoking connotations not only with Jewish history but also with the Israeli context. The artists argued that if, according to the United Nations, refugees are those who—for reasons of persecution—have been exiled and cannot return to their country, then the ancient Hebrews in the desert could be understood as early refugees and their sukkot (the shanties in the desert) as a refugee camp. The aim was to propose a contemporary reading of the sukkah both as a concrete object and as a symbol.[4] The artists decided to bring an "authentic," contemporary house from an Israeli Palestinian refugee camp to Hansen House in the city of Jerusalem and transform it into a kosher sukkah.

The project discussed here was first broached in an article published in the *Journal of Modern Jewish Studies* (2017). There, I examined concepts of home, identity, local history, and Israeli art history in relation to the cultural and political tensions that dominate the charged local landscape and topography of Israel/Palestine.[5] In this chapter I contextualize the Bedouin hut by framing it within discourses concerning the architecture of violence and architectural spolia. I describe the transformation of the Bedouin hut into a Jewish sukkah, examining the symbolic aspects that arose from the politics and poetics of its display in the former Jerusalem Leprosarium and in the Israel Museum.

I outline an output related to that transformation: the parallel development of an ecotourism initiative by the Bedouin community. This initiative led to a traditional Bedouin tent becoming an ethnographic object exhibited inside a Bedouin shack built exactly where the hut that became *The Eternal Sukkah* had once stood (though that hut became a museological object in a museum). This intertwined development of two culturally constructed structures for display—*The Eternal Sukkah* in the museum and the Bedouin tent displayed inside a Bedouin shanty—marked the introduction of both structures into two different arenas: an art museum and an ethno-enterprise. Those two structures do not compete but rather enrich one another, generating a long-term process of collaboration characterized by tactics of disguised display: The Jahalin hut entered the Israel Museum disguised as a Jewish sukkah and a piece of art, whereas the Bedouin tent, disguised as a "traditional" Bedouin tent, was displayed within an indoor structure in a desert that serves as a living museum for Western visitors.

Meeting Mohammed (Abu Suleiman) al-Korshan

As part of their efforts to bring a contemporary Israeli/Palestinian refugee family home to Hansen House in Jerusalem, a group of artists traveled to the Judean Desert, to the Palestinian Territories, to meet with Mohammed (Abu Suleiman) al-Korshan, the speaker for the Jahalin tribe in Jerusalem. This meeting was suggested by Alon Cohen-Lifshitz, an architect with Bimkom: Planners for Planning Rights, a nonprofit organization that works with the Jahalin community. The Jahalin are members of a Bedouin tribe that was uprooted from its lands in southern Israel in 1948 and relocated to the West Bank as refugees. The al-Korshan family settled in the Khan al-Ahmar area and pastured their animals on neighboring village lands. According to Abu Suleiman, "From that time we have become a minority group which is continuously exposed to the threat of forced displacement and discrimination."[6] After Israel occupied the West Bank in 1967, and as a consequence of the establishment and expansion of Ma'ale Adumim (a nearby settlement), the Israeli army increasingly restricted the tribe members' access to many of the grazing grounds.

The al-Korshans, as well as many other families of the Jahalin tribe, live in huts built with materials that they find. None of their homes or other structures are connected to potable water or electricity because the Israeli government considers them illegal, leaving them under the continuous threat of demolition by Israel's Civil Administration. Today there is a government plan to build a Bedouin town near Jericho that will accommodate about 12,500 people from three different tribes: Rashaida, Jahalin, and Kaabneh. However, this plan is yet another displacement attempt, similar to the processes that the Israeli state implemented in the Negev.[7] The

Bedouin families oppose "the plan to cram members of different tribes and clans altogether . . . in the same space [that] runs counter to their tradition, their way of life and their livelihood."[8]

The Bedouin Hut as Negative Spolia

The Bedouin huts in Area C,[9] the areas in the Occupied Territories that remain under Israeli control, are built with materials that they find: iron, wood taken from construction sites, metal from water heaters or from advertisement signs. The roof is made mostly of tin and is covered with sheets of plastic. The structure is constructed using wooden beams that are usually taken from older construction sites.

The reuse of construction materials and waste is a consequence of practical and economic considerations: Most of those materials are free of charge; they are easy to transport and can be used for speedy building; they are strong; and the only costs involved are transportation and labor, carried out by the experienced tribe members themselves. The construction usually takes about eight hours of collective work, depending on the size of the hut and the availability of community members. There is no use of any architectural plans; instead, the construction is based on experience, common sense, and improvisation given the availability of materials. The builders directing the construction generally work in the construction industry. The pieces are connected using hammers and nails. The walls are easily replaced or removed as a consequence of any damage or according to the season; during summer, walls might be dismantled and replaced with cloths. The interior is decorated with patterned fabrics that usually cover the metal pieces, selected by the women. Although the huts are not connected to water or electric services, there is an "advantage" to this type of construction: If the huts are destroyed by the Israeli Civil Administration, the community suffers less economic damage. However, destruction of huts, homes, solar electricity systems, or schools of course inflicts enormous psychological and emotional trauma on the community.[10]

These huts are not the type of home in which the Jahalin can take pride; they are not the structures they would like to inhabit. The mukhtar (head of the tribe) said that they would like to have structures made of concrete with open walls: this would preserve the traditional Bedouin way of life in a modern and stronger way, maintaining their traditional connection with the desert and creating space between the different homes.[11]

The structures themselves are both a consequence and a mirror of the political clash. They are the inverse side of territorial expropriation, the vernacular architecture of the "unsettled." These Bedouin structures, a result of territorial and ethnic politics, share common characteristics with architectural spolia. *Spolia* is an ancient term, originally related to booty, which became the common term for early Christian and medieval architectural reuse of stone building blocks dating from the Greco-Roman period.[12] "The primary motive for using spolia," writes Arnold Esch, "was to make use of second-hand structural elements in order to speed contemporary building projects and to reduce their cost."[13] In general, architectural spolia refers to the reuse of materials in new constructions that reflect domination. Following this logic, the Bedouin hut might be considered a photographic negative of spolia: homes and structures constructed not with fragments of a building from the defeated side but with unused or waste materials belonging to those in power or those who live in more favorable conditions.[14] Bedouin structures do not intend to refer to the "source" buildings; the builders are not interested in the history or origins of the different patches, materials, or fragments. The fragments are not from ruins but are instead from parts of former structures and had other uses and were reconfigured to construct a temporary home. The physical structure tells the story of political, ethnic, and economic subjugation. The reuse of building materials is not guided by a "green" approach; rather, it is a mode of survival.[15] Accordingly, the structures can be seen as forms of "embedded violence" in built artifacts, to paraphrase Runa Johannessen.[16]

As reflected in informal conversations and in social media, for the average Israeli citizen traveling to the Dead Sea and viewing the villages from the highway, these structures do not immediately express the politics of exclusion. Rather, they are perceived as the elected Bedouin way of life: their willingness to embrace "primitivity," social marginality, and poverty and their unwillingness to adapt to modern life and the laws of the State of Israel. This connection between the Bedouin, marginality, and poverty is a result of a state discourse and strategy that contradicts the other view of Bedouins in Israel as a particular culture, characterized by its hospitality and connection to nature. The clearest expression of Israel's approach to the Bedouin communities in Area C as marginal and worthless is the many governmental plans that insist on transferring Bedouin communities to locations next to garbage dumps or, as proposed recently, near a sewage treatment site where human habitation has been forbidden.[17] The present project attempted to challenge this bias.

The Transaction

During their first visit to the village where Mohammed (Abu Suleiman) al-Korshan resides, on the outskirts of the Palestinian village of Anata, the Israeli artists were hosted in a traditional open-sided Bedouin tent made of lamb's wool. They were served tea as they listened to Abu Suleiman tell the story of the Jahalin tribe and heard the tribe's concerns about the current threat of relocation, once again against their will.[18] The artists told Abu Suleiman about their wish to connect the ancient Jewish exile to the current exile suffered by the Jahalin. To do so, they related, they would like to transport a piece of this "hidden" Bedouin reality to another location, Jerusalem, and make it visible.

The artists offered to purchase a family shanty for 6,000 ILS (1,500 USD),[19] using funds the collective received from Hansen House to make a sukkah.[20] Abu Suleiman suggested renting the traditional Bedouin tent to the artists, the tent in which they met—the only one of this type that the community possessed—in order to share their heritage with the inhabitants of Jerusalem.[21] The artists clarified that they were interested in displaying a contemporary Bedouin home that reflects the current living conditions of the Jahalin, a consequence of Israeli ethnopolitics, converted into a Jewish sukkah. The artists said that they preferred to purchase one of the illegal structures, one of those destined for demolition, a shack, with all its signifiers and significance. The Jahalin considered the possibility of selling the structure, not just for financial reasons. The mukhtar and Abu Suleiman gave their blessing, arguing that this might be a good opportunity to publicize their situation more widely. They agreed to the idea of giving one of their huts such agency when placed in Jerusalem. The artists were offered three different cabins from the village in Khan al-Ahmar, uninhabited in the fall and used as storage, and the biggest was selected for its size and design.

FIGURE 1.1. Bedouin structure in Khan al Akhmar. Photo by Itamar Mendes-Flohr.

Dismantling and Translocating

Abu Suleiman offered to dismantle the hut for the artists, but the artists asked to be part of the process. They wanted to deconstruct and reconstruct it, to learn about the technique, and to make marks on the different fragments that would enable them to reconstruct it correctly. The structure was dismantled carefully, using conservation techniques applied to historical buildings as interpreted by the artists. The artists numbered each piece in relation to the other four pieces surrounding it. The marks were a clear reference to the techniques used in Jerusalem to mark façades of houses that are to be deconstructed but must retain their original façade for historical reasons. With the help of members of the Jahalin tribe, they dismantled the structure. This careful approach to the hut stood in stark contrast to the demolition process carried out by the Civil Administration.

The artists realized only much later that for Abu Suleiman the sale was more about the materials and not about the structure in its actual design. The specific order of the different fragments that composed the structure's walls have no special meaning for Abu Suleiman; the hut was valued for its technical and practical qualities. A reconstruction of the structure in a totally different place with the same material form would still be taken as a reconstruction; the idea of preservation was understood differently.

The huts are deconstructed and reconstructed by the Bedouin according to their needs and functionality, not for aesthetic reasons. The aesthetic approach to the home is expressed inside the structure, through fabrics and hanging objects, such as embroidery and pictures. This difference in approach evoked laughter among the Bedouin when the artists showed Abu Suleiman and other tribe members the first pictures of the hut reconstructed as a sukkah in a setting that differed starkly in terms of culture and nature. The structure was first reconstructed as a sukkah in the green garden of a former German hospital, very different from the setting of the Judean Desert.

The power relationships among the groups were clear to both parties. Both groups were taking different type of risks, related to their positions: the Jahalin with the Civil Administration (the artists told Abu Suleiman that if this action posed any risk to the community, they would prefer not to do it; however, Abu Suleiman asked to continue with the plan) and the artists with the directors of Hansen House, the institution where the art center is housed. The directors were not expecting a sukkah making such a strong political statement; it could potentially lead to conflicts and might serve as a reason to ask the artists to leave the compound and close their art center. The artists' feeling of risk is a consequence of life in Israel, where a critical political statement in the arts might be suppressed or censored or lead to economic ramifications.[22]

At Abu Suleiman's request, the artists agreed to dismantle the cabin in the dead of night to avoid the gaze of the Civil Administration.[23] By the time the artists would have started to reassemble the dismantled hut as a sukkah in Hansen House, the al-Korshan family would have begun building a new and sturdier cabin exactly where the old one had stood, using new wood beams purchased using the profit from the sale.

The deconstructed structure of the Bedouin home was transported to Jerusalem in a dump truck, passing the checkpoint as "construction waste." This process temporarily caused the structure to revert from the status of a home into raw materials. The home, at least as waste, can easily make its way to Jerusalem—a pilgrimage that cannot be freely undertaken by most of the Jahalin, who live in the Occupied Territories and have no permit to enter Israel. The legal economic transaction affected not only the shanty's value but also its illegal status. According to Israeli law, the illegal shanty became legal goods in the State of Israel.

The Transformation

The Bedouin structure was reconstructed in the gardens of Hansen House, the former Jerusalem Leprosarium. Some interventions were made to refer to the relocation and to transform the Bedouin structure into a kosher sukkah: The roof was exchanged for palm fronds (taken from the Hansen House gardens); the carpets were replaced with matting; and a paper decoration made by the daughter of one of the artists became a symbolic sukkah ornament. At the very moment that the ephemeral architecture of the Bedouin shack was changed, exchanging its recycled tin roof for fresh palm fronds, the exile of the Jahalin tribe materialized as a Jewish sukkah. The Jewish holiday's reenactment of exile took place in a temporary structure originally built as a family home by the Jahalin tribe. It became possible to experience the Jewish past through the Bedouin's present or through the connection between those two realities.

One senior staff member from the Jerusalem Authority understood that the artists' Bedouin sukkah was not actually an adaptation of a "traditional Bedouin tent" but instead of a Bedouin shack from Area C. This staff member telephoned the artists, attempting "to understand" the political implications. This person also expressed significant disappointment and shock at the possibility that such a political project funded by government

FIGURE 1.2. *The Eternal Sukkah* at Hansen House, Jerusalem. Photo by Diego Rotman.

money would evoke criticism and necessitate explanations. However, the staff member did not attempt to halt the construction.

The illegal Bedouin structure, originally destined for demolition, changed its status and became a legal and kosher Israeli sukkah. Thanks to this identity conversion, the translocation, and the change of ownership, this structure was able to survive. Ironically, to allow public access, the artists were forced to apply for a construction permit, which is granted by an engineer, legally authorizing the illegal structure. Once it was available for public access, a text was hung inside *The Eternal Sukkah* contextualizing the project.

The Former Leprosarium as a Symbolic Recontextualization

Hansen House, where *The Eternal Sukkah* was built, itself underwent a functional and identity transformation. The German Protestant Moravian community founded the Leprosarium "Jesus' Hilfe" as an isolated refuge for lepers in Jerusalem in 1867. For twenty years it operated in a building on what is now Agron Street. In 1887 the institute moved to a new building, designed by Conrad Schick, in the Talbiyeh neighborhood. Until 1948 most of the patients were Muslim Arabs and the nurses were Christians. Tawfiq Canaan, a Christian Palestinian, served as chief physician from 1919 until 1948. Following the establishment of the State of Israel, Canaan either left Jerusalem or was expelled.[24] The Jerusalem hospital at this point began to treat mostly Jewish patients. In 1950 the Jewish National Fund purchased the building and appointed the Israeli Ministry of Health to manage it. Its name, Leprosarium "Jesus' Hilfe," was changed to Hansen Government Hospital, named after Gerhard Henrik Armauer Hansen, the physician who discovered the bacteria responsible for leprosy. During the second half of the twentieth century, as antibiotic treatment succeeded, gradually reducing the number of patients, most of the patients with Hansen's disease were released from the hospital. Beginning in 2000, the hospital functioned solely as an outpatient clinic, and it finally closed its doors in 2009. The government then decided to transfer the building to the Jerusalem Municipality to be restored and turned into a cultural center. When the site opened in late 2013, it changed its identity once again and was named Hansen House, commemorating the scientific savior who replaced the spiritual healer, Jesus. Today, Hansen House is an art and design center and a tourist attraction that aims to show its visitors one of the city's most beautiful buildings and its "mysterious" history, opening its secret gardens and revealing its hidden beauty. Hansen House was converted from a former Christian institution directed by a Palestinian physician into a Jewish Israeli institution. Located in the Talbiyeh neighborhood, a former Palestinian neighborhood that today possesses a Jewish Israeli character, the building may have changed its official name but it retains the sign with the name of the former institution, "Jesus' Hilfe."

The former leprosarium was an institution for healing skin diseases. This adds another layer or symbolic dimension to the relocation of the hut, although it was not referred to in the artists' text or in the analysis or reviews written about it. Yet considering this background, it might be possible, following the recontextualization of the hut/sukkah in Hansen House, to approach the walls of the hut as a physical manifestation of a social and political disease provoked by the State of Israel's ethnopolitics as they manifest in the Bedouin home. The walls of this Bedouin home, understood as skin, are the manifestation of a tragic social disease, a disease that generates rejection, provokes marginality, and evokes fear among "healthy" citizens, a shack with *tsara'at* (leprosy).[25] The translocation process could be interpreted critically as an act of compassion by the empowered artists, or as an activist action attempting to expose "a victim" of the conflict, perhaps to generate healing, to spread knowledge and recognition about the causes of this social and political disease, or to confront "healthy" Israeli citizens with the results of their government's politics. Bringing the segregated hut into the center of the discourse in such a symbolic venue challenges the public to confront their values and ethics in relation to the other: The hut acts as a mirror.

Sukkot at *The Eternal Sukkah*

The launch of *The Eternal Sukkah* at the Hansen House was devoted to the situation of the Jahalin Bedouin tribe, which lives under the threat of displacement. It included the participation of architect and theoretician Haim Yaacovi, who worked with such communities in the past, and Rabbi

Milgrom, an activist in the organization Rabbis for Human Rights who works with Bedouin communities. After reading Leviticus 23, Rabbi Milgrom stated, "It is a very ironic verse for us today. Every citizen in Israel sits in a sukkah seven days, and they [the Jahalin], because of the fact that they are not citizens, they are sitting in a sukkah all year long." He wrote later on his Facebook page about *The Eternal Sukkah*: "It's a kosher *sukkah*, and dwelling in it during Sukkot totally transforms the mitzvah—emotionally, socially, politically—into a more religious act than I've ever felt."[26] *The Eternal Sukkah* can thus be seen as an ambivalent heterotopic dwelling representing both Bedouin and Jewish wandering. Jewish visitors to the Bedouin sukkah in the well-established Jewish neighborhood of Talbiyeh had an opportunity to experience the Bedouin diaspora through the commemoration of the Jewish holiday. Visitors could enter the "almost real" home of a refugee family, become familiar with their story through a text, and, of course, fulfill the Jewish commandment and experience their "own" history as refugees.

In December 2014 the fragments of *The Eternal Sukkah* were dismantled. They were subsequently exhibited in museological displays together

FIGURE 1.3. Interior of *The Eternal Sukkah*. Photo by Diego Rotman.

with a documentary film about the project and a model of *The Eternal Sukkah* built by Ktura Manor, a member of the Ethnographic Department of the Museum of the Contemporary at Mamuta.

From an Ethnographic Object to a Piece of Fine Art

After seeing the Bedouin sukkah in the gardens of Hansen House, the artists thought the next step in the project was to merchandise the sukkah as an art piece. Attributing the title "art object" to any piece of art is a museological invention; the museum in fact gives this formal recognition. In that sense, the transformation of the sukkah from a ritual object into a piece of contemporary art was a new challenge. Driven by a critical approach to the Western colonialist history of art and by the idea of artist ownership as added economic value to an object, the artists decided to attempt to sell *The Eternal Sukkah* to an art museum. Specifically, they aimed to sell it to the Israel Museum, the largest and most important museum in Israel.

The artists contacted two of the Israel Museum's curators, Amitai Mendelsohn (curator of Israeli art) and Rita Kersting (curator of contemporary art), who came to see the work. They were impressed by the structure and the project and were tempted by the idea of having it in the museum. During their visit, the curators asked the artists about the price of the object. Without having discussed this matter beforehand, the artists determined that the value of the piece was ten times higher than the price paid for the original dwelling. Half the sum, they told the curators, would be given to the al-Korshan family as a "copyright fee," and the other half would go to the Art Center. *The Eternal Sukkah* was reevaluated as a piece of art. In fact, through the appreciation of the object as something with historical and economic value, the hut became politicized, entering the arena of the symbolic.[27]

Both curators, together with Mira Lapidot, the museum's chief art curator, later watched the film and documentation of the project and accepted the artists' proposal to involve the museum in the process. This new addition to the process would add new layers and meanings to the history of the piece, provoked by another translocation of the object into a symbolic realm. The possible purchase of the object generated challenging questions from Lapidot regarding the nature of the object in its new recontextualization and economic considerations: To which department would this piece belong: contemporary art, Israeli art, or ethnography? Why not buy a hut directly from the Bedouin tribe? The sukkah was finally added to the wish list of art pieces that the curators presented to the museum's acquisitions committee.

The plan generated a great deal of thought among the artists about the meaning of such a step, including the dangers of cultural colonialism, Western manipulation, and the exploitation of a so-called weakened community.[28] Before making any final decision, the artists discussed the idea with Abu Suleiman and asked him to present the project not only to representatives of the community (as he had done previously) but also to a larger group of tribe members. A date was set and the project was presented to a group of twenty-five young men of the al-Korshan family (no women were present). The artists screened a documentary film about the project to discuss it and to explain the possible developments and meanings of the acquisition as understood by the artists in relation to possible further exhibition of the sukkah at the Israel Museum. The Jahalin and the artists discussed the project and its meanings and also the advantages and disadvantages that this move might afford. Besides the economic benefit—receiving half the amount the museum would pay—Abu Suleiman saw the project as another way of advocating for their cause: an additional channel to support the legal route they were pursuing, which would allow them to show their situation to a wider Israeli and international public. At another meeting, he said, "If you can bring it to the UN, bring it!" The artists thought that, to Abu Suleiman, the museum acquisition represented a type of semi-official Israeli recognition of the Bedouins' situation, a mode of advocacy and of encounter between the Jewish history as refugees and the Bedouins' present situation as refugees. The exhibition and possible media coverage would offer a way to let many others know about their situation. The al-Korshan family agreed to the idea of selling the hut to the museum and accepted on condition that every exhibition of the sukkah would be accompanied by an explanatory text regarding the context of the project, its origin and history, and the situation of the Jahalin. That day, Abu Suleiman said, half-amused, to the artists, "It would be great to invite the head of the Civil Administration [the government body in charge of the demolitions] to the museum in order to show him where our home is." After a long and heated debate with the acquisitions committee, the sukkah and the film (to be exhibited together in any further installation) were among the pieces slated for acquisition for the museum's permanent collection.

Translocation to the Israel Museum: Preservation and Exhibition

Perhaps the first and most literal moment of transforming *The Eternal Sukkah* into a piece of art occurred when the dismantled pieces were transported to the Israel Museum. At this point in the trajectory, instead of a dump truck transporting the pieces, as in its first move to Hansen House, a fine arts truck was used. At the beginning of the process, the professional movers treated the pieces with great respect, wearing the white gloves associated with their trade. When the job became harder, the movers' mood shifted: It seemed to them that they were transporting construction waste and not something that was part of an artwork. They lost their respect and professionalism, treating the fragments as mere pieces of old wood and metal sheets and throwing them one on top of the other. For a moment, the fragments lost their aura.

Pieces of construction waste became a Bedouin structure. They subsequently became a Jewish/Bedouin sukkah, and then the pieces became fragments of an art object. According to the museum's procedures, they first had to be disinfected (or purified) in a process of transformation from a ritual structure to an art piece. After the exhibit, *The Eternal Sukkah* was dismantled, again entering the sacred and "eternal" period of conservation. Upon entering the museum, it entered its "mythical" period.[29]

As in its translocation to Hansen House, the venue of the exhibit has a history of identity change, and the object again mirrored the local history of the hosting venue. The Israel Museum was established in 1967 on land that previously belonged to the Palestinian village Sheikh Bader. It was designed by Alfred Mansfeld, inspired by the Palestinian village of Malha. The image of a Palestinian village became, according to Zvi Efrat, the myth of origin that authenticates the Israel Museum: "Before it was a place, an object, a landscape, it was already a landmark . . . a fake relic of a (missing) past and at once a brave new model projected onto a white future."[30]

Along with the acquisition, the museum drew a precise map of instructions for the dismantling and reassembly of *The Eternal Sukkah*.

Construction waste that became a home, a storage space, and then a kosher sukkah was cataloged and conserved to prevent the deterioration of this cultural heritage object. Such preservation efforts are among the most obsessive and meticulous processes of conservation and canonization of an illegal building ever undertaken; the sukkah, further eternalized by the museum, would stand as an iconic symbol of Israeli ethnic politics: a process of canonizing the ephemeral.

The paradox is that this preservation process is nearly entirely symbolic: The object, and the politics attached to it, becomes part of the past. It encapsulates the architecture and way of living among the Bedouin community in the Occupied Territories, which are a result of Israeli policy. Through preservation, it is relegated to the past and removed from dominant consciousness as an undesirable present.

The sukkah was exhibited at the museum for the first time in "We the People," a collective indoor exhibition curated by Rita Kersting and held from September 2015 to March 2016. In this temporary exhibition, the sukkah, rendered useless as a ritual space, became a piece of art displayed indoors. Inside it, a short film that documented the process and the context in which the Jahalin live was screened. An explanatory text, as requested by the al-Korshan family, was added as well.[31] The exhibition coincided with a specific moment when the Jahalin faced the imminent threat of forced

FIGURE 1.4. *The Eternal Sukkah* at the Israel Museum, Jerusalem. Photo by Diego Rotman.

translocation. For this reason, politician and former parliamentarian Arie Eldad accused the Israeli Museum of crossing "a red line in supporting lawbreakers [and] covering that as art."[32] The sukkah brought a symbol of a population to be translocated to the margins of the margins into the center of the discourse. It introduced this population into the sacred space of Israeli art, so close to the Israeli Parliament, and this was interpreted as interference, an obstruction to the otherwise silent translocation process.

The Museum as Desert: Symposium, Discourse, and the Jahalin Children's Visit

During the exhibition, a symposium concerning the situation of the Jahalin and the other Bedouin tribes in Area C was held at the Israel Museum. Participants included scholars, activists, and Abu Suleiman himself, who was able to enter Israel after obtaining a special permit. When Abu Suleiman arrived at the Israel Museum for the symposium, he was asked if he would like to see the Bedouin shanty. He smiled politely and answered that he was not very interested in seeing it first, considering that he sees many such shanties every day. After touring the museum and visiting the archeological section and the Israeli and modern art galleries, he found the Bedouin structure in its new setup and in relation to other displayed objects and art pieces. The Jahalin hut was suddenly accorded the same status as historical and archeological objects from ancient Egypt and modern artworks by Picasso and Renoir. Abu Suleiman, smiling, approved the reconstruction of the hut. He entered the structure and immediately sat down in it with his relative Abu Jamal, the same way they sit at home.

James Snyder, the museum director, welcomed Abu Suleiman and, referring to the Bedouin hut/sukkah, told him, "It does not belong to us, we are just the custodians." Snyder's words were meant to express modesty and politeness. Abu Suleiman thanked him politely. According to Snyder, the museum paradoxically acquired an object that cannot be owned. To solve this problem ethically, the museum assumed the temporary role of custodian. This approach reflects the traditional colonialist practice and discourse of the Western museum. However, if we reflect on Snyder's words and contextualize them in the discourse of Israeli real estate and territorial politics, and more specifically in the context of the Absentee's Property Law of 5710/1950 enacted in Israel in 1950, the meaning of this approach may differ. "The primary purpose of this law," as Nir Hasson highlights, "was to enable use of lands belonging to Arabs who left Israel voluntarily or forcedly during the War of Independence."[33] Even though *The Eternal Sukkah* is not a Bedouin hut but a hybrid construction and even though it was legally purchased first by the artists as a hut and later by the museum with the consent of the Jahalin (who secured both income and political benefit from the act), Snyder's words reflect, probably unintentionally, the Israeli legal approach to Palestinian "abandoned" properties. The very act of being custodians of the Bedouin home makes reference to the Absentee's Property Law. Yet if Snyder's words indeed reflect a colonialist approach, it is also worthwhile mentioning Rita Kersting's comments in the leaflet for the exhibition that she curated and in which *The Eternal Sukkah* was exhibited. There she referred politely to the social background and embedded a critical approach toward the purchase: The "transformation passed by the construction from a Bedouin tent to a Jewish sukkah and later on to an art piece raises questions about refugees, the acceptance of the other, change of destiny and of an object, and about the complex relations between art and contemporary times." The museum, aware or not, performed an action that constitutes the inverse of the Civil Administration's act: Instead of declaring a Bedouin home illegal and destroying it, the museum bought it, legalized it, exhibited it, and preserved it.

Abu Suleiman's visit was an active performance of recognizing the hybrid sukkah as a piece that still belongs to his own heritage. If the hut was a performative set, Abu Suleiman and Abu Jamal were performing sovereignty. When Mira Lapidot, the museum's chief curator, came to welcome him half an hour before the beginning of the symposium, she entered the sukkah and approached Abu Suleiman, who greeted her with a warm "Welcome [home]." Through this rhetorical and performative act, the entire story of ownership was inverted. For a moment, the museum became the desert, *The Eternal Sukkah* became the Bedouin shanty in Khan al-Akhmar, the museum staff and public became Abu Suleiman's guests, and the museum director became a custodian.

During the symposium, Alon Cohen-Lifshitz and Abu Suleiman spoke about the political situation and current governmental plans; Rachel Elior discussed the connection to the Jewish holiday of Sukkot and the value of hospitality in Jewish and Bedouin cultures; and Daphna Ben-Shaul and Amitai Mendelsohn framed the discussion in the art and performative contexts. The advocate of the Jahalin, Moshe Lecker, added a comprehensive explanation of their legal situation and struggle.[34]

Three weeks later, at Abu Suleiman's suggestion, a day tour to the Israel Museum was organized for forty Jahalin children, having secured permits for them to enter Israel. They visited the archeology and contemporary art galleries as well as the sculpture garden; they attended a series of art workshops; and they ended their tour with a brief talk at the Bedouin sukkah, inverting again the role of visitor and host. The same day, the children went to the Jerusalem Zoo, at their request. During a break, I approached one of Abu Suleiman's sons, Suleiman, who had joined us on this tour and was sitting beside the zoo's reconstructed Noah's Ark. He and his younger brother, Tareq, were amazed when they discovered the sukkah at the museum. I asked him what he thinks about it now. He told me that it is an important project. However, he also found it sad to see the structure inside the building and not in the desert, in its natural setting. In this symbolic setting, his words assumed a profound meaning. Is the Bedouin hut in the museum akin to those animals in the zoo, an exemplar of exotic culture decontextualized for educational or aesthetic purposes? Is it a political statement attempting to call attention to the threat this community has lived under for so many years? Is it possible to display ethnography without the feeling that the displayed object and/or their owners are being betrayed?

Politicization and Politics: The Bedouin Structure at the Museum

The acquisition of *The Eternal Sukkah* generated a great deal of discussion in Israeli media. On the nationwide Israeli army radio network, Galey Tzahal, veteran journalist Rino Tsror interviewed Mira Lapidot and defined the acquisition of the sukkah as a historic act, "the first official recognition of the [Bedouin] diaspora." Many other positive reactions by artists and the general public were expressed on social media. Yet there were also some critical and negative voices, which I have discussed elsewhere.[35] The quantity of media attention and the polarized nature of these reactions to an artwork reflect this project's potential to tackle a major cause of tension in Israeli discourse: cultural borders, the "offense" of crossing them, and the anxiety related to any attempt to construct a hybrid historiography, house, land, or identity.

Daphna Ben-Shaul writes about the fusion between shack and sukkah as an action that turns displacement into a kind of common denominator but that is capable of giving

> rise to sense of solidarity between groups and individuals who live in a state of constant threat from the authorities (for reasons of national security or otherwise) within the confines of their homes. That shared homelessness also directs attention to the fact that the endless Jewish Israeli efforts to justify the nation's belonging to the land and to portray the Israeli state as a national home involves demolishing the homes of anyone who is perceived as a foreign element under its sovereignty.[36]

Ben-Shaul refers to the rhetoric used by the artists, who depicted the project in transgressive terms. She is interested in the practice of politicizing the domestic site, including the sukkah, and describes the project as a pro-civic practice—sometimes interpreted negatively or questionably by the right wing and the extreme left.

The artists, as expressed in private conversations, attempted to use the art system, its economy, and its power not only to confront the art system itself but also to publicize an urgent social and political matter: the situation of the Bedouin community. However, the Jahalin had slightly different objectives, as illustrated in several conversations with Abu Suleiman.[37] The Jahalin saw the project as a good opportunity to pursue an alternative method of advocacy and as a way to repair one of their structures. For the museum, the intention, as expressed by curator Amitai Mendelsohn, was to highlight practices of contemporary artists in Jerusalem and to approach social and political issues in a nondirect way (or at least, that was their expectation).

A Tent Within a Structure: The Bawadi Ecotourism Initiative

For a few hours the dismantled Bedouin hut in the desert left an empty space, which was filled that same night with a new and stronger cabin. This new cabin was built using wooden beams bought with the money made from selling the structure to the artists. The cabin was originally built to host a family returning to the area for the winter, but after a couple of months the al-Korshan family decided to intervene in the cabin. The walls were dismantled, leaving only the roof, and the structure was covered by a shade cloth. The interior was arranged with typical Bedouin carpets (some of them made in China), mattresses, and other new and old "folkloric" items. A large piece of new cloth was positioned to hide the ceiling, creating the feeling of being outdoors in a traditional Bedouin tent. The new cabin became a focal point for displaying Bedouin culture and hosting tourists visiting the "Bawadi ecotourism" project.[38] This was the entrance to what John Comaroff and Jean Comaroff refer to as an ethno-enterprise initiative: Those belonging to a particular ethnic group generate an enterprise to enhance "their autonomy, political presence, and their material circumstance by adroitly managing their tourist potential."[39]

"Bawadi," as its Facebook page states (also copied to the website that the Sala-Manca Group designed for them),

> is a Bedouin-driven eco-tourism initiative offering guided hikes along the ancient shepherding routes of the West Bank, Palestine, often known only to the Bedouin ... Bedouin youth ... [who] continue their traditional journeys through Palestine and give voice to their story.... Inviting guests to experience the song, the story and the silence of the desert, Bawadi is both a vehicle for advocacy and for income generation for Bedouin youth wishing to safeguard and promote their distinct culture and traditions. [It includes] traditional Bedouin lunches, dinners and overnights under the stars in local communities.... Sharing the little-explored and spectacular landscapes, flora and fauna of Palestine's deserts with visitors is a celebration of the Bedouin's living heritage.[40]

At the Israel Museum *The Eternal Sukkah* became a displayed ethnographic work of art out of its natural context. In the Bawadi experience, the desert, the real place, becomes a destination culture, an open-air museum for displaying and performing the Bedouin heritage under threat of forced exile.

The Bedouin villages and heritage, which are not recognized as legitimate by the Israeli government, undergo a process of self-recognition, re-creation, and interpretation, redefining Bedouin folklore and traditions through the active process of performing, textualization, and sharing.[41] Heritage and tourism, as Barbara Kirshenblatt-Gimblett argues, are collaborative industries: Heritage converts locations into destinations and tourism makes them economically viable as exhibits in themselves.[42] This applies to the case of Bawadi, an ecotourism initiative that might be included in the series of projects that Comaroff and Comaroff define as corporate identities, where culture is for sale and for survival, where a tribe becomes a corporation redefining a new identity, a new income.[43]

Bawadi is not only a *for*-profit project; it is also an activist initiative against the territorial and economic policies of the Israeli government; it is a counterperformance against the performance of hut demolitions. It is likewise activist in its ecological approach to home construction (based on recycled material) and in its attitude to the climate change crisis and the fight against consumerism. Bawadi also plays an opposing role to the Society for the Protection of Nature in Israel, which transforms natural areas into national parks in order to fulfill the duty of preserving the human heritage and to implement the Israeli politics of land confiscation. In this political process, ironically, the guard of the National Park was a member of the Jahalin tribe. Bawadi creates parks through performance, where heritage is performed to realize the Bedouins' rights. If a new settlement is going to be built in Khan al-Akhmar, it will be on the ruins of the Jahalin's intangible culture, or it may even coexist with it, perhaps unknowingly.[44]

FIGURE 1.5. Bawadi Ecotourist Initiative, Jerusalem. Photo: Bawadi Facebook Page.

According to Israeli law, the Jahalin do not legally own the lands on which they live and do not have the right to wholesome living conditions. Yet, according to their own beliefs and narrative, they own the secrets of the desert. They know and use the ancient shepherding routes that are being converted, through this initiative, into Bedouin heritage hiking routes. It is actually through the practice of walking or hiking that the Jahalin assert their sovereignty in the desert. They walk their heritage in order to share it, and share it in order to own it.

The Bawadi ecotourism initiative was created to generate income in times of economic and political trouble. In a post on its Facebook page, Bawadi stresses the fact that it is the first company to have an authorized guide licensed by the Palestinian Authority's Ministry of Tourism and Antiquities. The license is not only an important step in the company's development but also a legal recognition of the al-Korshan family as representatives of their own heritage.

According to Bawadi, the tours are a way of exploring the Bedouin landscape, its flora, and fauna—a process for shared celebration. To hike with the Jahalin, with the Bedouins, becomes a political statement, concurrent with their practice of performing Bedouin heritage. Tourists walk or hike in a pacific act of identification with the "natives." Bawadi hikes are part of a performative process of decolonizing, a walking practice contrary to a translocation process intended to proceed according to Israel's expansionist politics as manifest in the E1 Plan for the area east of Jerusalem.[45]

Conclusion

Both structures, *The Eternal Sukkah* at the Israel Museum and the Bedouin tent inside the shack structure in the Bawadi ecotourism project, are parallel developments in exhibiting the Jahalin heritage, past and present. Both refer to cultural ideas of home and are disguised as museological objects telling the stories of the Jahalin. Both are exhibitions displaying transient homes recontextualized. Both are structures inside structures.

The connection between *The Eternal Sukkah* and the Bawadi ecotourism initiative is not just symbolic. The money received from the sale of the hut to the museum was devoted to developing this tourist enterprise, which centered, at least at the time of this research, on the same symbolic landmark where the Bedouin hut was first acquired.

Both *The Eternal Sukkah* in the museum and the Bedouin tent displayed inside a Bedouin shanty mark the introduction of the Bedouin tent into two different arenas: the art discourse and the ethno-enterprise. These two structures coexist in such a way that enriches understandings of one another. They are part of a long-term process of collaboration that functions through strategies of disguised display. In the case of Bawadi, the traditional Bedouin tent is a symbol of a proud Bedouin heritage that acquires its specific power through its contrast with the contemporary shack hosting its display. The Israel Museum is itself a symbolic architectural spolia: Palestinian architectural heritage as a monument of the past exhibited by the new rulers. Yet in this context *The Eternal Sukkah* reveals (very quickly) that the sukkah is not only a sukkah but a contemporary disguised Jahalin home, a testimony to the Bedouins' political situation, which is ostensibly hidden.

Documentation of *The Eternal Sukkah* project was exhibited in Bergen, Aarhus, San Diego, Jerusalem, and Kfar Yehoshua. Presentations, screenings, and talks were conducted in Kingston (Ontario), Montreal, Toronto, Buenos Aires, Jerusalem, and Göttingen. At some of these presentations, when possible, guest speakers from the local Bedouin communities were invited to speak.

The Bawadi ecotourism initiative continued to be active on a small scale until the beginning of the COVID-19 pandemic. Since the end of the exhibition "We the People" in March 2016, *The Eternal Sukkah* has lain dismantled in the Israel Museum's storage room, far from public view, at a time when the threat of transfer is stronger than ever.[46]

Notes

1. See Hasan-Rokem, "Material Mobility." On contemporary sukkot in Israel, see Berlinger, *Framing Sukkot*.
2. *The Eternal Sukkah* discussed here is part of a series that began in 2006 consisting of four sukkot created by the Sala-Manca Group. For a brief introduction to these projects, see Mauas and Rotman, "Diary for a Landscape."

3 www.sukkahcity.com/ (accessed February 8, 2020).
4 From the text published for the exhibition; see www.Sala-manca.net/?p=99 (accessed April 8, 2015). In a text on the situation of the Jahalin in Khan al-Akhmar written in 2017, Orly Noy drew a similar connection between the Bedouin home and the sukkah: "Is there another way to awaken the Jewish-Israeli conscience, which instructs us to remember that the sukkah was an integral part of our forefathers' journey from slavery to freedom? That this is not so different from the dilapidated shacks that house the residents of Khan al-Ahmar, from which the state is trying to expel them? Will the fate of hundreds of people, children and elderly who live in deep poverty just a short drive away from the settlement of Kfar Adumim, be of any interest to us a moment before we go back to our daily routine after the holiday comes to an end?" (Noy, "Bedouin Village").
5 Rotman, "On the Architecture of the Ephemeral." For other scholarly work on *The Eternal Sukkah*, see Ben-Shaul, "Civic Bi-Longing"; and Cohen, "Wall and Tower." On the role of the sukkah as a symbolic icon in social protest in contemporary Israel, see Berlinger, "From Ritual to Protest."
6 Al-Korshan, "Written Submission to the UN Forum on Minority Issues."
7 Weizman and Sheikh, *Conflict Shoreline*, 41–45.
8 Hass, "Stop the Expulsion of the Bedouin." See also Hass, "West Bank Bedouin Fighting Israel's Plan."
9 "The Interim Agreements between Israel and the PLO, divided the West Bank into three categories: Area A, currently comprising about 18 percent of the land in the West Bank . . . ; the Palestinian Authority (PA) is endowed with most governmental powers in this area. Area B comprises approximately 22 percent of the West Bank and encompasses large rural areas; Israel retained security control of the area and transferred control of civil matters to the PA. Area C covers 60 percent of the West Bank. . . . Israel has retained almost complete control of this area, including security matters and all land-related civil matters, including land allocation, planning and construction, and infrastructure. The PA is responsible for providing education and medical services to the Palestinian population in Area C. . . . Civil matters remain under Israeli control in Area C and are the responsibility of the Civil Administration" ("Planning Policy in

the West Bank," B'Tselem, February 6, 2019, www.btselem.org/area_c/what_is_area_c; accessed July 15, 2015). See also Sharon, "Bedouins of the Judean Desert," 6.

10 See, for example, Zafrir, "Solar Power Is Great."
11 As stated by the mukhtar, Abu Raed al-Korshan, and Abu Suleiman al-Korshan in 2016 during a series of video interviews I conducted in 2016 in Khan al-Akhmar.
12 Kinney, "Introduction," 1–11.
13 Esch, "On the Reuse of Antiquity," 23.
14 Esch, "On the Reuse of Antiquity," 23.
15 See Kinney, "Introduction," 3.
16 Johannessen, "Unliveable Spaces," 8.
17 Hass, "Israel Tells West Bank Bedouin." This approach is not unique to Area C but is also evident in the Negev; see, for example, Ben Zikri, "Israeli Court Orders Bedouin to Pay Cost."
18 On the artists' approach as critical ethnography in reference to S. Ansky's ethnographic expedition, see Ben-Shaul, "Civic Bi-Longing."
19 The rest of the original budget (4,000 ILS) was used for transportation, permits, and symbolic fees for the participant artists and for the future storage of the sukkah.
20 The idea of a Palestinian house or village contained by a Jewish and Israeli art institution was not new in Israel, where the most notable example is the entire "artists' village" of Ein Hod. When Jews, most of them artists, came to live in the Palestinian houses of Ein Hod, the former Palestinian inhabitants relocated to a new village named Ein Chud on a nearby mountaintop from which their former village and homes are visible. See Yacobi, "Territory and Space"; and Jabareen, "Art and Spatial Disinheritance."
21 According to the al-Korshan family, traditional tents are no longer made, and there are no woman in the tribe who continue the tradition.
22 See, for example, Bishara, "Israel's Culture Minister Pushes Bill"; and "In Israel, It's 'Loyalty' or Culture: The Government Is Moving Forward with Its Brutish Attempt to Gag Artists and Cultural Institutions That Provide Vital Criticism," editorial, *Haaretz*, October 21, 2018.
23 Only some of the artists continued with the project: the Sala-Manca Group in collaboration with Itamar Mendes-Flohr and Yeshaiau Rabinowitz. The others continued developing other projects as part of the residency.

24 According to Salim Tamari, Canaan took the Arab patients from the city's leprosarium with him, and they all marched to the village of Silwan, where they remained until Canaan later founded a leprosarium north of Ramallah. The Moravian sisters Johanna Larsen and Ida Ressel reported that they led fifteen patients to Silwan in 1953 (at that time in Jordan) and stayed with them until the leprosarium north of Ramallah on Star Mountain was founded on June 12, 1960. See Rotman, "Fragile Boundaries of Paradise."
25 According to Maimonides, *tsara'at* could manifest in the walls of one's home. If the owner of the house sinned, colored streaks would appear on the wall of the house. This indicated that, as a consequence of his sin, God's presence had removed itself from the house. See Maimonides, *Mishneh Torah, N'gaim* 12:5.
26 Jeremy Milgrom, Facebook post, October 8, 2014, www.facebook.com/jeremy.milgrom (accessed January 20, 2021).
27 See Ben-Shaul, "Civic Bi-Longing."
28 Most of those reactions were expressed in the opening panel of *The Eternal Sukkah* project as reactions to the artists' expression of their desire to sell the sukkah to a museum. The entire session was videotaped and is part of the artists' archive.
29 See Baudrillard, *System of Objects*, 73–74.
30 See Efrat, "Land Marks."
31 For further discussion, see Ben-Shaul, "Civic Bi-longing"; Yahav, "Sala-Manca Artist Group"; and Rotman, "On the Architecture of the Ephemeral."
32 www.maariv.co.il/news/israel/Article-489570 (accessed February 11, 2020) [Hebrew].
33 In 1967, after the Six Day War, which saw the expansion of Jerusalem's municipal boundaries, Palestinians with assets in Jerusalem suddenly found themselves considered "absentee" owners, even though they never left their homes. Sometimes they were living only a few hundred meters away but outside the new Jerusalem city limits and officially in the West Bank, and they found their property confiscated only because Israel drew the new municipal border between them and their property, meaning that they were no longer residents of Jerusalem. For more information, see Hasson, "Supreme Court Rules." For the law in English, see knesset.gov.il/review/data/eng/law/kns1_property_eng.pdf (accessed February 11, 2020).

34 Video documentation (in Hebrew): www.youtube.com/watch?v=0PfvklpYjfE.
35 See Rotman, "On the Architecture of the Ephemeral."
36 Ben-Shaul, "Civic Bi-Longing," 253.
37 I conducted the interviews with Abu Suleiman between 2014 and 2017 and they were documented on video.
38 *Bawadi* in Arabic means "in the valley" and areas far from towns and villages. The enterprise started in 2012 under the name Sharai (desert) Eco-Tourism Company.
39 Comaroff and Comaroff, *Ethnicity, Inc.*, 24.
40 bawadi.org/ (accessed February 15, 2020). The website and the Facebook page are no longer active.
41 Heritage, writes Barbara Kirshenblatt-Gimblett, is a "value-added" industry; it produces the local for export. See Kirshenblatt-Gimblett, *Destination Culture*.
42 Kirshenblatt-Gimblett, *Destination Culture*, 151.
43 Comaroff and Comaroff, *Ethnicity, Inc.*
44 One of the posts on the Bawadi Facebook page stated, "The Palestinian desert is still the place to stroll away from confrontations with Israeli occupation." The desert becomes the photographic negative of confrontation, although it is in itself one of the arenas where colonization is actively taking place.
45 E1 is the name of a governmental plan to create an urban bloc between Ma'ale Adumim and Jerusalem, exacerbating the isolation of East Jerusalem from the rest of the West Bank and disrupting the territorial contiguity between the northern and southern parts of the West Bank. The Bedouin communities are within this area and they are to be translocated to carry out the plan. See "The E1 Plan and Its Implications for Human Rights in the West Bank," B'Tselem, November 27, 2013, www.btselem.org/settlements/20121202_e1_human_rights_ramifications.
46 Since the purchase of the structure by the Israel Museum, the artists tried to convince the museum to exhibit *The Eternal Sukkah* again at Sukkot, especially when there is still time to attempt to change the destiny of the Jahalin community. The dialogue between the Sala-Manca Group and Abu Suleiman continues. Likewise, I continue writing about the project.

Bibliography

al-Korshan, Mohammed. "Written Submission to the UN Forum on Minority Issues, December 14–15, 2010." www.ohchr.org/sites/default/files/Documents/HRBodies/HRCouncil/MinorityIssues/Session3/statements/MohammedalKorshanStatement.pdf (accessed September 20, 2023).

Baudrillard, Jean. *The System of Objects*, trans. James Benedict. London: Verso, 1996.

Ben-Shaul, Daphna. "Civic Bi-Longing: The Politicization of Domestic Site in Eternal Sukkah." In *Possession and Dispossession: Performing Jewish Ethnography in Jerusalem*, ed. Lea Mauas, Michelle MacQueen, and Diego Rotman, 231–67. Berlin: De Gruyter, 2022.

Ben Zikri, Almog. "Israeli Court Orders Bedouin to Pay Cost of Their Eviction from Unrecognized Village." *Haaretz*, August 8, 2019.

Berlinger, Gabrielle A. *Framing Sukkot: Tradition and Transformation in Jewish Vernacular Architecture*. Bloomington: Indiana University Press, 2017.

———. "From Ritual to Protest: Sukkot in the Garden of Hope." *Buildings and Landscapes: Journal of the Vernacular Architecture Forum* 24, no. 1 (2017): 1–25.

Bishara, Hakim. "Israel's Culture Minister Pushes Bill to Freeze Funds for Arts Organizations Highlighting Palestinian Narratives." *Hyperallergic*, August 10, 2018. hyperallergic.com/464763/israels-culture-minister-pushes-bill-to-freeze-funds-for-arts-organizations-highlighting-palestinian-narratives/ (accessed February 2, 2020).

Cohen, Mor. "Wall and Tower: Notes on Tactics and Tactical Experiments in Israeli Culture and Politics." *Networking Knowledge* 12, no. 2 (2019): 20–35.

Comaroff, John L., and Jean Comaroff. *Ethnicity, Inc*. Chicago: University of Chicago Press, 2009.

Efrat, Zvi. "Land Marks: The Emblematic Architecture of the Israel Museum and the Shrine of the Book." Draft ms. efrat-kowalsky.co.il/files/the-architecture-of-the-israel-museum.pdf (accessed December 10, 2014; URL unavailable).

Esch, Arnold. "On the Reuse of Antiquity: The Perspectives of the Archaeologist and of the Historian." In *Reuse Value: Spolia and Appropriation in Art and Architecture from Constantine to Sherrie Levine*, ed. Richard Brilliant and Dale Kinney, 13–31. Farnham, UK: Ashgate, 2011.

Hasan-Rokem, Galit. "Material Mobility Versus Concentric Cosmology in the Sukkah: The House of the Wandering Jew or a Ubiquitous Temple?"

In *Things: Religion and the Question of Materiality*, ed. Dick Houtman and Birgit Meyer, 153–79. New York: Fordham University Press, 2012.

Hass, Amira. "Israel Tells West Bank Bedouin: First Sign a Voluntary Eviction, Then We'll See If the New Location Stinks." *Haaretz*, September 1, 2018.

———. "Stop the Expulsion of the Bedouin." *Haaretz*, September 9, 2014, editorial section.

———. "West Bank Bedouin Fighting Israel's Plan for Forcible Relocation: High Court Petition Aims to Stop State Relocating 12,500 Bedouin to New Town." *Haaretz*, December 3, 2014, sec. A.

Hasson, Nir. "Supreme Court Rules: Israel Can Confiscate Palestinian Property in Jerusalem." *Haaretz*, April 16, 2015. www.haaretz.com/israel-news/1.652231 (accessed February 11, 2020).

Jabareen, Yosef. "Art and Spatial Disinheritance: The Uprooted Village of Ein Chud." *Block* 6, no. 6 (2008): 82–90 [Hebrew].

Johannessen, Runa. "Unliveable Spaces: Architecture and Violence in the West Bank." PhD diss., University of Copenhagen, 2018.

Kinney, Dale. "Introduction." In *Reuse Value: Spolia and Appropriation in Art and Architecture from Constantine to Sherrie Levine*, ed. Richard Brilliant and Dale Kinney, 1–11. Farnham, UK: Ashgate, 2011.

Kirshenblatt-Gimblett, Barbara. *Destination Culture: Tourism, Museums, and Heritage*. Berkeley: University of California Press, 1998.

Mauas, Lea, and Diego Rotman. "Diary for a Landscape to Take With." In *The Imaginary Republic*, ed. Brandon Labelle, 28–39. Berlin: Errant Bodies, 2020.

Noy, Orly. "The Bedouin Village Where Compassion Ends," *+972 Magazine*, October 6, 2017. www.972mag.com/the-bedouin-village-where-compassion-ends/ (accessed February 15, 2020).

Rotman, Diego. "The Fragile Boundaries of Paradise: On the Paradise Inn Resort at the Former Jerusalem Leprosarium." In *Borderlines: Essays on Mapping and the Logic of Place*, ed. Edwin Seroussi and Ruthie Abeliovich, 160–73. Warsaw: Sciendo De Gruyter, 2019.

———. "On the Architecture of the Ephemeral: The Eternal Sukkah of the Jahalin Tribe." *Journal of Modern Jewish Studies* 16, no. 3 (2017): 498–514.

Sharon, Moshe. "The Bedouins of the Judean Desert." Paper presented at the Symposium About the Bedouins in Memoriam of Yitzhak Nezer. www.snunit.k12.il/bedein/arti/0633.html (accessed October 4, 2015) [Hebrew].

Weizman, Eyal, and Fazal Sheikh. *The Conflict Shoreline: Colonialism as Climate Change*. Göttingen: Steidl, 2015.

Yacobi, Haim. "Territory and Space in Israeli Society and Politics." *Israel Studies* 13, no. 1 (2008): 94–118.

Yahav, Galia. "Sala-Manca Artist Group Wanted to Protest the Occupation—but Ended Up Joining It." *Haaretz*, November 12, 2015.

Zafrir, Rinta. "Solar Power Is Great, Unless You Are a Bedouin in the West Bank." *Haaretz*, January 1, 2016.

2

SOUND OBJECTS

Music, Material Culture, and the Sound Study of the Synagogue

Francesco Spagnolo

A Musical Prologue in Two Parts

In an essay emphatically titled "Music, The 'Jew' of Jewish Studies," musicologist Edwin Seroussi decried the marginality of music within the field of Jewish studies: "Within the modern scholarly discourses on Jewish culture . . . , music emerges as a relatively minor field of inquiry in comparison to other disciplines." Only in recent decades have scholars from a variety of fields and disciplines "addressed music from very diverse angles, as a vital component of Jewish religious experience, reactions to social shifts, and constructions of memory, place, identity, and gender."[1]

It is safe to say that the subject of material culture occupies an equally liminal place in the context of Jewish studies and that its consideration by scholars in a variety of fields and disciplines is still in its infancy. The liminality of both music and material culture in this arena can be certainly decried. But it can also be seen as an opportunity for the entirety of the field of Jewish studies itself—a field that originates from marginality, both cultural and epistemological—to rethink its tenets, to reframe itself in a broadened and epistemologically more inclusive perspective. In fostering such inclusivity, I am proposing to consider music and material culture not only as separate fields of inquiry within Jewish studies but also in their intersection with one another. A particular case study and locus of interest for such a consideration is the synagogue, past and present, as an intimate space for the negotiation of Jewish cultural identity and as a porous arena of intercultural dialogue. We can thus consider the "sound study" of the synagogue as an intersection of music *and* material culture and of music *as* material culture.[2] Studying the many dimensions of sound in the context of synagogue life means directly addressing several of the material cultures that make it up. These range from the activities of individuals and groups making sound (e.g., sounds from cantors, choruses, and congregants singing along or "creating" ritual noises with their bodies or with dedicated objects), to the objects that emit sound in the course of their ritual use (e.g., a variety of musical instruments and ritual objects with movable parts, such as the various decorations adorning the scrolls of the Hebrew Bible), to the choreographies of ritual music making and sound making across the cultures of the global Jewish Diaspora.

In considering some preliminary thoughts on how to structure a sound study of the synagogue, I would like to suggest two possible paths, or methodological entryways. Both stem from my own decades-long research interest in the synagogue music of the Jews of Italy, a field in which I have been able to study a wide variety of sources, ranging from written and literary ones to sound recordings, including my own fieldwork, conducted over the last two decades.

The first path I am proposing comes from my direct observation, as an ethnographer who is also a synagogue-goer. While attending Friday evening services at the main synagogue of Milan, Italy, I was particularly struck by the body language of the cantor, the late Rabbi Elia Richetti (1948–2021), during the recitation of the Kiddush, or sanctification of the Sabbath over wine. The Hebrew text he recited was the normative one in use among Jews following the Italian (or *italiyani*) rite. The cantor sang the blessings according to a melody he had acquired, as I later learned, from his maternal grandfather, Rabbi Ermanno (Ermin Zvi) Friedenthal (b. Bátaszék, Hungary, 1881; d. Milan, Italy, 1970).[3] It was, as the cantor told me in the course of an interview, a family tradition originating from Gorizia and a hauntingly beautiful example of the Ashkenazic *minhag* from Northern Italy, reminiscent of the intersection of late eighteenth-century opera and Central European *nusach*. Yet, what struck me the most about his rendition was not the melody but the gesture made by the cantor *immediately after* singing the words *bore peri ha-gefen* (creator of the fruit of the vine), that is, after the conclusion of the blessing over wine, which precedes the blessing over the Sabbath day. The cantor would hold up the silver Kiddush cup, bring it to his nose, take a brief pause (in the recitation of both text and melody), emphatically smell the scent of the wine emanating from the cup itself, and, invariably and almost inwardly to himself, smile.

This overtly self-conscious *gesture* of smelling the wine in the goblet, one that brings together text, music, body language, a ritual object (the goblet), and a food item (the wine), fascinates me to this day. On the one hand, this gesture could be understood according to Walter Benjamin's pioneering notion of an "aesthetics of the *gestus*." In discussing Kafka's *America* and its "Nature Theater of Oklahoma," Benjamin notes how gesture, when performed according to a set code, can act as a connector between the mundane and the heavenly.

> One of the most significant functions of this theater is to dissolve happenings into their gestic components. One can go even further and say that a good number of Kafka's shorter studies and stories are seen in their full light only when they are, so to speak, put on as acts in the "Nature Theater of Oklahoma." Only then will one recognize with certainty that Kafka's entire work constitutes a code of gestures. . . . Each gesture is an event—one might even say, a drama—in itself. The stage on which this drama takes place is the World Theater which opens up toward heaven.[4]

Furthering his analysis of gesture, Benjamin also seems to indicate how to understand its relationship with repetition and ritual, as forms of understanding and of transmission of knowledge that move beyond (or, at least, differently from) the linearity of intellectual processes.

> Experiments have proved that a man does not recognize his own walk on the screen or his own voice on the phonograph. The situation of the subject in such experiments is Kafka's situation. . . . He might catch hold of the lost *gestus* the way Peter Schlemihl caught hold of the shadow he had sold. He might understand himself, but what an enormous effort would be required! It is a tempest that blows from the land of oblivion, and learning is a cavalry attack against it.[5]

On the other hand, it should be pointed out that the cantor's gesture (raising the wine cup, pausing, smelling, and smiling) might also represent, de facto, a synesthetic performance of the discussion between the schools of Shammai and Hillel over the relationship (and possible hierarchy) between blessings and actions in Jewish ritual performance—a rabbinic rendition of speech-act theory—as chronicled in the Mishnah (*Berakhot* 8). The pause in the performance and the emphatic enjoyment of the wine before it is consumed (following the next blessing in the Kiddush ritual, the one over the Sabbath day) directly echo the disagreement between the two rabbinic schools: "These things are [disputed] between the school of Shammai and the school of Hillel about meals: The school of Shammai says, 'Bless the day, and afterward bless the wine.' The school of Hillel says, 'Bless the wine, and afterward bless the day.'"[6] In other words, the gesture—and the use of the wine cup—can be understood as a continuation and perhaps even as an interpretation of the rabbinic discussion by means of material culture. More broadly, the cantor's gesture in this particular ritual performance may serve as a reminder that, in approaching the topic of Jewish liturgy, one ought to cast a wide net, reaching far beyond text (or sound) alone and into the realm of *things*.

On a methodological level this approach can be defined as phenomenological, inasmuch as we acknowledge that *going back to the things themselves*, a leitmotif in the work of Edmund Husserl (1859–1938), involves considering the performance of prayers in the synagogue as a synesthetic experience, which encompasses time *and* form, space *and* architecture, text *and* literature, sound *and* music, and gesture *and* choreography, in bringing about the confluence of diverse and often conflicting aesthetic dimensions, representations of identity, and reconfigurations of the past.

My second proposed opening path comes from the comparative work that defines research in Jewish musicology and ethnomusicology, a field informed by the constant comparison of written and oral musical sources documenting the developments of Jewish oral traditions of synagogue song.[7] One of the most "famous" (or most widely performed) synagogue songs from Italy, which can also be heard in Conservative congregations across the United States, is a rendition of Psalm 29, *Mizmor le-david havu ladonai bene elim*, possibly composed by Michele Bolaffi (1768–1842) in 1826 for the Spanish-Portuguese synagogue of Livorno.[8] Written and recorded examples of this composition represent an array of variants of this melody in a variety of ritual traditions, including Livorno itself (Spanish-Portuguese), Casale Monferrato (Ashkenazic), Turin (Italian), Carpentras (Comtat Venaissin), and Eastern Mediterranean traditions from Salonica and Turkey.

This Livorno melody "wanders," as many melodies created or adopted in the context of Jewish life tend to do: It *travels* across communities, ritual identities, countries, and oceans. One could select many other examples to support this assertion, ranging from Hasidic melodies turned popular songs to the *incipit* of "La Marseillaise." In this context I am proposing to treat Jewish "wandering melodies" as musical objects, as commodities, with their history, biography, and currency across time and space.[9] Following this comparative approach appears to be conducive to the understanding of the circulation of material culture across the Jewish Diaspora. It also raises some crucial phenomenological questions: How does a musical object "travel," and what is it that actually "travels" so far and wide? What we hear through the comparative exercise of matching several variants of a given synagogue melody

FIGURE 2.1. Michele Bolaffi, "Mizmor ledavid" (1826), in *Versetti posti in musica dal Prof. Sig. M. Bolaffi. Dedicati al Sig. A. Crocolo.* Hebrew Union College, Birnbaum coll. Mus. Add. 11, no. 14:23–24.

is the sonic representation of a musical "structure" (the fact that a given melody under consideration, no matter how morphed in its varying environments, retains a certain basic pattern). At the same time, we also hear the very musical scores (which are tangible, not sonic, objects) that carry the melody across the Jewish Diaspora (by means of written or oral transmission), along with the relationship between the melody and the ritual gestures it accompanies (in the case of the Livornese example I used, the Torah processionals around the synagogue during the morning service of the Sabbath, when Psalm 29 is traditionally sung), and that define and mark one of the melody's constitutive elements, its rhythm and its connection with the body of those worshipping with it. These elements—musical structure, transmission, and gesture—*combined* define this and many other *wandering Jewish musical objects*. I do not hesitate to define this second approach in structuralist terms because its perspective can be applied to many other wandering objects of Jewish ritual life and beyond.

To summarize the methodological stance that I have outlined up to this point, I am thus proposing to:

1. Examine sounds (including music) in the synagogue as an essential aspect of Jewish material culture, intimately connected with Jewish everyday life (i.e., Jewish ritual is a *daily* occurrence).
2. Approach the study of the cultural history of the synagogue on the basis of *the observation and the reconstruction* of a set of complex interactions among sounds, texts, gestures (or body language), and objects (and thus space) in the present and in the past. This approach rests on the belief that what we call Jewish music (or Jewish musical traditions) is, along with other forms of material culture, the repository of unique information about relevant aspects of Jewish culture that are not necessarily found in other sources, typically written texts.
3. Appeal to a combined methodological framework that draws from concepts and practices derived from both phenomenological and structuralist analysis in order to carry out both an in-depth study of the synesthetic nature of Jewish ritual performance and the comparative understanding of its diasporic nature.

Musical Dimensions of Everyday Life

Jewish liturgical and paraliturgical music—namely, the array of ritual musical manifestations in the synagogue and the Jewish home—constitute one of the richest elements at play in the formation of cultural identity in the course of everyday life, as evidenced in the following realms:

- **Role of individuals and families in the shaping of communal life.** Liturgical music interacts with the cultural identity of individuals and families. It is passed on from one generation to the next and is intimately connected with the particular structure of the Jewish family. More than one oral tradition can coexist within the same family nucleus (if its members originate from different communities); or, vice versa, specific traditions can be kept within a single family, even when they differ from the customs followed by the surrounding community (e.g., if an individual family relocates to a different town). In the course of ethnomusicological research, the existence of mingled ritual identities should also be considered in assessing the social status of musical culture bearers and of their families within synagogue and communal life (rabbinic figures, *ba'ale tefilah* or cantorial figures, lay leaders, etc.).
- **Ritual, cultural, and social assets of a community.** Liturgical music also interacts with the *ritual identity* of a community. Often, however, the interaction between the text of the prayer book and the music connected to it in the liturgy may highlight the coexistence of different ritual identities within the same community (i.e., the music to which the text of the prayers is set may originate from a diverse array of musical repertoires, each marking distinct cultural and identitary traits). Liturgical music also relates to the cultural wealth of a community, because it concerns the background and the education of its leadership (rabbis, cantors, and lay leaders), as well as the relations with surrounding non-Jewish environments. Finally, liturgical music is connected with the socioeconomic status of a community and is a major factor at play in synagogue architecture, the hiring of professional (Jewish and non-Jewish) synagogue staff, the commissioning of liturgical compositions, the inclusion (or exclusion) of women and children in the performance of rituals, and so on.

- **Intercommunal networks.** Liturgical music is a relevant element in the interactions among communities, defining both contrasts and similarities. Communities that are geographically distant from one another may find a privileged channel of cultural exchange based on shared liturgical features; conversely, the hiring of a rabbi or a cantor from a different community may require the reconfiguration of the communal identity in relation to the newcomer's ritual and cultural backgrounds.

By considering individual, communal, and intercommunal dimensions, music can be seen not only as an *aspect* of Jewish everyday life but also as a *factor* that dynamically contributes to the shaping of cultural identity across time and place. As a crucial *locus* of communal interaction, and one that offers an intersection between normative Judaism and orally transmitted customs, liturgical musical practice offers a fertile terrain of investigation in which the cultural processes and changes occurring within a given community are fully represented. What emerges from the consideration of oral and written musical sources are the degrees to which older traditions have been preserved, the interplay between Jewish and non-Jewish repertoires, and the extent of openness to outside cultural influences manifested in synagogue life: in other words, a host of musical indicators of the relationship of a given Jewish group with its past and with the patterns of acculturation into mainstream Italian life. But the musical configuration of the ritual—which is always the result of an ongoing negotiation among the various components of a community—is also a strong indicator of the ideal image that a given community wants to present before its constituency as well as the surrounding host culture. This analysis may thus lead to highlighting extremely sensitive cultural traits, such as how a community strives to be perceived (by its members, by other communities, and by the surrounding non-Jewish world), how the role of tradition is conceived of as a part of social exchanges, and the degree of musical or cultural innovation deemed necessary to maintain a desirable level of cohesion among the different components of a Jewish group. Here, liturgical music seems to provide a highly charged context, in which social and political tensions, aesthetics and emotions, are both reflected and collectively performed.

From Synagogue Music to Sound Objects

Music in the synagogue exists within the broader context of a synagogue's soundscape. Aside from singing and instrumental performance, other sounds are intrinsically part of synagogue rituals. They can be created by bodies—congregants moving, shuffling, clapping, and, of course, humming along with cantors and prayer leaders—but also, most notably, by objects. Although noisemakers in use during the holiday of Purim and shofar horns, blown before and during the High Holy Days, are specifically created to emit sound, many Torah crowns, finials, pointers, shields, and other objects in Jewish ritual use do not exist primarily to make sound, and yet they often do. What constitutes a Jewish sound object?

In an attempt to answer this question, I worked closely with students in a seminar I taught at the University of California, Berkeley, in 2012 and eventually continued to explore the topic in an exhibition, titled "Sound Objects" (2013).[10] In both projects I combined the study of Jewish material culture with the emerging field of sound studies and investigated the role of objects that emit sound during synagogue rituals; also, I explored the general field of the study of the synagogue in terms of sound rather than under the more specific rubric of music. The exhibition included a selection of more than sixty objects, textiles, books, manuscripts, and photographs from the Magnes Collection of Jewish Art and Life, documenting ritual in the global Jewish Diaspora. It also integrated the on-site display with online resources consisting of images, texts, and the sounds recorded while "playing" several of the ritual objects on view. The exhibit was created, in part, in collaboration with the students of my undergraduate research seminar "Performing Texts: Music, Liturgy and Jewish Life," offered by the Department of Music of the University of California, Berkeley.[11] Over the course of the seminar, students worked closely with the holdings of the Magnes Collection and developed research projects describing select items included in the exhibition.

The project originated from the understanding that many of the objects used in the course of synagogue rituals generate sound. As mentioned, some ritual objects are designed to produce specific sounds, such as the shofar, the horn blown in the synagogue during the month of Elul (preceding the New Year) on Rosh Hashanah and Yom Kippur, or the noisemakers used in conjunction with the public reading of the name

Haman from the book of Esther. Since the process of Jewish Emancipation in nineteenth-century Europe, many synagogues have also incorporated musical instruments into the ritual, including the organ, and contemporary worship might also include a variety of musical instruments. In a variety of synagogue contexts, musical instruments can also be evoked, even though they are not physically played: "Imitation of musical instruments was part of the cantorial improvisation style and mannerisms in the Ashkenazi communities during the eighteenth century and the early nineteenth. Some cantors accompanied their improvisations with facial grimaces and body movements."[12]

Many other ritual objects are often designed to emit sound—the ones dedicated to the embellishing, storing, carrying, and reading of the Torah scrolls, as well as those used in the Havdalah ceremony that marks the end of the Sabbath and holidays—even though sound making is not their primary function. These ritual sound objects are not musical instruments per se. Rather, they are at times adorned with pendants or bells or made with movable parts that rattle, ring, or otherwise make sound when the objects are used (and moved around in the context of ritual performance). The sonic power of these objects is only apparently unintentional. The sounds they emit cannot be avoided, and sound-making parts are constitutive of their shapes, forms, and functions.

Although the sounds made by voices and musical instruments during ritual are closely regulated by rabbinic authorities, those sounds made by ritual objects typically are not. A performative approach to the study of ritual objects might thus shed a different light on an important aspect of Jewish life outside the scope of normative religion and yet one that is located at its very core: ritual, including the public reading of the Hebrew Bible in synagogue liturgy. In the following sections I provide some examples drawn from the exhibition.

The Voice of the Shofar

The shofar, an animal's horn prepared for use as a musical instrument, is the only ancient Jewish liturgical instrument that survived the destruction of the Second Temple of Jerusalem in the year 70 CE, and it is still in use. First mentioned in Exodus 19:16, it was sounded outside the synagogue to proclaim the new year and the jubilee year and was used as a signal and a call to war. In synagogue liturgy the shofar is sounded on Rosh Hashanah,

Yom Kippur, and in the month preceding them (Elul). According to the Talmud and the *Shulchan Aruch*, a shofar should be made of a ram's or wild goat's horn, both of which are naturally curved.[13] The horn should not be painted, but it can be gilded or carved with artistic designs, without modifying the mouthpiece. Shofar horns are produced around the Jewish world in many different shapes, from the horns of different animals, and their use may differ slightly (e.g., whether they are played daily during the month of Elul or not, depending on the liturgical custom) according to the biblical texts, prayers, and meditations that accompany its sounding. Size and weight of the materials equally affect both the sound and the gestures made by its player (*ba'al toqea'*, "master of the [shofar] blast"). The sounds emitted by a shofar are classified according to specific terminologies and can also be represented through written symbols.

Ritual Noise
According to the book of Esther, the holiday of Purim was instituted to remember the deliverance of the Jews from Haman's plot to kill them. It is celebrated in the month of Adar by sending portions of food to friends, making gifts to the poor, eating a festive meal, and reading the book of Esther (*megillah*) in the synagogue. Whenever the name of Haman is read, children and adult congregants often make loud noises with rattles to blot out the character's memory, along with that of other evildoers who are considered descendants of 'Amalek.[14] Special objects have been created across the Jewish Diaspora to assist in this action, a rare case in which noisemaking in the context of synagogue ritual is tolerated by religious authorities. At times, hammers or rocks are used to smash other rocks on which the name Haman had been previously inscribed. Again, the shape and fashion of ritual noisemakers changes across the Jewish world, affecting both the relationship with the world outside the synagogue (some noisemakers are adapted from those used in the secular world, e.g., to sound fire alarms, etc.), and the individual dynamics of noise production.

Cantors
The role of the synagogue cantor (in Hebrew, *chazan*) evolved over time into a musical, pastoral, and educational profession (or one of voluntary service to the community). The cantor's primary purpose, however, is that of *sounding out*—rather than "setting to music"—the liturgy, including the

texts of the prayers, of liturgical poetry, and of the Hebrew Bible. To this day, cantors embody the tension between the dimensions of sound and of music in Jewish ritual. Not every sound emitted by a cantor can necessarily be classified as music—chanting, spoken word, and vocal improvisations are all part of their sound repertoire. At times, cantors and prayer leaders also wish to influence the pace of the liturgy and do so by using the reading stand—and, on some occasions, the prayer books—as percussive devices, marking the rhythm of the music or chant they perform along with the congregations.

Sounds of the Torah

In order to be read during synagogue liturgy, the scrolls of the Hebrew Bible are carried from their storage location to the reading area and then returned after use. Ritual performance is, at times, accompanied by the sounds created by those objects dedicated to adorn the scrolls—cases, crowns, finials, and shields and at times also the garments used to dress the scrolls—or by Torah pointers, objects specifically designed to assist the reading by pointing at the text, which are often made of metal or wood and include movable parts and often bells or clappers in varying shapes. These sound devices are ubiquitous across the global Jewish Diaspora and are attested through time, indicating that sound production is somewhat coessential, albeit not mandatory, to the Torah scroll in its synagogue use. A manuscript dating from 1159, found in the Cairo Genizah, for example, already mentions Torah finials having bells.[15]

In this respect, the rituals surrounding the public reading of the Hebrew Bible in the synagogue can be also connected, through specific sound objects, to the ceremony that marks the end of Sabbaths and festivals (Havdalah), a ritual that can be celebrated both in the synagogue and in the Jewish home. The Havdalah service is introduced by blessings over wine, aromatic spices, and light, each marked by objects that assist in the ritual. Spice boxes and candle holders might also be complemented by bells or made of movable parts, which create sound during use. To better understand the sound of the Torah as an *object*, the "Sound Objects" exhibition was complemented by a digital playlist, hosted on the Soundcloud platform.[16] To create this playlist, a veritable example of *musique concrète*[17] made with Jewish ritual objects, each museum object was carefully handled as though it was being used in a ritual setting, and the sounds it emitted were recorded in short representative sound clips. The comparative listening of their sounds is coessential to their nature as things and will hopefully become an item of consideration in future comprehensive studies of Torah-related ritual objects.

Conclusion

Shifting the study of "music" in the synagogue to that of "sounds" implies a series of epistemological and methodological turns. In this essay I have attempted to create a methodological field that includes the daily musical practice of the synagogue under the rubric of material culture and consequently investigated the modes of sound production that characterize synagogue rituals. This shift has far-reaching consequences for the study of both music and material culture. In the context of musicology, musical praxis in the synagogue appears to be connected to a variety of sound-making functions and objects that are not often part of its field of investigation. In the context of the study of Jewish material culture, sound production emerges as a yet-undeveloped area of consideration.

Notes

1. Seroussi, "Music," 3–4.
2. On sound studies, see the foundational volume by R. Murray Schafer: Schafer, *Soundscape*.
3. Elia Richetti, personal communication, February 22, 2017, New York City. A public performance of the "Friedenthal family Kiddush" was performed by Rabbi Richetti in the course of a live concert I curated at Kehila Kedosha Janina Synagogue that same day.
4. Benjamin, "Franz Kafka," 120–21.
5. Benjamin, "Franz Kafka," 137–38. See also section 5 ("'The Quotable Gesture") of Benjamin, "What Is Epic Theater," 151.
6. *m. Berakhot* 8:1, Sefaria, www.sefaria.org/Mishnah_Berakhot.8?lang=bi (accessed January 1, 2020). See also BT *Berakhot* 51b:11–20.
7. See, for example, two classic studies by Hanoch Avenary: "Persistence and Transformation" and "Aspects of Time and Environment."

8 The earliest written sources of this melody, signed by Bolaffi, were unearthed by Eduard Birnbaum, and later by Israel Adler, and were researched by Edwin Seroussi in his study of Livornese synagogue music; see Seroussi, "Livorno." See also my additional research on the diffusion of this melody (and of its contemporary variants in Casale Monferrato) in Spagnolo, "Musical Traditions," 239–69.
9 On persistence and transformation of synagogue songs, see Avenary, "Aspects of Time and Environment." On the biography of objects, see Kopytoff, "Cultural Biography of Things."
10 Spagnolo, "Sound Objects."
11 Spagnolo, "Performing Texts."
12 Schleifer, "Synagogue Music."
13 TB *Rosh ha-shanah* 26a; *Shulchan Aruch, Orach Chayim* 586:17.
14 See Horowitz, "The Rite to Be Reckless."
15 See "List of silver vessels and precious textiles belonging to the two Rabbanite synagogues of Old Cairo" (dated 1159), MS, Univ. Library Cambridge, Taylor Schechter Collection, NS J 296, described by S. D. Goiten, "Synagogue Building." See also Yaniv, "Mystery of the Flat Torah Finials."
16 Spagnolo, "Sound Objects."
17 On the development of *musique concrète*, see Palombini, "Musique Concrète Revisited."

Bibliography

Avenary, Hanoch. "The Aspects of Time and Environment in Jewish Traditional Music." *Israel Studies in Musicology* 4 (1987): 93–123.

———. "Persistence and Transformation of a Sephardi Penitential Hymn Under Changing Environmental Conditions." *Yuval: Studies of the Jewish Music Research Centre* 5 (1986): 181–237.

Benjamin, Walter. "Franz Kafka: On the Tenth Anniversary of His Death" (1934). In *Illuminations: Essays and Reflections*, by Walter Benjamin, ed. Hannah Arendt, PAGES. New York: Harcourt, Brace, 1968:111–40.

———. "What Is Epic Theater?" (1939). In *Illuminations: Essays and Reflections*, by Walter Benjamin, ed. Hannah Arendt, 147–54. New York: Harcourt, Brace, 1968.

Goiten, S. D. "The Synagogue Building and Its Furnishings According to the Records of the Cairo Geniza." *Eretz-Israel: Archaeological, Historical, and Geographical Studies* 7 (1964): 169–72.

Horowitz, Elliott. "The Rite to Be Reckless: On the Perpetration and Interpretation of Purim Violence." *Poetics Today* 15, no. 1 (1994): 9–54.

Kopytoff, Igor. "The Cultural Biography of Things." In *The Social Life of Things: Commodities in Cultural Perspective*, ed. Arjun Appadurai, 64–90. Cambridge, UK: Cambridge University Press, 1986.

Palombini, Carlos. "Musique Concrète Revisited." *Electronic Musicological Review* 4 (June 1999). www.rem.ufpr.br/_REM/REMv4/vol4/arti-palombini.htm (accessed January 1, 2020).

Schafer, R. Murray. *The Soundscape: The Tuning of the World*. Rochester, VT: Destiny Books, 1994.

Schleifer, Eliyahu. "Synagogue Music and Its Development." In *Grove Music Online*, s.v. "Jewish Music." www.oxfordmusiconline.com/grovemusic/view/10.1093/gmo/9781561592630.001.0001/omo-9781561592630-e-0000041322 (accessed June 23, 2022).

Seroussi, Edwin. "Livorno: A Crossroads in the History of Sephardic Religious Music." In *The Mediterranean and the Jews: Society, Culture, and Economy in Early Modern Times*, ed. Elliot Horowitz and Moises Orfali, 131–54. Ramat Gan: Bar-Ilan University Press, 2002.

———. "Music: The 'Jew' of Jewish Studies." *Jewish Studies* 46, no. 11 (2009): 3–84.

Spagnolo, Francesco. "The Musical Traditions of the Jews in Piedmont (Italy)." PhD diss., Hebrew University of Jerusalem, 2007.

———. "Performing Texts: Music, Liturgy, and Jewish Life." Course notes, Fall 2012, University of California, Berkeley. performingtexts.wordpress.com (accessed January 1, 2020).

———. "Sound Objects: Case Study No. 3." Exhibit at the Magnes Collection of Jewish Art and Life, 2013, University of California, Berkeley. https://magnes.berkeley.edu/exhibitions/past-exhibitions/case-study-no-3-sound-objects/ (accessed January 1, 2020).

Yaniv, Bracha. "The Mystery of the Flat Torah Finials from East Persia." *Padyavand: Judeo-Iranian and Jewish Studies* 1 (1996): 63–74.

3

PLEASE BE SEATED

Benches and the Infrastructure of Judaism

Juliana Ochs Dweck

> The way we choose to sit, and what we choose to sit on, says a lot about us: our values, our tastes, the things we hold dear.
>
> —WITOLD RYBCZYNSKI, *Now I Sit Me Down*[1]

Benches, the humblest of seats, are among the most ubiquitous, so ordinary as to go almost unnoticed or at least to be taken for granted.[2] In cityscapes benches are places of repose, platforms on which to pause, perch, and view the world. In public spaces these long and sometimes portable pieces of plank seating provide fleeting moments of relief and surfaces of convenience during periods of transition. Park benches, traditionally made of stone or wood, and more recently of powder-coated steel or thermoplastic, are spots for both solitude and shared spectatorship; they mediate between the public realm of the city and the more intimate time and space of the individual and negotiate between competing temporalities, interjecting stasis into a bustling city. But off the street and outside the public domain, benches have another role, supporting not only bodies but also traditions. This is the case for the benches that have punctuated Jewish history and culture in spaces of study, prayer, and communal gathering. Since ancient times, benches have been objects that have not only embodied Jewish values and tastes but also played a supporting role in conferring sacrality and facilitating relationships.

In Jewish ritual and life, benches hide in plain sight, stealth objects that hover below the radar until they are summoned for use. In his memoir of

Jewish life in the 1870s in what is now Belarus, Shmaryahu Levin recalled his days as a student in the local Jewish elementary school.

> There I was, on a small, hard wooden bench with nine other children. . . . The table in front of the bench consisted of rough, unplaned planks, and the heads of the big nails which fastened them together stuck out, so that it was easy to get caught on them. The children sat on two benches, five on each side of the table, and Mottye the *melamed* sat at one end. . . . He did not sit still, but swayed back and forth as he taught. He bade us keep our hands above the table, look out for the nails, and sit respectfully.[3]

The sensation of the wooden benches of the *heder* lingered evocatively in Levin's mind, intermingling with his memories of teacher and texts. The small, hard wooden bench made learning a haptic experience, both mnemonic and metonymic of the discipline of his early childhood Jewish learning. A century later, cultural historian Marcie Cohen Ferris described a Jewish bench that lingered redolently in her own childhood memory of the synagogue in Blytheville, Arkansas, in the 1960s: "Benches—particularly pews—are the most visceral memory I have of my Jewish upbringing. The feeling of sitting in *our* Cohen seats each Friday night in Temple Israel. I knew every detail of that Jewish real estate, and made-up imaginary worlds about those spaces as my mind wandered during services."[4] In her memory, as in Levine's, the bench was a space to inhabit and an object recalled in embodied ways, with material qualities that signaled cultural values of solemnity and stability. The pew in her midcentury midwestern American synagogue defined Jewish time and space, demarcating a personal and familial realm within the larger sanctuary and creating a bridge between the liturgy of the service and the wandering imagination of a young girl finding her place in Jewish life.[5]

Aesthetically and haptically, benches are often associated with austerity: They are somber and stiff, the structural minimum needed to suspend a body off the ground. As landscape architect Laurie Olin has said about seats, benches perform "their parts quietly";[6] they recede—by design—into the background, quite unlike a gleaming pair of filigreed silver Torah finials, an engraved Kiddush cup held aloft for all to see, or a gilded Hanukkah lamp aglow in flickering light. Unassuming benches retreat into the background of Jewish ritual and practice, but they still, in common with these more illustrious ritual objects, have enabling qualities: supporting interaction, transmitting values and identities, and facilitating experiences of sacrality. Benches have a social agility, connecting people to the divine and to texts, to histories, and to other human bodies. Although there is nothing inherently Jewish about benches, their capacity to demarcate time and space and to bind Jews to each other, to texts, to traditions, to a shared peoplehood but equally to enact segregation and marginalization, suggests that they might be a Jewish cultural object worthy of investigation. Seating and the arrangement of seats in Jewish life have significance well beyond the communal bench, whether it is the arrangement of dining chairs around a holiday table or the stack of folding chairs set out before a synagogue Kiddush lunch. Samuel Heilman's classic 1976 sociological analysis of the social and theological drama that unfolds in an American Orthodox synagogue brought attention to the diverse modes in which people occupy space in a synagogue, from the ways congregational regulars consistently place themselves in the sanctuary's folding chairs to the moments and spaces for social gathering outside the sanctuary, with different compositions cementing social alliances and levels of religious observance.[7] My interest, however, is specifically in the objectness of benches: the physical presence, material qualities, aesthetic attributes, and haptic sensations of these portable yet enduring things. In this essay I offer an intentionally eclectic exploration of benches as Jewish material culture through ancient, early modern, modern, and contemporary examples spanning Europe, North America, and the Caribbean, divided into four interrelated taxonomies: (1) benches of learning, (2) benches as ritual objects for life-cycle events, (3) benches for prayer, and (4) benches of exclusion.

The focus on benches diverges from traditional categories of Judaica, whether Torah scrolls or Sabbath lamps, to experiment with a new object type that possesses its own ritual power to mark sacred time and space. Part of that ritual power derives from the capacity that benches have to contribute to what we might call an infrastructure of Judaism. Sociologist Susan Leigh Star has defined infrastructure as something that is "invisible [and] part of the background for other kinds of work"[8] but that operates as a cultural object and agent in its own right. Recent work in anthropology has examined how public infrastructures such as roads, pipes, or electrical wires circulate and distribute materials and technologies in ways that enable and sometimes constrain a range of social and political possibilities. One might consider the infrastructure that supports Jewish ritual life, encompassing the social networks, communal relationships, and circulations of products that facilitate adherence to tradition. *Eruv* enclosures can be said to function in this capacity, as physical and symbolic delineations made for the purpose of allowing activities normally prohibited on the Sabbath to occur within a proscribed space.[9] Benches also serve in an infrastructural capacity within the flow of Jewish life, demarcating time and social structure, facilitating flows of ideas and texts, and mediating the connections between humans that sustain and are sustained by religious traditions.[10]

Benches of Learning

The role that benches play in the infrastructure of Jewish education has a long history, the arrangement of wooden benches in Shmaryahu Levin's modest schoolhouse linked, in fact, to an ancient tradition of Jewish learning. The Talmud records the transformative role that benches played in Jewish learning in Babylon (present-day Iraq) in the first century CE.[11] When Rabbi Elazar ben Azarya succeeded Rabbi Gamliel as the *nasi*, the highest rabbinic position, the first change he instituted was to add benches to the house of study. The Gemara relates that, on his first day, several benches were added to the study hall to accommodate the numerous students eager to learn, but the rabbis dispute this number. According to one Talmudic opinion, four hundred benches were added, whereas another view suggests that it was seven hundred benches; the commentary that mediates between these opinions underscores the value that Jewish tradition places on seating capacity.[12] Although four hundred benches may have been the actual number, it is said that seven hundred was cited for hyperbolic effect to highlight metaphorically the new leader's radical embrace of open learning: A vast number of benches would signal the countless numbers of new interpretations, commentaries, and insights that would expand and enhance Torah study. The Talmud's numeration of additional seats—not additional students—is what symbolizes this radical hospitality as a broader range of Jewish society was welcomed into the *beit midrash* (house of learning and interpretation) that day.

To this day, the concept of seven hundred benches resonates as a symbol of inclusive learning. In 2018 in Piedmont, California, Rabbi Dev Noily, of Kehilla Community Synagogue, in collaboration with SVARA ("a traditionally radical yeshiva dedicated to the serious study of Talmud and committed to the Queer experience")[13] announced the launch of an initiative called 700 Benches. It would be a "radically inclusive" house of study that invited anyone who can read Hebrew into a "direct, un-translated relationship with the Hebrew and Aramaic texts of our tradition." An advertisement for the program displayed a sea of park benches in a multi-hued array of red, blue, yellow, and green to underscore their embodiment of inclusion.

Sacred texts may be the principal conduits of Jewish learning, but—whether in Babylonia or Piedmont, California—benches create conditions of possibility for textual transmission and communal engagement. Affordable, durable, accessible, and portable, benches have a collectivizing quality that gives this piece of furniture a pedagogic utility: When inhabited by a pair or a group of students, they turn individuals into equals for the duration of their sit. They also promote particular forms of comportment and attention. Historian Kenneth Ames proposed posture as an artifact in itself, something shaped as much by furniture and culture as physiology. For example, "When sitters conformed to the postures asserted by [Victorian parlor chairs and sofas], they sat bold upright or nearly so, in a position that confirmed their status as competent human beings and projected both gentility and control."[14] The colorful sea of park benches advertised by SVARA are of the traditional park variety, with angled backs that place bodies in a posture of repose. In contrast, Levin's Belarussian backless plank wooden bench was a type more typically associated with indoor learning, never truly conforming to the human body, although they may have been worn down by touch over time. Anatomically, plank benches set the spine in a near vertical position, placing legs and hips at about 90 degrees, thighs parallel to the floor, and feet flat on the ground. They inevitably promote an engaged posture that, unlike the upright Victorian chairs Ames described, demands neither frontal nor static comportment but rather compels sitters to shift, lean, and, most important, participate.

Rustic benches found in American Jewish summer camps facilitated learning that was interactive, democratic, and, indeed, bucolic.[15] In the mid-twentieth century, when Jewish camps were presenting themselves as an escape from industrial and then suburban centers, a way of maintaining tradition while ensuring relevance, the aesthetic of benches—unadorned, undomesticated, neither urban nor suburban—can be said to have played a role in that process of communal reinvention.[16] In a photograph from about 1946, girls in an updated New York Jewish sleepaway camp pose in the camp's wood and clay shop, a bench running diagonally into the foreground. Given the carefully staged tableau, one cannot help but consider the prominent long wooden bench occupied by just one girl, incised and splattered with the paint and clay of campers' self-expression. This photograph is but one example, because everything at Jewish camp seemingly involved rough-hewn benches: dining, learning, praying, singing. This bench's protuberance underscores benches' broader role in the infrastructure of summer camp, one among an assemblage of midcentury artifacts that worked in June and July to undo baby boomer assimilation and fashion as distinct American Jewish culture—interactive, collaborative, and

FIGURE 3.1. Girls working in the wood and clay shop, ca. 1946. Jewish Community Center of Greater Buffalo and Summer Camps Records, 1915–2009. Courtesy University Archives, State University of New York, Buffalo.

encouraging forms of Jewish learning and material engagement beyond religious texts.

Benches as Ritual Objects

Benches' material qualities are more distinctive in the context of life-cycle events, where they function as ritual objects to support ceremony, demarcate sacred time and space, and give material form to spiritual symbols. The sixteenth-century compilation of Jewish ritual and law, the *Shulchan Aruch*, dictates in *Yoreh Deah* 265:11 that during the foundational Jewish life-cycle ritual of circumcision, a bench or a chair should be reserved for Elijah the Prophet, who, according to Jewish lore, attends all circumcisions as an angel of the covenant to protect and bless the child. A tradition with origins in the tenth century, a physical Chair of Elijah (*kiseh shel Eliyahu*) is usually an elevated seat placed centrally but left unoccupied; many synagogues have an ornamental chair for this purpose.[17] In some traditions the eight-day-old baby boy is placed on this chair while the ritual circumciser (mohel) recites the opening prayer that begins, "This is the Chair of Elijah." Since at least the tenth century, the godfather (*sandek*), the family or community member who is honored with holding the child during the *brit*, would sit in a special chair, usually located to the left of the Chair of Elijah but often difficult to distinguish from it. According to Shalom Sabar, "At times the chair of Elijah is identical with that of the *sandek* but in other cases the latter chair has a different design. Thus, it may be higher and occasionally fitted with a special footrest for the *sandek*'s feet."[18]

Some Chairs of Elijah are distinctly intended for the prophet, such as one richly carved and ornamented chair in the collection of the Israel Museum in Jerusalem, considered one of the most sumptuous items produced by the Bezalel School. Designed by Ze'ev Raban (born in Poland, active in Israel, 1890–1970), it is made of walnut wood, leather, woolen carpet, embroidery on silk and velvet, ivory, shell, silver filigree, enamel, and brass. The chair's regal decoration features biblical scenes, emblems of the twelve tribes, and cherubs in the classic Bezalel style.[19] In some synagogues the *sandek* sits in the Chair of Elijah; others use a separate chair, and still others use a chair that is wide enough for both the *sandek* and Elijah. For ceremonial efficiency and decorative impact, the chair of the godfather and the symbolic seat reserved for the prophet are united to become, in these cases, a double seat or a bench. According to Sabar, "Among Ashkenazi Jews it became common to join the two seats together into a bench divided in the center: on one side (usually the left) sits the *sandek*, while the other remains empty for Elijah."[20]

One double wooden seat in the collection of the Israel Museum was made in Dermbach, Germany, before 1768, with one seat intended for the godfather, the other reserved for Elijah.[21] As exemplified by this carved, painted, inscribed, and padded bench, Chairs of Elijah are not humble objects but rather rare comfortable benches in Jewish tradition, embellished seats of honor frequently adorned with embroidered upholstery, velvet cushioning, or satin pillows. The beautification perhaps stimulates the religious imagination, for indeed the Chair of Elijah becomes that because the Jewish community declares it so: Through a speech act and an act of the imagination, it sees Elijah sitting on that bench, just as it conjures him drinking the wine set out in a goblet on the Passover table. Notwithstanding the workings of the imagination, the bench has a weighty physical presence, typically owned by and housed in a synagogue, to be pulled from the wall or taken out of storage and placed in the center of

FIGURE 3.2. Elijah's Chair for a circumcision ceremony, before 1768; carved and painted wood; 110 × 112 × 55 cm. The Feuchtwanger Collection, Israel Museum, Jerusalem (HF 0009 197/003), purchased and donated by Baruch and Ruth Rappaport, Geneva. © Israel Museum, Jerusalem. Photo by David Harris.

the room on the right occasion. During a circumcision, although the godfather physically cradles the child, Elijah would symbolically guard the newborn from harm at this particularly precarious moment. There is a tradition of leaving Elijah's chair or bench in this position for three days, allowing the furniture to do its protective work, functioning not unlike the amulets surrounding childbirth that are among the most common talismans in Jewish tradition. There is thus a temporal dimension to the bench's work of sanctification and protection.

In contrast to this splendor, the humblest of benches is what American Jews often refer to as a shiva bench, a seat typically provided to families by a synagogue or funeral home to be used during the seven-day period of Jewish ritual mourning. If seats for Elijah are the rare Jewish chairs that make their way into museum collections, the same cannot be said for simple shiva stools. Seats for mourning have a distinctly unassuming presence: not just low to the ground but also small in size and if not uncomfortable, then at least self-effacing in form and feel. Along with other Jewish ritual mourning practices, such as covering mirrors or not wearing makeup, the mourning seat serves both as a symbol and as an enactment of the pain of grief, a gesture of reverence for the dead. Unornamented, undecorated, nontechnical, a bare essential for support, the mourning bench is about "doing without."[22] Simultaneously substantive but insignificant, material but ephemeral, it embodies qualities of the human at its most fragile. The shiva bench, like the Chair of Elijah used in life-cycle rituals but unlike communal benches, is a repository for a joining of the material and the immaterial world, a mediator between the human and the divine, the earthly and the mystical.[23]

Jewish law for mourning derives from the life and book of Job: "They sat *to* the ground" (Job 2:13). Querying the words "to the ground" rather than "on the ground," the Jerusalem Talmud (*Moed Katan* 3:5) interprets this to mean that mourners should sit near but not on the ground, placing them in a posture of humility and differentiating them from the visitors who come to console. Whether made of carved wood or sometimes folded cardboard, shiva seats are small to encourage intimate spacing among mourners and low enough to signal the need for distance from the non-mourning public. As a ritual object, an array of shiva seat sets the space of the house of mourning and the time of shiva as a hallowed realm. Like Chairs of Elijah, as objects within a community, they appear and recede at particular ritual moments to support the body and provide a structure for Jewish mourning, an artifact that mirrors a mourner's emotional state while mediating between the individual mourner and the community.[24] Mourning benches play an infrastructural role in Jewish ritual; they are drawn out at particular moments to create community, define time, and facilitate transitions between stages of life and feeling, and in this way they serve as a lens into the ways that Jews "attached meaning to space, or transform 'space' into 'place.'"[25]

Benches for Prayer

If benches are ritual objects in life-cycle events, then in the context of regular weekly prayer in the synagogue, benches—or more specifically, pews—provide a more architectural infrastructure for daily and holiday services.[26] Pews, backed benches for communal prayer, are perches from which to read, pray, chant, sing, and see. They are perhaps foremost spots for communication: stations in which to listen to divine or rabbinic word, to speak in return, and probably also to whisper with one's neighbor.[27] For centuries and around the world, synagogue benches have turned individual Jews into a congregation not only by choreographing worship but also by placing congregants in physical proximity to each other, combining the decorum afforded by forward-facing rows of bodies with the intimacy of adjacent seating.[28] In the context of a synagogue, pews have a "connective capacity," linking people to each other, to the liturgy and cadence of the service, and to texts.[29] And yet prayer benches, set within a complex matrix not only of faith, ideology, and community but also of social aspiration and finance, become critical sites of deliberation over what and whose social and theological categories will receive communal sanction. The debate over mixed seating in the synagogue, a metonym for debate over gender equality in Jewish life more broadly, is a subject that has received considerable attention in the public discourse since the late eighteenth century and in scholarship since the 1980s. Whether women's pews are to the left of men's pews, behind them, above them on a second-floor gallery, or entirely outside the building; whether women have a view of the bimah or not; whether or not women had acoustic access to the liturgy; whether the women's section was demarcated with a physical partition (*mechitsa*)—all give material form to a range of social and theological priorities. The signification of mixed seating has shifted over time, embodying—depending on the societal views prevailing in any given moment—family values, modernity, or the place of women in Jewish ritual life and often serving as a primary symbol of denominational differences.[30] But in addition to the gendered aspect of synagogue seating, pews have structured and maintained differences, particularly differences of class or social hierarchy or race, within Jewish communities in other ways—concerns I turn to after a brief consideration of Judaism's long history of seated prayer.

References to prayer in the New Testament, rabbinic sources, and writings of the Hellenistic philosopher Philo of Alexandria paint a picture of Jews seated during portions of prayer in ancient synagogues.[31] More tangibly, excavations of ancient synagogues reveal a common pattern of permanent stone benches built around some or all of the synagogues' inside walls, sometime rising in two or three tiers. Permanent furniture alone did not accommodate all of the ancient worshipers, with evidence in the Babylonian and Jerusalem Talmud attesting to the use of portable benches in Jewish communal settings; these benches were made of wood and were "arranged according to the whim of the congregation,"[32] although many worshippers would have still sat on floor mats.[33] Benches positioned congregants' bodies to face the focal element of prayer, the Torah, as it passed from the ark to the bimah and then back again—a physical infrastructure that facilitated the flow of texts and attention. This arrangement of seats was conducive to worship but also to social hierarchy. In synagogues from the second century CE, a throne-like seat of honor (Greek *kathedrai* or Aramaic *korsea*) was located along the uppermost tier in a synagogue to indicate a person's rank or position in distinction to ordinary benches or chairs.[34]

The use of benches in the ancient synagogues of Palestine to support both devotion and social distinction is a practice that continued through to the medieval synagogues of Eastern Europe—from the gothic masonry of the Staronova Synagogue in Prague, built in 1270 (the oldest synagogue in Central Europe), to the Golden Rose Synagogue in Lvov, built in 1582.[35] The origins of seated Jewish prayer are ancient, but the form and materiality of synagogue pews and the role they play in mapping social hierarchies were influenced by church architecture. The pew was introduced into Christian houses of worship in the fourteenth century and became common in the next century, when wood supplanted stone seats.[36] The Protestant Reformation in the sixteenth century further transformed church architecture: With the sacrament replaced by longer services and formal sermons, the pulpit rather than the altar table became the focal point of prayer and pews became a standard piece of furniture.[37] During a period of increased European wealth in the eighteenth century, family box pews in Protestant churches—which could be furnished with cushioned seats, carpets, and other accessories—became popular, sold to families as private property.[38]

Synagogues adopted church pews, sometimes literally. In late nineteenth- and early twentieth-century synagogues in the former Polish-Lithuanian Commonwealth region of Volhynia, in what is now Ukraine, pews in uniform rows faced eastward toward the Torah ark and toward Jerusalem, the traditional direction that diasporic Jews face during prayer.[39] Seats along the eastern wall (called *mizrah*, meaning "east") were reserved for wealthy or revered community members and, mirroring Catholic churches at the time, each pew had a pulpit with a book shelf.[40] The Vilna shul in Boston, founded in 1903 by a congregation of Yiddish-speaking Lithuanian immigrants, adopted the space of the Twelfth Baptist Church of Boston, a Black church, including their pews. They adapted the church's symbolism by removing—literally scraping off—the horizontal lines of the crosses marking each pew.[41] (A mid-nineteenth-century wooden pew from the Twelfth Baptist Church, with a tall upright back and five small oval numbered seat plates, is in the collection of the National Museum of African American History and Culture in Washington, DC, a gift of the Vilna Shul and Boston's Center for Jewish Culture Inc.).

Pews have long played a role in synagogues not only in supporting the architecture of a service but also in creating senses of belonging and, simultaneously, in symbolizing differentiated membership within a congregation. In early modern European synagogues, pews were purchased by congregants as real estate, and even when the benches themselves are no longer with us, they leave an archival trace in the *shtar* (Aramaic, a legal contract). One contract printed in Amsterdam in 1671 records the purchase by Yosef ben Harav Liber of a seat in the new Ashkenazic synagogue of Amsterdam, completed in 1671 for a congregation of refugees of the Thirty Years War from the Rhine region and signed by six synagogue trustees (*parnassim*).[42] We know precisely where the seat holder would have sat each week: in the men's section, "the seventh row, north side, ninth place, known by its borders, between Rabbi Itzik Katz on the one side and the assembly [*kohelet*] on the other." This last designation suggests that one of the adjacent spots had not yet been sold and therefore belonged to the community—a bench for guests. On the back of this printed sales record is a subsequent handwritten contract of sale of the same seat to yet another owner in 1689.

Although conversations about class are often concealed in Jewish communities, the arrangement of pews and the people in them often created a map of socioeconomic hierarchy and contributed to structures of social and financial inclusion or exclusion. Synagogue "seating patterns," according to Samuel Heilman, "are not simply physical arrangements but reflect social belongingness."[43] The right to sit in certain pews conferred status in the earliest of American synagogues, where pew assignments historically have gone hand in hand with congregational membership. In Kehal Adath Jeshurun—known as the Eldridge Street synagogue, founded in 1887 as the first Orthodox house of worship built by Eastern European Jews in America—congregants embraced an American Presbyterian aesthetic of decorum, one reflected not only in its numbered pews but also in its financial structure for seating. From the synagogue's founding, membership was synonymous with the purchase of a seat, the first seat of status going to Isidor Abrahamin 1887 for over $1,000; seat prices decreased considerably the further one sat from the ark.[44] As historian Jeffrey Gurock explains, "Ownership of a seat was not only a sign of status and of belonging, it was also an investment" that had resale value as the congregation grew in size and renown; seats would be passed down to children in wills or even traded up for ones more expensive and desirable.[45]

Purchased pews thus not only created private space but also functioned as private property,[46] as codified in seating contracts with legal clout in the eyes of the congregation and the state. Hundreds of such contracts are filed in the archives of Temple Emanu-El, founded by German Jewish immigrants on the Lower East Side in 1845 as the first Reform congregation in New York City. One lavishly ornamented agreement signed in 1869 between Temple Emanu-El and Max Rau documents the congregant's purchase for $750 of pew 35: "situated on the northeasterly corner of the 5th avenue and 33rd street in the city of New York." Once folded into eighths, the contract was likely safeguarded by Mr. Rau and the subsequent inheritors of the pew seat in 1920 and 1930, as suggested by pew transfers handwritten on the back of the contract. Pew purchases and seat transfers were carefully logged in synagogue ledgers, and the ledgers remain active to this day, repeatedly refreshed with lawyers' letters inserted over the years to record transfers. The accounting was complex in part because Temple Emanu-El's seat owners paid New York State real estate taxes on their pews or pew fractions thereof. As cautioned in Mr. Rau's contract, "Any default in the payment of rent or taxes and all the right, title and interest of the said party of the second part to the pew conveyed . . . shall be liable to forfeiture . . . in accordance to the rules and regulations." Inevitably, there are numerous instances where pews essentially went into foreclosure for unpaid taxes, in which case the congregation recovered ownership. For example, at a meeting of the Board of Trustees held on October 3, 1937, a vote accepted Mrs. Noah Schwab's offer to transfer her seat in pew 110 to the congregation as a means of canceling the accumulated pew taxes; in turn, the synagogue allowed her to use pew 210, seats 1–2, during her lifetime without any obligation to her heirs.

By this point, Temple Emanu-El had merged with Temple Beth-El, and both became equal parents of the present building in the current location on the Upper East Side of New York City, completed in 1929 with 2,500 seats (still the largest Jewish house of worship in the world). Despite or because of the luxurious building, discontent lingers in the synagogue archive. Temple Emanu-El's new sanctuary had not even been dedicated when the seating committee reported in 1929 that "dissatisfaction was expressed" by specific members (who together owned four seats valued at $6,400 in 1929, recorded presumably to give credence to their objection) whose views from their seats in the front side and side balconies were obstructed by lecterns.[47] The next year, as the congregation continued to adjust to the new building, "considerable complaint" was expressed that the front rows of pews interfered with the handling of funeral caskets.[48]

As status-conferring objects, pews could fulfill or alternatively challenge congregants' desires for comfort and elegance. The upholstery wrapping of Temple Emanu-El's pew seat and seat back, as Katherine Grier has argued about the French style of domestic furniture in the second half of the nineteenth century in America, "seemed to mediate the apparently incompatible demands of the cultured facade and bodily comfort."[49] As objects of decorative art, the pews are beautifully crafted; many feature carved foliate bench ends (not unlike the most upscale of church pews built at the same time) and also conveniently conceal heating vents below to keep worshipers warm. A small extant selection of locked pew boxes—added independently by certain members to safeguard personal prayer books at their seats, which would otherwise periodically go missing—further created a sense of well-being and privacy within the voluminous sanctuary. The pews' aesthetic was part of a larger social statement underpinning the new structure's lavish Romanesque revival style, the idea that, in the words of the institution's own history, "Having left persecution and fear behind, New York City's Jewry had carved out its place in the mainstream of American life and reached the upper echelons."[50]

It was in the thick of the congregational merger and move to a new building that membership in the synagogue shifted from a system of pew purchases to an annual fee, which predominates today, even though grandfathered property rights to pews persist for certain seats.[51] Today, most Temple Emanu-El congregants add onto their membership dues a payment for assigned seats for the High Holidays, which are priced according to eight price points (A–M) according to seating sections detailed in an online seating chart.[52] Even as financial structures shift, the system of synagogue pews continues to be charged with meaning and to provide an infrastructure for communal prayer, an infrastructure with both social and material effects that reflects the ways blurred boundaries between material and immaterial structures generate and sustain Jewish life.

Benches of Exclusion

Synagogue pews are rarely preserved as artifacts in museum collections, but in the Jewish Art and Life Wing of the Israel Museum in Jerusalem—one of the few places where one can examine synagogue pews with the aid of museum lighting—four original, reconstructed synagogues from three continents are displayed. One of the displaced sanctuaries is Tzedek v'Shalom, the Sephardic synagogue built in 1736 in Paramaribo, Suriname, for one of the oldest Jewish communities in the Caribbean, established in the 1650s by Sephardic Jews of Iberian origin.[53] Built of wood in a neoclassical style, the symmetric sanctuary is painted white with arched windows. Original brass chandeliers, crafted in the Netherlands in the eighteenth century, hang from its ceiling and between the colonnades. A wide hall and a reader's platform stand opposite the Torah ark, itself surrounded by areas of differentiated bench seating. Rows of congregational pews—some with minimal horizontal slat backs and others with ornate vertical slatwork—face inward toward the ark. Benches facing outward are also incorporated into the exterior of a central dais from which the Torah was read. The grandest pews are incorporated into elevated platforms with decorated arched backs, reserved for leaders of the community (*parnassim*) and for the rabbi.

Despite the precision of this synagogue's reassembly, what the benches do not record in this museum setting is the fact that, in Suriname's prosperous Jewish community of plantation owners and slaveholders, it was not purchase price that dictated their allocation but racial categories. Among the first nonindigenous settlers in this former Dutch colony in the eighteenth century, many Jews were plantation owners who owned land in Jodensavanne (Jews' Savannah) worked by enslaved Africans.[54] As was common in colonial societies, a low proportion of women and interracial sexual relations and marriage between Jewish and blacks in

FIGURE 3.3. Pews in the reconstructed 1736 Tzedek v'Shalom Synagogue of Suriname. Israel Museum, Jerusalem; permanent loan from the Jewish Community of Suriname. Photograph by author, July 2017.

Suriname, led, as Aviva Ben-Ur has noted in her study, to a bifurcated social structure defined by the community in 1663: A *jahid* denoted a full member of the Jewish community; and a *congregante* described either a child of an African mother and Sephardic father, who converted to Judaism and was legally recognized as Jewish within the Jewish patriarchal system adopted in Suriname, or a white Jewish member "who had been demoted to a lower social status as a penalty for marrying a Jewish female of African descent."[55]

According to furniture historian Ken Ames, sitting is a "culturally constructed performance," one that reveals aspects of a person's "character, gender, social class, and power," and it has presented occasion for social stratification since antiquity.[56] In Suriname's synagogues, reflecting the depths of communal anxieties and biases, pews served as a physical and symbolic infrastructure for Jewish colonial demarcations of race and class; benches for prayer were a primary site in which racial classes were reinforced and belonging was conferred or denied. Aviva Ben-Ur studied Neve Shalom, the Ashkenazic congregation in Paramaribo, which in 1734 stipulated in its bylaws that Euro-African Jews were required to sit behind the reader's lectern,[57] benches where white Jews were prohibited, or on what was called the mourner's bench (pews otherwise used during congregants' period of mourning); and the ordinance likely imitated the legislation of Portuguese Jews at Tzedek v'Shalom.[58] The elevated benches situated between the pillars were afforded only to white members of the community who successfully petitioned for a spot there. By the end of the eighteenth century, Euro-African Jews began to petition for seats between the pillars, to no avail; *jahidim* who attempted to occupy the seats of *congregantes* were fined.[59] Only by the end of the eighteenth century, when Tzedek v'Shalom's community had shifted almost entirely away from a slave-based agricultural economy and the Euro-African population had grown exponentially, did the mapping of communal boundaries onto benches came slowly to an end.[60] In the intervening century in this Caribbean Jewish community, benches of prayer, under the guise of maintaining communal stability, provided an infrastructure for racism and inequity.

Benches as Things and Relations between Things

In Jewish life benches function in a range of often competing capacities: as a source of cohesion or of exclusion, as legal objects and as art, as stability and as portability, as comfort and as violence—binaries that underscore the durability and multivalence of benches as an object type that is constantly recentered, reframed, and invested with new meaning over time. Although benches are among the humblest of decorative arts, over hundreds of years and around the world, they have organized Jews, their sacred and secular things, their values and ethics, and their feelings in space and in relation to one another, drawing people in with their symbolism and their offer of support forces. Not only do benches have a meaningful material presence in their own right, but they also—in supporting an infrastructure of Judaism—serve as the background for social, ideological, and ritual work.

Like large-scale infrastructure projects—known for their tendency to break down, fail, collapse, and leak[61]—the inevitable breakdown of benches causes its own anxiety in Jewish legal commentary. In the sixteenth-century Code of Jewish Law (*Shulchan Aruch*), the Sabbath laws detail what is permissible or forbidden when it comes to using and fixing broken benches on the Sabbath. We are advised, for example, that if using a broken bench on the day of rest, "It is forbidden to use the leg as a support for the bench, or to rest the broken bench on another bench, for fear that one would come to reattach the leg and wedge it in tightly"—which is to say, for fear that one would effectively be fixing the bench, in violation of the prohibition against labor of any kind on the Sabbath. If a broken bench might cause harm to a person, however, "it is permitted to remove it or to rest it on another bench in order to sit on it," because there are leniencies within Sabbath observance when a life could be in danger. Still, one cannot replace a broken bench leg on the Sabbath or let the bench plank be supported by another bench unless, as an exception "one already sat on it before the Sabbath while it was in this condition." One can also, if it has been prepared in advance before the Sabbath, rest a board on two stools or blocks of wood to function as a bench, but one cannot build such a bench on the Sabbath.[62] To have been given such consideration and rabbinic dispensation reaffirms the outsized role that benches play. We might describe benches the way Brian Larkin has described infrastructure, as both "things and also the relation between things"[63]—that is, as things with material presence in prayer, ritual, and study and as things with a connective role in communal sociality and in mediating relations between everyday and spiritual realms.

Anthropologists have underscored infrastructure's inescapably unfinished qualities: "They expand and retreat; they evolve over periods," according to Andrew Barry, their very fragility and instability enabling them to evolve over time.[64] As with anything iterative and unfinished, Jewish communal benches contain within them a promise for something more in the future; this is not a verbal contract but a material, performative pledge.[65] Whether in summer camps, houses of mourning, or the microcosm of a synagogue, benches are a promise: of knowledge, of camaraderie and community, and, of course, of support.

Notes

I am grateful to Gabrielle Berlinger, Gabriel Goldstein, and Ruth von Bernuth for organizing the "Wandering Objects" conference in 2018. Their capacious premise prompted my thinking about benches as Jewish material culture. Conversations and rich material from Barbara Kirshenblatt-Gimblett, Jenna Weissman Joselit, Shalom Sabar, and Laura Arnold Leibman inform this paper. William Gross generously shared rare sources and wisdom from his collection. Avi Decter and Vanessa Ochs offered astute editorial guidance. I thank Ira Rezak for the invitation to speak about benches to the Friedman Society and Warren Klein for providing insight and access to the Temple Emanu-El synagogue archive.

1 Rybczynski, *Now I Sit Me Down*, 205.
2 The English word *bench* comes from the Germanic word *banc*, originally referring to a riverbank.
3 Levin, *Childhood in Exile*, 50. Levin would go on to study at Berlin University and at the Hochschule für die Wissenschaft des Judentums in the same city, becoming an adherent of Ahad Ha'am in the movement for Jewish nationalism.
4 Marcie Cohen Ferris, panel introduction at the "Wandering Objects" conference, North Carolina Museum of Art, November 2018.
5 Katherine Grier studies domestic textiles and upholstery in mid-nineteenth-century American domestic interiors, but the concept of

upholstery demarcating the safety of interior spaces applies to religious contexts as well: "Ownership of decorative objects presented the possibility of the private house as a 'memory place' of culture, where the potentially dangerous outside worlds, not just of commerce but also of secular knowledge, could be tamed and made domestic by bringing them under the softening hand of familial influence" (Grier, *Culture and Comfort*, 15).

6 Olin, *Be Seated*, 94.
7 Heilman, *Synagogue Life*.
8 Star, "Ethnography of Infrastructure," 380.
9 See, for example, Siemiatycki, "Contesting Sacred Urban Space"; and Rapoport, "Creating Place."
10 AbdouMaliq Simone writes that infrastructure "exerts a force: not simply in the materials and energies it avails, but also the way it attracts people, draws them in, coalesces and expends their capacities" (Simone, "Infrastructure").
11 BT, *Berakhot* 28a.
12 Contemporary scholars have calculated the seating capacity of synagogues, whether in nineteenth-century American synagogues, such as Mikveh Israel in Philadelphia or Temple Emanu-El in New York, or ancient synagogues in first century CE Palestine. From seating capacities, Chad S. Spigel extrapolates the sizes and growth of ancient synagogue membership, the ways synagogues are used, and, more broadly, the relationship between architecture and community. See Wischnitzer, *Synagogue Architecture*; and Spigel, *Ancient Synagogue Seating Capacities*.
13 SVARA, "Mission and Vision."
14 Ames, *Death in the Dining Room*, 191.
15 Attending to the nuances of seating, one might argue that benches are a far cry from the summer seats that Jenna Weissman Joselit observes in her archeology of Jewish life in the Catskills, where the plentitude of chairs that graced the elegantly campy grounds of Jewish summer resorts "reflect one of the most characteristic of all Catskills experiences: sitting." In chairs, American Jews in the twentieth century "slouched . . . their bodies splayed and relaxed; no one gave a fig about sitting up straight, ankles neatly crossed. Chairs were for getting up close and for nestling even closer, for generating talk, for playing cards, for eavesdropping. Proximity and portability were their hallmarks, not propriety. Chairs made for a good time; chairs made for sociability. They were, quite literally, the conversation pieces" (Joselit, "In the Frame," 22–23).

16 According to anthropologist Riv-Ellen Prell, American Jewish summer camp leaders worked purposefully against the suburban Judaism of their campers' parents, void, in their minds, of sufficient education and understanding. See Prell, *Jewish Summer Camping*. See also Nosowitz, "Evolving Ideologies."

17 The freestanding stone chairs discovered in ancient synagogues have sparked considerable scholarly debate since the 1920s over the question of whether the "Seat of Moses" refers to a real chair of honor for one or more leaders of a congregation, a symbolic seat dedicated to Moses (like the Chair of Elijah), or perhaps a seat where a Torah scroll (the Five Books of Moses) would be placed during the reading of the Haftarah. See Rahimi, "Stone Synagogue Chairs." Cecil Roth proposes controversially that the Chair of Elijah has its origins in the ceremonial Chair of Moses, whose original use was forgotten. See Roth, "Chair of Moses."

18 Sabar, "Prophet Elijah Visits Venice," 100. This type of chair, complete with footrest, is depicted in Moritz Daniel Oppenheim's oil painting *The Godfather Awaits the Child* (*Der Gevatter erwartet das Kind*) (1867), which is set in the old synagogue in Frankfurt; the painting documents a circumcision, with the mohel in the center and, next to him, the godfather, sitting in an upright carved wooden chair, raised enough off the ground so as to require a footstool, waiting to receive the eight-day-old child. The painting is in the collection of the Jewish Museum.

19 In the two oldest synagogues in France, the fifteenth-century synagogues of Carpentras and Cavaillon (rebuilt in rococo style in the eighteenth century), a niche several feet above the ark contained a miniature chair known as Elijah's chair, standing only about 20 inches tall. Too small to be sat upon, the chair remained symbolic but may have been brought down and placed near the ark during the circumcision ceremony. Krinsky, *Synagogues of Europe*, 241.

20 Sabar, "Prophet Elijah Visits Venice," 100.

21 The bench is inscribed with the name Zelig Hendel Fach, who commissioned it. For photographs of the double-seated Elijah's chairs that were housed with some permanence on *bimot* in the great synagogues of Dubno, Kremenets, and Lukiv in the former Polish-Lithuanian Commonwealth region of Volhynia (present-day Ukraine), see Kravtsov and Levin, *Synagogues in Ukraine*, 89.

22 Engelke, "Sticky Subjects," 122.

23 McDannell, "Interpreting Things."
24 In proxemics, the anthropological study of the amount of space that people in a given culture feel is necessary to set between themselves and other humans, sociopetal forces or spaces, such as cafés and domestic dining rooms, are designed to bring people together; whereas sociofugal spaces, such as library carrels and church pews, frequently cited examples, are designed to minimize contact between people. Seats for mourning are uniquely an object that enables both simultaneously.
25 Low and Lawrence-Zuniga, *Anthropology of Space and Place*, 185.
26 Chairs rather than benches provide flexibility, convenience, and comfort in a range of synagogue settings and denominations. For a discussion of the arrangement of chairs in a midcentury American Orthodox synagogue, see Heilman, *Synagogue Life*.
27 Heilman's sociology of an Orthodox synagogue is as much a study of gossip as it is of Halacha, and there is no more active location for the transmission of secret gossip than at one's seat in the sanctuary. Heilman, *Synagogue Life*, 181.
28 A large scholarly field has studied the relationship between Jewish identity and synagogue architecture, much focused on exterior built form and style. See, for example, Weissbach, "Buildings Fraught with Meaning," the introduction to a special issue of *Jewish History* on the symbolism of synagogue architecture, situated within the spatial turn in Jewish historiography. In a noteworthy study of synagogue architecture in Galicia and Bukovina, Kravtsov ("Jewish Identities") shows how Jewish identities in the Hapsburg Empire in the nineteenth century were constructed and denominations demarcated by synagogue architecture.
29 Harvey, "Introduction," 3.
30 Sarna, "Debate over Mixed Seating." In Karla Goldman's analysis the shift from secluded women's balconies to open galleries for women with tiered seating (thought to negatively showcase "disreputable behavior among women") and finally to family pews (later called mixed seating) in the 1870s and later in America as in Germany reflected desires for decorum rather than a rethinking of women's roles and rights in Judaism. See Goldman, *Beyond the Synagogue Gallery*, 80. See also Zangenberg, "Will the Real Women Please Sit Down."
31 Spigel, *Ancient Synagogue Seating Capacities*, 38.
32 Spigel, *Ancient Synagogue Seating Capacities*, 42.

33 Rahimi, "Stone Synagogue Chairs"; Spigel, *Ancient Synagogue Seating Capacities*, 41.
34 Rahimi, "Stone Synagogue Chairs," 192.
35 Kravtsov, "Jewish Identities."
36 Backless stone benches were introduced in English parish buildings in the thirteenth century and were placed against walls for the elderly and sick. Over time, they were moved into the body of the building, first in a semicircle around the pulpit and then fixed in rows to the floor. Davies, *Secular Use of Church Buildings*, 101.
37 See Davies, *Secular Use of Church Buildings*, 138; and Viola and Barna, *Pagan Christianity*, 35.
38 Viola and Barna, *Pagan Christianity*.
39 The basic orientation of synagogue prayer developed over the course of about five centuries in Roman Mediterranean communities after the destruction of the Second Temple in 70 CE and migrated to Eastern Europe. Hubka, *Resplendent Synagogue*, 29.
40 Kravtsov and Levin, *Synagogues in Ukraine*, 89.
41 Harvard University Pluralism Project Archive, "Vilna Shul."
42 This contract is held in the Gross Family Collection (item 118.011.080). It was translated by William Gross.
43 In the context of the Orthodox synagogue he studied, Samuel Heilman observed that finding one's regular seat in the synagogue not only symbolizes but also affects one's place in the community: "As they enter the shul, the members—new and old alike—have little choice with regard to where each will sit or with whom each will become associated. Those who challenge such informally assigned associations, who fail to find their niche—both actually and figuratively—in the community . . . soon find that they never become fully integrated into the congregation" (Heilman, *Synagogue Life*, 39, 190).
44 Pollard, *Landmark of the Spirit*, 70.
45 Gurock, "Stage in the Emergence of the Americanized Synagogue," 10. An array of payment plans accommodated some members, whereas others could rent seats for $10, paid in quarterly installments, although Annie Pollard observed that purchasers rarely paid in full. The membership signified by seat ownership or rental entitled congregants to a range of benefits, including attending general meetings, voting rights, and access to the synagogue library and study sessions; only seat owners

could hold office for the first twenty-five years until a constitutional change in 1913. See Pollard, *Landmark of the Spirit*, 70.
46 Although the sale of assigned pew seats in American synagogues is attributed to Presbyterian influence and aspiration, it is a tradition that nineteenth-century Eastern European synagogue congregations participated in as well. In the Gwozdziec Synagogue, built in the early eighteenth century, the names of former congregants are inscribed on the painted decorative arches behind a ring of built-in benches, although it is not known whether these inscriptions were honorific, acknowledged donor contributions, or marked purchased seats. According to Thomas Hubka, the usage may have changed over time. See Hubka, *Resplendent Synagogue*, 37.
47 Temple Emanu-El, "Trustee Minutes, 1926–1930" (1929), 207.
48 Temple Emanu-El, "Trustee Minutes, 1926–1930" (1930), 255.
49 Grier, *Culture and Comfort*, 177.
50 Temple Emanu-El, "Our History."
51 At that time, existing pew values were applied to membership, but for the families that demanded to retain their pews—twenty-seven families still own seats to this day—seats needed to be transferred to the new sanctuary. These processes leave traces in the congregation's pew record book. For example, in the ledger begun in 1929, the notes for pew 11, seat 2, indicate that in the original Emanu-El building the family owned one-quarter of pew 507, valued at $400; the new assessed value is $1,200 for each pew, and the new location in the new building is pew 100, seat 5. Adding to the complexity, the synagogue removed these seats to create an aisle, moving the congregant to new seats with a higher value of $1,666. The pews were subsequently sold and the record has been crossed off.
52 Temple Emanu-El, "Membership Options."
53 In the late 1990s, with the synagogue no longer in use, permission was granted to transfer its interior and all its original contents—including six Torah scrolls, silver *rimonim*, and silver *yads*—to the Israel Museum on long-term loan from the congregation. See Coen-Uzzielli, *Tzedek ve-Shalom*.
54 According to Aviva Ben-Ur, "As early as 1684, 4,200 African slaves resided in Suriname, and the colony's 232 Jewish householders, comprising 28.6 percent of Suriname's European population, owned slightly more (30.3 percent or 1,298) than their share of slaves" (Ben-Ur, "Peripheral Inclusion," 187).
55 Ben-Ur, "Peripheral Inclusion," 188.

56 Ames, *Death in the Dining Room*, 189. "They are designed to allow or suppress a variety of postures. Once created, chairs are used by people who conform to or violate the postures enabled by and asserted by these objects."
57 Ben-Ur, "Peripheral Inclusion," 190.
58 Aviva Ben-Ur, personal correspondence, January 8, 2020.
59 The petitions, as Ben-Ur explains, may have been less a revolt for overarching racial equality or for more desirous seats than a wish for European-origin Jews to "publicly claim *congregantes* as their own flesh and blood." Ben-Ur, "Peripheral Inclusion," 190, 195.
60 Ben-Ur, "Matriarchal Matter," 152. The community shifted toward some patterns of inclusion emerging among Caribbean Jewish societies, with the social status of Euro-African Jews rising, as reflected in inheritance and burial locations. See Ben-Ur, *Peripheral Inclusion*, 197.
61 Barry, "Discussion: Infrastructural Times."
62 Appel, *Concise Code of Jewish Law*, 276.
63 Larkin, "Politics and Poetics of Infrastructure," 3329. Benches evince a constant tension, as Penny Harvey describes infrastructure, "between the material form (the 'thing' and its constitutive relations) and the connective capacity of such forms that are built to enable circulation or to sustain particular life projects" (Harvey, "Introduction," 1).
64 Barry, "Discussion: Infrastructural Times."
65 Simone Abram and Gisa Weszkalnys describe city or national planning as a promise that "has effects and brings about an obligation on the part of the promisor" (Abram and Weszkalnys, *Elusive Promises*, 9).

Bibliography

Abram, Simone, and Gisa Weszkalnys. *Elusive Promises: Planning in the Contemporary World*. New York: Berghahn, 2016.

Ames, Kenneth. *Death in the Dining Room and Other Tales of Victorian Culture*. Philadelphia: Temple University Press, 1994.

Appel, Gersian. *The Concise Code of Jewish Law*, vol. 2, *A Guide to Prayer and Religious Observance on the Sabbath*. Brooklyn: KTAV, 1989.

Barry, Andrew. "Discussion: Infrastructural Times." Society for Cultural Anthropology, September 24, 2015. culanth.org/fieldsights/discussion-infrastructural-times (accessed May 7, 2024).

Ben-Ur, Aviva. "A Matriarchal Matter: Slavery, Conversion, and Upward Mobility in Colonial Suriname." In *Atlantic Diasporas: Jews, Conversos, and Crypto-Jews in the Age of Mercantilism, 1500–1800*, ed. Richard L. Kagan and Philip D. Morgan, 152–69. Baltimore: Johns Hopkins University Press, 2009.

———. "Peripheral Inclusion: Communal Belonging in Suriname's Sephardic Community." In *Religion, Gender, and Culture in the Pre-Modern World*, ed. Alexandra Cuffel and Brian Britt, 185–210. New York: Palgrave Macmillan, 2007.

Coen-Uzzielli, Tania, ed. *Tzedek ve-Shalom: A Synagogue from Suriname in the Israel Museum, Jerusalem*, trans. Dani Barkai and Carol Sutherland. Jerusalem: Israel Museum, 2010.

Davies, J. G. *The Secular Use of Church Buildings*. London: SCM Press, 1968.

Engelke, Matthew. "Sticky Subjects and Sticky Objects: The Substance of African Christian Healing." In *Materiality*, ed. Daniel Miller, 118–39. Durham, NC: Duke University Press, 2005.

Goldman, Karla. *Beyond the Synagogue Gallery: Finding a Place for Women in American Judaism*. Cambridge, MA: Harvard University Press, 2000.

Grier, Katherine. *Culture and Comfort: Parlor Making and Middle-Class Identity, 1850–1930*. Washington, DC: Smithsonian Institution Press, 1988.

Gurock, Jeffrey S. "A Stage in the Emergence of the Americanized Synagogue Among East European Jews: 1890–1910." *Journal of American Ethnic History* 9, no. 1 (1990): 7–25.

Harvard University Pluralism Project Archive. "Vilna Shul." https://hwpi.harvard.edu/pluralismarchive/vilna-shul (last updated September 25, 2018; accessed May 7, 2024).

Harvey, Penny. "Introduction: Attention to Infrastructure Offers a Welcome Reconfiguration of Anthropological Approaches to the Political." *Critique of Anthropology* 38, no. 1 (2016): 3–52. https://eprints.lse.ac.uk/79722/.

Heilman, Samuel. *Synagogue Life: A Study in Symbolic Interaction*. New Brunswick, NJ: Transaction, 1998.

Hubka, Thomas. *Resplendent Synagogue: Architecture and Worship in an Eighteenth-Century Polish Community*. Waltham, MA: Brandeis University Press, 2003.

Joselit, Jenna Weissman. "In the Frame." In *The Borscht Belt: Revisiting the Remains of America's Jewish Vacationland*, ed. Marisa Scheinfeld, 21–28. Ithaca, NY: Cornell University Press, 2016.

Kravtsov, Sergey. "Jewish Identities in Synagogue Architecture of Galicia and Bukovina." *Ars Judaica: The Bar-Ilan Journal of Jewish Art* 6 (2010): 81–100.

Kravtsov, Sergey R., and Vladimir Levin. *Synagogues in Ukraine: Volhynia*, vol. 1. Jerusalem: Zalman Shazar Center and Center for Jewish Art, 2017.

Krinsky, Carol Herselle. *Synagogues of Europe: Architecture, History, Meaning*. New York: Dover, 1996.

Larkin, Brian. "The Politics and Poetics of Infrastructure." *Annual Review of Anthropology* 42, no. 1 (2013): 3327–43.

Levin, Shmarya. *Childhood in Exile*, trans. Maurice Samuel. New York: Harcourt, 1929.

Low, Setha M., and Denise Lawrence-Zuniga, eds. *The Anthropology of Space and Place: Locating Culture*. London: Wiley-Blackwell, 2003.

McDannell, Colleen. "Interpreting Things: Material Culture Studies and American Religion." *Religion* 21, no. 4 (1991): 371–87.

Nosowitz, Dan. "The Evolving Ideologies of American Jewish Summer Camp." Atlas Obscura, August 9, 2018. www.atlasobscura.com/articles/jewish-summer-camps. (accessed May 7, 2024).

Olin, Laurie. *Be Seated*. New York: Applied Research + Design, 2017.

Pollard, Annie, *Landmark of the Spirit: The Eldridge Street Synagogue*. New Haven, CT: Yale University Press, 2009.

Prell, Riv-Ellen. *Jewish Summer Camping and Civil Rights: How Summer Camps Launched a Transformation in American Jewish Culture*. Ann Arbor: Michigan Publishing, University of Michigan Library, 2006.

Rahimi, L. Y. "Stone Synagogue Chairs: Their Identification, Use, and Significance." *Israel Exploration Journal* 40, no. 2/3 (1990): 192–214.

Rapoport M. "Creating Place, Creating Community: The Intangible Boundaries of the Jewish 'Eruv.'" *Environment and Planning D: Society and Space* 29, no. 5 (2011): 891–904.

Roth, Cecil. "The Chair of Moses and Its Survivals." *Palestine Exploration Quarterly* 81, no. 2 (1949): 100–111.

Rybczynski, Witold. *Now I Sit Me Down: From Klismos to Plastic Chair—A Natural History*. New York: Farrar, Straus & Giroux, 2016.

Sabar, Shalom. "Prophet Elijah Visits Venice: A Rare Italian Elijah Chair from Early Nineteenth Century Venice." In *La nascita nella tradizione ebraica: Birth in Jewish Tradition*, ed. Silvia Guastalla, 98–123. Livorno: Belforte Salomone, 2005.

Sarna, Jonathan D. "The Debate over Mixed Seating in the American Synagogue." In *The American Synagogue: A Sanctuary Transformed*, ed. Jack Wertheimer, 363–94. New York: Cambridge University Press, 1987.

Siemiatycki, M. "Contesting Sacred Urban Space: The Case of the *Eruv*." *Journal of International Migration and Integration* 6 (2005): 255–70.

Simone, AbdouMaliq. "Infrastructure: Commentary by AbdouMaliq Simone." *Cultural Anthropology* (2012). https://journal.culanth.org/index.php/ca/catalog/category/infrastructure (accessed May 7, 2024).

Spigel, Chad S. *Ancient Synagogue Seating Capacities: Methodology, Analysis, and Limits*. Tübingen: Mohr Siebeck, 2012.

Star, Susan Leigh. "The Ethnography of Infrastructure." *American Behavioral Scientist* 43, no. 3 (1999): 377–91.

SVARA. "Mission and Vision." svara.org/about-svara/ (accessed December 19, 2019).

Temple Emanu-El. "Membership Options." www.emanuelnyc.org/membership/membership-options/#toggle-id-2 (accessed January 6, 2020).

———. "Our History." www.emanuelnyc.org/about-us/our-history/ (accessed October 2, 2023).

———. "Trustee Minutes, 1926–1930." Temple Emanu-El Archives, New York.

Viola, Frank, and George Barna. *Pagan Christianity? Exploring the Roots of Our Church Practices*. Carol Stream, IL: Tyndale House, 2008.

Weissbach, Lee Shai. "Buildings Fraught with Meaning: An Introduction to a Special Issue on Synagogue Architecture in Context." *Jewish History* 25 (2011): 1–11.

Wischnitzer, Rachel. *Synagogue Architecture in the United States*. Philadelphia: Jewish Publication Society, 1955.

Zangenberg, Jurgen. "Will the Real Women Please Sit Down: Interior Space, Seating Arrangements, and Female Presence in the Byzantine Synagogue of Horvat Kur in Galilee." In *Gender and Social Norms in Ancient Israel, Early Judaism, and Early Christianity: Texts and Material Culture*, ed. Michaela Bauks, Katharina Galor, and Judith Hartenstein, 91–117. Gottingen: Vandenhoeck & Ruprecht, 2019.

Part II
JEWISH THINGS ON DISPLAY

4

THE EVIDENCE ROOM

Contemporary Holocaust Reliquary

Laura Levitt

As a scholar of religion, of Holocaust memory, and increasingly of material culture and the work of commemoration, I bring some of my reflections on *The Evidence Room*, Robert Jan van Pelt and the University of Waterloo team's contribution to the 2016 Architectural Biennale, into this interdisciplinary conversation about Jewish objects.[1] My reflections emerge out of my engagement with this room as part of the final chapter of my book *The Objects That Remain*.[2] I became obsessed with this work after hearing van Pelt interviewed on CBC radio about *The Evidence Room* in the spring of 2016.[3] That interview led me to Venice, then to Toronto (on three different occasions), and finally to the Hirshhorn Museum in Washington, DC, to attend *The Evidence Room*'s US premier during the summer of 2019. I wanted to see and experience this work firsthand in different settings, where its meaning deepens and changes. In what follows I reflect on some of the ways that I understand *The Evidence Room* as a holder, a container of memory, a forensic reliquary construction that combines the exactitude of the techniques and technologies of architectural forensics with the delicacy and reverence of the religious reliquary, a container of sacred objects.

Holdings

Holding is a process. We do not necessarily "arrest" the past or keep it captive. To hold on to especially tainted pasts and keep their memories alive

FIGURE 4.1. A uniform from Auschwitz-Birkenau. Reprinted with permission from the United States Holocaust Memorial Museum.

requires a certain delicacy. Holding on too tightly can take away that which makes these memories compelling and animate. Part of what attracts me to this notion of holding is the way it signals the relationship between objects and memory: not only the delicacy of this term but also its palpable qualities. Holding demands that we pay attention to the details. Like vulnerable objects, memories can break, and painful memories are often tied up in the objects that both hold and carry such legacies forward. These are the very qualities that mark how Robert Jan van Pelt and the Waterloo team broached their efforts to create *The Evidence Room*. They mark their efforts to recreate forensically the various pieces of evidence that make up this project and then, in so doing, reanimate them.[4]

Touching the past is implicit in the act of holding. Even metaphorically, we tap into a discourse of the tangible. We hold objects, pieces of all kinds of painful pasts, in our hands and, if we are attentive, careful, we can keep their memories alive. Not unlike the barrister in the 2016 film *Denial*,[5] who picks up a piece of mangled wire in the ruins of the crematoria at Auschwitz-Birkenau and holds it in his hands, only to keep it nearby as he goes on to defend Deborah Lipstadt in the British High

Court of Justice, such objects can keep us from forgetting. Although a fictional embellishment, this talismanic gesture makes visible how objects often work to animate and compel memory. The film, strangely released during the same year as *The Evidence Room*, taps into this all-too-familiar tactile enactment. Memory objects often function as prompts, as physical reminders that keep memory present even when such objects are recreated. And in this spirit or reconstruction, the Waterloo team has allowed visitors to *The Evidence Room* to touch this past and its echoes. They do this through their careful efforts to forensically reproduce the evidence in new tactile forms. In this way we are reminded not only of the horrors of the Holocaust and the enactment of the Final Solution at Auschwitz but also of its ugly contestation in the 2000 Lipstadt libel trial. We are reminded of the power of these pieces of forensic and architectural evidence that, in that instance, proved that the Holocaust happened.[6]

Although we keep vast storehouses of objects in places that serve as containers for all those memories, they are not always easily within our reach.

FIGURE 4.2. A bin of rings. Reprinted with permission from the United States Holocaust Memorial Museum.

As a plural noun, the term *holdings* itself refers to legally owned properties, usually capital or stock assets but also the materials that make up a library or an archival collection. The documents that were cast to make *The Evidence Room* come from the archival holdings of Auschwitz-Birkenau, a collection that was in Soviet hands and was only belatedly made available to scholars and researchers such as van Pelt in the late 1990s, well after the war. Holocaust archives, libraries, and museums of all kinds are committed to the preservation of a broad range of fragile holdings. These are also not so easily touched.

So, how do we keep the memory of these horrific events alive in an ever-shifting present? How do we make them available to whole new publics and place them in our reach? How do the labors of architects, designers, and engineers who used these materials in the present enable us to touch and to reinhabit these terrible places? And, in so doing, what kinds of stories and lessons do they impart?

Not unlike an earlier generation of artists who recreated classical sculpture to be displayed and handled by a broader public, van Pelt and the Waterloo team not only recreated objects in three dimensions—a column, a door, a gas mask—but also rendered two-dimensional objects—drawings, plans, and architectural designs—anew.[7] They made even those documents into tangible three-dimensional objects. And like their historical predecessors, these pieces of *The Evidence Room* call attention to their status as reproductions explicitly built to be handled. The whole exhibit is rendered in stark white plaster like those reproductions of classical figures in such places as the Crystal Palace.[8] They are meant to be edifying.

In my book, the work that led me to seek out *The Evidence Room*, I was interested in the objects of memory: literal but also figurative objects that prompt especially painful memories and the ways that these materials come to us.[9] The past, even when we are able to touch its traces, is always already mediated. We come to these artifacts through any number of frames and templates, explanatory stories and legends, and critical theories from the works of poets, literary scholars, historians, sociologists, and architects whose writings and creations often introduce us to these materials in the first place. *The Evidence Room*, as I have already indicated, is an explicit reconstruction of the evidence at hand.[10] And in many ways all works of Holocaust scholarship are re-creations, mediations that offer only indirect access to what is otherwise inaccessible even as castings. As scholars, writers, artists, and lawyers, our work is in turn shaped by these stories and descriptions. We hold and convey stories about these terrible pasts with the hope that we might approximate some sense of what it was like. And yet the pasts that we transmit have not just our fingerprints all over them but also the traces of larger explanatory stories, including what Jacques Derrida has called the laws of common usage.[11] Common usage is, in part, how we try to contain these otherwise unruly stories. And so with *The Evidence Room* I want to challenge the seemingly self-evident explanation of this piece as a container of vital evidence but consider some of the ways that this powerful work conveys other kinds of meaning. Although this piece is literally about the empirical evidence that was used in court to prove that the Holocaust happened, it also allows us to experience other things.

Although the room is built out of castings of the evidence from the Lipstadt trial, including recreated pieces of that edifice of destruction, and embodies that evidence, it also creates a new container, a new space of contemplation and critical engagement. In this room we consider the evidence before us as both Holocaust memory and a memory formed in relation to those who denied this reality; we are asked to see this work well after the Lipstadt trial in 2000. And so it is that here in *The Evidence Room* we contemplate a familiar story about what it means to hold Holocaust evidence so that justice can be done. And in this case there was indeed a juridical reckoning. After the trial, however, the story did not end. We find ourselves returning to the juridical to learn something else: the ongoing challenge of the ethics of architecture, the status of truth claims, and some of the questions not contained in the legal case.

The stories we tell and retell carry the traces of both common and less common narratives. The past—*this past*—and the legacy of Auschwitz-Birkenau continue to resonate, speaking to us in both familiar and less familiar ways. The challenge of keeping these memories alive is, in part, bound to our efforts to take seriously our own contemporary preoccupations and commitments, the things that we need to address for whatever reasons in the present that continue to draw us back to this past and this evidence. In this instance van Pelt and the Waterloo team returned to the evidence at the heart of the 2000 trial to consider the ways that evidence continues to speak with urgency about things that matter, the obligations of those who make architecture.

The occasion of the 2016 Architectural Biennale and its concern with the ethics of architecture drew the Waterloo team to find a new way of conveying this story,[12] breathing new life into this material using the practices of art, architecture, and engineering to offer another rendering.

The Talismanic and the Evidentiary

The fragile shards, the very pieces of paper held in the archive that van Pelt ultimately brought to light in that British courtroom, become yet again the critical building blocks for this new holder of memory, *The Evidence Room*. In part, I want to suggest that these horrible documents have both talismanic and evidentiary qualities. They are not necessarily protective or magical, as the term *talisman* might suggest, but something more. They carry compelling properties that are less easy to explain; these archival documents are not settled. Their meanings have not been contained or put to rest, even well after their days in court where they played such a crucial role. The documents still have much more to teach us, to show us. To get at these lingering elusive qualities, I now turn to what art historian Alexander Nagel describes as the afterlives of reliquary.[13] The language of relics and their containers can usher us into the sacred nature of the evidence and the archive.

Collecting and preserving evidence is both a science and an art, a custodial routine and a rite. The ongoing encounters between object entities and those who care for them in all different ways is animating. Conservators and custodians on the one hand and scholars, architects, artists, and poets on the other work in tandem to hold these unruly objects, to protect and to preserve them, even as they build new containers—both in storage and in exhibition—to carry their legacies forward. New vessels and venues offer a kind of nesting that is perhaps less about the evidence (object) and more about the talismanic (meaning). These containers are, through their proximity to the shards they contain, reliquaries. They carry memory forward. These enactments happen within both the museological and the juridical practices that shape works such as *The Evidence Room*; new audiences, new publics, are able to confront the history of the Holocaust as well as the ongoing history of its memory. The room also helps us grasp—to literally touch—the urgent and abiding sense of the sacred nature of these enactments. To address them in such terms, however, we need to reconsider enduring cultural discomforts with the notion that animate objects have sacred or talismanic properties.

Animate Objects: The Return of the Religious

As literary scholars Peter Stallybrass and Rosalind Jones explain, the challenge posed by such objects dates back to when "Europe rejected objects that were attributed with animating powers,"[14] often describing, for example, a long-standing discomfort with both the African fetish and the "true spiritual power of relics, indulgences, and sacraments."[15] In this way, Dutch Protestants in the seventeenth century linked both Catholic and Akan beliefs in animate objects as forms of "demonized idolatry."[16] These are some of the historical antecedents for a whole series of lingering discomforts around all kinds of objects. It is with many of these scholars that I turn to the language of relics and their containers to make more vivid some of what *The Evidence Room* does. And as I do so, I want to make clear that the sacred quality of relics is proliferative: Touching relics, caring for them, and making their containers and new displays of all kinds extend their sacred qualities. Even when sheltered or otherwise protected, touch is crucial. Even reproductions cast from the original become secondary relics.

Housing Afterlives

As we consider more fully the physical fragility of pieces of Holocaust evidence, this notion of the reliquary has a related but somewhat different resonance. Preserving Holocaust artifacts has required creating reproductions and, under the guise of new containers, transformed how we handle the artifacts. Special archival boxes hold delicate pieces of clothing, such as a child's sweater or a postwar wedding gown made from a found parachute. The parachute was made of rayon, a fabric never meant to last, and so the wedding gown cannot be touched by hands or exposed to light. These requirements have meant creating whole new facilities, such as the United States Holocaust Memorial Museum's state-of-the-art storage facility, the David and Fela Shapell Family Collections, Conservation and Research Center in Bowie, Maryland.[17] This impulse to preserve is also expressed in new works of Holocaust commemoration, new monuments and memorials, and new poems and plays, novels, and historical studies.

And so in 2016 we witnessed the construction of what might be figured as a contemporary Holocaust reliquary when Robert Jan van Pelt and

FIGURE 4.3. Part of the interior of *The Evidence Room*. Reprinted with permission from The Evidence Room Foundation. Photo by Theodore Bogosian.

the team from the University of Waterloo returned to the forensic evidence that van Pelt had gathered at Auschwitz-Birkenau and later deployed as a key component in the 1996–2000 trial. They built *The Evidence Room*, a new container of Holocaust memory.[18]

As I have already suggested, and as you might have already gleaned, the Waterloo team used copies of those horrific documents from Auschwitz-Birkenau to reconstruct what van Pelt had found in the archive. The team painstakingly recreated the material in three dimensions and produced an architectural space where, as Holocaust survivor Elly Gotz explained, visitors could touch this past: "Most people know about the Holocaust. It is possible to know things, to be aware of them, but not feel them. This exhibition lets people touch the metal of the gas column, run their fingers over the drawings, and connect in that mysterious way that sometimes happens when reality overwhelms us by becoming part of us."[19]

By casting the documents at the heart of van Pelt's testimony in plaster, the team made these texts tactile. They become the walls of this stark holding space that revolve around key reconstructed elements of that lost architecture of destruction: the door to the gas chamber and the gas

FIGURE 4.4. Recreated image, 2:5 scale, of crematorium 3 in action. Reprinted with permission from The Evidence Room Foundation. Photo by Theodore Bogosian.

column—"the double grates that protected the bucket filled with poison pellets."[20] They used the designs, the specifications from those documents, and key elements of the case, to rebuild these pieces and house them.

Whereas the film *Denial* revived and revisited this case about Holocaust memory and the role of the historian in verifying "historical facts," *The Evidence Room* made van Pelt's critical testimony newly material and tangible. This painstaking forensic exhibition was created for and first displayed in Venice as an evidentiary reliquary, where it was nested within the many diverse rooms that contained other stories from the Front, other enactments of the ethics of architecture, its pasts and its futures.[21]

How do we house the afterlives of objects and the palpable memory of those places that are no longer standing? What do relics and their reliquaries teach us about these efforts? Like those forensic documents that became tactile in *The Evidence Room*, relics are often housed in beautifully crafted containers. They are held in vast storage facilities, ephemeral exhibition halls, and in private collections. And in these venues they are displayed in various smaller containers—display cases or locked vaults—each one a form of reliquary.

Contact between relics and the materials that brush up against them—that wipe and polish, display and contain them—is transformative,

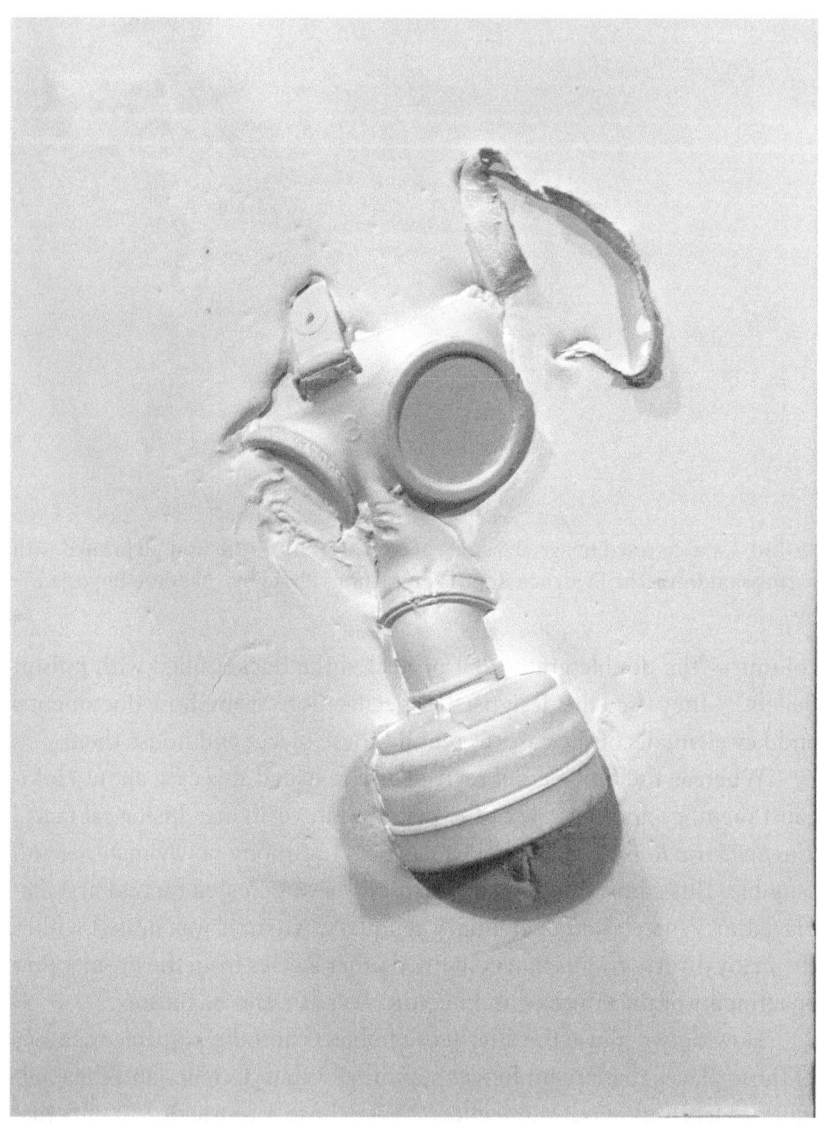

FIGURE 4.5. Recreated gas mask from *The Evidence Room*, 2:3 scale. Reprinted with permission from The Evidence Room Foundation. Photo by Theodore Bogosian.

FIGURE 4.6. Recreated photo of the architects of Auschwitz-Birkenau, 3:1 scale. Reprinted with permission from The Evidence Room Foundation. Photo by Theodore Bogosian.

like the very process of forensic casting. As art and architectural historian Shelley Hornstein explains, the Waterloo team used forensic casting techniques "to make present something that is absent. Typically, a cast would be made to preserve bodies at crime scenes, archeological sites, or architectural elements for later analysis."[22]

Touch makes these objects into living matter. By virtue of their proximity to those sacred shards, they become secondary relics. In other words, the reliquary itself, the room in this case, participates in the ongoing life of the relics it houses. In this way, the architectural space that van Pelt and the Waterloo team created is such a tactile sacred space.

The ritual acts, the performative labors of the Waterloo team in making *The Evidence Room*, are themselves part of the story. Its labors make and remake, or repurpose, that which has been stored, breathing new life into these documents. In turn, these enactments are also layered, similar to the act of casting, often one atop another. And placed together, the various casts of the documents come to create an even larger container, the room. Writing in the catalog for a major contemporary exhibit of sacred art at the British Museum, "Treasures of Heaven," Alexander Nagel explains that "the display of relics typically assumed a nested structure: reliquaries were kept inside larger housings, and these were placed in structures that functioned both as buildings and macro-reliquaries."[23] These holders are both beautiful and functional.[24]

In the book that accompanies *The Evidence Room*, Anne Bordeleau, the architect and historian in charge of making the casts of all the archival records, wrote, "It displays drawings, constructions, and artifacts as intentional productions, indexes pointing to the hands that made them. It strips architecture of its mundane veil and reveals it in its bleakest light."[25] By casting these documents in plaster, visitors are able to touch the traces of these horrific enactments.

The ability to touch these traces connects the labor of the Waterloo team to the sacred nature of this reliquary. As craftspeople, their labors help to revive these materials and to enable them to be shared with those who visit the room. The curators who produced "Treasures of Heaven" for the British Museum worried about visitors wanting to touch the sacred objects on display there. Writing about this challenge, curator James Clifton explained that the Plexiglas cases performed "a doubling of the reliquaries in which they [the relics] are already housed"[26] but that "visitors were free to touch, kiss, or otherwise engage in religious *frottage*[27] with the relic-related gifts in the gift shop situated at the end of the exhibition."[28] This is the kind of tactile longing that *The Evidence Room* embraces and fulfills as a forensic reliquary. In this room, touch—sacred experience through physical connection—is encouraged and not contained. And like so many sacred relics, the memories attached to them are violent and horrific, and this is part of why they demand our attention.

In his catalog essay for *Treasures of Heaven*, Nagel makes reference to an eclectic historical collection also housed in Venice.

> The Gualdo collection, assembled in Venice in the sixteenth and seventeenth centuries, contained an impressive collection of relics, including a piece of the True Cross, saints' body parts, fragments of the tombs of Lazarus, Jesus, and the Virgin Mary, as well as stones from Mount Sinai and from the spring of Cedron—a collection of stones presumably like those in the box from the Sancta Sanctorum. These mingled with "profane" relics such as the turtle from the Vendramin collection and the claw of a great beast given by the king of

Poland, and also with examples of ancient epigraphy, paintings, and antiquities. Sometimes the reliquary itself consisted of natural marvels, such as ostrich eggs or nautilus shells, which were duly adorned with settings in silver and gold. More than simple containers for the sacred, reliquaries were multiple structures worthy of attention as *curiosa* in their own right.[29]

Venice has a long history of art and of reverence for reliquaries—both lasting and ephemeral—despite the seemingly secular nature of its art and architectural biennales. These links between Venice, containers, rooms, and memory seem to have shaped van Pelt's vision for *The Evidence Room*.

Inspired by his mentor Dame Frances Yates, the author of *The Art of Memory* (1966) and *Theatre of the World* (1969), van Pelt explains that he considered "the concept of a building as a vessel of memory." What he hoped to accomplish in *The Evidence Room* is "most perfectly exemplified in Giulio Camillo's Theatre of Memory, a room filled with images that allow the visitor to 'at once perceive with his eyes everything that is otherwise hidden in the depths of the human mind.'"[30] Strangely enough, that memory palace had its own historical relationship to Venice, enabling van Pelt to return to his teacher and that memory room to conclude his essay. Writing from his studio in Canada in February 2016, amid the collection of all "the elements of *The Evidence Room*, which will come together in Venice," he tells readers that Camillo's Theatre of Memory was also "a temporary installation" and "for the few months that it existed, five centuries ago, it too stood in Venice."[31] Both of these rooms were ephemeral structures built and exhibited in Venice.

Addressing the longer history of Venetian reliquary art, Nagel writes:

> Museological commemoration was thus layered over the cult of relics, sometimes even on the sites of religious foundations. During the French invasion of Italy, the Venetian priest Gugliemo Wambel scrambled to save the sacred objects of Venice, amassing a collection of close to ten thousand items, including thousands of reliquaries, which shortly after his death were installed in a newly built rotunda attached to the Church of San Toma. Although still in a cult-setting, this new construction was just as importantly a proto-museum of religious art.[32]

Like the biennale itself, these objects were preserved and displayed on sacred ground. These were containers within containers, another iteration of the *wunderkammer*, the theme of the 2012 Architectural Biennale.[33] The biennale's vast venues house a full array of such nested reliquary objects, each a carefully crafted installation in and of itself. But, like *The Evidence Room*, these are layered pieces that each call attention to the workmanship, the arts out of which they were created and recreated. These are provocative, compelling, and often beautiful architectural containers that made the rituals of creation and conservation manifest. They were on full display both there and later at the Royal Ontario Museum in Toronto, and then, in a different way, at the Hirshhorn Museum in Washington, DC.[34]

The reconstituting and display of *The Evidence Room* at the Royal Ontario Museum from June 25, 2017, to September 3, 2018, made even more explicit the reliquary logic of this powerful piece. Here again *The Evidence Room* found itself nested within a vast collection, a collection perhaps not that unlike those Nagel writes about in Venice. But in moving and reconstituting *The Evidence Room* in Toronto, the work had already changed. It had taken on new resonances and meanings, both the same as and different from what they were in Venice. In Toronto the work spoke to a broader public who could easily visit it in this major Canadian museum. The room was no longer bound by the context of the Architectural Biennale. In Toronto *The Evidence Room* eloquently and reverentially highlighted and addressed Canadian survivors and their families. There was also a room set up outside the exhibit for visitors to contemplate the powerful connections made inside.

Careful signs signaled to visitors that this was a sober site. Decorum was requested. These elements were not a part of the exhibit in Venice. Here, too, there were added layers: New spaces shaped one's entry and exit from the exhibit, and knowledgeable docents explained the work, the history of the camp, and the room's more explicit relationship to the 2000 trial. For this exhibition, new casts were made of the newspaper headlines announcing the outcome of the trial. There were also new scale models of the camp and a short video that helped make more vivid this layered history. These were all a part of the added spaces that framed one's entry and exit from *The Evidence Room* at the Royal Ontario Museum.

Canada and Holocaust Memory

There is something else about this work that was also strangely resonant in Canada, the place of its creation and design. In this version *The Evidence Room* also spoke to the promise of Canada. For those in the camps, "Canada" was itself the name for a site of holding, the place where all of the precious possessions taken from those who died and those who survived Auschwitz-Birkenau were stored. It was a site of strange abundance in the midst of profound degradation and deprivation. To think of "Canada" as the name given to that place, one can hardly take in the power of the actual country in the imagination of those in the camp—ironic and hopeful.[35] Canada was a place that contained multitudes. This seemingly contrasting meaning of the name Canada echoes an earlier series of installations by the artist Christian Boltanski, his 1988 series *Canada*, as art historian Ernst van Alphen explains:

> "Canada" here stands for the country of excess and exuberance to which one wants to emigrate, because it can offer a living to everybody. In the works with the title *Canada* Boltanski showed piles of second-hand garments. For the first version of this installation at the Ydessa Hendels Art Foundation in Toronto, he used six thousand garments. The brightly colored clothes were hung by nails on all four walls. Every inch of the room was covered by them. The installation not only brought to mind the warehouses in the concentration camps, but by the sheer number of garments it also evoked the incredible number of people who died in the camps and whose possessions were stored in "Canada."[36]

Like *The Evidence Room*, Boltanski created a room, a container of Holocaust memory in Toronto. In his case Boltanski made visceral this connection between Canada and those holding places within the camps. He brought a semblance of that other "Canada" to Canada as an act of commemoration and provocation. And now more recently, *The Evidence Room* speaks to a different Canadian legacy of Holocaust memory. It taps into van Pelt's archival work as a Canadian forensic architect at Auschwitz-Birkenau and his powerful testimony in the 2000 trial. Its design also speaks to the Waterloo team's own profound and abiding commitment to teaching the ethics of architecture.

A Foundation: More Iterations

The Evidence Room makes a new space of and for ongoing Holocaust memory. Recently, these efforts to remember not only the Holocaust itself but also the legacy of preserving Holocaust memory have been institutionalized through the creation of The Evidence Room Foundation. This American institution is committed to making sure that *The Evidence Room* continues to circulate, that it continues to be displayed and discussed and otherwise engaged in different venues across the globe, beginning with its US premiere in Washington, DC, in 2019.

Like the ship *Argo*, the inspiration for poet Maggie Nelson's award-winning 2015 book, *The Argonauts*, from the pavilions and exhibition halls of Venice and the space of the Royal Ontario Museum's vast collections, *The Evidence Room* continues to be remade and reconstituted. Having left Canada for the United States, this forensic reliquary construction continues to keep Holocaust memory alive for ever new audiences and visitors.

In the summer of 2019 *The Evidence Room* came to the Hirshhorn Museum and Sculpture Garden in Washington, DC, a leading voice for contemporary art and culture located on the National Mall, a part of the Smithsonian Institution.[37] In this context the work took its place as a piece of art and architecture. At the Hirshhorn, without the antechambers and overt links to the trial and a survivor community, the stark simplicity of *The Evidence Room* took on yet other new meanings. In Washington, DC, it came to speak eloquently to American audiences about the status of evidence, truth, and the rule of law in the United States at a particularly charged moment of national reckoning around these questions. But it also suggested the power of art. As I wrote about the piece in this setting, the work stands in critical conversation with the various works of contemporary art on display all around it.[38] At the Hirshhorn *The Evidence Room* was a part of the "What Absence Is Made Of" exhibition, a constellation of avant-garde works that addressed issues of memory, disappearance, and death.[39] Here the work insists on not forgetting.

Given the creation of The Evidence Room Foundation and its mission to keep *The Evidence Room* in circulation, the piece will continue to be made and remade as a warning of the dangers of the evidence it houses. It will be refurbished and reconstituted again and again, bit by bit as art and architecture in other venues going forward.

Notes

1 Bordeleau et al., *Evidence Room*. Robert Jan van Pelt's *The Evidence Room* was his contribution to the 2016 Architectural Biennale in Venice. The title refers to both the exhibition and the companion book about the creation of this work. See the biennale's two-volume exhibition catalog information: International Architectural Exhibition, *Reporting from the Front*.
2 Portions of this essay are taken from chapters 4 and 6 of my book *The Objects That Remain*. They appear here in altered form. I am grateful to Penn State University Press for permission to use this material.
3 "Chilling Exhibit," *CBC Radio*.
4 Marks, *The Skin of Film*; Olin, *Touching Photographs*. Scholars of photography and film recognize how we handle, hold in our hands, and, at the same time, capture the haptic qualities of both photographic and cinematic film in notions of haptic visuality and haptic photographic practices.
5 The film *Denial* was directed by Mick Jackson and released in 2016. See Lipstadt, *History on Trial*. Lipstadt describes how her team had to prove that the Holocaust happened in order to refute the claims of David Irving in the British High Court of Justice.
6 Lipstadt, *Denying the Holocaust*. This text and Lipstadt's claims about David Irving were at the heart of this trial.
7 For more about these connections, see Hornstein, "Representing Evidence," 604. I thank an anonymous reviewer for reminding me of this important connection. Hornstein also considers the connections between this work and the "white cube" in powerful ways. For more on these connections, see Hornstein, "Representing Evidence," 603. These art historical connections make special sense in the context of the Hirshhorn exhibit in 2019.
8 Drawing this connection, Hornstein looks specifically to the work of art historian Kate Nicholes, who writes about "the presentation of plaster casts of Greek and Roman sculptures as a democratizing approach to educate the masses who visited the Crystal Palace for 20 years after it was relocated from Hyde Park (the Great Exhibition in 1851) to Sydenham in South London (1854)" (Hornstein, "Representing Evidence," 604). See Nichols, *Greece and Rome at the Crystal Palace*. On the history of

the Metropolitan Museum of Art's cast collection, see Milleker, "Brief History of the Cast Collection."
9. Levitt, *The Objects That Remain*.
10. For a digital virtual tour of *The Evidence Room*, provided here with permission from The Evidence Room Foundation, go to https://theweitzman.org/exhibitions/the-evidence-room/.
11. Stallybrass and Jones, "Fetishizing the Glove."
12. International Architectural Exhibition, *Reporting from the Front*.
13. Nagel, "Afterlife of Reliquary."
14. Stallybrass and Jones, "Fetishizing the Glove," 174. See also Young, *Texture of Memory*. Although Young draws some of these connections to the fetish, he offers a somewhat different take.
15. Stallybrass and Jones, "Fetishizing the Glove," 175.
16. Stallybrass and Jones, "Fetishizing the Glove," 175.
17. McNamara, "U.S. Holocaust Museum Research Center Opens." The center opened in April 2017.
18. See Jackson, *Denial*. It is also strangely notable that in the same year that *The Evidence Room* was created, 2016, and in a quite different vein, the Lipstadt trial was brought back to life as the subject of the film *Denial*. This film itself becomes another kind of holder of this story, making it available to new generations who might not know this story.
19. Bordeleau et al., *The Evidence Room*, 76.
20. Bordeleau et al., *The Evidence Room*, 76.
21. International Architectural Exhibition, *Reporting from the Front*. Hornstein powerfully describes *The Evidence Room*'s place in the Central Pavilion. As she explains, the work stood in sharp contrast to the pieces all around it. Here was a space "without audio track, no voice-overs, no video: a space of near-to-silence save for the whisper of visitors" (Hornstein, "Representing Evidence," 599). As she goes on to explain, "Color abounds, acoustic soundtracks hum, and the din of visitors hangs in the atmosphere and even overwhelms at times, in sharp contradistinction to van Pelt's whitewashed, silent, curated space" (599). My own reaction to this placement was less positive. I found that the piece was overshadowed at times by the loud and colorful displays that surrounded it in that central pavilion.
22. Hornstein, "Representing Evidence," 598. These are notions I explore further in my book *The Objects That Remain*. See especially chapter 4 and

the haunting images of Mike Mandel and Larry Sultan from *Evidence, 1977*.
23 Nagel, "Afterlife of Reliquary," 212.
24 Schuessler, "The Evidence Room." I keep thinking about the way that *The Evidence Room* was critiqued for being perhaps too beautiful. It is after all a stark and striking forensic production. And yet, how else do we show respect and reverence? See, for example, Jennifer Schuessler's critique in popular news media. I am also reminded of the magnificent boxes at the United States Holocaust Memorial Museum designed to hold the utterly fragile nylon parachute wedding dresses made in displaced persons' camps just after the war. These hopeful repurposed garments created by survivors in order to celebrate life after, to ritually enact the promise of a future, of love and family, are themselves kept for safekeeping in those reliquaries.
25 Bordeleau et al., *Evidence Room*, 118.
26 Clifton, "Conversations in Museums," 210. Clifton goes on to say that these vitrines in fact "augment the objects' special status and the viewers' longing to experience their sacred force, even in the context of a secular museum" (210).
27 Iversen, *Photography*, esp. 48–66 for a discussion about rubbing.
28 Clifton, "Conversations in Museums," 210. As Clifton explains, this "may have provided an outlet for pent-up tactile yearnings" (210).
29 Nagel, "Afterlife of Reliquary," 213.
30 Bordeleau et al., *The Evidence Room*, 79.
31 Bordeleau et al., *The Evidence Room*, 86.
32 Nagel, "Afterlife of Reliquary," 212.
33 Saieh, "Venice Biennale 2012"; Williams and Tsien, *Wunderkammer*.
34 As Hornstein argues, part of the power of *The Evidence Room* is that the horrific evidence it gathers and uses—the architecture of genocidal destruction—can be recreated, in fact, anywhere. The plans, the drawings, the inventories can be reproduced in Venice and elsewhere. Van Pelt and the Waterloo team demonstrate this potential in their construction of *The Evidence Room* itself.
35 van Alphen, "Deadly Historians." Some argue that the name Canada was ironically given to this storage facility by the Nazis, whereas others attribute this designation to the camp inmates themselves. Art historian Ernst van Alphen writes that Canada was "the euphemistic name the

Nazis gave to the warehouses that stored all the personal belongings of those who were killed in the gas chambers or interned in the labor camps" (62). Others suggest that Canada was the name given to these places by the inmates for whom Canada was a country that symbolized wealth and promise.

36 van Alphen, "Deadly Historians," 62.
37 See hirshhorn.si.edu/.
38 Levitt, "(Holocaust Memory) Laura Levitt Guest-Blog."
39 Small, "History of Holocaust Denial." As Zachary Small writes in his review of the installation at the Hirshhorn, "The juxtaposition is instructive, illustrating how the political has become its own aesthetic category over the last few generations. And whereas *Absence* predominantly represents memory as the dematerialization of history, *The Evidence Room* argues the opposite: memory as the manifestation of history."

Bibliography

Bordeleau, Ann, Sascha Hastings, Donald McKay, and Robert Jan van Pelt. *The Evidence Room*. Toronto: New Jewish Press, 2016.

"Chilling Exhibit 'The Evidence Room' Recreates a Nazi Gas Chamber." *CBC Radio*, March 2, 2016. www.cbc.ca/radio/q/schedule-for-wednesday-march-2-2015-1.3472195/chilling-exhibit-the-evidence-room-recreates-a-nazi-gas-chamber-1.3472244 (accessed July 10, 2022).

Clifton, James. "Conversations in Museums." In *Sensational Religion: Sensory Cultures in Material Practice*, ed. Sally Promey, 205–13. New Haven, CT: Yale University Press, 2014.

Hornstein, Shelley. "Representing Evidence." *Memory Studies* 15, no. 3 (2022): 595–609.

International Architectural Exhibition. *Reporting from the Front: Biennale Architettura 2016, 28.05-27.11, Venice*, 2 vols., curated by Alejandro Aravena Mori. Venice: Marsilio, 2016.

Iverson, Margaret, *Photography, Trace, and Trauma*. Chicago: University of Chicago Press, 2017.

Jackson, Mick, dir. *Denial*, 2016. New York: Bleecker Street Films, 2017. DVD.

Levitt, Laura. "(Holocaust Memory) Laura Levitt Guest-Blog (The Evidence Room)." *Jewish Philosophy Place* (blog), July 1, 2019. jewishphilosophyplace.com/2019/07/01/holocaust-memory-laura-levitt-guest-blog-the-evidence-room/ (accessed October 11, 2019).

———. *The Objects That Remain*. University Park: Penn State University Press, 2020.

Lipstadt, Deborah. *Denying the Holocaust: The Growing Assault on Truth and Memory*. New York: Plume, 1994.

———. *History on Trial: My Day in Court with a Holocaust Denier*. New York: Harper Perennial, 2006.

Marks, Laura. *The Skin of Film: Intercultural Cinema, Embodiment, and the Senses*. Durham, NC: Duke University Press, 2000.

McNamara, John. "U.S. Holocaust Museum Research Center Opens in Bowie." *Capital Gazette*, April 24, 2017. www.capitalgazette.com/maryland/bowie/ph-ac-bb-holocaust-facility-0425-20170424-story.html (accessed October 15, 2019).

Milleker, Elizabeth. "A Brief History of the Cast Collection." Metropolitan Museum of Art, 2006. www.classicist.org/assets/images/resources-students/A-Brief-History-of-the-Cast-Collection.pdf?fbclid=IwAR2hAkeahLcbTfPe9AuojZFf6-5msurbn-hyz-mop5ksKsW0BdGeRbA3vG4 (accessed July 10, 2022).

Nagel, Alexander. "The Afterlife of Reliquary." In *Treasures of Heaven: Saints, Relics, and Devotion in Medieval Europe*, ed. Martina Bagnoli, Holder A. Klein, C. Griffith Mann, and James Robinson, 211–22. New Haven, CT: Yale University Press, 2010.

Nelson, Maggie. *The Argonauts*. Minneapolis: Graywolf Press, 2015.

Nichols, Kate. *Greece and Rome at the Crystal Palace: Classical Sculpture and Modern Britain, 1954–1936*. Oxford, UK: Oxford University Press, 2015.

Olin, Margaret. *Touching Photographs*. Chicago: University of Chicago Press, 2012.

Saieh, Nico. "Venice Biennale 2012: Wunderkammer / Tod Williams Billie Tsien Architects." *ArchDaily*, November 22, 2012. www.archdaily.com/272440/venice-biennale-2012-wunderkammer-tod-williams-billie-tsien-architects (accessed July 12, 2022).

Schuessler, Jennifer. "'The Evidence Room': Architects Examine the Horrors of Auschwitz." *New York Times*, June 14, 2016. www.nytimes.com/2016/06/15/arts/design/the-evidence-room-architects-examine-the-horrors-of-auschwitz.html?mcubz=1&_r=0 (accessed June 18, 2017).

Small, Zachary. "A History of Holocaust Denial Comes Under Scrutiny in 'The Evidence Room.'" *Hyperallergic*, August 28, 2019. hyperallergic.com/513169/the-evidence-room-hirshhorn-museum/ (accessed July 12, 2022).

Stallybrass, Peter, and Rosalind Jones. "Fetishizing the Glove in Renaissance Europe." In *Things*, ed. Bill Brown, 174–92. Chicago: University of Chicago Press, 2004.

van Alphen, Ernst. "Deadly Historians: Boltanski's Intervention in Holocaust Historiography." In *Visual Culture and the Holocaust*, ed. Barbie Zelizer, 45–73. New Brunswick, NJ: Rutgers University Press, 2001.

Williams, Tod, and Billie Tsien. *Wunderkammer*. New Haven, CT: Yale University Press, 2012.

Young, James. *The Texture of Memory: Holocaust Memorials and Meaning*. New Haven, CT: Yale University Press, 1994.

5

MAKING SPACE FOR JEWISH CULTURE IN POLISH FOLK AND ETHNOGRAPHIC MUSEUMS

Curating Social Diversity after Ethnic Cleansing

Erica Lehrer and Monika Murzyn-Kupisz

In a volume dedicated to collecting and interpreting "Jewish things," the standard question inevitably arises about what constitutes a thing's Jewishness. Work on and in post-Holocaust Poland requires confrontation with a most complex and painful version of this question. The historically shifting entanglements, national identifications, and intergroup conflicts among Jewish and Christian Poles were further complicated by the sudden brutality by which these social relations—both among people and between people and things—were severed during the Holocaust. The cataclysm involved the separation of an entire community from its world of things, from pocket-sized personal objects to immovable communal property. This Jewish "material culture"—things locally known in the postwar era as "post-Jewish" (*pożydowskie*)—was thus orphaned and in the intervening years has undergone a partial, contested, and ongoing "re-inheritance" by others, often by the original Jewish owners' Catholic neighbors (both literally and more broadly construed).

Today, the relationships that such "awkward objects" might have with both Jews and other communities demand theorization and an expanded vocabulary. The notion of "implication," borrowed from Michael Rothberg,[1] has been suggestive for an enhanced approach to theorizing things that "involves shifting the focus away from the agency of the 'subjects' . . .

and transpos[ing] it instead to the agency of the 'objects,' recognizing the material world's ability to depict, to move, to connect, to remind, even to accuse."[2] Polish museums are a domain in which objects implicating Jews (whether formerly owned by them, representing them, or otherwise indexing them) have proved particularly challenging. "Jewish things" in this broadest sense can be "unruly" for Polish museums that house them, because they point to Jewish absence and difference and to the fraught and affectively freighted histories that are attached to them.[3] They thus illuminate biases embedded in museum epistemologies, taxonomies, and curatorial practices, potentially provoking calls to change these. Jewish things present challenges for nationally oriented museums, because the question of where Jewish objects fit forces questions about Jewish belonging in the nation more broadly. The treatment of "Jewish things" in museums thus offers a window into both debates about the nation and shifting trends in museology, particularly regarding the role of such institutions in shaping ideas about national heritage.

Postsocialist Poland has seen a boom in new museum activity—including the opening of new institutions and the renovation and expansion of existing ones—in a trend particularly visible since the accession of the country to the European Union (EU) in 2004.[4] This moment of growth in the Polish museum sector is taking place as new museological paradigms are developing internationally. A pluralistic trend emanating from the West emphasizes the "European" values of supranational integration and minority inclusion and the deeply critical postcolonial rethinkings of museums' fundamental raison d'être. In Poland we see the confrontation of two political tendencies that map onto two divergent conceptions of national heritage: one that celebrates Polish ethnonationalism and attempts to reclaim heroic Polish history, and another favoring discourses of pluralism and multiculturalism (and addressing darker historical chapters). Both formulations were in different ways and at different times marginalized and appropriated by the postwar communist state.

Ethnographic museology, one thread of which was taken up in Poland in the late nineteenth century as part of broader ethnonational consolidation projects that were also influenced by developing "scientific" disciplinary categories, tends toward the first narrative.[5] Although the state's territory had been at most 60 percent ethnically Polish before World War II and although Jews constituted 10 percent of the population, ethnographers largely held the "Jewish question" aside from the question of ethnic Polish cultural autonomy, whose territorial aspirations they rooted in ideas of a distinct Slavic peasantry.[6] The postwar socialist state with its class-conscious mandate repurposed and refreshed the earlier tradition of celebrating the national peasantry in the context of the prewar museum institutions and collections they inherited. Poland's historical multiethnicity was further obscured by the Holocaust and the postwar redrawing of Polish borders along with associated, sometimes violent, population transfers. These events almost completely destroyed the historically integral, almost one-thousand-year-old Jewish presence. Indeed, it was during the period of the postwar Polish People's Republic that the country first existed as an almost entirely monoethnic polity, a condition largely maintained in its post-1989 Third Republic.[7] Yet despite a wide range of important efforts by activists, including a few significant institutions such as those described later, the country's amnesia regarding its prior cultural heterogeneity is profound, extending across both public and private domains.[8] This is particularly true in terms of the more critical recognition of complex relations between ethnic Poles and their historically multiethnic neighbors. Given the significance of Jews to the social fabric of the Polish countryside, prominent sociologist Jan Gross observed with consternation in 2016 that "on the whole, you don't know, *even if you look at the local ethnographic museums* . . . that there had been a Jewish population" in Poland's towns and villages.[9]

Gross and other scholars (e.g., Barbara Engelking and Joanna Tokarska-Bakir) have brought challenging historical and cultural revelations to light, contributing to a two-decades-long public debate regarding the ability of the country to embrace Jewishness as part of the imagined national "we."[10] The treatment of Jewish subject matter in public museums can be seen as a barometer of attendant social and political changes. And there has indeed been a clear increase in the visibility of Jews as a component of Poland's heritage landscape, including in important, purpose-built new Jewish museums, which serve as diplomatic gestures on the national and international stage.[11] Today this country of perhaps twenty thousand Jews is home to no fewer than seven Jewish-themed museums (with two more under construction), from modest but significant projects in Chmielnik, Płock, Kraków, and Lublin[12] to the world-class multimillion-dollar POLIN Museum of the History of Polish Jews in Warsaw, which was heralded in the Polish and international press as a watershed moment for Poland's version of *Vergangenheitsbewältigung* and Polish-Jewish reconciliation when it opened in 2014. *The Economist* predicted that this new institution—born of both local and international impulses, with North American folklorist Barbara Kirshenblatt-Gimblett at its curatorial helm—would "intensify the debate about how museums should think about depicting issues of national identity," which indeed it has.[13]

But museums are diverse in their histories, epistemologies, audiences, social roles and values, and organizational and funding structures. Łukasz Bukowiecki recently noted that "although public opinion concentrates [on] the less than 20 'most important' Polish museums, the whole sector consists of almost one thousand institutions, whose activities are often discursively ignored, but are appreciated by visitors."[14] A 2011 survey of Polish museums posits over 220 institutions with Judaica collections or exhibitions that include Jewish content.[15] Thus it is worth considering the much broader range of *non-Jewish* museums where Polish and other visitors might encounter Jewish materials, beyond the relatively few specifically Jewish ones that have been celebrated. In this essay we focus on three Polish museums—two of the country's largest ethnographic museums and one much more marginal folk museum—asking how these types of institutions are responding to the country's broader recent trends of integrating Jewish subject matter into Polish national heritage.

Little attention has been paid to the transformation of such *preexisting* museum institutions, those not distinctly focused on Jewish heritage, as they begin to include, or increase their integration of, Jewish themes in their displays. We argue that these more "universal" civic cultural institutions—with their more deeply entrenched local audiences, collections, infrastructures, museum staff, and museological paradigms—better reflect the structural and political challenges, shifting disciplinary formations, cultural inertia, and human anxieties that accompany attempts to embrace Jewishness in its diverse expressions as an integral part of Polish heritage. The museums' evolving approaches to the incorporation and framing of Jewish materials offer a new perspective on navigating the *transition* from past and status quo paradigms to a range of newly unfolding national self-conceptions.[16]

Jews in Poland's Ethnographic Museums

In Central and Eastern Europe ethnographic museums have traditionally been understood as the keepers of national culture and tools of nation building, bound up as they were with the rise of nineteenth-century nations and the delineation of the cultural groups (ethnos or folk) that justified them.[17] In multicultural cities such as Lviv/Lwów, Vilnus, Kraków, and Warsaw under the Russian and Austro-Hungarian empires, such museums were founded as a part of a Polish nation-building process. Carried out during a period of foreign rule when Poland did not exist as a sovereign state, they were thus grassroots citizens' rather than state-sponsored initiatives and were under increased pressure to carry the torch of the imagined and aspired-to territorial Polish ethnonation.

Polish Jews—in an attempt to constitute themselves as a legitimate, "normal" nation within the dominant paradigm of the day—created their own traditions of ethnographic documentation and collection, whether they were pursuing a vision of parallel national sovereignty or an integral place in a pluralistic Polish collectivity.[18] They were occasionally supported by and at least in dialogue with their "ethnic" Polish colleagues in the broader development of ethnographic museology. But the aspirations embodied in their traditions died along with the majority of Jews in Europe in the war. Their collections were scattered: Some were stolen or destroyed by the Nazis; some were nationalized by local postwar regimes; and some were reappropriated by the new State of Israel or the United States in the name of a distinct Jewish ethnonational communal patrimony. Today's fragmentary Jewish collections in ethnographic museums speak to a truncated earlier history of (re)imagining Jews' place in Poland.

In museums in the postwar Polish People's Republic, pressure for an ethnonational Polish imaginary continued in line with general state politics stressing the uniform, monocultural character of the Polish state. These politics were expressed in discourses and practices of a Polish national brand of communism that was developed to domesticate and legitimize what might otherwise be resisted as a foreign, Soviet imposition. In museums in the postwar period, national minorities were occasionally visible for strategic purposes, but exhibits mentioning them were curated to reflect these politics.[19]

Today's Polish ethnographic museums, then, are fundamentally tied to ideologized disciplines that at least between 1945 and 1989 saw Jews, along with other "national minorities," as either largely external to their concerns or problematic obstacles to overcome in their quest for ideal (ethnic) nationhood. The Jewish question that troubled the division of Europe into ethnonational states is reflected in such institutions in a still largely romantically constituted museum ethnography that continues to define national collectivities monoethnically. Attempts to add Jewish subject matter to these museums today must thus go hand in hand with broader redefinitions of nation, culture, and ethnography. Ethnographic museums in the West, whose existence was closely linked with nineteenth-century attempts to define culture and link it to human groups for purposes of colonial expansion, have in recent years been fundamentally thrown into question as legitimate keepers of and authorities on culture, and they have been pushed to redefine their approaches to presenting it.[20]

Yet if ethnographic museums elsewhere are losing the kind of authority they once had as definitive, scientifically constituted containers of identity in today's diversified representational landscape, they still play a significant social role in Poland. That lasting relevance may be attributed to several factors: (1) their dedication not to elite culture but to the lifeways of so-called common people and thus their popular perception as representing democratic culture; (2) their function as attractive destinations for school groups, with after-school or weekend "informal education" events for Polish children and families; and (3) the renaissance of interest they are experiencing because of the fashion for reinterpreted folk, ethno-design, and do-it-yourself aesthetics (which was somewhat dampened during the 1990s because of the association of these themes with the ideology of the former communist regime but which has been strongly present since the nineteenth century in Polish art and design).[21]

For this reason our inquiry addresses the representation of Jews in non-Jewish-specific museums in Poland by focusing on three ethnographic or folk museums: the National Ethnographic Museum in Warsaw (Państwowe Muzeum Etnograficzne w Warszawie), the Seweryn Udziela Ethnographic Museum in Kraków (Muzeum Etnograficzne im. Seweryna Udzieli w Krakowie), and the Przedbórz Regional Folk Museum (Muzeum Ludowe Ziemi Przedborskiej). New critical or decolonial approaches have been the primary analytical tools for assessing and driving the changes in ethnographic museums in the West. But there has been little public discussion regarding the practical application—and indeed the applicability—of such approaches to ethnographic (or any) museology in Poland,[22] despite the broadly shared epistemological and curatorial foundations of Polish ethnographic museums and their Western counterparts.[23] These debates have just begun to touch Polish soil through the travels and exchanges of Polish and foreign scholars, artists, curators, and community activists—ourselves included. In what follows, we ask what challenges these imported new approaches confront and which preexisting, local paradigms and sources of innovation they might find themselves in creative tension with. We are interested in understanding the drivers of and constraints on progressive change in Polish ethnographic museums as well as the interplay among external and internal sources as they confront the weight and complexity of Polish history.

"Cabinet of Jewish Curiosities": Przedbórz Regional Folk Museum

The Przedbórz Regional Folk Museum is in many ways an outlier among our three selected museums. It is not a "registered" museum[24] but a labor of love by a single individual in a deeply provincial locale, and it functions largely outside current trends in global museological discourse. In its status as largely unmediated by disciplinarily norms, it illustrates a common vernacular approach to the display of Jewish culture in Polish contexts. It also points to the broader commodification of "picturesque," "folkloric" Jewish culture for the purpose of tourist consumption in private-sector contexts and as such is a window onto popular ideas about Jews that underlie this trend.[25]

Przedbórz is a small municipality in the current Łódź region with 7,300 inhabitants in 2015, of which 3,600 resided in the town proper. A typical former shtetl, it has had city rights since the fourteenth century and a Jewish community existing there since the end of the sixteenth century. The first mention of a synagogue in Przedbórz was in 1638, a structure considered one of the most beautiful wooden synagogues in Poland.[26] Before World War II almost two-thirds of the town's seven thousand residents were Jewish, most living in the central, oldest part of the town and on adjacent streets. The town suffered major destruction during the first days of the war in September 1939, including the burning down of the synagogue by the German Nazi occupiers. In January 1940 a ghetto was established for Jewish residents of the area. It was liquidated in October 1942, when the Jews were moved to the ghetto in Radomsko and later to the Treblinka extermination camp. After the war, at the turn of 1945–46, nine local Jews returned to Przedbórz; all were killed in the forest of Radoszyce by underground right-wing Polish partisans.[27]

The museum is the only public representation of Jews in the town. The project was initiated by Tadeusz Michalski, a teacher at the local secondary vocational agricultural school (*technikum rolnicze*), who began collecting artifacts in the region in the 1970s and organized an initial display of them in one of the rooms of the local school—a so-called folk room (*izba ludowa*)—in 1983.[28] From 1986 to 1997 the museum continued to function as a private initiative that grew with Michalski's travels in the surrounding countryside, though it was renamed the Civic Folk Museum (Społeczne Muzeum Ludowe) and moved to the Przedbórz market square. In 1998 it became a municipal institution, and in the following year it was moved to the building of a former (presumably Jewish) inn at 9 Kielecka Street, one of nineteen such inns that had existed in Przedbórz in the prewar era.[29] At that time, ownership of the museum was officially taken over by the municipality and renamed the Przedbórz Regional Folk Museum (Muzeum Ludowe Ziemi Przedborskiej). The museum's founder became its director, and he continues to function as its sole curator.[30] Michalski is also a locally known poet, writer of collections of *szmonces* ("Jewish-style" jokes, or jokes making references to Jewish culture), and a *znachor*, or traditional village healer. He identifies fully with the institution he built: "The museum is me and I am the museum."[31]

According to its founder, the Przedbórz Regional Folk Museum collection includes over 8,000 artifacts (the museum's report to the national Office of Statistics in 2016 listed 1,638 inventory entries), and boasts approximately 2,700 visitors per year (per 2016–18 data). Most of these are locals (half of them schoolchildren from the region); some are Polish tourists (there is some online chatter about the museum), and a few are foreign Jews. The museum has a yearly budget of 132,000 zlotys (about €31,000), which is relatively large for the small municipality but tiny in comparison to the two major urban institutions we describe later. The museum has three employees, each working part-time.

The museum's overall curatorial strategy is that of a typical *skansen*,[32] with individual rooms curated in naturalistic-style displays of conventional local domestic settings (kitchen, sitting room, bedroom) and rooms depicting village craft production (blacksmith's shop, cooper's workshop, weaving and spinning, pottery making, fishnet making), as well as rooms devoted to specific themes (World War II partisan bunker, Christian religious art, locally prominent persons). The domestic spaces are presented as normatively Catholic. In places, however, the self-taught curator has put "similar" religious ritual objects from Jewish and Catholic traditions side by side, for example, a mezuzah and a font for holy water—both of which were traditionally found at the entrances to local Przedbórz homes—without explanation.

The visibly Jewish portions of the museum, though clearly demarcated as "other," are relatively prominent, as they are situated at the beginning and end of the museum's visitor path. Upon entering the museum's courtyard, one encounters a display of locally salvaged tombstones propped against one wall, which is accompanied by a large interpretive plaque

FIGURE 5.1. Jewish headstones and wooden figures in the courtyard of the Przedbórz Regional Folk Museum. Photo courtesy of Erica Lehrer.

describing "The history and annihilation of Przedbórz Jews" ("Historia i zagłada Żydów przedborskich"). Interspersed among the stones are carved wooden figurines depicting Hasidic Jews, a popular object in the Polish postwar (and particularly postcommunist) folk art industry.[33] Boards on the wall above the display of objects provide basic information on the rituals, holidays, and history of Jews in Przedbórz, including the symbolism of Jewish headstones and the destruction of the Przedbórz synagogue during World War II. Elsewhere in the courtyard are boards titled, for example, "From the atmosphere of old Przedbórz" ("Z klimatu dawnego Przedborza"), which includes photographs of prewar Jews and quotations from Michalski's own poems, which refer to Jewish themes.[34]

After progressing through the museum's other rooms, visitors end at the "Jewish inn," a room marked with a sign stating "Judaica" (*Judaika*), the term used for all material things (artifacts, documents, etc.) relating to Jews and Jewish culture in Poland. Curated in quasi-diorama style to give the feeling of entering an actual inn, from outside the small room one can see a life-size mannequin of a religious Jew with cap and beard standing behind the counter—a historic wooden *szynkwas* typical for Jewish taverns and, according to Michalski, salvaged from a real historic inn. One of the few mannequins in the museum, it is a metonym for the absent Jewish population. Yet it also reinforces the popular yet ambivalent Polish stereotype of the Jew as tavern keeper, with his ledger book and abacus to keep track of debts and his jugs to serve alcohol; his religious and cultural difference is further underlined by way of a Sabbath challah on the counter and bulbs of garlic and dried herring hanging above. It is an image repeated in major works of Polish national literature, cinema, and theater (as well as folk sayings), thus interrupting any direct reference to history.

The Jewish-tended "inn" also functions as an undifferentiated repository of all "things Jewish" from Michalski's collection. The rest of the room contains a veritable jumble of "Jewish" objects of widely varying time periods, functions, and aesthetic qualities, which is devoid of interpretive context. These include more carved wooden figurines of Jews and headstone fragments, historical photographs, prayer books left by recent Hasidic Jewish pilgrims to the area, pennants left by Israeli school groups visiting nearby heritage sites, a promotional folder of the Berkeley California Jewish congregation that had unrealized plans to rebuild Przedbórz's famous synagogue in Berkeley, an academic article about the Holocaust, and a

FIGURE 5.2. Entrance to the "Jewish inn" room at the Przedbórz Regional Folk Museum. Photo courtesy of Erica Lehrer.

scrap of parchment from a Torah scroll, inscribed with Hebrew lettering, irreverently pinned to the wall.

Seemingly selected less for any link to a coherent historical cultural formation and more for a combination of visual impact and as a mode of open storage (all surfaces were used, including floor, walls, tables, and even the ceiling), it recalls a Renaissance cabinet of curiosities, suggesting the exploratory reach of its owner. Michalski himself seems unaware of the meaning(s) of all the objects he has collected; his own idiosyncratic sense of Jewishness seems to be the criterion for inclusion in this motley display.

Adjacent to the Jewish inn are two rooms that contain displays that further break the otherwise typical timeless cultural tableaux that characterize traditional ethnographic curatorial strategies. The first is the inclusion in a flat glass case of a page of the local newspaper *Głos Przedborska* (*The Przedbórz Voice*) from May 1930 describing the unscrupulous ways of the local Hasidim in their attempts to influence municipal elections. The second is the presence of an underground "bunker" featuring mannequins representing local World War II Polish Home Army partisan fighters.

Although not an ethnographic museum in a strict sense, the Przedbórz museum represents a significant trend visible in Poland's provinces in the last thirty years, in which orphaned Jewish cultural materials are preserved and brought to public attention in specific locales because of the visionary, countercultural, and often heroic efforts of a single person.[35] Michalski fits the profile: "I did it for the needs of heart." In Michalski's case the presentation of Jewish heritage was part of his broader efforts as a local schoolteacher to preserve the memory of old Przedbórz. His father was an apprentice in a local Jewish shoemaker's workshop before World War II and had recounted good memories of the experience, and Michalski's discovery of numerous objects linked to the former local Jewish community (including fragments of headstones and Torah scrolls) made clear to him the importance of including the Jewish presence in his museum. Michalski took it upon himself to collect and preserve vestiges of local Jewish heritage, and he feels it is his moral duty to remind others of this past.

This museum thus represents, in part, an ethical impulse to preserve Jewish heritage. It claims Jews as integral to the regional national imaginary constructed by the museum. And, however accidentally, it links past and present in its undisciplined curatorial strategy. The objects left by contemporary American and Israeli travelers, the presence of

Holocaust scholarship, the Torah fragment—even the antisemitic newspaper article—point to multiple historical moments and forces and a range of past and ongoing Jewish lives, making it more difficult to separate Jews as only an "object of ethnography"[36] and part of Poland's oft-invoked nostalgic, colorful, and peacefully coexisting neighbors.

Yet, given the prevailing cultural and political climate, Michalski seems to realize that he is taking a risk, which sets unspoken, perhaps unconscious parameters on what and how he curates. For example, he was disinclined to discuss difficult issues (Where were the tombstones from? How did he get the pieces of Torah scroll?). Indeed, he did not seem to think there were, on the whole, difficult issues to discuss in any broad historical sense ("Polish-Jewish relations? What relations? They complemented each other and were condemned to each other, to a symbiotic life."). Yet it was clear that he understood his own perspective as different from and more tolerant than the norm. "I always strive to include the Jewish element," he said, "not [as] blood-suckers but [as] normal people."

Further, for Michalski, Jewish heritage functions as a personal inspiration that supports his own idiosyncratic artistic vision and worldview ("Thank goodness I am not an ethnographer, I had talent and sensitivity") rather than as any established research or pedagogical project. Animated by a cosmology filled with dybbuks who inform him about the past, during our tour he repeated a litany of antisemitic jokes and superstitions that perpetuate romanticized and magical ideas about Jews and Jewish objects common to Polish folk culture.[37] The Jew as innkeeper, while denoting a certain social reality, also reproduces the most mythic of Polish images, including the idea that Jews inebriated an innocent Catholic peasant population.[38]

Although Michalski described some minimal consultations with Jews regarding the information listed on the courtyard plaques, the exhibition as a whole is rather an expression of a highly fetishized though culturally widespread vision of Jews and Jewish culture, completely out of touch with any insider Jewish view of their own lifeways or any professional scholarly understanding, whether Polish or foreign.

"Two Solitudes": The National Ethnographic Museum in Warsaw

Established in 1888, the National Ethnographic Museum in Warsaw (Państwowe Muzeum Etnograficzne w Warszawie; PME) is the oldest institution of its type in Poland.[39] Most of its original collection was destroyed during World War II and was developed anew in the postwar period. After the war the museum was initially housed in a palace outside Warsaw, and since 1973 the collection has been housed in a reconstructed former building of a credit society in the heart of Warsaw at the corner of Kredytowa and Mazowiecka Streets, across from the famous Zachęta National Gallery of Art. Plans for the basic galleries and their thematic configurations, which were devised by art historian and ethnographer Ksawery Piwocki in 1961, were innovative for the time, as they were organized to highlight the links among cultural, historical, and political processes, including the "former ethnic situation" and the "historic misfortunes" of the country.[40] But due to a lack of renovations, growing collections, and financial problems, by the 1990s the museum was largely invisible among the city's cultural offerings. Major changes began to be implemented in the early 2000s and especially since 2008, when a new director was appointed.[41] These involved renovation of the building, new exhibitions, and the opening of the Museum of Children (2013), a small separate section of the museum focused on providing workshops for young people. The museum contains over 80,000 objects, including 2,300 custodial deposits. It has 72 employees (2015) and a yearly budget of 8.8 million zlotys (€2,062,500) (2015), including 6.1 million zlotys (€1,429,700) from the Mazovian regional government. It saw 76,300 visitors in 2015.

In 2013 the museum completed a major renovation of the building involving more than 60 percent of its usable surface. In December 2013 an entirely new installation of the museum's main permanent gallery was unveiled under the title "Celebration Time in Polish and European Folk Cultures" ("Czas Świętowania w kulturach ludowych Polski i Europy"), spanning over 850 square meters. Based on director Adam Czyżewski's comprehensive new vision, the new exhibition "fulfills one of the basic methodological proposals of contemporary cultural anthropology and museology," building its narration so as to achieve a balance between textual and performative understanding... of culture. It enriches the attendee's knowledge but at the same time stimulates his sensitivity, emotions, [and] becomes an object of aesthetic experience. It uses words as a commentary but the message is effective most of all thanks to images, objects, scenography and architecture. It is not a lecture, which would describe in a linear, finished, closed and *de facto* way only one of the possible visions of reality. It is thus a tale about folk cultures [in the plural] and not about folk culture [in the singular]. It shows these through a multiplicity of accounts [and] narratives, which are ever changing in time.[42]

The result is an attractive, gleaming two-story display of Polish village rituals and costumes. More of a mall than a cabinet of curiosities, the objects are supplemented by videos that connect past practices to the ongoing present. The updated, postmodern theoretical underpinnings of the new installation can be seen, for example, in the inclusion of a section on the state-run folk arts commission Cepelia, which is announced by the presence of a neon sign from one of its shops, which had been ubiquitous in communist Poland since the 1950s.

FIGURE 5.3. "Celebration Time" gallery in the National Ethnographic Museum in Warsaw. Photo courtesy of Monika Murzyn-Kupisz.

The PME website bills the new display as "the biggest and most important exhibition in the 125-year history of the Warsaw National Ethnographic Museum. It is a colorful, multi-vocal story showing the rituals, customs, and various holiday accessories of different religious rites and traditions in Poland."[43] Followers of the Eastern Orthodox Church or the Greek Catholic Church, Armenians, and, other, smaller Polish minority communities are included in the main gallery, although in a separate section, and their distinctiveness—displayed in the form of a single holy book to represent each group—is limited to religious beliefs and customs.

Jewish cultural content has been included in a different, highly visible way, though separated entirely from the main space. Just outside the entrance to the main "Celebration Time" exhibit is a second entrance to the right leading to an exhibit listed as "Jewish Festivities in Poland," but which Czyżewski affectionately calls the Annex.[44] In stark contrast to the spacious bright-white main hall, the walls of the cavelike Jewish annex—which covers only 36 square meters, or 4 percent of the floor space used by "Celebration Time"—are painted flat black. Glass display cases flank the gallery, containing an array of Jewish ritual objects, both historical and contemporary, donated or on loan from Warsaw's present-day Jewish community, including Hanukkah menorahs and dreidels, Passover seder plates, tefillin, and prayer books. Also present are a series of paintings by Polish Jewish artists from the nineteenth and twentieth centuries, such as Artur Markowicz, Henryk Lewensztadt, Max Haneman, Henryk Gotlib, and Artur Szyk, and a few contemporary creations, such as contemporary local artist Monika Krajewska's paper cutouts (*wycinanki*). A video loop in the gallery screens prewar black-and-white Yiddish films—including the famous *Dybbuk* (Michal Waszynski, 1937)—illustrating various Jewish holiday rituals.

According to the director, although the Annex was intended to accompany the main exhibition from its conception in 2010, it was modified after opening to include a wooden scale model of the main, wooden synagogue from the town of Gąbin (Gombin in Yiddish) and a documentary film about it. Since 2015 one has to enter the Annex by walking through the entryway of a sukkah from the town of Szydłowiec.[45]

The PME has made a quantum leap forward with this new exhibition. The simple move to include Jews in Poland's flagship ethnographic museum is a clear statement that Jewish culture is part of Polish national heritage. The contemporary objects in the display cases and the scale model and sukkah reconstruction further communicate that ethnography is not only about either the past or an abstracted, idealized culture but also about taking a newer approach that is particularist and historically contextualized.

However, the question of whether Jews should be seen as "similarly different" to other national minorities in Poland or "differently different" from them is a subject of ongoing scholarly debate.[46] By segregating Jews entirely from "Celebration Time," the PME places itself in the latter camp. According to the PME director, Adam Czyżewski, the Jewish exhibition is displayed separately because it reflects an actual historical separation of communal cultures. He also refers to an asymmetry reflecting how Jews, as the subaltern minority group, were exposed to and familiar with Polish culture far more than Catholic Poles were in relation to Jewish culture and particularly Jewish religion, which thus remained obscured for the Catholic Poles. In embracing this perspective, the museum automatically positions visitors as normative, Catholic Poles. Finally, Czyżewski suggests that the stark distinction suits both Polish Catholic and perhaps even more so Jewish communal sensitivities regarding their own mutual distinctness; if he had chosen to integrate the two groups, he anticipated receiving complaints from both sides.

Yet the downsides of the new configuration are clear: The separate space gives Jewishness a feeling of clear otherness that is distinguished from what is hard not to read as "real," normative Polishness. Although perhaps an understandable sign of mourning for a tragically lost community, the choice of black paint, contrasting with the core exhibit's bright white, echoes long-standing associations in Polish folk culture (and European Christianity more generally) of Jewishness as obscurantist and associated with dark forces, and the gallery itself can produce a haunting sensation. The strict division also reinforces retrograde anthropological ideas of cultural boundedness and homogeneity, falling short of both contemporary historiography and cultural theory that could help illuminate the interpenetration and mutual cultural influences among Polish Catholics and Polish Jews.

The rather static, staid, traditional display of Jewish heritage contrasts not only with the bright, animated tone of "Celebration Time" but also with a number of the PME's other new exhibitions, for example, "Granice"

("Borders"; 2008–9), a provocative show of photographs of people of color dressed in Polish folk costume, which was created by two Poles living in New York.[47] In a 2014 interview Czyżewski discussed bolder displays that he had considered, in particular the idea to include a 1979 documentary film depicting the hanging, beating, burning, and drowning of the Jewish effigy of Judas from the southern Polish town of Pruchnik, a ritual that was stopped as a result of protests in recent years but that has seen a subsequent resurgence.[48] Czyżewski had envisioned placing this film as a kind of "doorway" connecting the main "Polish" section with the Jewish Annex.[49] But visionary museum directors are limited in their influence, particularly on controversial topics.

The city's broader, shifting museumscape also bears consideration. The opening of the POLIN Museum of the History of Polish Jews in 2014 may have both catalyzed and troubled Czyżewski's move to create the Jewish Annex at the PME. To some museum employees and casual observers, the emergence of a specialized institution nearby dealing with Jewish issues relieved the PME of any obligation to treat what appeared to be clearly demarcated as someone else's history and culture. As Czyżewski notes, "People [still] don't connect Jewish culture with ethnography," a discipline strongly associated with ethnonational culture.[50]

A 2015 exhibit of Warsaw Jewish community member Monika Krajewska's contemporary Jewish paper cutouts and a conference in the same year on Jewish folklore further signal the museum's commitment to Jewish themes. But they also suggest (perhaps self-imposed) constraints on what approaches to Jewishness are palatable to audiences, government funders, and museum staff.[51] Czyżewski's choice to move ahead with the particular curatorial approach of the Annex reflects both the significance and the limitations of this attempt to embrace Jews as an integral, if parallel part of broader Polish (folk) culture.

"Ambivalent Externalizing": The Seweryn Udziela Ethnographic Museum in Kraków

Kraków's Seweryn Udziela Ethnographic Museum (Muzeum Etnograficzne im. Seweryna Udzieli w Krakowie; MEK) was established as a separate private museum run by the Society for the Ethnographic Museum in 1911.

Converted into a public, state-owned institution in 1945, since 1948 it has been housed in the former town hall of Kazimierz in the heart of Kraków's historically Jewish quarter. In 2015 the museum had fifty-three employees and a 4.1 million zloty (€960,775) budget, most of which was supplied by the Małopolska regional authority, which is its supervising body. More than seventy-four thousand people per year make use of the museum's diverse offerings.[52] Of the three museums we surveyed, the MEK is the only one whose vast collection (eighty thousand objects) was inherited from the prewar era; it is thus the largest, oldest, and best-preserved collection in Poland. With the exception of the ground floor's cottage interiors (1951), one completely renovated gallery of springtime customs (2011), and the addition of an entirely new exhibition of folk art on the second floor ("Unattainable Earth," 2015), the basic structure and curatorial approach of today's core "permanent" exhibition on folklife and culture ("The Rhythm of Life and Human Objects") was curated in the late 1960s, with piecemeal changes introduced in the early 2000s, 2015, and 2019.[53] Recent changes are linked to the hiring of a new director in 2008, and since then the museum has been engaged in a process of halting transformation.[54]

Despite numerous progressive changes, Jews are notably absent as agents in the nation imagined by the core exhibition.[55] Although they are not entirely missing from the permanent exhibit, out of more than forty thematic sections regarding Polish folklife, Jews appear as subjects in a single photograph in the larger display in only six of them, a presence introduced in the late 1980s or early 1990s.[56] Displays on tavern keeping, folk music,[57] and paper cutting seem conspicuously lacking, as these were domains in which Jews were widespread and influential and in which they retain a strong presence in popular cultural memory. In arrangements of photos and artifacts illustrating village social and economic life, in a long display case of Polish regional costume, and most clearly in the content of the large second-floor galleries dedicated to daily life and seasonal rituals, the Poland envisioned by the museum is fundamentally a Slavic, Catholic one. Jews appear most visibly in the museum through the gaze of their ethnic Polish neighbors as costumes and masks donned for seasonal caroling and Carnival and as puppets in Christmas crèches or Jewish figurines sold at an Easter fair.

Before 2011 the museum's curatorial approach was traditionally "scientific," offering brief, general overviews of galleries with diverse materials, providing largely symbolic interpretations of the cultural practices and products presented. Costumes depicting Jews were framed solely in terms of their magical, mediating role in peasant cosmologies, with no reference to Jewish experience or intergroup conflict. The texts were also almost exclusively in Polish, and their tone and content suggested that the imagined audience was Catholic and presumed to be uncritical of the materials on display. As recently as the late 1990s, a mannequin wearing a cloak and a caricatured mask of an Orthodox Jewish man was labeled simply *Żyd* (Jew).

Since 2008, when the MEK brought in a new director, Antoni Bartosz (accompanied by the hiring of a number of new young museum workers), the museum's discursive and aesthetic approach to ethnographic museology saw a leap forward in both curatorial strategies and user-friendliness, evident in the museum's addition of a gift shop, public outdoor furniture and displays, and façade decoration. The museum's new slogan, "My museum, a museum about me," seemed a clear response to growing calls for relevance, participation, and democratization in the museum world in the West (and to critiques of ethnographic museums in particular) and to internal Polish debates about the repression of the peasant roots of Polish post-1945 society.[58] On their website and in other promotional materials, the museum has begun to frame itself in progressive terms, highlighting a number of unorthodox, experimental initiatives aimed at engaging the local population, particularly children, in marginalized city heritage, including Jewish heritage.[59]

The core exhibition has undergone a significant material change as well: the complete revision of the gallery of springtime customs under the banner of the "Re-newal" (*Od-nowa*) project, which took a radical turn away from a traditional, "scientific" curatorial approach. Emphasis has been placed instead on aesthetic experience, with a colorful "total environment" replacing dull specimen cases. The room today offers visitors a *sense* of Polish village spring, with bright wooden walls and an enormous tree trunk that grows up into the ceiling painted in a rainbow motif suggesting Polish folk crafts and surrounded by comfortable, foliage-green couches. The number of objects on display has been drastically cut, with individual highlights curated in whimsical, custom-shaped vitrines embedded in the walls, for example, a lightning bolt suggesting a spring storm. A few related archival images and quotes from ethnographic reports and village memoires are engraved in the surrounding walls. The row of delicate hand-painted Easter eggs is fitted with an antique-looking magnifying glass on metal tracks that visitors can slide along to inspect each egg. The wall panels covering two recessed display cases of wooden toy figurines from Kraków's age-old annual "Emaus" Easter-time fair—including ever-popular Jews—are movable, so visitors can uncover hidden sections. Mirrors and magnifying glasses are also used in these cases, enhancing the playful feel of the display.

But this aesthetic evolution, though representing a form of progress, has created new problems, especially with regard to Jewish themes. The changes in the springtime customs gallery arguably leave Jews *more* rather than less obfuscated. The decrease in explanatory texts leaves the objects on display at the mercy of whatever ambient, preexisting interpretations visitors bring with them, further limiting access to new perspectives. In addition, although the playful participatory choice of providing a loupe to examine an object is fine for a painted egg, a Jew under a magnifying glass raises exoticizing, even racist resonances.

Given the museum's progressive discourse and its responsiveness to popular themes, and the significance and popularity that Jewish culture has come to garner in Poland and in Kraków in recent years, one might expect the MEK to have a dedicated Judaica section, if not a more challenging integrated embrace of Jewish culture in its presentation of the "Polish folk."[60] This would align not only with reference to broader, postcolonial critiques of ethnographic museology that the museum seems, in broad terms, to be responding to, with its calls for dismantling cultural hierarchies and privileging multivocality, but also with reference to the MEK's local conditions: as an institution situated directly in Kraków's historical Jewish quarter, in a building that once served as a Jewish school, with a plaque on its exterior wall showing King Kazimierz the Great's medieval welcome of the Jews to Poland, and with a prominent postwar director (Tadeusz Seweryn) who was recognized for being "righteous among the nations" for his work to save Jews during the World War II Nazi occupation of Poland.[61]

It is worth noting that since Bartosz's tenure began, Jewish themes—even a few emotionally and politically challenging ones—have been featured almost annually in *temporary* exhibitions at the MEK. These were, with one recent exception, developed in response to external impulses

FIGURE 5.4. Jewish figurine behind peephole in the springtime customs gallery in the Seweryn Udziela Ethnographic Museum. Photo courtesy of Erica Lehrer and Jason Francisco.

and partnerships and prepared by external artists and curators, with the MEK offering gallery space in the museum's annex, a block away from the main seat.[62] The MEK has also agreed to a series of critical "interventions" addressing their curation of Jewish materials, which was also initiated by outsiders.[63] These latter projects and events both give evidence of and increase the staff's and especially the director's growing sensitivity to the museum's representation (and lack) of Jewish culture. Yet when left to their own devices—and particularly when engaging their own core collections and displays—MEK curators have often seemed ambivalent and inhibited, occasionally gesturing toward more critical engagement with Jewish subject matter but tentative, muffled, or abortive in their attempts to manifest these as enduring changes in their permanent galleries.[64]

The 2011 exhibit "Passages and Repassages" was a radical curatorial departure for the MEK and in clear conversation with critical Western audience expectations.[65] The exhibition (and its bi- and trilingual catalogs in Polish and German and in Polish, French, and English) was made at the invitation of La Maison de l'Artisanat et des Métiers d'art in Marseilles and traveled to Berlin after its Kraków premiere.[66] Curated by a team of forty MEK ethnographers, psychologists, sociologists, philosophers, art historians, and writers, the approach was to start from the objects' personal resonances and the memories they evoke and then to "dig out subjects and themes that remain relevant and contemporary, sometimes disturbing, even scandalous."[67] Yet it was silent on the contested nature of Jewish materials that it prominently featured. The aesthetic innovations—a curtain of keys visitors had to pass through and a street made of figural beehives—evoked folk culture's magical sensibilities, including those regarding otherness. But ideas about magic when applied to outsiders in the Polish folk context contain unexamined prejudices and violence.[68] The image selected for the exhibit's promotional poster (in both Polish and French iterations) was one of the show's two figural beehives depicting Orthodox Jews. Yet the catalog text made no mention at all of the variety of contemporary debates raging at the time about Poland's Jewish past or about the difficult emotions that the object itself—a wooden Jew made by Polish peasants to produce a wealth of honey—might evoke.[69]

Equally ambiguous is the incremental disappearance of Jewish-related materials, particularly those that might be seen as more contentious, from the MEK's permanent exhibition over the past decade. First to vanish was a framed photograph of an effigy of an Orthodox Jew hanging from a tree. Taken in the village of Pruchnik, it documented the 1979 iteration of the annual ritual involving the torture of the biblical Judas rendered as a prewar Polish Jew. As mentioned earlier, this tradition has seen a resurgence, and it has also become politicized in relation to anti-immigrant sentiment and Jewish property restitution claims.[70] Leading up to the 2011 transformation of the springtime customs gallery, a number of mannequins dressed in ritual garb representing social others were removed, including the aforementioned Jewish male mannequin and a "Gypsy" (Roma) woman. Further updates to the wintertime customs gallery have included the removal of the caroling group in 2017 (among them a Jewish character with stereotypical mask and long cloak) and the sets of Christmas crèche puppets that typically included one or more Jewish characters. Some of the accompanying documentary photographs, including one featuring Polish villagers laughing at a man dressed as a Jew riding on a puppet *turoń* (a kind of ram), are also no longer on display.[71]

The ambivalence surrounding Jewish themes must be understood with reference to multiple, entangled anxieties, gaps, and stumbling blocks, some invoked in conversation with members of the museum staff, others intuited by us. These include (1) Jewish content being the purview of other local museums (e.g., the Museum of Kraków, Old Synagogue and Schindler Factory branches; the National Museum; and the Galicia Jewish Museum); (2) the MEK's modest number of relevant objects; (3) MEK curators feeling underequipped in this particular subject domain;[72] (4) passive or active disinterest in Jewish subject matter on the part of some museum staff; (5) the museum's sense that highlighting and/or integrating Jewish subject matter would not be welcomed by their usual audience; (6) lack of local Jewish communal interest in the ethnographic museum and thus a lack of political will to push for Jewish cultural inclusion there; and (7) political anxieties surrounding Jewish subject matter, which have increased since the fall of 2015 with the return to power of the conservative, right-wing Law and Justice Party. Although Bartosz has publicly stated his belonging to the ranks of Poland's "philosemites,"[73] it is impossible to fully ascertain the MEK leadership's deep motivations, fears, and strategies. What is clear is that even if the museum were committed to taking on this topic, the changing cultural and political context in which it operates make engaging Jewishness increasingly risky, and indeed the most obvious challenge (and the one most consistently invoked by the museum) remains funding.[74]

The disappearance of Jewish-related material from MEK's permanent galleries might be seen negatively. It could suggest that, because such material has come to be understood as contentious as a result of the more demanding gaze of new audiences and critics and shifting museum norms, it is being swept under the rug rather than openly confronted with a critical curatorial approach. Yet the MEK's halting, piecemeal efforts to both acknowledge and contain the potency of Jewish materials and themes surely points to delicate negotiations of personal, disciplinary, and political opinions and commitments among both museum staff and funders. Welcoming external partners to initiate periodic, boundary-pushing projects on the margins of the institution may be less an abrogation of responsibility than a shrewd navigation of treacherous political waters.

Conclusion

Museums and their practitioners are important loci of both activism and conservatism. Through them, ambient cultural, political, and disciplinary discourses—and resistance to these—find curatorial expression. Ethnographic museums in particular offer a unique perspective on the opportunities and limitations presented by such symbolically and materially dense institutions in efforts to shift from a more exclusive, ethnonational model of the (Polish) nation to one that accommodates both past and present civic-national diversity. Our main concern is understanding the challenges that stand in the way of progressive change.

The two more standard "disciplinary" museums suffer from the lack of a robust model for multiethnic integration in a museological tradition of *Volkskunde* that has, across Europe, been almost exclusively ethnonational in its approach to ethnographic classification. In "Austrian" Poland in particular—where Kraków is located—Polish elites used developing cultural sciences to focus on regional rural peasantries, whom they attempted to mobilize and integrate to help articulate an essential Polish culture and "national spirit" and to claim deep ties to particular territories.[75] Jews were primarily urban (town dwellers) and involved in crafts and commerce, as opposed to the more rural Slavic peasants who lived near their fields, and as a Diaspora, Jews were transregional rather than regional. Thus they defy, for example, the common curatorial logic seen in the MEK's corridor of "regional peasant costume" and are thus absent there despite the iconic status of Jewish ritual costume in Poland. But nor do Jews fit comfortably in the parallel tradition of *Völkerkunde*, the ethnography of the "exotic other" encountered on foreign expeditions; although Jews were conspicuously different, they were also local and familiar.

The present-day struggle to invent a language for the display of Jewish culture in ethnographic museums requires that Jews be newly constituted as an ethnographic subject. This is, of course, taking place in parallel with the postsocialist reinvention of something called "Polish culture" at a moment in time when anthropologists and cultural critics have dismissed the very idea of unitary, homogeneous "cultures" as outmoded and oppressive. Attempts to curate Polish Jews in Polish ethnographic museums after the Holocaust raise a host of additional practical, political, and emotional issues. The range of approaches to (and frequently the lack of) inclusion of Jews in such museums mirrors their uncertain and sometimes outright unwanted place in dominant visions of the Polish nation, a community itself embattled and periodically suppressed or attacked.

Analogous Western European and North American museums are broadly if unevenly responding to demands for pluralization that have accompanied demographic shifts and associated political expectations on the part of minority communities and their allies. But in today's largely monoethnic Poland, the discourse of multiculturalism is new and has shaky foundations, inasmuch as it is rooted in an unevenly emerging social imaginary that takes recourse at turns to a historical situation of cultural diversity, a Europeanizing identity, and the need to address a traumatic wartime history. Powerful forces—conservative and regressive—also obfuscate or oppose these claims.

New discourses promulgated by progressive directors (e.g., "a museum about me") are difficult to operationalize in a truly critical way in a society in which the constitution of the collective "me" is in heated dispute. The issue of museums' approaches to ethnic minorities is broader than just the Jewish issue and points to the representation of other others who lived in historically Polish lands (Roma, Ukrainians, Belarussians, Germans).[76] With the increased number of Ukrainian immigrants in Poland, for example, fraught issues relating to expressions of Ukrainian history and culture have been coming to the fore. At the very moment that the International Council of Museums was debating a radically progressive new definition of what a "museum" is for, Poland's Law and Justice government was aggressively promoting celebratory, patriotic expressions of heritage and censuring anything less. In such a climate, pro-pluralist directors and curatorial staff in Polish museums have an unenviable task.[77]

Art critic and curator Magdalena Ujma praised the MEK's bold post-2008 changes but noted the limitations in Bartosz's embrace of a "general humanistic approach," which hearkens back to museum founder Seweryn Udziela's turn-of-the-century discourse of "curiosity" and "respect." By reaching backward and inward, instead of forward and outward, to newer and more diverse sources of museum theory and critique, the MEK forgoes the opportunity, perhaps the responsibility, to take "a sharper look at itself" and the more transformative potential that such self-criticism would unlock.[78] Ujma calls the MEK's approach "therapeutic" rather than

FIGURE 5.5. Winter customs room with empty white frames where the now-missing masks had hung in the Seweryn Udziela Ethnographic Museum, September 2019. Photo courtesy of Erica Lehrer.

"critical," as it encourages individual ("me") rather than social reflection, which requires truly encountering the other.

But new social forces may be catalyzing this reflection. In September 2019 the display of carolers' masks at the MEK—including the most negatively caricatured depictions of Jews—was taken down from the wall. The removal took place in the wake of an open discussion with the museum's director initiated that summer by the local organization FestivALT: New Currents in Contemporary Jewish Art as part of a series of critical events in Kraków titled "Re-Jewing Polish Folk Culture."[79] Based on Bartosz's response to the pain and anger expressed by the mostly Jewish audience at this event, it seems clear that he was led to the conclusion that the masks are simply too volatile to display as they are.

It is here that we will see how far the museum is prepared to go in honoring its new mandate of multivocality, dialogue, self-questioning, and respect for others,[80] particularly in relation to those social groups personally affected by the materials on display. Although temporary exhibitions with challenging perspectives are important, they come and go. But the meanings attributed to objects in the permanent collection through truly critical curatorial approaches are stickier, disrupting the museums' inherited taxonomies and display traditions in ways that bring uneasy politics deeper into the museums' interior, on their gallery walls, but "backstage" as well, where human and material agents might be animated in new, unruly ways.

Whether or not Polish ethnographic museums embrace the demands of a critical, decolonial museological avant-garde, a shift in their approach seems overdue, moving from what Barbara Kirshenblatt-Gimblett calls in situ curating, where objects are presented as parts of putative, often utopian cultural wholes, to "in context" curating, which creates a pedagogical frame for the viewer through historical background, questions, comparisons, and circumstances of collecting and which rescues the objects from triviality.[81] Such a shift would require a *highlighting* of the contested nature of Jewish material culture rather than its ignoring, containment, or removal, making its historical and political specificity, as well as the social violence surrounding it, inescapable.

Given the deep ambivalence toward Jewish heritage and history in Poland, the sometimes awkward curatorial approaches to Jewish topics in ethnographic museums that we describe cannot but point to an understandable lack of confidence on the part of museum directors and staff around these issues in an atmosphere of great social, structural, and political change. In today's Poland, where the government deploys a celebratory politics of history with a heavy hand, dismisses directors, and forcibly recurates museums whose narratives they find insufficiently supportive of Polish national pride[82]—and traffics in sanitized forms of Jewish heritage for their own, cynical ends—both Jewish presence and Jewish absence are topics of anxious significance.

Postscript

Just as this article was going to print,[83] Erica Lehrer, on her way to the next in a series of critical interventions in the Kraków Ethnographic Museum undertaken in partnership with MEK curator Magdalena Zych, received images of the brand new (November 2019) installation that replaced the empty space where the caricatured Jewish masks had long hung. They include a new, personal text written and signed by Zych. Printed on a sheet of laminated yellow paper affixed to the wall with metal binder rings, this supplement to the gallery's larger, main interpretive text (which appears on the gallery's standard, poster-sized black board), is written in a new kind of voice. It questions the innocence of the masks and the larger traditions they belong to; it describes the historical antisemitism they continue today to support. The new display has also replaced the masks themselves—and their visceral ability to hurt—with a larger number of small-scale archival photographs of similar masks in use, spanning the years 1938–87. The new text asks, self-reflexively, whether the museum cared about the feelings of Jewish and Roma visitors who received ironically MEK's "my museum" slogan. This outcome speaks to the necessity and potential for museum-community dialogue and for the progressive change that only listening, over time, will bring.

Notes

A version of this text was published as Erica Lehrer and Monika Murzyn-Kupisz, "Making Space for Jewish Culture in Polish 'Folk' and 'Ethnographic' Museums: Curating Social Diversity after Ethnic Cleansing," in the special issue of *Museum*

Worlds, "Festschrift for Barbara Kirshenblatt-Gimblett," ed. Conal Macarthy, 7 (2019): 82–108. We would like to acknowledge the inspiration (and for Erica Lehrer also the mentorship) of Barbara Kirshenblatt-Gimblett. We would also like to thank Magdalena Waligórska, Joanna Wawrzyniak, and Sarah Zarrow for their comments on an earlier draft of this chapter.

1 See Rothberg, *Implicated Subject*.
2 Lehrer, "Material Kin," 306.
3 Lehrer, "Material Kin," 288–323.
4 Jagodzińska, *Museums*. Many of the new museums are history museums on themes censored under communism (e.g., interwar achievements, World War II's Home Army, and the Warsaw Uprising).
5 Linkiewicz, "Scientific Ideals."
6 Stauter-Halstead, "Peasant as Literary and Ethnographic Trope."
7 Lukowski and Zawadzki, *Concise History of Poland*; Porter-Szücs, *Poland in the Modern World*. Some 69.2 percent of residents of Poland in 1921 declared their nationality as Polish, and 68.9 percent declared Polish as a native language in 1931 (Ukrainian and Yiddish being the most important other native languages). Religious identification in 1931 was Roman Catholic, 64.8 percent; Orthodox, 11.8 percent; Greek Catholic, 10.4 percent; and Jewish, 9.8 percent.
8 Nowak et al., *Banality of Forgetting*.
9 Aderet, "Historian Who Shed Light on WWII Massacres"; emphasis added.
10 See, for example, Engelking, *Such a Beautiful Sunny Day*; and Tokarska-Bakir, "The Hanging of Judas."
11 With the loosening of the late socialist government's grip on culture in the 1980s, a few extraordinary museum projects on Jewish topics came to fruition. Two exhibitions in the months surrounding the 1989–90 political transformation—"Polish Jews" (December 1989 to February 1990) in Kraków's National Museum and "Jews of Wrocław, 1850–1944," which opened in March 1989 in Wrocław's Museum of Architecture—drew significant crowds and attention to the issue of the historical presence of Jews in Poland (Kretschmann, "Entangled Heritage").
12 These Jewish museums are the Świętokrzyski Shtetl Education and Museum Centre in Chmielnik, the Galicia Jewish Museum in Kraków,

the Grodzka Gate NN Theatre Centre in Lublin, and the new branch of the Gliwice Museum focused on the history of Jews in Silesia. References to the presence of Jews in Poland are common in new regional history museums, such as the spectacular Silesian Museum in Katowice (opened 2015) and more modest sites such as the Pieniny Museum in Szlachtowa (reopened 2014), which includes Jewish residents and visitors in their exhibit on the history and culture of the Pieniny Mountains and the Szczawnica spa resort.

13 See "Shtetl of Honour," *The Economist*, October 18, 2014, www.economist.com/books-and-arts/2014/10/18/shtetl-of-honour (accessed November 9, 2019).

14 Bukowiecki, *Things of Warsaw*, 10.

15 Folga-Januszewska, *1,000 Museums*. For comparison, a 1979 source indicates the presence of objects of Jewish art in more than sixty Polish museums (Rejduch-Samkowa, "Sztuka Żydowska"), and a list compiled in cooperation with the POLIN Museum of the History of Polish Jews (Kryciński et al., *Zabytki kultury żydowskiej*) included more than sixty museums and exhibitions worth visiting for tourists interested in Jewish culture.

16 The organizational structure of museums in Polish society has also undergone significant change since 1989, especially since 1999, because at the end of 1998 (effective January 1, 1999) there was a major administrative reform in Poland that assigned each museum, often arbitrarily, to a specific level of territorial government oversight (i.e., national, regional, county, local/municipality). These new divisions have meant that few museums are still financed directly by the Ministry of Culture and National Heritage. Most museums, including the three we discuss, are currently supervised and financed by a regional, county, or municipal government. New EU cofunding programs also prioritize regional identity.

17 Linkiewicz, "Scientific Ideals." This approach flowed from a nineteenth-century Herderian romantic notion of essential singular ethnonational identities.

18 Kilcher and Safran 2016; Veidlinger 2016.

19 See, for example, Woleńska, *Wystawa sztuki ludowej zamieszkałych*. In April 1960, "an exhibition on the folk art of Belarussians, Lithuanians, Russians, Slovaks, Ukrainians and Jews who live in Poland," containing

about five hundred "folk art" objects, was curated at the Kraków Ethnographic Museum by Maria Woleńska from the National Museum in Kraków. It was initiated by the Polish Ministry of Culture and Art to celebrate the millennium of the Polish state. Whether intended to rival the Catholic Church's celebration of one thousand years of Polish Christianity in the same year or to be part of the post-Stalinist thaw, a few years later Jews would be vilified again in the events of 1967–68.

20 See, for example, Boursiquot "Ethnographic Museums"; Durrans, "Future of Ethnographic Exhibitions"; Harris and O'Hanlon, "Future of the Ethnographic Museum"; Modest et al., *Matters of Belonging*; and Thomas, *Museums in Postcolonial Europe*.

21 Brzezińska, "Made in a Polish Village"; Klekot, "Seventh Life."

22 Cf. Bukowiecki, *Things of Warsaw*; Bukowiecki and Wawrzyniak, *Dealing with Difficult Pasts*; Murawska-Muthesius, "Love of Beauty"; Murawska-Muthesius and Piotrowski, "Introduction"; and Piotrowski, *Muzeum Krytyczne*.

23 For a discussion of the complexities of applying postcolonial analysis to the Polish case, including a reference to the broader European colonial mind shared by Warsaw National Ethnographic Museum founder Stefan Szolc-Rogoziński, see Grzechnik, "Missing Second World."

24 According to the Polish Museum Law of November 21, 1996, a *muzeum rejestrowane* is a museum with a significant, valuable collection that adheres to the highest museum management standards, has a statute or regulations document formally approved by the Minister of Culture and National Heritage, and is included in the Ministry's National Register of Museums. In 2019 only 128 Polish museums were listed, including the Warsaw and Kraków ethnographic museums (Ministerstwo Kultury i Dziedzictwa Narodowego, "Rejestr Muzeów").

25 The Przedbórz museum is not entirely isolated, however, as the director has contracted some work with a professionally trained art historian, and the local municipal tourism office promotes the museum on their website.

26 Piechotka and Piechotka, *Heaven's Gates*.

27 According to the museum's director, Tadeusz Michalski, local lore holds that they were killed because they collaborated with the hated Communist Party Security Services, the Urząd Bezpieczeństwa. Anthropologist Joanna Tokarska-Bakir's 2018 study *Under a Curse* debunks these myths, which were frequently used as a justification for such murders.

28 Such small-scale folk rooms were a common approach to displaying local artifacts in Poland in lieu of a self-standing museum.
29 Michalski described it as a Jewish inn from the eighteenth century, which was reconstructed in 1898, and claims it was frequented by Nobel Prize–winning Polish author Władysław Reymont, who was born in nearby Kobiele Wielkie. Since 1994 the building has been listed on the National Register of Museums as "an inn from the sixteenth–seventeenth century."
30 The museum is presently financed from the municipal budget, but the director has a relatively free hand in designing the exhibition and associated activities. Apart from minor renovations and repairs done with the help of student volunteers, no major investments have ever been made in the building.
31 Tadeusz Michalski, personal communication, Przedbórz, July 21, 2014.
32 A skansen is an (originally Swedish) open-air museum consisting of collections of historic structures; they are particularly popular in Central and Eastern Europe. See Czajkowski, *Muzeum Budownictwa Ludowego w Sanoku*.
33 These particular figures are the product of Polish-Jewish-themed wood-carving competitions that were run by the museum for several years.
34 For example: "Small windows with a side glance / into the gist of street hassle / . . . where every Jew had his own little corner / Just like as the cinnamon-like Berdichev / cherishing the love of small-town simplicity."
35 "Leaders of Dialogue," Forum for Dialogue, 2019, dialog.org.pl/liderzy-dialogu/en/leaders/ (accessed November 1, 2019); Marzynski, *Frontline*.
36 Kirshenblatt-Gimblett, "Objects of Ethnography."
37 Cała, *Image of the Jew*.
38 Dynner, *Yankel's Tavern*; Goldberg, "Żyd i karczma na Podlasiu"; Goldberg, "Żyd a karczma wiejska"; Opalski, *Jewish Tavern-Keeper*.
39 Referring to the title of this section, the expression "Two Solitudes" originally referred (and still does refer) to a perceived lack of communication, and a lack of will to communicate, between Anglophone and Francophone people in Canada. The term was popularized by Hugh MacLennan's 1945 novel *Two Solitudes*. We use it here as an evocative metaphor rather than as a strict parallel.
40 Czyżewski, "Czas świętowania"; Piwocki, "Ethnographical Museum in Warsaw."

41 Since 1999 the museum has been overseen by the regional government.
42 Czyżewski, "Transformation," 11.
43 Państwowe Muzeum Etnograficzne w Warszawie, "Czas świętowania." Currently the PME webpage states that the display is closed for renovations.
44 Bielawski and Stankowski, "Czyżewski."
45 POLIN Museum of the History of the Jewish People, "Ocalona kuczka." Until recently the only object of this kind in a Polish museum collection, the sukkah is on loan from the nearby POLIN Museum of the History of Polish Jews. According to Czyżewski, it did not fit in POLIN's exhibition.
46 On this debate, see, for example, Avrutin et al., *Photographing the Jewish Nation*; Gottesman, *Defining the Yiddish Nation*; and Zarrow, "Object Lessons." We thank Sarah Zarrow for this distinction between "similarly different" and "differently different." Zarrow holds the former stance, whereas Itzik Gottesman holds the latter stance.
47 Czyżewska, "Introduction." A catalog produced for a traveling version of the show contains the images along with a short essay by Elżbieta Czyżewska.
48 Kazimierczuk, "Sąd nad Judaszem"; Tokarska-Bakir, "The Hanging of Judas."
49 Bielawski and Stankowski, "Czyżewski."
50 Bielawski and Stankowski, "Czyżewski."
51 Krajewska's exhibit was titled "Seeking Paradise" ("Szukam raju"). The proceedings of the conference "Jewish Ethnography and Folklore in Poland Until 1945" ("Etnografia i folklorystyka żydowska w Polsce do roku 1945") were published in *Etnografia Nowa / The New Ethnography*, 7 (2015) and 8 (2016).
52 Departament Kultury i Dziedzictwa Narodowego, *Kultura*.
53 For the 1960s changes, see Dolińska, "Muzeum Etnograficzne." For the changes in the twenty-first century, see Szczurek, *Sto i pół*.
54 Bartosz, "Słowo wstępne"; Bartosz, "Ethnographic Museums"; Bartosz, "Szumi coś i gwarzy."
55 Lehrer, *Jewish Poland Revisited*; Lehrer, "Most Disturbing Souvenirs."
56 Dolińska, "Muzeum Etnograficzne"; Dolińska and Gruszka, *Sto i pół*. In 1985 the decision was made to "modernize" the exhibition and remove explicit communist content from it.
57 Waligórska, *Klezmer's Afterlife*.

58 Leder, *Prześniona rewolucja*.
59 Murzyn-Kupisz and Działek, "Muzea a budowanie kapitału społecznego"; Piszczkiewicz, "Ethnography in the Public Space." Temporary exhibitions have treated topics that might be seen as boundary pushing in the local context, such as Islam or refugees or the inclusion of a gay couple in an exhibit about weddings. They have also used new approaches such as long-term field research with denizens of the city's communist-era garden allotments or an exhibition with object selection and interpretation based on memories of a range of MEK employees.
60 Wasilewska-Prędki, "Judaika." Although there was no systematic Judaica acquisition, the MEK owns ten Judaica items (clothing and flags) and hundreds of photographs and archival documents, including postcards.
61 There is also some evidence that, during the Nazi occupation, Jews may have been hidden in the building that is now the museum's annex (Ester's House).
62 Robert Gądek, personal communication, August 12, 2019. Gądek is the associate director of the Kraków Jewish Culture Festival. Exhibits initiated and organized by the festival include Wojciech Wilczyk's "There Is No Such Thing as an Innocent Eye" (2009); "Becoming Acquainted with Jerusalem: Photographs, 1857–1900" (2010); Roger Bennett, David Katznelson, and Josh Kun's "Jews on Vinyl" (2011) (the only exhibit to take place in the main building, in the educational activities room); Łukasz Baksik's "*Mazevot* for Everyday Use" (2012); and Erica Lehrer's "Souvenir, Talisman, Toy: Poland's Jewish Figurines" (2013). In 2018–19 the MEK formally partnered with Erica Lehrer, Roma Sendyka, Wojciech Wilczyk, and the MEK curator Magdalena Zych on the exhibition "Terribly Close: Polish Vernacular Artists Face the Holocaust," which was one outcome of these curators' international research project, TRACES, sponsored by the EU Horizon 2020 program (ec.europa.eu/programmes/horizon2020/en).
63 Lehrer, *Na Szczęscie To Żyd*; Lehrer, "Most Disturbing Souvenirs"; Lehrer and Sendyka, *Różnicowanie narodowego "my."*
64 The International Council of Museums' (ICOM) 2017 theme "Museums and Contested Histories: Saying the Unspeakable in Museums" was taken up by young MEK curators during Kraków's 2017 "Night of Museums" (*Noc Muzeów*) festival in a set of posters and postcards highlighting "difficult issues" in the MEK's galleries. One of the posters came and went

but finally returned and remained near the carolers' masks, and though somewhat buried in a few paragraphs of text, it did contain the museum's first ever mention of antisemitism as a relevant interpretive framework for these materials. The MEK also recently experimented with multiethnic integration offsite in "Kto To Wie(ś)—Na Własną Rękę, Na Własną Miarę," an intervention on the grounds of the Szymbark *skansen*, two hours from Kraków, where photographs of former ethnically and religiously diverse local inhabitants were to "remind us of the close and interdependent existence upon which the rural sense of community was based—not free from crises and tensions" (Muzeum Dwory Karwacjanów i Gładyszów, "Kto To Wie(ś)").

65 The catalog stated that the "idea [was] to create an exhibition that would show the Museum's collection to foreign audiences in a fresh and original way" (Szczurek, *Przejścia i powroty* [2010], 11).

66 Szczurek, *Przejścia i powroty* (2010 and 2013). The exhibit opened in Marseilles in 2011 and in Berlin's Museum Europäischer Kulturen (Staatliche Museen zu Berlin) in 2013.

67 "Passage et Repassage: Małopolska in Marseille," Events from the Adam Mickiewicz Institute, 2011, https://culture.pl/en/event/passage-et-repassage-malopolska-in-marseille (accessed October 31, 2019).

68 Cała, *Image of the Jew*; Tokarska-Bakir, "The Hanging of Judas."

69 "Passage et Repassage." In addition, the keys' suggestion of dispossession, forced migrations, loss of homes, and the Polish appropriation of Jewish and German property is not alluded to (Jan Grabowski and Dariusz Libionka's pioneering 2014 study on dispossession of Jews is titled *The Keys and the Cash Box* [*Klucze i kasa*]).

70 On anti-immigrant sentiment, see JTA, "Polish Anti-Refugee Protesters." On Jewish property restitution claims, see Mikrut-Majeranek, "Kontrowersyjne wieszanie Judasza." The climax of an anti-(Muslim) immigrant rally in the Polish city of Wrocław in November 2015 involved the burning of an effigy of a Hasidic Jew—virtually the same as the "Judas" hanging—holding the flag of the EU while the crowd chanted "God, Honor, and Fatherland." And on Good Friday in 2019, inhabitants of Pruchnik revived the "hanging of Judas" tradition, with members of the crowd (which included many children) shouting to deliver the straw Jewish effigy an extra five lashes for "reparations" (referring to contemporary debates over Jewish reparations for expropriated World War II property).

71 Also worth mentioning is the clear, if brief, description of (unflattering) images of and ideas about Jews in a discussion of Polish Christian rituals in a 1995 edition of the Kraków Ethnographic Museum's annual scholarly journal, and the museum's lack of any mention or image relating to such Christian folk depictions of Jews fifteen years later in their more public sesquicentennial anniversary volume *A Hundred and a Half: Stories from the Kraków Ethnographic Museum* (Dolińska and Gruszka, *Sto i pół*).

72 Since 2009, though, the MEK has had an archivist on staff, Kamila Wasilewska-Prędki, who has a master's degree in Jewish studies from the Jagiellonian University.

73 "Every Museum Is a Story: A Conversation with the Museum Director, Antoni Bartosz," open meeting held on June 26, 2019, at the Ethnographic Museum Seweryna Udziela in Kraków. www.festivalt.com/event/every-museum-is-a-story-a-conversation-with-the-museum-director/.

74 Higher government powers, which are increasingly conservative and nationalist, determine the museum's opportunities and resources, and the MEK has recently struggled with the stalling of a major EU cofunded renovation and refurbishment project (see Kursa, "Jak Wam się kojarzy Kobierzyn").

75 Stauter-Halstead, "Peasant as Literary and Ethnographic Trope."

76 Kapusta and Kapusta, "Obiekty romskie." The MEK has not organized any exhibitions on Roma people, who have been present in Kraków since the fifteenth century, despite holding more than seventy photographs, postcards, and engravings documenting Roma everyday life in their collection.

77 At the time of this publication, the Law and Justice (PiS) government is no longer in power, having been voted out in the country's parliamentary elections in October 2023. The country's national museums remain in a liminal state as many PiS-backed staff members remain in these institutions.

78 Ujma, "Muzeum Etnograficzne."

79 "Every Museum Is a Story."

80 Bartosz "Ethnographic Museums."

81 Kirshenblatt-Gimblett, "Objects of Ethnography," 19–23.

82 On such dismissals, replacements, and recurations, see, for example, Gessen, "Poland's Ruling Party"; Machcewicz, *Muzeum*; and Polska, "Cultural Emergency in Warsaw."

83 This refers to the first printing, in *Museum Worlds* (Lehrer and Murzyn-Kupisz, "Making Space for Jewish Culture").

Bibliography

Aderet, Ofer. "Historian Who Shed Light on WWII Massacres Goes from Honoree to 'Pole Hater.'" *Haaretz*, March 1, 2016. www.haaretz.com/jewish/.premium-the-pole-who-is-breaking-the-silence-1.5410809 (accessed April 18, 2024).

Avrutin, Eugene M., Valerii A. Dymshits, Alexander Ivanov, and Harriet Murav, eds. *Photographing the Jewish Nation: Pictures from S. An-sky's Ethnographic Expeditions*. Hanover, NH: University Press of New England, 2009.

Bartosz, Antoni. "Ethnographic Museums: The Invaluable Mirrors." In *Polish Museums*, ed. Dorota Folga-Januszewska, 134–55. Olszanica: Bosz, 2012.

———. "Słowo wstępne" [Introductory Words]. In *Rocznik Muzeum Etnograficznego im. Seweryna Udzieli w Krakowie* [Yearbook of the Seweryn Udziela Ethnographic Museum in Kraków], vol. 16, *Wspólnota poszukujących* [A Community of Seekers], ed. Małgorzata Szczurek, 5–6. Kraków: Seweryn Udziela Ethnographic Museum in Kraków, 2010.

———. "Szumi coś i gwarzy" [Something Hums and Chatters]. In *Lokalne Muzeum w globalnym świecie: Poradnik praktyczny* [The Local Museum in a Global World: A Practical Guide], ed. Joanna Hajduk, Łucja Piekarska-Duraj, Piotr Idziak, and Sebastian Wacięga, 146–50. Kraków: Małopolski Instytut Kultury, 2013.

Bielawski, Krzysztof, and Albert Stankowski. "Czyżewski: Ludzie nie kojarzą kultury żydowskiej z etnografią" [Czyżewski: The Public Does Not Associate Jewish Culture with Ethnography]. *Wirtualny Sztetl*, October 29, 2014. sztetl.org.pl/pl/tradycja-i-kultura-zydowska/wywiady/czyzewski-ludzie-nie-kojarza-kultury-zydowskiej-z-etnografia (accessed April 18, 2024).

Boursiquot, Fabienne. "Ethnographic Museums: From Colonial Exposition to Intercultural Dialogue." In *The Postcolonial Museum: The Arts of Memory and the Pressures of History*, ed. Iain Chambers, Alessandra de Angelis, Celeste Ianniciello, Mariangela Orabona, and Michaela Quadraro, 76–83. Burlington, VT: Ashgate, 2014.

Brzezińska, Anna. "Made in a 'Polish Village': Modern Ethno-Design vs. Traditional Culture of the Polish Countryside." In *Art in Contemporary Cultural Systems*, ed. Waldemar Kuligowski and Adam Pomieciński, 49–62. Poznań: Wydawnictwo Nauka i Innowacje, 2014.

Bukowiecki, Łukasz. *Things of Warsaw and Things of the Past: Evolution and Priorities of the Museum of Warsaw*. Museum of Warsaw Report 1. Warsaw: University of Warsaw, 2019. projectechoes.eu/wp-content/uploads/Bukowiecki-Museum-of-Warsaw-Report-1.pdf (accessed November 2, 2019).

Bukowiecki, Łukasz, and Joanna Wawrzyniak. *Dealing with Difficult Pasts at the Museum of Warsaw: Implications of Curatorial Memory Practices*. Museum of Warsaw Report 2. Warsaw: University of Warsaw, 2019. projectechoes.eu/wp-content/uploads/Bukowiecki-Wawrzyniak-Museum-Of-Warsaw-Report-2_compressed.pdf (accessed November 24, 2019).

Cała, Alina. *The Image of the Jew in Polish Folk Culture*. Jerusalem: Hebrew University Magnes Press, 1995.

Czajkowski, Jerzy, ed. *Muzeum Budownictwa Ludowego w Sanoku* [Open-Air Museums in Poland]. Poznań: Państwowe Wydawnictwo Rolnicze i Leśne, 1981.

Czyżewska, Elżbieta. "Introduction." In *Border Exhibition, Ulster Museum, Belfast, 6 May–12 June 2010*, ed. Elżbieta Czyżewska, 2–3. Warsaw: Adam Mickiewicz Institute, 2010.

Czyżewski, Adam. "Czas świętowania: założenia metodologiczne wystawy" [Celebration Time: Methodological Underpinnings of the Exhibition]. In *Czas świętowania w kulturach Polski i Europy* [Celebration Time in Polish and European Cultures], ed. Adam Czyżewski, 9–12. Warsaw: Państwowe Muzeum Etnograficzne w Warszawie, 2013.

———. "Transformation of the State Ethnographic Museum in Warsaw, 2008–2012." *Etnografia Nowa / The New Ethnography* 5 (2013): 10–33.

Departament Kultury i Dziedzictwa Narodowego [Department of Culture and National Heritage]. *Kultura i Dziedzictwo Narodowe Województwo małopolskie: Raport za 2015 rok* [Culture and National Heritage, Małopolska Region: Report for 2015]. Kraków: Urząd Marszałkowski Województwa Małopolskiego, 2016.

Dolińska, Magdalena. "Muzeum Etnograficzne w Krakowie: wierność tradycji" [Ethnographic Museum in Kraków: Loyalty to Tradition]. *Lud* 87 (2003): 83–109.

Dolińska, Magdalena, and Dorota Gruszka. *Sto i pół: opowieści z Muzeum Etnograficznego w Krakowie* [One Hundred and a Half: Stories from the Ethnographic Museum in Kraków]. Kraków: Muzeum Etnograficzne im. Seweryna Udzieli, 2011.

Durrans, Brian. 1993. "The Future of Ethnographic Exhibitions." *Zeitschrift für Ethnologie* 118, no. 1 (1993): 125–39. www.jstor.org/stable/25842302.

Dynner, Glenn. *Yankel's Tavern: Jews, Liquor, and Life in the Kingdom of Poland*. Oxford, UK: Oxford University Press, 2013.

Engelking, Barbara. *Such a Beautiful Sunny Day: Jews Seeking Refuge in the Polish Countryside, 1942–1945*. Jerusalem: Yad Vashem, 2016.

Folga-Januszewska, Dorota. *1,000 Museums in Poland: A Guide*. Olszanica: Bosz, 2011.

Gessen, Masha. "Poland's Ruling Party Puts an Extraordinary Museum of Polish-Jewish History into Limbo." *New Yorker*, September 23, 2019. www.newyorker.com/news/our-columnists/polands-ruling-party-puts-an-extraordinary-museum-of-polish-jewish-history-into-limbo (accessed November 1, 2019).

Goldberg, Jacob. "Żyd a karczma wiejska w XVIII wieku" [The Jew and the Village Tavern in the Eighteenth Century]. *Wiek Oświecenia* 9 (1993): 205–13.

———. "Żyd i karczma na Podlasiu w XVIII wieku" [The Jew and the Tavern in the Podlasie Region in the Eighteenth Century]. *Studia Podlaskie* 2 (1989): 27–38.

Gottesman, Itzik Nakhmen. *Defining the Yiddish Nation: The Yiddish Folklorists of Poland*. Detroit: Wayne State University Press, 2003.

Grabowski, Jan, and Dariusz Libionka, eds. *Klucze i kasa: O mieniu żydowskim w Polsce pod okupacją niemiecką i we wczesnych latach powojennych 1939–1950* [The Keys and the Cash Box: On Jewish Property in Poland Under German Occupation and in the Early Postwar Years 1939–1950]. Wydawnictwo: Stowarzyszenie Centrum Badań nad Zagładą Żydów, 2014.

Grzechnik, Marta. "The Missing Second World: On Poland and Postcolonial Studies." *Interventions* 21, no. 7 (2019): 998–1014.

Harris, Clare, and Michael O'Hanlon. "The Future of the Ethnographic Museum." *Anthropology Today* 29, no. 1 (2013): 1–32. www.jstor.org/stable/23486436.

Jagodzińska, Katarzyna. *Museums and Centres of Contemporary Art in Central Europe after 1989*. New York: Routledge, 2019.

JTA. 2015. "Polish Anti-Refugee Protesters Burn Effigy of Orthodox Jew." *Times of Israel*, November 19, 2015. www.timesofisrael.com/polish-anti-refugee-protesters-burn-effigy-of-orthodox-jew/ (accessed April 18, 2024).

Kapusta, Anna, and Piotr Kapusta. "Obiekty romskie w archiwum Muzeum Etnograficznego im. Seweryna Udzieli w Krakowie: Rekonesans antropologiczny" [Roma Objects in the Archives of the Seweryn Udziela Ethnographic Museum in Kraków: Anthropological Reconnaissance]. *Studia Romologica* 11 (2018): 299–336.

Kazimierczuk, Agnieszka. "'Sąd nad Judaszem' wrócił do Pruchnika: Spalono kukłę Żyda" ["The Judgement of Judas" Returned to Pruchnik: A Jewish Effigy Was Burned]. *Rzeczpospolita*, April 21, 2019. www.rp.pl/Spoleczenstwo/190429961-Sad-nad-Judaszem-wrocil-do-Pruchnika-Spalono-kukle-Zyda.html (accessed April 18, 2024).

Kilcher, Andreas, and Gabriella Safran, eds. *Writing Jewish Culture: Paradoxes in Ethnography*. Bloomington: Indiana University Press, 2016.

Kirshenblatt-Gimblett, Barbara. "Objects of Ethnography." In *Exhibiting Cultures: The Poetics and Politics of Museum Display*, ed. Ivan Karp and Steven D. Lavine, 386–443. Washington, DC: Smithsonian Institution Press, 1991.

Klekot, Ewa. "The Seventh Life of Polish Folk Art and Craft." *Etnološka Tribina* 33, no. 40 (2010): 71–85. https://hrcak.srce.hr/63180.

Kretschmann, Vasco. "Entangled Heritage: Wrocław's German-Jewish and Polish-Jewish History Exhibitions, 1920–2010." *Kultura Popularna* 1, no. 50 (2017): 92–102. doi:10.5604/01.3001.0010.4078.

Kryciński, Stanisław, Olej-Kobus Anna, and Kobus Krzysztof. *Zabytki kultury żydowskiej w Polsce: przewodnik* [Monuments of Jewish Culture in Poland: A Guide]. Warsaw: Carta Blanca, 2011.

Kursa, Magdalena. "Jak Wam się kojarzy Kobierzyn? Wkrótce zmienicie zdanie" [What Do You Associate Kobierzyn With? You Will Change Your Mind Soon]. *Wyborcza.pl*, May 13. 2017. krakow.wyborcza.pl/krakow/7,44425,21803348,jak-wam-sie-kojarzy-kobierzyn-wkrotce-zmienicie-zdanie.html (accessed April 18, 2024).

Leder, Andrzej. *Prześniona rewolucja: Ćwiczenia z logiki historycznej* [An Unnoticed Revolution: Exercises in Historic Logic]. Warsaw: Wydawnictwo Krytyki Politycznej, 2014.

Lehrer, Erica. *Jewish Poland Revisited: Heritage Tourism in Unquiet Places*. Bloomington: Indiana University Press, 2013.

———. "Material Kin: 'Awkward Objects' and 'Communities of Implication' in Post-Colonial, Post-Holocaust Polish Ethnographic Collections." In *Across Anthropology: Convergences through Museums, Colonial Legacies, and the Curatorial*, ed. Margareta von Oswald and Jonas Tinius, 289–322. Leuven: Leuven University Press, 2020.

———. "'Most Disturbing Souvenirs': Curative Museology in a Cultural Conflict Zone." In *Curatorial Dreams: Critics Imagine Exhibitions*, ed. Shelley Ruth Butler and Erica Lehrer, 46–63. Montreal: McGill-Queen's University Press, 2016.

———. *Na Szczęscie To Żyd / Lucky Jews*. Kraków: Ha!art Press, 2014.

Lehrer, Erica, and Monika Murzyn-Kupisz. "Making Space for Jewish Culture in Polish 'Folk' and 'Ethnographic' Museums: Curating Social Diversity After Ethnic Cleansing." *Museum Worlds*, special issue "Festschrift for Barbara Kirshenblatt-Gimblett," 7 (2019): 82–108.

Lehrer, Erica, and Roma Sendyka, eds. *Różnicowanie narodowego "my": marzenia kuratorskie* [Differentiating the National "We": Curatorial Dreams]. Kraków: Wydawnictwo Uniwersytetu Jagiellońskiego, 2019.

Linkiewicz, Olga. "Scientific Ideals and Political Engagement: Polish Ethnology and the 'Ethnic Question' Between the Wars." *Acta Poloniae Historica* 114 (2016): 5–27.

Lukowski, Jerzy, and Hubert Zawadzki. *A Concise History of Poland*, 2nd ed. Cambridge, UK: Cambridge University Press, 2006.

Machcewicz, Paweł. *Muzeum* [Museum]. Kraków: Znak Horyzont, 2017.

Marzynski, Marian, dir. *Frontline*. Season 14, Episode 9, "Shtetl." Aired April 17, 1996. www.pbs.org/wgbh/frontline/film/shtetl/ (accessed April 18, 2024).

Mikrut-Majeranek, Magdalena. "Kontrowersyjne 'wieszanie Judasza' w Pruchniku" [Controversial 'Hanging of Judas' in Pruchnik]. Histmag.org, April 23, 2019. histmag.org/Kontrowersyjne-wieszanie-Judasza-w-Pruchniku-18609 (accessed December 16, 2019).

Ministerstwo Kultury i Dziedzictwa Narodowego [Ministry of Culture and National Heritage]. "Rejestr Muzeów" [Register of Museums]. February 8, 2019. https://bip.mkidn.gov.pl/pages/rejestry-ewidencje-archiwa-wykazy/rejestry-muzeow.php (accessed December 16, 2019).

Modest, Wayne, Nicholas Thomas, Doris Prlić, and Claudia Augustat, eds. *Matters of Belonging: Ethnographic Museums in a Changing Europe*. Leiden: Sidestone Press, 2019.

Murawska-Muthesius, Katarzyna. "Love of Beauty in the Tsarist Colonial Capital: The Museum of Fine Arts in Warsaw (1862–1916)." *Centropa* 12, no. 2 (2012): 179–93.

Murawska-Muthesius, Katarzyna, and Piotr Piotrowski. "Introduction." In their *From Museum Critique to the Critical Museum*, 1–14. London: Routledge, 2017.

Murzyn-Kupisz, Monika, and Jarosław Działek. "Muzea a budowanie kapitału społecznego w środowisku lokalnym" [Museums and the Development of Social Capital in the Local Context]. *Rocznik Muzeum Wsi Mazowieckiej w Sierpcu* 5 (2014): 19–40.

Muzeum Dwory Karwacjanów i Gładyszów [Museum of the Karwacjanów and Gładyszów Manors]. "Kto To Wie(ś): Na Własną Rękę, Na Własną Miarę" [Who Knows It (the Village): On Your Own, by Your Own Measure]. 2019. www.muzeum.gorlice.pl/wydarzenia-kulturalne/art/qkto-to-wie-na-wasn-rk-na-wasn-miarq (accessed July 29, 2019).

Nowak, Jacek, Sławomir Kapralski, and Dariusz Niedźwiedzki. *On the Banality of Forgetting: Tracing the Memory of Jewish Culture in Poland*. New York: Peter Lang, 2018.

Opalski, Magdalena. *The Jewish Tavern-Keeper and His Tavern in Nineteenth-Century Polish Literature*. Jerusalem: Zalman Shazar Center for the Furtherance of the Study of Jewish History, 1986.

Państwowe Muzeum Etnograficzne w Warszawie [National Ethnographic Museum in Warsaw]. "Czas świętowania: Remont" [Celebration Time: Renovation]. Wystawa Stała [permanent exhibition], 2016. ethnomuseum.pl/wystawy/czas-swietowania/ (accessed July 16, 2016).

Piechotka, Maria, and Kazimierz Piechotka. *Heaven's Gates: Wooden Synagogues in the Territories of the Former Polish-Lithuanian Commonwealth*. Warsaw: Wydawnictwo Krupski i S-ka, 2004.

Piotrowski, Piotr. *Muzeum Krytyczne* [The Critical Museum]. Poznań: Dom Wydawniczy "Rebis," 2011.

Piszczkiewicz, Katarzyna. "Ethnography in the Public Space, or How to Respond to Life." In *Extended Museum in Its Milieu*, ed. Dorota Folga-Januszewska, 181–87. Kraków: Universitas, 2018.

Piwocki, Ksawery. "Ethnographical Museum in Warsaw." *Etnografia Nowa / The New Ethnography* 5 (2013): 34–53.

POLIN Museum of the History of the Jewish People. "Ocalona kuczka z Szydłowca została przywrócona publiczności" [Jewish Sukkah Saved from

Szydłowiec Returned to the Public]. POLIN Museum of the History of the Jewish People, March 6, 2015. www.polin.pl/pl/aktualnosci/2015/03/06/ocalona-kuczka-z-szydlowca-zostala-przywrocona-publicznosci (accessed October 31, 2019).

Polska, Agnieszka. "A Cultural Emergency in Warsaw: Artist Agnieszka Polska Speaks Out." *Frieze*, November 22, 2019. frieze.com/article/cultural-emergency-warsaw-artist-agnieszka-polska-speaks-out (accessed November 22, 2019).

Porter-Szücs, Brian. *Poland in the Modern World: Beyond Martyrdom*. Chichester, UK: Wiley-Blackwell, 2014.

Rejduch-Samkowa, Izabella. "Sztuka Żydowska w Polsce" [Jewish Art in Poland]. *Judaica*, 2011. judaica-art.com.pl/ (accessed November 1, 2019).

Rothberg, Michael. *The Implicated Subject: Beyond Victims and Perpetrators*. Stanford, CA: Stanford University Press, 2019.

Stauter-Halstead, Keely. "The Peasant as Literary and Ethnographic Trope." In *The Nation in the Village: The Genesis of Peasant Identity in Austrian Poland, 1848–1914*, by Keely Stauter-Halstead, 97–114. Ithaca, NY: Cornell University Press: 2001.

Szczurek, Małgorzata. *Przejścia i powroty / Passages et repassages / Passages and Repassages*. Kraków: Muzeum Etnograficzne w Krakowie, 2010.

———, ed. *Przejścia i powroty: ze zbiorów Muzeum Etnograficznego w Krakowie* [Passages and Repassages: From the Collection of the Ethnographic Museum in Kraków]. Kraków: Muzeum Etnograficzne w Krakowie, 2013.

———. *Sto i pół: opowieści z Muzeum Etnograficznego w Krakowie* [A Hundred and One Tales from the Ethnographic Museum in Kraków]. Kraków: Muzeum Etnograficzne im. Seweryna Udzieli w Krakowie, 2011.

Thomas, Dominic, ed. *Museums in Postcolonial Europe*. Abingdon, UK: Routledge, 2009.

Tokarska-Bakir, Joanna. "'The Hanging of Judas'; or, Contemporary Jewish Topics." *Polin: Studies in Polish Jewry* 24 (2011): 381–400.

———. *Pod klątwą: Społeczny portret pogromu kieleckiego* [Under a Curse: A Social Portrait of the Kielce Pogrom]. Warsaw: Czarna Owca, 2018.

Ujma, Magdalena. "Muzeum Etnograficzne: świeże spojrzenie" [The Ethnographic Museum: A Fresh Look]. *Obieg*, March 29, 2012. https://archiwum-obieg.u-jazdowski.pl/teksty/24505 (accessed April 18, 2024).

Veidlinger, Jeffrey, ed. *Going to the People: Jews and the Ethnographic Impulse.* Bloomington: Indiana University Press, 2016.

Waligórska, Magdalena. *Klezmer's Afterlife: An Ethnography of the Jewish Music Revival in Poland and Germany.* New York: Oxford University Press, 2013.

Wasilewska-Prędki, Kamila. "Judaika w zbiorach Muzeum Etnograficznego im. Seweryna Udzieli w Krakowie: przegląd najważniejszych obiektów" [Judaica in the Seweryn Udziela Ethnographic Museum in Kraków: A Review of the Most Important Objects]. *Krzysztofory* 35 (2017): 451–62. www.muzeumkrakowa.pl/images/upload/WYDAWNICTWA/Krzysztofory%2035/KRZY.2017.24.Wasilewska-Predki.Kamila.pdf (accessed December 16, 2019; URL unavailable).

Woleńska, Maria. *Wystawa sztuki ludowej zamieszkałych w Polsce Białorusinów, Litwinów, Rosjan, Słowaków, Ukraińców, Żydów* [Exhibition of Folk Art of Belarussians, Lithuanians, Russians, Slovaks, Ukrainians, and Jews Living in Poland]. Kraków: Muzeum Etnograficzne im. Seweryna Udzieli, 1960.

Zarrow, Sarah Ellen. "Object Lessons: Art Collection and Display as Historical Practice in Inter-War Lwów." *Polin: Studies in Polish Jewry* 29 (2017): 157–75. muse.jhu.edu/article/695129 (accessed April 18, 2024).

6

JEWISH THINGS AT THE MUSEUM OF FINE ARTS BOSTON

A History

Simona Di Nepi

The Museum of Fine Arts (MFA) in Boston houses an enviable encyclopedic collection built on the foundational principle of showing art from across time, across cultures, and across the globe.[1] Its holdings of Egyptian, Greek, Roman, and Japanese art in particular are some of the best in the world. They testify to an early and profound interest on the part of museum trustees, curators, and donors in ancient civilizations from faraway lands. The Greek and Roman art collection was given its boost in 1900 by trustee Francis Bartlett, who donated $100,000 (more than $3 million today) for the purchase of classical antiquities. The extensive collection of Egyptian and Nubian art was the result of the museum's own archeological excavations, launched in 1905 with Harvard University. Its Asian art collection had its legendary champion in William Bigelow, who traveled to Japan in the 1870s and 1880s and donated more than fifty thousand works of art to the MFA.[2] Judaica, as I demonstrate in this essay, followed an entirely different trajectory, broadly characterized by the absence of purposeful collecting and, until recently, by an abandonment to chance. It would take well over a century for the museum to invest in its first intentional Judaica purchase and, most important, the vision and generosity of two women—Jetskalina H. Phillips and Lynn Schusterman—to take Judaica into a new and ambitious direction. My goal is to reconstruct the history of the museum's relationship with Jewish ceremonial objects and Jewish art in general. I do so chronologically, by highlighting landmark moments, individual objects, and visionary donors and by discussing the museum's methodology for the display of its Jewish collection.

Ephraim Benguiat: A Missed Opportunity?

In 1888 a flamboyantly dressed antique dealer and discerning Judaica collector by the name of Hadji Ephraim Benguiat arrived in Boston. A Turkish-born Jew, Benguiat moved to the United States from Gibraltar to expand his international rug and textile business.[3] The city's Museum of Fine Arts was then in its infancy in Copley Square, before a rapidly growing collection would push it to a new and larger building in the then muddy Fenway area. Shortly after settling in Boston, Benguiat approached Major General Charles Greely Loring, the museum's first director, and, recognizing the man's connoisseurship and connections, began a long-lasting correspondence. His numerous letters show that, starting in 1889, Benguiat regularly sought Loring's advice on his myriad plans and ideas. Most important, along with the museum's annual reports, these letters show that, between the spring of 1889 and the fall of 1892, Ephraim Benguiat loaned the museum "a collection of the utensils and table decorations used by a Jewish family in celebrating the Feast of Passover; five pieces of embroidery, and an illuminated scroll in a silver case, 'The Book of Esther.'"[4] This was a pioneering display that, only two years after the landmark 1887 Anglo-Jewish Historical exhibition in London, showed the young Boston museum's commitment to displaying Jewish ritual objects. This glorious premise might have led to a permanent presence of Benguiat's Judaica collection at the MFA, possibly even to its ultimate acquisition, but the determination of a Washington curator changed the course of events. After seeing the objects in Boston, curator Cyrus Adler of the United States National Museum in Washington, DC, approached Benguiat and persuaded him, first, "to exhibit them at the World's Columbian exposition in Chicago, and ultimately to bring them together for installation in the National Museum."[5]

Following Benguiat's death in 1924, Adler would eventually succeed in purchasing the collection in his new role as president of the Jewish

Theological Seminary in New York, making it the centerpiece of the new Jewish Museum, at the time housed in the seminary's library.[6]

Accidental Judaica

In the course of the following 120 years, a small number of Jewish objects entered the MFA in a distinctly haphazard fashion. As individual gifts rather than the fruits of a strategic plan, they seemed to access the building almost undetected, at times with no apparent recognition of their Jewishness. Three factors contributed to this: (1) As gifts rather than purchases, they were not actively sought out and as thoroughly researched; (2) they were often part of donations containing hundreds, if not thousands of non-Jewish objects; and (3) their wide-ranging materials, origin, and periods placed them in different departments, thus making it difficult to be viewed as products of a shared culture. It is one of the joys of the encyclopedic museum's Judaica curator to unearth and catalog these objects, which were hiding for decades in the departments of ancient art, prints, books, drawings, paintings, and textiles.

Five important Judaica acquisitions are fitting case studies of this phenomenon, starting with the first known Jewish item to enter the museum's collection—incidentally also the most recent to have been identified. In 1895 James William Paige bequeathed 284 "pieces of laces, embroidery, brocades, and other textiles" to the MFA.[7] In this wealth of fabric, there was also a long strip of white linen cataloged, until recently, as "Point Lace, Italy, 17th century" (95.992).[8] Recent examination allowed me to rediscover the lace as an early Italian Torah binder, probably from the Veneto region, datable to the early seventeenth century.[9] The Hebrew inscription (*Ishmael Colonia May the Rock Keep Him and Esther Colonia with Joy of Torah*) indicates that a married couple donated this binder to wrap the Torah scroll during the festival of Simchat Torah.[10] Twenty years after this earliest known acquisition, on May 7, 1915, the ocean liner *Lusitania*, sailing from New York to Liverpool, was sunk by a German U-boat off the Irish coast. Among the 1,198 people who drowned was Leslie Lindsey Mason, a young Bostonian on her honeymoon with her English husband. A year later, Leslie's father, local industrialist and MFA trustee William Lindsey, bought 560 musical instruments in England from Reverend Francis W. Galpin, to be donated to the MFA in memory of his daughter.[11] Amid the hundreds of instruments, was a shofar (17.1961), cataloged as nineteenth-century Polish, which can be seen in the MFA's Musical Instruments gallery.[12] A few months later, Harvard art professor and painter Denman Waldo Ross donated two volumes of an eighteenth-century Hebrew Bible, to this day the most important items in the museum's Hebraica collection (17.512, 17.513).[13] The volumes were printed in Amsterdam in 1762 and 1767 by the Jewish Propps family, owners of the city's most important printing house. Professor Ross, an insatiable collector in an exceptionally wide range of fields, would proceed to donate to the museum some eleven thousand objects over the course of forty years, but no other known Judaica piece is among them. Silent Judaica donations came from Jewish donors too: In 1938 New York banker Philip Lehman, of Lehman Brothers fame, gave the MFA 371 textiles and costume accessories from the collection of his recently deceased wife, Carrie Lehman.[14] Two pieces in Carrie Lehman's collection were made for Jewish ritual purpose: a German 1745 Torah binder (38.1148), embroidered with the names of baby Meyer and his father Rabbi Yosef, and a shimmering silk *tallit katan* (38.1093), its small size indicating it was made for a child.[15] During the twentieth century, thousands of gifts also streamed into the museum's Art of the Americas Department, which is today the depository of one of the finest collections in the country. Martha and Max Karolik, Boston lovers of so-called folk art, donated more than five thousand objects over thirty years, including paintings, sculpture, and works on paper. In 1960 South End dealer Henry Gray sold Max Karolik a gilded wood lion (60.488) previously bought from the recently demolished synagogue of Anshei Poland in Boston's South End.[16] The naturalistically sculpted lion was one of a pair flanking the Tablets of the Law atop a Torah ark carved by Sam Katz, a Galician Jewish immigrant known for his twenty-four Torah arks in synagogues in and around Boston.

These objects, noteworthy in both their quality and historic significance, did not receive attention at the time of their acquisition and, apart from the shofar, were never displayed.[17] As mentioned, this can be attributed to the circumstances surrounding their acquisition, as single Judaica objects that were part of large donations, and to a lack of interest in Jewish material culture by the museum world at large.

The dearth of Jewish art in the MFA's galleries did not go unnoticed, at least not by Alexander Brin, publisher and editor of *The Jewish Advocate* weekly of Boston. In 1926 Brin launched in a fund-raising campaign to purchase Jacob Binder's 1919 painting *The Talmudist* (26.201) for the "the great reservoir which is the pride of the city of Boston."[18] For Brin, the portrait of an old Jew dressed in a tallit would give MFA visitors "the most typical presentation that a dignified, self-respecting artistic Jewry could make."[19] As argued by Steven Fine, Brin's impassioned plea to the Jewish community must have been, at least in part, a response to John Singer Sargent's depiction of the Jewish faith in his 1919 *Triumph of Religion* murals in the Boston Public Library.[20] It is un unclear whether the famous painter realized that the European illuminated manuscripts and cathedral façades that inspired his personification of *Synagoga* as a dethroned and blind-folded woman were visual expressions of the medieval antisemitic tradition. Although Brin's efforts succeeded and the gift was accepted, the MFA never granted its donors the satisfaction of seeing the painting on its walls.[21]

Against this backdrop, it is somewhat surprising to find that, in the second half of the twentieth century, the MFA appeared to break its silence on Jewish art with two exhibitions organized in cooperation with the American Jewish Historical Society. For one month in 1953, "Early American Jewish Portraits and Silver" presented eighteenth- and nineteenth-century Jewish life through fifty-three works, including many by famed New York Jewish silversmith Myer Myers.[22] A similar subject was explored in 1990 by American paintings curator Erica Hirshler in "The Levy-Franks Family Colonial Portraits" exhibition, which explored the story of these prominent merchants in mid-eighteenth-century New York.[23] Although seminal for shedding light on early American Jewish life, these two temporary exhibitions did not alter the museum's collecting policy. It would take four decades for a new era to begin.

Time for Change

By the turn of the twenty-first century the age of accidental Judaica was coming to an end, and in a mere four years (2009–13) the MFA dramatically changed its approach: It made its first deliberate Judaica purchase, was bequeathed an important dedicated Judaica fund, established a Judaica curatorship, and was given a core collection of 120 objects. It all began in the fall of 2009, when the chair of the Art of Europe Department, George Shackelford, and the senior curator of European decorative arts, Thomas Michie, spotted in the Sotheby's New York November Judaica sale a splendid German Hanukkah lamp, probably made in Augsburg in about 1750.[24]

It had long been the MFA's ambition to acquire a great example of historic Judaica and, once a fitting candidate was identified, the fund-raising

FIGURE 6.1. Hanukkah lamp, about 1750, silver gilt. MFA purchase (2009) with donated funds.

machine was put into motion. Thanks to a number of private donors and an unusually long list of smaller museum funds, the MFA was able to quickly raise a significant sum and win its first Judaica auction purchase.[25] As a remarkable example of both Jewish ceremonial art and German Rococo silver, the lamp was promptly installed in a temporary Hanukkah display by the museum's Fenway entrance. In 2010 it was repositioned to form a bold juxtaposition with the *Crosier of Abbot Gerhard Saint Mang* (2004.569), in the Angelica and Lloyd Russel Gallery for eighteenth-century European art, where it can still be seen. The Hanukkah lamp is an exemplary illustration of Judaica's chameleon-like quality, that is, the ability to transform itself and assume the visual language of the surrounding artistic culture. Every inch of its surface is filled with exuberant Rococo decoration: the dense diaper design pattern across the backplate; the scrollwork and acanthus leaves along the edges; the palm leaves and shells framing the central cartouche; passages of deep relief in the cornucopias spilling fruits and flowers. Pairs of evidently added putti appear at the top, raising what may have been a crown, now missing.[26] Smaller putti are seen hanging on to the pilasters' flower pendants, as though to keep from slipping. In addition to the opulent ornamentation, one of the lamp's most distinctive features is the two small figures on the pilasters: Judith, seen dangling Holofernes' severed head, and Judah Maccabee, advancing toward battle with a tall spear.[27] These defiant Jewish heroes, symbols of rebellion against the foreign oppressor, appear together in other German Hanukkah lamps of the same period.[28]

In line with a phenomenon all too common in Judaica, the original lamp may have been modified or refashioned, possibly at different stages.[29] Besides the evident signs of alteration around the putti in the top section, other additions are also likely to have occurred, such as in the small central lion with the Tablets of the Law; they also cannot be excluded for the side pilasters, as well as the figures of Judith and Judah Maccabee (although probably at an earlier date than the lion). It is possible that through these modifications some components were removed or lost, such as the servant light.[30]

The *hanukkiah* has a notable and—a rare occurrence in the Judaica market—uninterrupted provenance for over 150 years.[31] From the nineteenth century until its sale in November 2009, its owners were the Goldschmidts of Frankfurt, a prominent family of collectors and antiquarians with ties to the Rothschilds. Although the role of the first recorded owner, Selig Meier Goldschmidt (1828–96), as an art dealer would suggest that the lamp had not been in the family since the beginning—but rather that he had purchased it—his prestigious name imbues the piece with additional allure.[32]

Less than one month after the purchase of the Augsburg lamp at the Sotheby's sale, an unexpected letter marked the watershed moment for Judaica at the MFA: The missive informed the Development Department that the recently deceased Jetskalina H. Phillips had left the bulk of her estate to the museum for the study, acquisition, and display of Judaica.[33] The news caught the staff by surprise. Until then, nobody at the museum had ever heard of the generous benefactor, let alone of her plans for a bequest. A decision was soon made to use the gift in two ways: to create an acquisition fund and to establish the Jetskalina H. Phillips Curatorship of Judaica, to which Marietta Cambareri—already curator of European decorative arts and sculpture—was appointed on a part-time basis.[34] By checking records at nearby Temple Israel, Cambareri soon found that Phillips, a retired school teacher living Kansas, had worked in Boston in the 1960s as a medical technologist. Most interestingly, these records showed that the she was born in Holland and had converted to Judaism on February 8, 1964, the day before her wedding to Jewish physician Robert M. Phillips.[35] This information helped to build a more complete picture of Jetskalina H. Phillips, one that might in part explain the motivations behind her extraordinary gesture.

Amid the astonishment and excitement that accompanied news of the Phillips gift, then MFA director Malcom Rogers came to terms with past inadequacies in conversation with a journalist.[36] He openly admitted that, "while the MFA showcases the artistic achievements of world cultures, it has not made much of an effort to collect, study or showcase Jewish ceremonial art," meaningfully adding, "It has not been seen as an essential part of the museum's mission to diverse communities." Because of what he granted were underdeveloped Judaica holdings, Rogers was also aware that the Phillips purchase funds would not be sufficient and that it would be imperative to engage collectors.

A direct result of the momentous shift was the installation in the same year of Myer Myers's silver Torah finials (ca. 1766–76), on loan from the historic Touro Synagogue in Newport, Rhode Island.[37] The finials, made by the Jewish silversmith who led the market in eighteenth-century New

York, are a particularly rare example of colonial American Judaica. They were used by the two earliest communities in the country, congregations Shearith Israel and Jeshuat Israel, founded by Sephardic Jews in New York and Newport, respectively.[38] The opportunity arose for the MFA to include this major loan for the opening in November 2010 of the Art of the Americas Wing, a project that had been many years in the making. The new wing featured a gallery dedicated to Newport colonial furniture, offering the ideal setting for the Myers Torah finials, where at the time of this writing they can still be admired.

It was not too long after these two Judaica installations that another extraordinary woman would pick up Jetskalina Phillips's baton. In 2011 Lynn Schusterman, a Tulsa philanthropist and collector, visited Boston to see the MFA's newly opened Linde Family Wing for Contemporary Art, made possible by her good friend—museum trustee Joyce Linde. As the creator, with her late husband Charles, of a philanthropic global foundation with special focus on Jewish causes,[39] Lynn Schusterman was struck by a conspicuous hole in the museum's vast holdings. Upon hearing of Phillips's bequest and the museum's ensuing interest in collecting Judaica, she promptly offered her own collection of Jewish art.[40] Two successive trips by curator Marietta Cambareri to Tulsa—the first with former curator of contemporary decorative arts Emily Zilber and Sotheby's senior consultant Sharon Liberman Mintz,[41] and the second with former head of objects conservation Pamela Hatchfield—resulted in the gift of the Charles and Lynn Schusterman Collection to the MFA in 2013. The transformational gift consisted of 121 objects with a broad chronological, geographic, and material range.[42] Dating from the eighteenth through the late twentieth century and originating in Europe, Asia, North Africa, and America, the collection includes seventy-one pieces of silver and metalwork, five works on paper, seven textiles, four paintings, three sculptures, and many examples of ceramics. By offering additional funds for the care and documentation of the collection, Schusterman set an example of an enlightened donor who fully understood the challenges of large collections donations. In the museum's press release Malcom Rogers proudly stressed, "The gift establishes the MFA as one of the very few encyclopedic art museums in America working to build a Judaica collection."[43] Cambareri spoke of a foundational gift that put the museum on a footing nationally.[44] These were not overstatements. At the time, only two other nonspecialist art museums in the United States—the North Carolina Museum of Art and the Minneapolis Institute of Art—had been purposefully purchasing and displaying Judaica, in both cases with dedicated galleries.[45] The Metropolitan Museum of Art had recently started to seriously collect in the field, with the outstanding purchases in the same year of an eighteenth-century Venetian silver Torah crown and a fifteenth-century illuminated manuscript of Maimonides' *Mishneh Torah*, the latter jointly acquired with the Israel Museum in Jerusalem.[46] Although there is no doubt that these institutions represented weighty competitors, with the Shusterman gift Boston's MFA gained a core collection to build on. The next step would be the realization of its display vision.

The Integrated Display: Principle and Examples

One of the key factors that contributed to Lynn Schusterman's decision to donate her collection to the MFA in 2013 was the idea that Judaica would be integrated into the rest of the museum's holdings and displayed in galleries across the building. As is often the case in the life of a museum, this display approach started in part as a necessity, a practical response to the absence of a collection. The Augsburg lamp and Myer Myers's finials, the first two Jewish pieces to go on display in 2010, were shown in the European and American galleries because, quite simply, they had to. The success of these two installations and the subsequent Schusterman gift helped to shape the display method into a more cohesive plan for the future. For the following ten years, rather than living in a separate space, the objects would continue to be shown exclusively alongside non-Jewish works from the same region and period. This methodology, resting on the fundamental notion that Jewish art is in no small part the fruit of exchange with the wider culture, is particularly suited to encyclopedic collections of the scope and range of the MFA. Indeed, curators at the Metropolitan Museum of Art have also been working with this model, for example, by displaying illuminated manuscripts on loan from the Jewish Theological Seminary and the Library of Congress in the broader context of their European medieval galleries.

The MFA display plan soon gained praise from highly respected voices in the field. The late Vivian B. Mann, professor emerita of Jewish art and visual culture at the Jewish Theological Seminary and former chair of Judaica at the Jewish Museum in New York, declared unequivocal support for integrating Judaica: "Since there are few restrictions on the forms of ceremonial art in Jewish law, Judaica reflects the style of surrounding culture."[47] American Jewish history professor Jonathan Sarna of Brandeis University appreciated the opportunity to see "Jewish materials side by side with other materials from the same place and the same era."[48]

In the following months and years, curator Marietta Cambareri collaborated with colleagues across curatorial departments to integrate highlights from the Schusterman gift. The choice naturally fell on areas of strengths of the collection. The thirty-one Hanukkah lamps and twenty-two spice containers (out of a total of 121 objects) made ritual items for the home indisputable candidates. The Angelica and Lloyd Russel Gallery for eighteenth-century European art gradually became the hub of domestic Judaica, carefully positioned alongside non-Jewish decorative and religious objects. In late 2013 two silver Hanukkah lamps and two spice towers from Central and Eastern Europe[49] were added to the aforementioned display of the Augsburg lamp. In my own, later experience, visitors' responses to this unusual pairing proved to be a key part of the experiment. Many visitors acknowledged that this arrangement defied expectation; some admitted to a slight discomfort, and others pointed to the shared decorative flourish of the Augsburg lamp and the crosier. Nearby, the earliest and most remarkable silver pieces from the Schusterman gift—a pair of late seventeenth-century German candlesticks and a 1722 Parisian cup—were grouped with luxury household items.[50] The Rothschild's coat of arms and Hebrew inscription engraved on the Kiddush cup[51] created the opportunity to associate it with snuff boxes and other small treasures donated in the same year by the heirs of the Viennese branch of the Rothschild family.[52] In October 2014, on the opposite wall, two Dutch blue-and-white plates painted in Hebrew with *Pesach* (2013.961) and *Succoth* (2013.962) found a home amid eighteenth-century ceramic dishes from Delft.[53] Since the early seventeenth century the Dutch city has made its fortune by producing imitations of fashionable Chinese porcelain in the less costly tin-glazed earthenware. As testified by the Hebrew inscriptions, Jews were not immune to the European craze for the white glaze and blue floral designs and loved to decorate their homes with Jewish-adapted Delftware.[54]

Another sizable group of works in the Shusterman gift consists of metalwork, rugs, and low-relief sculptures from the Bezalel School of Arts and Crafts.[55] The hybrid ornamentation of the Eretz Israel aesthetic—a mélange of motifs from different periods and regions—allowed curators to install ceremonial objects from early twentieth-century Jerusalem in a European gallery dedicated to a wide swath of nineteenth-century styles. The case contained works by silversmith Yehia Yemini (1897–1983) and designer-sculptor Zeev Raban (1890–1970). Yemini's silver Hanukkah lamp and cone-shaped spice box featured the intricate filigree work, swirling patterns, and applied turquoise of centuries-old Yemenite techniques.[56] Alongside were Raban's *hanukkiot*, their embossed surfaces boasting ancient Judean coins, spiraled columns, and a menorah guarded by lions.[57] The gallery hosted another Judaica intervention, that of a gold enameled wedding ring (69.1096),[58] whose acquisition predated the Schusterman gift. Donated in 1969 as a "late 16th century marriage ring" and only later understood to be a nineteenth-century piece made in Renaissance style, the jewel was displayed with revival-style objects from the European collection.[59] However, the star of this gallery's Judaica—and of the entire Schusterman collection—was a painting.

The painting is an arresting portrait by Isidor Kaufmann (1853–1921) of a young woman gazing out at the viewer with a stern, defiant expression. Previous Chilean owner Jacobo Furman must have held it in great admiration when he chose it for the cover of his hefty collection catalog.[60] The artist, born in the Austro-Hungarian city of Arad, found success in Vienna with Jewish genre scenes and portraits. Today, his piercing likenesses of bearded rabbis, Hasidic boys, and, more seldom, young Orthodox women achieve hammer prices well above expectations even in slow auction sales. In *Hannah* he demonstrates a total command of his medium: the naturalistic rendition of the woman's delicate features and pink hue of her complexion; the close observation of detail in the *sterntichel*, the satin cap decorated with lace and pearls; the burgundy backdrop used to enhance the impact of the luminous figure; the sense of immediacy in the woman's position, her body in profile and her eyes turning as though caught in a fleeting moment. Once described as the painter's daughter or more generically as a young bride, the sitter's identity is still shrouded in mystery.[61] She is shown in the traditional clothing that a married woman would have worn for festive occasions. And yet the fact that Kaufmann

FIGURE 6.2. *Hannah*, Isidor Kaufmann (Hungarian, active in Austria, 1853–1921), late nineteenth or early twentieth century; oil on panel. Charles and Lynn Schusterman Collection. Photograph © Museum of Fine Arts, Boston.

kept the garments in his studio and used them as props would point to the possibility that the sitter was in fact a model. It is also not clear whether the gilded Hebrew letters spelling out "Hannah" in the top-left corner refer to her name or perhaps to the biblical Hannah, mother of the prophet Samuel, who long struggled to conceive a child.

After three years the Bezalel case and *Hannah* were de-installed to make room for a blockbuster gallery filled with Monet paintings (the MFA Boston has one of the world's strongest holdings of Claude Monet, with thirty-six works). In 2018 the fluidity of the twenty-first-century permanent collection galleries allowed me to reinstall the works in different contexts and new locations. The Jerusalem Bezalel School pieces were put on view near the museum's Fenway entrance, beside a lanky Giacometti statue and slick Viennese silver objects, and Kaufmann's *Hannah* emerged from storage to peer out at visitors next to another Schusterman treasure: Edouard Brandon's diminutive painting *Jewish Man Reading* (2013.973).[62]

A New Momentum and Broadened Vision

A new chapter of the MFA Judaica story began in 2017, with my appointment as the Charles and Lynn Schusterman Curator of Judaica, the newly established and first full-time curatorship of its type in the country. This shift resulted in numerous acquisitions, the expansion of Jewish displays to fourteen galleries, and an overall new impetus of the Judaica program.

With a mandate to shape an increasingly ambitious and comprehensive vision for Judaica that would encompass multiple objectives—fundraising and acquisitions, gallery displays and exhibitions, education and outreach—it soon became clear just how vital prioritization would be. Building the Judaica collection emerged as the highest priority, the fundamental condition at the core of all aspirations. This primary goal has been pursued in two ways: by actively seeking new acquisitions—through purchases and gifts—and by searching "hidden" Judaica items among the existing five hundred thousand MFA objects. At the time of this writing, this dual approach has resulted in the addition of 141 items to the previously known 135 objects. These new additions include 47 new acquisitions and 94 items identified in the museum's existing holdings.

Among the recent purchases is the MFA's most important Judaica acquisition to date: a spectacular silver Torah shield, made in late eighteenth-century modern-day Ukraine, bought in December 2020 at Sotheby's single-owner sale from the Sassoon collection.[63] This jewel-like object is exceptional for many reasons. First, it was made, signed, and dated by a Jewish silversmith; his inscription is engraved in Hebrew letters: "This is the work of my hands, Elimelekh Tzoref of Stanislav, in the year 5542."[64] Unusually for a Torah shield, the artist lavishly decorated it on both sides. On the front the traditional iconography of the Tablets of the Law, surmounted by the crown (representing the Torah) and flanked by the figures of Moses and Aaron, is enriched by an intricate silver-gilt pierced screen. In the thick, exuberant scrollwork, fantastical animals with leafy tails hide—dragons, reptiles, and, in the center, sea creatures seemingly munching on the Decalogue. The decorated back sets this shield apart; breastplates were almost never decorated on the reverse and certainly never with narrative scenes. Here, the superbly engraved scenes of the sacrifice of Isaac and of Isaac blessing Jacob are encased within exuberant Rococo frames. Beyond this iconographic innovation, no single Judaica object in the MFA's collection shows such a wealth of techniques and materials—engraving, pierced silver, gilding, enamel.

The Sassoon auction made instant noise worldwide—and not just among Judaica specialists. In articles that appeared before the sale in *The Wall Street Journal* and *The Guardian*,[65] the Torah shield was singled out as the most important lot; after the sale, Richard McBee delved into its iconography for *Mosaic* magazine.[66] One year after the purchase, *Apollo: The International Art Magazine* chose the shield as one of its "2021 Top Museum Acquisitions," no doubt thanks to its ability to illustrate "the drive to diversify museum collections" and "present a more inclusive history of art."[67]

Another major recent acquisition is a magnificent set of silver Torah finials marked Hamburg 1688–89. Purchased in June 2019 at a Sotheby's auction in New York, the pair is exceptional both for its quality and for its early date.[68] Jurgen Richels, the prolific silversmith who made it, was a renowned chaser with a wide body of work, including domestic objects (a silver canister at the Metropolitan Museum of Art), liturgical works (reliquary busts for the Paderborn Treasury), and precious *Kunstkammer* pieces (a standing cup mounted on shell at the Victoria

FIGURE 6.3. Torah shield, Elimelekh Tzoref (Ukrainian [Stanislav], active 1782), 1781–82 (Hebrew year 5542); silver, parcel gilt, with enamel, niello, and stones. Museum purchase with funds donated by the Phillip Leonian and Edith Rosenbaum Leonian Charitable Trust, Jacques Aaron Preis, Trustee. Photograph © Museum of Fine Arts, Boston.

and Albert Museum). Except for a second, almost identical pair of Torah finials formerly in the Sassoon collection, no other Jewish ritual items by Richels survive.[69] For the MFA's *rimonim*, he used as a model the three-tiered hexagonal shape of seventeenth-century Dutch sets. However, he personalized and "revolutionized" this type to create a far more sculptural, dynamic, and ultimately exciting pair of finials that reflects the boldness of German Baroque silver. This is best seen in the lowest tier, with its large, cavelike opening, and the clever use of shells, acanthus leaves, and trefoils to enliven the surface.

June 2019 was an especially fruitful month for the MFA; at the same Sotheby's auction, the museum purchased another exceptional pair of silver *rimonim*.[70] Marked with the initials of Edward Aldridge, the date letter of 1764, and the London assay office mark, these towering Torah finials were the first piece of English Judaica to enter the museum's collection. The slender and unusually tall ornaments were entirely silver gilt, perhaps later than their date of manufacture and to suit the desire of voracious and celebrated Judaica collector Philip Salomons (1796–1867), whose name is engraved on the staves.[71] The distinguished ownership history carried on after Salomons's death in 1867; the *rimonim* were bought by or donated to the historic Central Synagogue in London, which ultimately consigned them at the 2019 auction.[72] At the time of acquisition, these *rimonim* were also the earliest known English Torah finials in America[73]—a fact that is hardly surprising when one considers that the first *rimonim* known to have been made in England are dated 1712.[74] The MFA's pair is a prime example of the work of an established silversmith adapting the distinctive style of his secular, domestic production on a Jewish ceremonial object. Aldridge applied to Judaica his trademark Rococo style, characterized by fanciful and exuberant openwork designs, typical of the cake baskets his shop specialized in.[75] Although the juxtaposition of the *rimonim* with Aldridge's silver inkstand in the MFA's collection (1976.662a–c) would have offered the opportunity to make a comparison between the artist's secular and religious silver, in December 2019 curators opted for an alternative display, exhibiting in a glass case the shimmering London Torah finials on the top shelf and, below them, a group of sober Protestant chalices from England, Wales, and Scotland. The British religious silver case stands proud in the original wall-paneled dining room from Hamilton Palace, a grand Scottish country house built in the late seventeenth century.

FIGURE 6.4. Torah finials, Jurgen Richels (German, 1664–1711), 1688–89; silver, parcel gilt. Museum purchase with funds donated by the Charles and Lynn Schusterman Family Foundation and Jetskalina H. Phillips Fund. Photograph © Museum of Fine Arts, Boston.

With the same objective of broadening the domestic focus of the Schusterman collection, two other pieces of synagogue Judaica were purchased at auction earlier in 2018: a pair of silver Torah finials from Morocco and a silver Torah shield from the former Kingdom of Hungary (modern-day Slovakia).[76] The beautifully crafted parcel gilt Moroccan Torah finials

FIGURE 6.5. Torah finials, Edward Aldridge (first mark 1724, died by 1766), 1764; silver, parcel gilt. Jetskalina H. Phillips Fund. Photograph © Museum of Fine Arts, Boston.

(2019.10.1&2) are a fine example of a popular late nineteenth-century type from Meknes, also found in other collections.[77] With the typical motifs of Hispano-Islamic architecture, such as the octagonal domed shape and the horseshoe arches, these finials would make a fitting installation in the new Art of Islamic Cultures galleries at the MFA. These galleries currently host a striking late nineteenth-century silver Algerian Hanukkah lamp

(2013.1006)⁷⁸ from the Schusterman gift that, with its crescent and star, colonnades, and pointed arches, is strongly reminiscent of North African mosques and palaces. The style of the Hungarian Torah breastplate (2019.9) could not be any different. Exquisitely chased with pendants of fruits and flowers, this eighteenth-century Torah shield still has its original reversible plaque showing the Hebrew abbreviations for Simchat Torah on one side and Yom Kippur on the other.⁷⁹ Although silver examples of synagogue Judaica—and particularly Torah ornaments—have been a clear priority, there has also been a conscious effort to broaden the scope of the collection by pursuing works of disparate typology and in different media. In fact, the first objects in the quick succession of new Judaica acquisitions were a group of works on paper and a textile. Although highly sensitive to light, these acquisitions achieved a fundamental goal for the Judaica collection: to collect broadly across cultures. The decorative Shabbat cloth and two *ketubbot* purchased at Sotheby's December 2017 Important Judaica sale were the first Jewish items from Iran to enter the MFA's collection.⁸⁰ Embroidered with colorful floral motifs and Hebrew biblical verses, the large, round cloth (2018.10) once decorated the festive table of the too often neglected Kurdish communities.⁸¹ On the back, a handwritten label dated November 1932 indicates that Isaac Sassoon of London loaned the piece to the city's Jewish Museum. The two early twentieth-century Iranian *ketubbot* (2018.45, 2018.46)⁸² are distinguished instead by the booklet form and text layout of Muslim wedding contracts, testifying to the incorporation of local artistic traditions by the Jews of Tehran. The same seamless absorption of the surrounding visual culture is convincingly illustrated by another *ketubbah* (2018.463), purchased shortly after; signed in The Hague and dated 1742, this marriage contract is engraved on its borders with flowers, birds, and animals in the tradition of still-life Dutch paintings.⁸³ The Mahrati script and Sahri-dressed women depicted on another 2018 acquisition—an 1874 Haggadah from Poona, India (2018.465)—function similarly to the flowers of the Dutch *ketubbah*: as reminders that Judaica is as varied as the Jewish communities it represents. Yet, in my view this incontestable truth cannot be the sole message conveyed by a modern Judaica collection. There also must be scope for more complicated works, such as the newly acquired Aachen Haggadah (2019.11.1–53), perhaps the most subversive piece in the collection. In what appears to be a daring act of rebellion to the safe domestic images of Jewish life associated with

Passover, Ukrainian-Israeli artist Zoya Cherkassky populated her 2004 Haggadah with hybrid creatures sporting heads of ultra-Orthodox men and bodies of birds.[84] The three silver works bought in 2018 from Israeli jewelry designer Tamar Paley also seek to break with tradition: *A Sign upon Your Hand*, *Hamavdil*, and *Between Sacred and Not* reinterpret ritual items worn by men (such as tefillin and tallit) in a feminist spirit, offering both Orthodox and secular women wearable Judaica jewelry.[85]

With a luxury that only large encyclopedic museums enjoy, the MFA's Judaica collection is currently also being built from within, through the rediscovery and reinterpretation of objects scattered in various departments. The earliest and most exciting pieces have emerged from the Textile and Fashion Arts superb collection. In 2019, in addition to the aforementioned Italian Torah binder (95.992) and *tallit katan* (38.1093), curators also rediscovered an eighteenth-century Torah mantle (41.179) and a seventeenth-century fabric embroidered with Hebrew, stylized blossoms, and pomegranates (43.484).[86] Although a number of findings also surfaced in the Art of Europe and Art of the Americas collections, the record for the highest number of museum items recently assigned to Jewish art is held by the Prints and Drawings Department. As the repository of a staggering two hundred thousand works, this part of the MFA's collection is one of the richest in the world. Determining what, in these vast holdings, qualifies as Jewish art is a complex, at times challenging question. Whereas the Jewishness of decorative arts tends to be determined by the objects' function, for prints and drawings (as for paintings and sculpture) the artist's origin and subject matter are usually the deciding factors. Just as the artist's identity alone is not sufficient to qualify a work as Jewish—as shown by the twenty-nine works by Ben Shahn in the MFA's holdings—a mere thematic approach is not satisfactory. Although the winning formula is often found in the combination of these two, dozens of prints and drawings were added to the Judaica collection by considering each piece individually.[87] These include works by both Jewish American and Israeli artists, such as David Aaronson's *Rabbi III*, Jack Levine's *Saul and David*, Mordechai Avniel's *Safed, Old City*, and Yitzhak Greenfield's *Jerusalem and Letters*.[88] The Prints and Drawings Department also houses the Leonard A. Lauder Postcard Archive, containing 120,000 items, many with Jewish themes. The museum's holdings no doubt still hold many surprises, but this broad summary should convey the fundamental decision to widen curatorial interest beyond ceremonial items so as to include works in all media related to Jewish life and culture.

Purchases and curatorial rediscoveries are not the only new acquisitions to have entered the museum's collection in this busy Judaica season. Thanks to the growing momentum, between 2017 and 2022 the MFA received a series of remarkable gifts, some of which I highlight here. The master metalsmith and teacher Linda Threadgill donated her *Garden of Lights* (2018.167.1), a large silver Hanukkah lamp whose flower-shaped candle holders, thin stems, and intricately etched leaves reveal her lifelong love of plants and botany.[89] Eric Zafran, former MFA associate curator of French paintings, purchased for the museum at auction two original so-called folk art objects: *Ten Commandments Flanked by Lions* (2019.13), a carved and painted Torah ark fragment, probably made for a Brooklyn synagogue in the 1920s; and the charming *Bottle with Synagogue Tableau* (2019.1815), a late nineteenth-century vignette showing Moses and Aaron standing by a Torah scroll.[90] The museum also received an exquisite Torah binder (2019.12)[91] made in 1736 in Germany, arguably the superior example in the MFA's existing group of wimples; embroidered in silk and silver thread with an outstanding eye for detail and exhibiting the traditional iconography of the chuppah and Torah scroll, the binder also features humorous passages with deer and birds chewing leaves. Thanks to the generosity of the Schlager family, the MFA was also able to add to its collection a Kiddush cup by the great Israeli silversmith Moshe Zabari.[92] In a career spanning more than sixty years, Zabari made Judaica history as one of the creators of a new, modernist style. His bold 1993 *Holiday Kiddush Cup* (2019.493)[93] is now fittingly displayed with Shabbat candlesticks by his teacher Ludwig Wolpert. Last but by no means least, a different kind of gift was offered to the MFA in late 2019, with the donation by the children of the late Vivian B. Mann of her vast Judaica library. Mann's book collection is a living testament to the extraordinary scholar's breadth and depth of knowledge as well as a daily and tangible reminder of her inestimable contribution to the field.[94]

As both the Judaica collection and resources continue to grow, curators will keep asking themselves essential questions: What kind of Jewish art collection do we want to shape? What is the best way to display it (in the context of the encyclopedic museum)? And, most important, how can Judaica be and stay relevant for our visitors?

I can only attempt to provide answers as they present themselves in this moment: MFA Judaica must acquire broadly; collecting comprehensively not only honors the foundational principle of the MFA's encyclopedic collection but also, most important, reflects the diversity of Jewish art and culture. Such an inclusive approach to acquisitions must seek multiple and varied display possibilities, aimed at integrating Judaica with the rest of the collection to show connections and affinities while also presenting it in a dedicated space—to deepen questions of meaning and function. This is why in December 2023, just before the publication of this volume, the MFA reached a milestone in its history by opening its first Judaica gallery.[95] Only this combined display approach, it might be argued, can mirror the dual historic nature of Jewish communities: their simultaneous ability to be an integral part of the surrounding local cultures while also retaining a core autonomous identity. What about relevance? At a time when encyclopedic museums across the world must question and radically revisit their role in the communities they hope to serve, Jewish objects and their untold stories can speak to issues that are at the heart of social and cultural change.

Notes

I would like to thank Marietta Cambareri, Senior Curator of Sculpture, and Jetskalina H. Phillips, Curator of Judaica, for reading this essay and offering helpful suggestions.

1. Martin Brimmer, the museum's first president and founding trustee, expressed this notion by stating, "The museums of today open their doors to all of the world, and the scope of their collections has broadened to meet the public needs." Brimmer, "Museum of Fine Arts."
2. For a comprehensive history of the MFA, see Whitehill, *Museum of Fine Arts Boston*.
3. Benguiat's letterhead boasted that he was "patronized by and Decorator to H.R.H. the Duke of Connaught, Manufacturers of Rugs and Art Embroideries, Constantinople and Smyrne and Collector of Laces and Very old European Embroideries and Tapestries" (with an address in both London and Boston). Letter to MFA Director Major General

Charles Greely Loring, March 6, 1889, Benguiat correspondence, MFA Archives, Boston.

4 Brimmer, "Contributions to the Loan Exhibitions," 46. A handwritten full list of all the pieces is in loan receipt no. 1304, May 15, 1889 (Benguiat file, MFA Archives).

5 Adler and Casanowicz, *Collection of Jewish Ceremonial Objects*, 701.

6 Grossman and Ahlborn, *Judaica at the Smithsonian*, 55.

7 Brimmer, "Contributions to the Loan Exhibitions," 50.

8 To see an image, type object number 95.992 in the collection search box of mfa.org. Thanks to Judaica intern Dahlia Sokolov, in 2019 we discovered the existence of this piece in the MFA Textile and Fashion Arts Department.

9 Several comparable examples are found in Italian Jewish museums. See Bemporad and Melasecchi, *Tutti i colori dell'Italia Ebraica*, cat. 45 166, cat. 56 172.

10 This recent discovery can be added to the MFA's three known Torah binders, currently on view for the first time in the Andrew and Russel Gallery of European Art (Gallery 142).

11 Lindsey purchased all the instruments from collector Reverend Francis W. Galpin (1858–1945), Hatfield Regis. Files archive of the Musical Instruments Department, MFA, Boston.

12 To see an image, type object number 17.1961 in the collection search box of mfa.org.

13 To see an image, type these volume numbers in the collection search box of mfa.org.

14 Philip and Carrie Lehman amassed a large collection of European paintings and decorative arts, later expanded by his son Robert Lehman. In 1969 Robert bequeathed the collection to the Metropolitan Museum of Art, which displays it in the Robert Lehman Wing. See Koeppe et al., *Decorative Arts in the Robert Lehman Collection*.

15 See Di Nepi, "Treasures from Storage."

16 To see a photo of the lion, type its object number in the collection search box of mfa.org.

17 The lion has been recently displayed in the exhibition "Collecting Stories: The Invention of Folk Art" (February 6, 2021–January 10, 2022) devoted to Max Karolik's gift; the Torah binder is currently shown in a case with Judaica textiles made by women in the Andrew and Russel Gallery of European Art (Gallery 142).

18 For an image of the portrait, type its object number in the collection search box of mfa.org.
19 Brin, "Binder's Artistic Creation."
20 Fine, *Art, History, and the Historiography*, 2–3.
21 As stated in the credit line, the painting was the gift "of a group of art lovers through a committee consisting of Alexander Brin, Carl Dreyfus, Louis E. Kirstein, A. J. Philpott, and A.C. Ratshesky." The painting is now on view at the MFA for the first time, in the museum's first Judaica gallery (inaugurated on December 8, 2023).
22 The exhibit "Early American Jewish Portraits and Silver" ran from February 15 to March 15, 1953. See also "Jewish Silver, Portraits Shown at Art Museum," *Boston Globe*, February 15, 1953, p. 29.
23 For the occasion an exhibition brochure was produced: *The Levy-Franks Family Colonial Portraits, August 30–December 9, 1990* (Boston: Museum of Fine Arts, 1990).
24 MFA accession number 2009.5022, December 16, 2009. Based on stylistic grounds, MFA curators concurred with the origin and dating established by Sotheby's experts. The lamp bears a large and small Austrian control mark for Brünn (now Brno, Czech Republic), 1806–7, and two Dutch control marks for foreign work (used 1813–93). The item was listed in the Sotheby's catalog for November 24, 2009, by an anonymous seller ("descendent of Selig Meier Goldschmidt"), Sotheby's, New York, lot 86.
25 The funds were donated by Lizbeth and George Krupp; Joyce and Edward Linde; Scott Nathan and Laura DeBonis; Barbara L. and Theodore B. Alfond; the Cordover Family Foundation; Judith P. and S. Lawrence Schlager; Susan B. Kaplan; Clay Barr; Irving W. Rabb; an exchange from an anonymous gift in memory of Charlotte Beebe Wilbour (1833–1914); the William Francis Warden Fund, made possible by the generous assistance of John Axelrod; bequest of Charles Cobb Walker; General Funds, The John Axelrod Collection; bequest of Maxim Karolik; gift of Mrs. Sidney T. Allen; gift in memory of Dr. William Hewson Baltzell by his wife, Alice Cheney Baltzell; the John Gardner Coolidge Collection; bequest of Frank Brewer Bemis; gift of Mrs. Dows Dunham; gift of Edward Jackson Holmes; gift of Mrs. Forsyth Wickes; gift of Mrs. George Linder; the Juliana Cheney Edwards Collection; gift of the Walpole Society; gift of Mr. and Mrs. Stephen C. Greene; gift of Mrs. Albert J. Beveridge; bequest of Helen S. Coolidge; gift of Mr. and

Mrs. John Templeman Coolidge; bequest of Charles Hitchcock Tyler; gift of Miss M. H. Jewell; gift of Mrs. Joseph Newhall Smith in memory of her husband; gift of the Western Art Visiting Committee; gift of the John Gardner Greene Trust; the Otis Norcross Fund; gift of Mrs. Francis B. Lothrop; gift of the Trustees of the Reservation Estate of Mrs. John Gardner Coolidge; gift of Dr. Henry J. Bigelow; gift of Mrs. Albertine W. F. Valentine, residuary legatee under the will of Hervey E. Wetzel; the Denman Waldo Ross Collection; gift of Mrs. Henrietta Page; gift of Frank Gair Macomber; the Elizabeth Day McCormick Collection; gift of the estate of Gertrude T. Taft; the Susan Greene Dexter Fund; bequest of Maxim Karolik; bequest of Miss Amy M. Sacker; gift of Mrs. Frances E. Perry; gift of Mrs. Horatio Appleton Lamb in memory of Mrs. Winthrop Sargent; gift of Mr. Edward Jackson Holmes; bequest of George Nixon Black; gift of Mrs. Frederick T. Bradbury; gift of Mr. and Mrs. William de Forest Thomson; bequest of Susan Greene Dexter in memory of Charles and Martha Babcock Amory; gift of Francis H. Bigelow; gift of Bloomingdale's; the John Wheelock Elliot and John Morse Elliot Fund; bequest of Forsyth Wickes, The Forsyth Wickes Collection; the Swan Collection; gift of Miss Elizabeth Howard Bartol; gift of Mrs. H. P. Sturgis; gift of Mrs. Abbott Lawrence; bequest of George Washington Wales; the Alfred Greenough Collection; gift of Mrs. Guy Lowell in memory of her husband, Guy Lowell; gift of the Collection of Edward Jackson Holmes; bequest of Gertrude T. Taft; bequest of James W. Paige; gift of Mrs. Henry Mason; bequest of Mrs. John H. Thorndike; gift of Richard Edwards; gift of Miss Louise M. Nathurst; the Jessie and Sigmund Katz Collection; the Phillip Leffingwell Spalding Collection, given in his memory by Katharine Ames Spalding, Philip Spalding, Oakes Ames Spalding, and Hobart Ames Spalding; gift of Roland Nickerson; gift of George E. Cabot in memory of Eliza Hemenway Cabot; bequest of Mrs. M. A. Elton; the Turner Sargent Collection, bequest of Mrs. Turner Sargent (Amelia J. Holmes); gift of Dr. George L. Walton; bequest of Emma M. Dimond; gift of Mrs. Thomas P. Rich; gift of Misses Catharine Langdon Rogers and Clara Bates Rogers; bequest of Mrs. Edna H. Howe; the Mary S. and Edward J. Holmes Fund; the William Francis Warden Fund; and an anonymous donor.

26 This hypothesis is based on contemporaneous iconography of both Jewish and non-Jewish objects (see, e.g., the *ketubbah* from 1763 in

Melasecchi and Spagnoletto, *Marriage Contracts*, cat. 9, 104–5; and *Coat of Arms with Two Putti Holding a Crown*, German seventeenth-century drawing at the Metropolitan Museum of Art in New York, acc. no. 52.570.153). The Sotheby's sale catalog listing the Hanukkah lamp identified the missing piece held by the putti as a servant light. This is unlikely, as German lamps of the period always featured their servant light on the side (see Jewish Museum examples F 197 and JM 27-53).

27 The male figure is shown in Greek military garb. In the Sotheby's auction catalog he was identified as "David, with sling and spear." His presence on a Hanukkah lamp makes it far more likely to be Judah Maccabee.

28 See Jewish Museum, New York, accession numbers F 197 and JM 27-53. Judith on her own is found as early as the sixteenth or seventeenth century, on Italian bronze Hanukkah lamps (Victoria and Albert Museum, London, M.28-1965), or with her maidservant on German examples of the seventeenth–eighteenth centuries (Jewish Museum, New York, JM 26-64; Israel Museum, no. B86.0029 and B13.0634).

29 Scientific testing carried out on the silver alloys of different parts has not offered definitive answers. Marietta Cambareri presented these observations in an unpublished paper for the annual Moldovan Symposium held by the Friedman Society at the Jewish Museum in New York in March 2012.

30 Although the servant light was not always present, in German lamps of the same period it is usually found attached to the backplate or as a separate component on the side. See examples in the Jewish Museum, New York, acc. nos. JM 26-64 and JM 27-53.

31 Selig Meier Goldschmidt (1828–96), Frankfurt; by descent to his son, Meier Selig Goldschmidt (1865–1922), Frankfurt; by descent to his daughter, Alice Goldschmidt Eisemann (1896–1965), Frankfurt and London; by descent to her son, Meier Selig Eisemann, Minnesota and Israel; by descent to an anonymous family member; then the November 24, 2009, anonymous seller ("descendent of Selig Meier Goldschmidt") at Sotheby's.

32 See obituary of Selig Meier Goldschmidt, founder of the antique firm J & S Goldschmidt, in the *Frankfurter General Anzeiger*, 1896. Cembalest, "Out of the Ghetto."

33 The letter was dated December 22, 2009. The MFA would learn the extent of the bequest in 2010.

34 This appointment was in addition to Cambareri's regular full-time position in sculpture and decorative arts. For more information, see Wecker, "8 Questions."
35 The Temple Israel certificate indicates that Jetskalina Phillips converted under the tutelage of Rabbi Roland B. Gittelson (1910–95), known for the eulogy delivered at the graveyard at Iwo Jima during World War II. The conversion and wedding certificates are cited in McGinity, *Marrying Out*, 238n74.
36 Cembalest, "Out of the Ghetto."
37 For a photo of the finials, type object number L-R 44.2019.1-2 into the collection search box of mfa.org.
38 Since the 2010 installation and following a legal dispute between the two congregations, the First US Circuit Court of Appeals ruled that Shearith Israel of New York owns both Touro Synagogue and the Myer Myers Torah finials. The credit line in the MFA's object label was amended accordingly to "from the Touro Synagogue, Newport, R.I. Collection of Congregation Shearith Israel, N.Y."
39 The foundation was launched in 1987 with the aim of strengthening Jewish life across the world and supporting local causes in Oklahoma. See Cardin, *First 30 Years*.
40 The collection was mainly formed in the 1990s and 2000s through auction purchases in America and Israel.
41 At the behest of Lynn Schusterman, Sharon Mintz joined the trip to provide her expertise and to advise on the collection.
42 In 2013 the gift included 120 objects, with the addition the following year of Isidor Kaufmann's *Hannah* (2014.513), whose accession was delayed by provenance research.
43 MFA press release, November 25, 2013.
44 Edgers, "Benefactor."
45 The Walters Art Museum in Baltimore had also shown interest in Judaica. It received a gift of Jewish Yemenite jewelry by Benjamin Zucker and jointly acquired with the Yeshiva University Art Museum in New York a wooden door believed to be from the Ben Ezra Synagogue in Cairo.
46 Accession numbers 2013.443 and 2013.495. For these two acquisitions, see *A Treasured Legacy: The Michael and Judy Steinhardt Judaica Collection*, Sotheby's, New York, April 29, 2013, lots 113 and 55. Like the MFA, throughout its long history the Metropolitan Museum of Art has

received a number of Judaica gifts; in 1906 it also purchased German pewter plates, namely, a Passover plate and a pair of redemption of firstborn ceremony plates (06.780 and 06.745).

47 Cembalest, "Out of the Ghetto."
48 Edgers, "Benefactor."
49 Accession numbers 2013.910, 2013.915, 2013.916, and 2013.919.
50 Shabbat candlesticks, 2013.911.1–2; Kiddush cup, 2013.912.
51 The inscription reads, "Remember the Shabbat and keep it holy, to Salomon Anselm from his rabbi on 6th Shvat 5576 [February 5, 1816]."
52 Gift of the heirs of Bettina Looram de Rothschild. These objects were confiscated by the Nazis in 1938 with the rest of the collection of Baron and Baroness Alphonse and Clarice de Rothschild of Vienna. They were recovered after the war.
53 For photos of the plates, type the object numbers into the collection search box of mfa.org.
54 The Israel Museum, Jerusalem, holds a 1672 plate with "Hatimah Tova'" (acc. no. B42.06.0386) painted on it, with an identical design and the same potter's mark as the MFA's Sukkot dish. For other Hebrew inscribed plates, see Jewish Museum, acc. nos. F 2978 and F 3707 (1981–28).
55 These include two watercolors (2013.996, 2013.997), two Hanukkah lamps (2013.934, 2013.938), an exhibition poster (2013.998), and a terracotta low-relief (2013.976) by Zeev Raban; a bronze low-relief by Boris Schatz (2013.975), a spice box and Hanukkah lamp by Yehia Yemini (2013.1024, 2013.940), two pairs of candlesticks (2013.935, 2013.939), and three rugs (2013.1000, 2013.1001, 2013.1028).
56 Accession numbers 2013.940 and 2013.1024.
57 Accession numbers 2013.934 and 2013.938.
58 For a photo of the ring, type this object number into the collections search box of mfa.org.
59 The donor of the ring was Genoese dealer Ferdinando Ildebrando Bossi, who in the same year illegally sold the so-called Boston Raphael to the MFA, plunging director Perry T. Rathbone into an international controversy that ultimately led to his resignation.
60 MFA accession number 2014.513. See Furman, *Treasures of Jewish Art*, 266–67. See also the catalog of New York's Jewish Museum exhibition: Braunstein, *Personal Vision*, 38 no. 40. The MFA painting was bought by

the Schustermans at the New York Sotheby's sale on December 2, 2000 (lot 9).
61 A similar portrait of the same woman titled *The Jewish Bride* was sold on December 19, 2007, at Sotheby's New York (lot 223). For the identification with the painter's daughter, see *Christie's, London, Important 19th- and 20th-Century Pictures*, sale catalog, March 19, 1982, lot 83; Braunstein, *Personal Vision*, 30 no. 40; and Natter and Cohen, *Bilder des Wiener Malers*, 192–93. A portrait of a different woman sold at Kestenbaum (March 16, 2017, lot 1) was affixed on the reverse with a letter written by the artist's son, Philipp Kaufmann, identifying the sitter as Marie Pauline Kaufmann, the artist's daughter.
62 In December 2023, I reinstalled *Hannah* in the museum's first Judaica gallery. For the Brandon painting, see Smee, "Tiny Painting."
63 MFA accession number 2021.58. See *Sassoon: A Golden Legacy*, Sotheby's New York, December 17, 2020, lot 26.
64 Stanislav is the former name for Ivano-Frankivsk, a town about two hours south of Lvov, now western Ukraine. The signature also allows us to attribute to Elimelekh Tzoref two other similar but unsigned Torah shields from the Sassoon collection, the first in the Israel Museum, Jerusalem (B13.0558), and the second with a private collector.
65 "Treasures of Judaica from the Sassoon Family Collection," *Wall Street Journal*, December 11, 2020; "Sassoon Family Collection of Jewish Artefacts to Be Sold at Auction," *The Guardian*, October 29, 2020.
66 "The Mystery of the Sassoon Shields," *Mosaic*, February 10, 2021.
67 *Apollo: The International Art Magazine*, December 2021, 60–67.
68 MFA accession numbers 2019.634.1&2. See also *Sotheby's Important Judaica: Featuring the Serque Collection*, Sotheby's New York, June 5, 2019, lot 79. MFA Boston now owns two exceedingly rare seventeenth-century Torah finial sets: The first was made in 1649 in Rotterdam, acquired in 2021 (2021.60.1&2), and the second is the 1688 German pair discussed in this essay. See Di Nepi, "Torah Finials"; and Di Nepi, "Itinerant Sephardic Judaica." The same model is followed by Pieter van Hoven; see, for example, his 1705 pair at the Jewish Museum, New York. See Grafman and Mann, *Crowning Glory*, 235–36, no. 383 (F 2827 a&b). In Europe, there are several earlier examples; the oldest extant set dates to 1638 and is in the Museo Ebraico, Rome. See Di Castro, *I Tesori del museo ebraico di Roma*, 116, inv. 82.

69 *Sotheby's Important Judaica from the Sassoon Estate*, Tel Aviv, April 9, 1999, lot 15. The current whereabouts of this pair is unknown.
70 MFA Accession number 2019.635.1&2. *Sotheby's Important Judaica: Featuring the Serque Collection*, June 5, 2019, lot 3. See also Grimwade, *Treasures of a London Temple*, 18.
71 Philip Salomons was a wealthy banker and the brother of David Salomons, the first Jewish mayor of London. He amassed a large Judaica collection, which he displayed in his private synagogue atop his Hove residence. After his death, most of his collection was acquired by Reuben D. Sassoon. See *Sotheby's Important Judaica*, 14.
72 It is unclear whether Salomons himself donated the finials to the newly founded Central Synagogue, the congregation bought them at the sale held after his death, or they were bought by another individual who donated them to Central Synagogue. See the synagogue's history in *Sotheby's Important Judaica*, 8–9.
73 In 2023 the MFA and the Jewish Museum in New York purchased jointly an earlier pair of London Torah finials, made in 1729 by Abraham Lopes de Oliveyra (2023.452.1-2), making the MFA the owner of two of the earliest English pairs in the country.
74 Three pairs made in London in 1712 survive: two sets at Bevis Marks synagogue (the first by Samuel Wastell and the other probably by Richard Edwards) and one by Samuel Edlin at the Jewish Museum in London. Before the 1710s, English congregations imported Judaica from other European countries (especially Holland and Germany) or commissioned foreign silversmiths. See Grimwade, "Anglo-Jewish Silver," 113–25.
75 Edward Aldridge's silver cake basket at the Rhode Island School of Design Museum in Providence (object 60.102) provides the closest parallel to the design of the *rimonim*'s openwork. In addition to the MFA's new acquisition, Aldridge produced at least three additional Judaica pieces: a Torah pointer (lot 4 of the June 2019 Sotheby's sale) and two smaller Torah finials pairs from 1761 and 1764, still at Central Synagogue.
76 These were lots 10 and 131, respectively, at the Sotheby's Important Judaica sale in New York on December 19, 2018. The Torah shield bears the mark of the medieval town of Banská Štiavnica in central Slovakia (named Selmecbánya as part of the Kingdom of Hungary at the time).
77 For a photo, search under object number 2019.10.1&2 in mfa.org. Other similar examples are in the Gross Family Collection, Tel Aviv, and the

Israel Museum, Jerusalem. One of the pairs in the Israel Museum is attributed to the Jewish silversmiths Mordecai Attia and Isaac Aravatz (accession number B86.0163(a–b) 147/330(a–b)), making it most likely that the MFA finials were made by one of the Jewish metalsmiths working in that area.

78 For a photo, search this object number in the collection search field at mfa.org.

79 For an image, search 2019.9 in the collection search box at mfa.org. Although the Sotheby's catalog dates it to 1825 on stylistic grounds, the city mark (with two crossed hammers, an S, and the number thirteen) was in use only until 1800.

80 Lots 103 and 117, respectively, in *Sotheby's Important Judaica*, December 20, 2017, New York.

81 See photos of the Shabbat cloth by typing 2018.10 into the collection search box at mfa.org. For comparative examples, see Jewish Museum, New York (F 6033) and the Israel Museum (161/4).

82 For images, type these object numbers into the collection search box at mfa.org.

83 See discussion and image of the Dutch *ketubbah* in Di Nepi, "Itinerant Sephardic Judaica." The engraved borders are variations on a copper design (possibly for two *ketubbot*, in 1648 and 1654) by Shalom Mordechai Italia. This iconography became part of a highly popular type of Dutch-Spanish *ketubbot* produced in several European communities between the second half of the seventeenth century and the mid-nineteenth century.

84 Search images under accession number 2019.11.1–53 at mfa.org. See Sorek, "Zoya Cherkassky's Aachen Passover Haggadah."

85 Search images at mfa.org, collection search, accession numbers 2018.2186, 2018.2187.1&2. See Bolton-Fasman, "MFA Acquires Tamar Paley's Feminist Judaica Art." The MFA's first acquisition of feminist Judaica was Cynthia Eid's *Miriam's Cup* in 2015 (2015.112).

86 In the old object file this piece is described as "Italian valance." These textiles were traced in the museum database in 2019 as part of the work project of Judaica intern Dahlia Sokolov.

87 The decision ultimately rests in the hands of the curator, who must carefully balance the traditional ideas around "visual Jewishness" with a more expansive three-dimensional approach.

88 Accession numbers 64.217, 1993.652, 53.2111, and 1981.384.
89 A photo of the Hanukkah lamp (accession number 2018.167.1) can be seen by entering the accession number into the collections search box at mfa.org. This work was made for the 1999 exhibition "Magic and Ritual: Hanukkiahs Seen Through Contemporary Eyes" at the Steinbaum-Krauss Gallery in New York, which showcased the work of twenty-nine artists and focused on pieces with religious symbolism related to Hanukkah. It was also shown in the 2015 retrospective "Cultivating Ornament: Linda Threadgill Master Metalsmith" at the Metal Museum in Memphis.
90 Find photos of both gifts through a collection search at mfa.org.
91 Search for the image at mfa.org.
92 The credit line for the cup reads, "Museum purchase with funds donated by the children and grandchildren of Judith P. and S. Lawrence Schlager in honor of their 60th wedding anniversary and their 80th and 85th birthdays." The cup is illustrated in Berman, *Moshe Zabari*, 41.
93 Search image with this accession number at mfa.org.
94 I am especially grateful to Miriam L. Wallach for the time and effort she offered to assist with the library donation.
95 This gallery, named "Intentional Beauty: Jewish Ritual Art from the Collection," is one of only four such spaces in encyclopedic museums in the country, and the first in the Northeast.

Bibliography

Adler, Cyrus, and Immanuel M. Casanowicz. *The Collection of Jewish Ceremonial Objects in the United States National Museum*. Washington, DC: US Government Printing Office, 1908.

Bemporad, Dora Liscia, and Olga Melasecchi. *Tutti i colori dell'Italia Ebraica: Tessuti preziosi dal Tempio di Gerusalemme al prêt-à-porter*. Florence: Giunti, 2019.

Berman, Nancy M. *Moshe Zabari: A Twenty-Five Year Retrospective*. New York: Jewish Museum; and Los Angeles: Skirball Museum, 1986.

Bolton-Fasman, Judy. "MFA Acquires Tamar Paley's Feminist Judaica Art." *Jewish Boston*, July 22, 2019. www.jewishboston.com/read/mfa-acquires-tamar-paleys-feminist-judaica-art/ (accessed May 7, 2024).

Braunstein, Susan L. *Personal Vision: The Furman Collection of Jewish Ceremonial Art.* New York: Jewish Museum, 1985.

Brimmer, Martin. "Contributions to the Loan Exhibitions." *Annual Report for the Year 1889* (Museum of Fine Arts, Boston) 14 (1889): 46–50.

———. "The Museum of Fine Arts, Boston." *American Architect and Building News* 8, no. 253 (October 30, 1880): 205–15.

Brin, Alexander. "Binder's Artistic Creation 'The Talmudist' to Be Presented to the Museum of Fine Arts in Boston Through Public Subscription." *Jewish Advocate*, November 1926.

Cardin, Sandy. *The First 30 Years of Making It Possible: The Story of the Charles and Lynn Schusterman Family Foundation.* Atlanta: 30 Point Press, 2019.

Cembalest, Robin. "Out of the Ghetto." *Tablet Magazine*, May 25, 2011. www.tabletmag.com/sections/arts-letters/articles/out-of-the-ghetto (accessed May 7, 2024).

Di Castro, Daniela. *I Tesori del museo ebraico di Roma.* Rome: Araldo de Luca, 2010.

Di Nepi, Simona. "Itinerant Sephardic Judaica: From Dutch Ports to the Harbors of Europe and the Americas." In *The Routledge Companion to the Global Renaissance*, ed. S. Campbell and S. Porras, 546–59. Oxfordshire, UK: Routledge, 2024.

———. "Torah Finials." In *Dutch Art in a Global Age*, ed. Christopher Atkins and Antien Knapp, 98–101. Boston: MFA Publications, 2023.

———. "Treasures from Storage: Two Rediscovered Italian Jewish Textiles at the Museum of Fine Arts Boston." In *Jewish Italy: Rediscovered Stories*, vol. 2, *Italia Ebraica: Storie Ritrovate*, ed. Olga Melasecchi, 15–24. Rome: Artemide Edizioni, 2023.

Edgers, Geoff. "Benefactor Gives MFA a Solid Base in Judaica." *Boston Globe*, November 5, 2013.

Fine, Steven. *Art, History, and the Historiography of Judaism on Roman Antiquity.* Leiden: Brill, 2013.

Furman, Jacobo. *Treasures of Jewish Art: From the Jacobo and Asea Furman Collection of Judaica.* New York: Hugh Lauter Levin Associates, 1997.

Grafman, Rafi, and Vivian B. Mann. *Crowning Glory: Silver Torah Ornaments of the Jewish Museum, New York.* New York: Jewish Museum, 1996.

Grimwade, Arthur G. "Anglo-Jewish Silver." *Transactions (Jewish Historical Society of England)* 18 (1953–55): 113–25.

———, comp. *Treasures of a London Temple*. London: Taylor's Foreign Press, 1951.

Grossman, Grace Cohen, and Richard E. Ahlborn. *Judaica at the Smithsonian: Cultural Politics as Cultural Model*. Washington, DC: Smithsonian Institution Press, 1997.

Koeppe, Wolfram, Clare Le Corbeiller, William Rieder, Charles Truman, Suzanne G. Valenstein, and Clare Vincent. *Decorative Arts in the Robert Lehman Collection*. Princeton, NJ: Princeton University Press, 2012.

McGinity, Keren R. *Marrying Out: Jewish Men, Intermarriage, and Fatherhood*. Bloomington: Indiana University Press, 2014.

Melasecchi, Olga, and Amedeo Spagnoletto. *The Marriage Contracts of the Jewish Community of Rome*. Rome: Campisano Editore, 2018.

Natter, Tobias G., and Richard I. Cohen. *Bilder des Wiener Malers, Isidor Kaufmann, 1853–1921*. Vienna: Jüdisches Museum der Stadt Wien, 1995.

Smee, Sebastian. "Tiny Painting, Big Book." *Washington Post*, January 29, 2020.

Sorek, Ronit. "Zoya Cherkassky's Aachen Passover Haggadah: A Subversive Illuminated Manuscript." *Ars Judaica: The Bar-Ilan Journal of Jewish Art* 12 (2016): 135–42.

Wecker, Menachem. "8 Questions for MFA Judaica Curator Marietta Cambareri." *Iconia* (blog), July 22, 2010. https://web.archive.org/web/20120802030823/https:/blog.chron.com/iconia/2010/07/8-questions-for-mfa-boston-judaica-curator-marietta-cambareri/ (accessed May 7, 2024).

Whitehill, Walter M. *Museum of Fine Arts Boston: A Centennial History*, 2 vols. Cambridge, MA: Harvard University Press, 1970.

7

NOTES FOR A HISTORY OF THE JUDAIC ART GALLERY OF THE NORTH CAROLINA MUSEUM OF ART

John Coffey

For much of the twentieth century, Judaica as a distinct field of the visual arts has been largely ignored by American art museums. One can speculate on the reasons: a dearth of curatorial expertise, a poor regard for the aesthetic quality of the objects, and surely here and there antisemitism. But the result is that in 2023 only a small number of art museums in the United States have coherent, meaningful collections of Jewish ceremonial art. Among those collections only two are displayed in dedicated galleries. And of these two, the larger and more active collection is at the North Carolina Museum of Art (NCMA). How the NCMA's Judaic Art Gallery came to be in a region of the country distant from the major centers of Jewish American culture is largely the achievement of one determined and visionary individual: Abram Kanof.

    Abram Kanof's life, which spanned the twentieth century, followed the familiar trajectory of the striving, intellectually precocious immigrant son.[1] Kanof was born in 1903 in the Russian Empire, the son of a kosher butcher. Fleeing pogroms, the Kanof family arrived at Ellis Island in 1905. With characteristic humor, Kanof recalled, "I was brought up in the Brownsville section of Brooklyn, where one either grew up to be an atheist or a traditional Jew. I chose the latter."[2] After graduating from medical school in 1928, Kanof pursued a distinguished career as a pediatrician, medical researcher, and clinical professor. A man of energy and deep commitment to his community, he also lent his support to a wide variety of charities and

FIGURE 7.1. Dr. Abram Kanof. Photo: North Carolina Museum of Art.

cultural institutions, often rising to leadership positions. He served as a trustee of the American Jewish Historical Society (president, 1961–64) and the B'nai B'rith Museum in Washington, DC (president, 1954–60). He sat on the board of the Jewish Theological Seminary in New York and served as the chairman of the governing board of the Jewish Museum (1948–62).[3]

At the Jewish Museum Kanof created one of his most enduring legacies, establishing in 1956 the Tobe Pascher Workshop to promote contemporary design in Judaica. As he later explained, "The modern synagogue and home demand modern appurtenances and modern ceremonial objects. Each age has generated its own view of Judaism and has modified its modes of worship, and there is no reason why our age should not produce its own form of sacred accessories."[4] The workshop, housed in the basement of the Jewish Museum, provided studio space for artists-in-residence and classrooms where several generations of American metalsmiths learned to apply modernist design principles to the creation of Jewish ceremonial art.[5] The impact of the workshop can be seen in synagogues and Jewish homes across the country.

Kanof and his wife, Frances, were also passionate collectors and donors.[6] They donated their extensive collection of books and Haggadot to Duke University, a collection of Yiddish theater and film posters to the American Jewish Historical Society, and numerous pieces of modern ceremonial art to the Jewish Museum, the B'nai B'rith Museum, and the Museum of Modern Art.

Primarily through his association with the Jewish Museum and its staff, Kanof became a dedicated student of Jewish history, culture, and art. He published extensively in these fields and was the author of several books, notably *Jewish Ceremonial Art and Religious Observance*, published by Harry Abrams in 1970 and the first coffee table book on the subject.[7] By the time he retired from teaching, Abram Kanof was nationally recognized for his expertise in Judaica and much in demand as a speaker.

In his mideighties, when he was asked to reflect on his long and crowded life, Kanof noted that outside his medical career, he was proudest of three accomplishments: the founding of the Tobe Pascher Workshop; the donation of the Abram and Frances Pascher Kanof Collection of Jewish Art, Archaeology, and Symbolism to Duke University; and the creation of the Judaic Art Gallery at the North Carolina Museum of Art.[8]

Following their retirement in 1971, Abram and Frances Kanof moved to Raleigh, home to their elder daughter and her family. Although officially retired, he was anything but. Kanof immersed himself in the life of his adopted community. And as the author of *Jewish Ceremonial Art and Religious Observance*, he came to the attention of the North Carolina Museum of Art.

According to Kanof, his involvement with the NCMA began in 1973 with a phone call from director Moussa M. Domit. Temperamentally unalike, the Lebanon-born museum director and the New York Jewish physician shared a sense of otherness in what was then a small and provincial southern city. The two men became fast friends. As Kanof recalled that initial conversation: "[Domit] could talk and I could talk. He said, 'Why don't we have a Judaica exhibit here?' I said 'Fine.'" Founded as a traditional museum of Western (i.e., European and American) art, the NCMA by the early 1970s had significantly extended the boundaries of its collection, adding ancient Egyptian and Classical art, as well as the beginnings of meaningful collections of sub-Saharan African and pre-Columbian art.[9] In this context an exhibition of Jewish ceremonial art was not such a novelty, especially given the presence in Raleigh of a national authority on the subject. Domit and Kanof could also call on the enthusiastic support of the state's Jewish community. Although Jews had lived in North Carolina since colonial days, the Jewish population in the early 1970s was quite small—0.02 percent of the total population—and widely dispersed.[10]

Even so, two of the twelve members of the North Carolina Museum of Art Commission, the forerunner of the Board of Trustees, were Jewish.[11]

The exhibit "Ceremonial Art in the Judaic Tradition" opened at the NCMA on April 27, 1975. Kanof served as guest curator. Described by Domit as "the most ambitious of the shows organized at the museum during the biennium," the exhibition featured a catalog with an essay by Kanof and a checklist of 184 items.[12] Among the lenders were the Metropolitan Museum of Art, the Brooklyn Museum, and the Jewish Museum, as well as twenty-nine private collectors. The Kanof family lent twenty-six pieces.

Almost fifty years later, the exhibition remains the largest museum presentation of Judaica in the South. Local media coverage was favorable, if somewhat perplexed. When the writer for the Raleigh *News and Observer* asked himself, "Why is this show being produced in North Carolina where the Jewish population is so small?" he conceded that "the art of the Jews, a people very much a part of American society, perhaps warrants a closer look than other groups."[13]

The exhibition attracted 9,099 visitors—an impressive attendance for the time.[14] Defying expectations, the show proved popular among non-Jews, especially church groups, confirming the appeal of Jewish art and culture in the Bible Belt. Deftly leveraging the popularity of the exhibition, Domit proposed that the NCMA acquire a permanent collection of Judaic art. The trustees unanimously agreed. Kanof had already seized the opportunity: Even before the exhibition opened, it was announced that "Dr. Abram Kanof has raised $9,000 to be used to acquire Judaic ceremonial art objects."[15]

The arrangement with the NCMA was straightforward: Kanof would volunteer his time as curator with primary responsibility for acquiring a permanent collection of Jewish ceremonial art. He would also be chiefly responsible for raising the necessary funds. With his long years of experience on institutional boards and his deep knowledge of Jewish philanthropy, Kanof accepted the assignment with relish. For him, it was the perfect retirement project, active and full of purpose, and would happily engage him for the rest of his life. Although he was past seventy when he began his "crusade" (his term), Kanof was indefatigable as a curator, educator, promoter, and rainmaker.

Kanof's first challenge was to determine the scope and character of the proposed collection. Of course, an encyclopedic collection of Judaica of the kind held by New York's Jewish Museum was not possible, or even desirable given the mission of a general art museum. Instead, Kanof proposed a modest-size ensemble of objects that assist and enhance the spiritual life and religious observance of the Jewish people. (To preserve coherence, paintings and sculpture and other nonutilitarian art forms were not included.) The collection as envisioned by Kanof would embrace four broad categories, defined by purpose or function: synagogue and the Torah; Sabbath and holidays; life cycle; and home.[16] The collection would also survey an array of aesthetic styles, historical and modern. Not surprising, modernist objects from the Tobe Pascher Workshop formed a major group. As noted, Kanof very much believed that reinterpreting traditional ritual objects through contemporary design affirmed the vitality of Judaism. Equally important, Kanof insisted that the Judaic collection be first and foremost an *art* collection with each new acquisition considered by the same criteria that would be applied to the evaluation of fine silver and other decorative arts: foremost, excellence of concept, design, and execution. This undeniably elitist approach, in line with traditional art curatorial practice, focused only on that small percentage of Judaica deemed to be of "art museum quality."

To raise acquisition funds, Kanof crisscrossed the length of the state lecturing to civic and religious groups and calling on potential donors. Governor James B. Hunt lent enthusiastic support, as did Grace Rohrer, secretary of the North Carolina Department of Cultural Resources, the NCMA's parent agency. In 1976 the North Carolina Bicentennial Commission adopted the Judaic art collection as a special project. The Committee of '76, composed of prominent Jewish business and civic leaders, canvassed the state, soliciting funds from private individuals, foundations, and corporations. To provide additional venues for fund-raising, the NCMA packaged small traveling exhibitions of Judaica and toured them to museums in Charlotte, Greenville, Wilmington, Fayetteville, and other North Carolina cities.[17]

As funds came available, Kanof acquired more objects, primarily from dealers in New York. To these he added gifts from his own collection, a few credited to his extended family. By the time the Judaic Art Gallery opened in 1983, the NCMA's Judaic art collection included eighty-one accessioned pieces.[18]

The original Judaic art collection was true to Kanof's concept of a gallery representing the major types of Jewish ceremonial art as interpreted over generations and across the Jewish Diaspora and Israel. However, the strength of the collection was the core group of twentieth-century pieces by Ludwig Y. Wolpert and Moshe Zabari of the Tobe Pascher Workshop and Ilya Schor. Wolpert's *Passover Seder Set with Plates, Dishes, and Wine Cup*, originally created in 1930, destroyed by the Nazis, and recreated in 1975, is an early exemplar of Bauhaus-inflected modernist Judaica. Zabari, who succeeded Wolpert as director of the Tobe Pascher Workshop, designed a cosmic version of a Torah crown with loops of silver and dangling starlike pearls. In contrast, Ilya Schor's large *Passover Seder Plate* with appliqué of cut and pierced silver was inspired by the folk art traditions of his native Poland.[19]

The Judaic Art Gallery opened on December 18, 1983, in a small polygonal space in the new museum building designed by New York architect Edward Durrell Stone. Featuring thirty-five objects, the

FIGURE 7.2. *Passover Seder Set with Plates, Dishes, and Wine Cup*, Ludwig Yehuda Wolpert (American, born Germany, 1900–1981), designed 1930, fabricated 1975; silver, glass, ebony; height overall with cup, 9¾ in. (24.8 cm); height of plates, 4 in. (10.2 cm); diameter of plates, 13¾ in. (34.9 cm); height of cup, 6 in. (15.2 cm); diameter of cup, 2¾ in. (7.0 cm); height of dishes, ⅞ in. (2.2 cm); diameter of dishes, 2⅞ in. (7.3 cm). Museum purchase, Judaic Art Fund, 1976 (76.4.6/a–j).

original installation emphasized aesthetics over content—a battle Kanof lost to the NCMA's chief designer. In 1996 the gallery was redesigned with an arrangement more aligned with the functional purpose of the objects. The gray walls were repainted in a deep plum color with dramatic use of spotlight and shadow that imparted a jewel box character to the gallery. To mark the reopening of the gallery, the NCMA published the fully illustrated *Guide to the Judaic Art Collection* with an essay by the ninety-two-year-old Kanof.[20]

Once the gallery opened, Kanof assumed the role of the gallery's principal educator and promoter.[21] He instructed the NCMA's docent corps and delivered numerous public lectures throughout the state. Rarely did he turn down a request to lead a tour group.[22] Through his knowledge and passion for art and Judaism, his gift of storytelling, and the warmth of his personality, Kanof created a devoted constituency for the Judaic Art Gallery. Although many contributed to the success of the gallery, Kanof provided the essential vision, expertise, and boundless enthusiasm. He was the indispensable man. When he died in 1999 at the age of ninety-five, the Judaic Art Gallery faced an existential crisis.

Because Kanof left behind no real protégé, management of the Judaic Art Gallery passed to John W. Coffey, the deputy director and curator of American and Modern Art. Coffey had served as the NCMA's liaison to Kanof. Although he honored the founder's vision, Coffey recognized that the collection was still very much a work in progress with glaring weaknesses, notably a number of objects of uneven quality or questionable authenticity. (Here it must be admitted that, as a curator, Kanof was an amateur who made his share of mistakes. However, scholarship and connoisseurship in the field of Judaica were less developed then, and the inconsistencies that marked the NCMA's original collection can be found in most Judaica collections, public and private, from this period.)

Remedying the deficiencies would require patience and commitment as well as resources many times greater than the funds raised so far. In 2001 Coffey invited friends, family, and other supporters of Abram Kanof to form an affiliate group, the Friends of the Judaic Art Gallery, and charged it with one critical mission: funding the future development of the Judaic art collection and its programs.[23] In large measure, the present success of the Judaic Art Gallery testifies to the zeal and generosity of an ever-expanding circle of Friends.

As a first step in the renewed development of the Judaic art collection, the NCMA contracted the services of Gabriel M. Goldstein, curator and later associate director of the Yeshiva University Museum, to evaluate each object in the existing collection in terms of authenticity, aesthetic quality, historical significance, condition, and appropriateness. Goldstein also provided general guidance for acquisitions going forward. Since 2003 the NCMA has retained Goldstein as a consulting curator of Judaic art. Additional expertise has been generously volunteered by Dr. Roger M. Berkowitz, director emeritus of the Toledo Museum of Art and an NCMA trustee.

Guided by Goldstein's report, the NCMA resumed its acquisition program of Judaic art in 2004. The immediate goal was to build a collection of such quality and importance that would justify a place for the Judaic Art Gallery in the planned new gallery building. The longer-term goal—a natural expansion of Kanof's original concept—was to shape a balanced survey of Jewish ceremonial art ranging across the past four centuries and embracing the major centers of Jewish culture worldwide.[24]

The first notable acquisition was a silver standing Hanukkah lamp, designed in the mid-1920s by Ze'ev Raban of Jerusalem's Bezalel Workshop and a masterwork of the "Hebrew Style."[25] This lamp, so expressive of Jewish national aspiration, has become emblematic of the NCMA's Judaic art collection, and in 2015 it was loaned to the White House for the national Hanukkah celebration. Each new acquisition stoked the enthusiasm of the Friends of the Judaic Art Gallery, encouraging ever higher levels of giving and enabling in turn the pursuit of truly exceptional objects on the international art market. Historical highlights of the collection include splendid pieces from eighteenth-century Europe: a gilded silver Torah shield by the Augsburg master Hieronymus Mittnacht, and a pair of silver architectural Torah finials from Amsterdam's Grote Synagoge.[26] Among the Judaic objects from communities beyond Europe is an opulent silver Torah case made in Guangzhou for a Baghdadi synagogue in Mumbai.[27] The acquisition of each of these objects was made possible with funds donated by North Carolinians from the Friends of the Judaic Art Gallery.

Although most attention—and acquisition funds—have been directed to laying the historical foundation of the collection, the NCMA continues to honor Dr. Kanof's precept to acquire Judaica of our own time. Recent acquisitions have included works by Israeli artists Zelig Segal, Iris

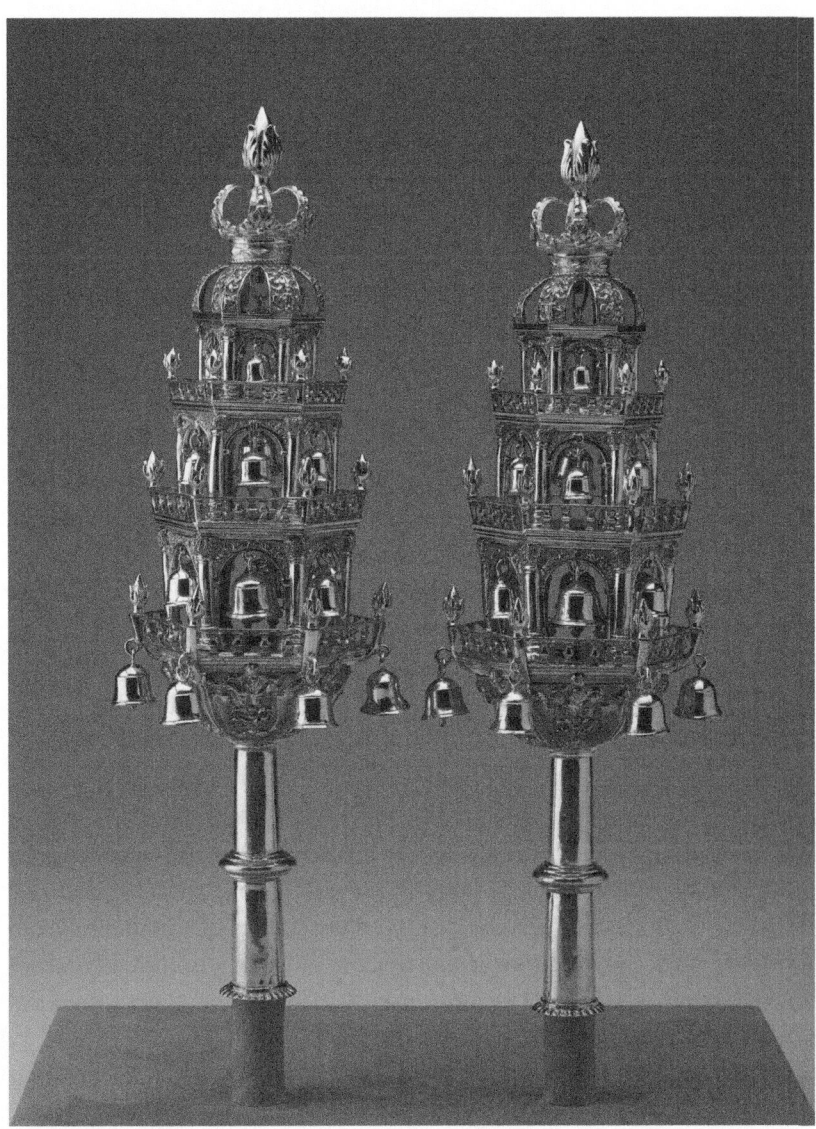

FIGURE 7.3. Pair of Torah finials, attributed to Willem Hendrik Rosier (Dutch, Amsterdam, 1707–75), ca. 1765; silver, partly gilded; (each) 16⅝ × 5½ in. (42.2 × 14 cm). Purchased with funds from Margaret and Douglas Abrams, Marion Meyer-Robboy and Stanley Robboy, Connie C. and Robert D. Shertz, Laura and David Brody, Joan and Kalman Cohen, David C. Falk Sr., Elizabeth Kanof Levine and Ronald Levine, and other Friends of the Judaic Art Gallery, 2007 (2007.1/a–b).

Tutnauer, and Sari Srulovitch.[28] Srulovitch was commissioned to create a complete ensemble of Torah ornaments—crown, shield, and pointer—and to design the accompanying silk Torah mantle.

The acquisition program achieved its first goal in April 2010 when the Judaic Art Gallery moved to an expansive (1,152 square feet) gallery in the NCMA's new West Building. The design is spare and flexible, allowing the uncluttered display of more than seventy objects in custom-made glass cases. Skylights bathe the gallery with filtered natural light. In 2015 the gallery expanded into an adjacent space, increasing its footprint to 1,728 square feet—more than twice the size of the original Judaic Art Gallery.

The new iteration of the gallery was divided into three spaces, separated by translucent textile scrims imprinted with a charming detail of the Kanof daughters from a prayer book cover by Ilya Schor in the collection. The first space provides an introduction and features a selection of visually impressive objects, such as a large standing Hanukkah lamp for an Eastern European synagogue and a Baroque Venetian Torah crown. The second space displays objects used in the observance of the Sabbath and other holidays and festivals, as well as objects related to events marking the life cycle from birth to burial. The third space is devoted to the art of the synagogue, especially ornamental objects to enshrine and adorn the Torah. The focus of the gallery—positioned at the end of the gallery's long central axis (thus affirming its importance)—is a pedimented "Ark" case presenting a group of three "mannequin Torahs," each dressed in a historically accurate facsimile mantle on which are displayed ensembles of ornaments from modern Israel, Enlightenment Amsterdam, and early twentieth-century North Carolina.[29] Following traditional practice, the colors of the mantles are changed seasonally.

Conceptually, the Judaic Art Gallery occupies a resonant position within the NCMA. Even though, of course, the objects are Jewish in content, they have meaningful affinities with works of art across the museum's collection through ritual, history, and aesthetics. The Judaic objects make up the NCMA's only significant decorative arts collection, offering superb examples, of metalsmithing in particular, that complement the European, American, and modern art in other galleries. Moreover, the Judaic art collection embraces cultures and geographic regions not otherwise represented in the museum, for example, Eastern Europe and Asia.

Integral to the experience of the gallery is an interpretive program offering the visitor multiple ways to engage with the objects. Because most visitors are not Jewish and are presumed to have only passing familiarity with Judaism and its ritual observance, wall panels explain the principal holidays and festivals and the decoration of the synagogue and Torah scroll. Individual labels touch on various aspects of the object, such as its specific ritual use, iconography, artistic style, or provenance. Translations of most Hebrew inscriptions are provided. Volunteer docents receive special training in Jewish history, culture, and ceremonial life.

Public programming features family-oriented activities centered on holidays and a popular Purim celebration hosted by the Friends of the Judaic Art Gallery and open to the local Jewish community. The annual Abram and Frances Pascher Kanof Lecture, endowed by the Kanof-Levine family, presents substantive programs by national and international scholars and curators on subjects of special interest to the Jewish community. In recent years the NCMA has forged strong relationships with area colleges and universities, and undergraduate and graduate students receive object-based training in the Judaic Art Gallery. In 2018 the NCMA and the Carolina Center for Jewish Studies of the University of North Carolina at Chapel Hill co-organized the important national symposium "Wandering Objects: Collecting and Interpreting Jewish Things."

The NCMA proudly embraces the Judaic Art Gallery as an extraordinary aesthetic, intellectual, and spiritual experience and as a venue for religious and cultural understanding. Among the Jewish communities in the state and the southeast, the gallery is also a source of pride, hope, and renewal. The museum strikingly demonstrated its sympathy with the state's Jewish citizens by its response to the tragic shooting at the Tree of Life synagogue in Pittsburgh in 2018. Arriving on Monday after the incident, the museum's staff paused in their work to relocate to the main entrance the eighteenth-century Hanukkah lamp, made for an Eastern European synagogue and formerly owned by a Pittsburgh family.[30] Marking the place of the missing lamp, they pinned to the gallery wall a sable cloth, ripped in grief.

From modest beginnings in the late 1970s, the Judaic Art Gallery has evolved into—arguably—the most visible expression of Jewish culture in the South. In the two decades since Abram Kanof's death, the collection has been thoughtfully and patiently nurtured to elevate the overall artistic quality of the objects and to extend the range of stories told.[31] Frequently, acquisitions have addressed both needs. Purchased in 2017, an early eighteenth-century Torah crown, made in Venice for a synagogue in Mantua, not only exemplifies the height of baroque design and artisanry but also testifies to the cultural prestige and brilliance of the Italian Jewish community at that time.

Having nothing to represent the rituals attendant on death and dying, the NCMA acquired in 2019 a magnificent ceremonial beaker from the Darmstadt Burial Society.[32] Made in Augsburg in the early eighteenth century and engraved with the names and personal emblems of successive generations of society members, this beaker possesses an imposing presence and an equally engaging history, having descended in a Darmstadt rabbinic family and spirited out of Germany in the wake of Kristallnacht. The crown and the beaker, objects of supreme artistry, dignity, and spiritual presence, affirm the museum's aspirations for the Judaic art collection.

John Coffey retired from the NCMA in January 2021, and Gabriel Goldstein assumed interim curatorial responsibilities for the Judaic art program. As part of a museum-wide reinstallation of the permanent collection, the Judaic Art Gallery was moved to a more prominent location within the suite of European art galleries. This, the gallery's fourth iteration, opened in October 2022. The new layout of the gallery generally adheres to the previous design but with more in-depth interpretation and the addition of such new acquisitions as a pair of Torah finials, the epitome of Georgian elegance, from the workshop of Hester Bateman, the preeminent woman silversmith in eighteenth-century London.

The onset of COVID provided the incentive—really, the imperative—for greater outreach and connection to a more diverse community. Perhaps the most successful new venture is the annual online Freedom Seder, which presents Passover as a universal celebration of the human spirit available to all. Religious and civic leaders from across North Carolina come together to share the importance of renewal, storytelling, community, and social action. If any program points the way forward for the NCMA's Judaic Art Gallery, it is the Freedom Seder.

In 2023—a half-century after the opening of the Judaic Art Gallery—the director and trustees of the NCMA reaffirmed their commitment to the gallery by establishing a permanent curatorial position to oversee the future development of the gallery and its programs. In July 2023 Sean P. Burrus

FIGURE 7.4. Torah crown, attributed to Zuanne Cottini (Italian, Venice, active 1682–1736), early eighteenth century; silver with gilded silver attachments; height, 9 in. (22.9 cm), diameter, 8⅝ in. (21.9 cm). Gift of Steven and Lisa Feierstein in memory of their forebears; Ugo Goetzl and family in memory of Alberto and Amalia Goetzl and Arrigo and Itala Ravenna of Trieste, Italy; Elaine Sandman; Jennifer and Andrew Sandman; Dana and Scott Gorelick; Barry Sandman; and Lisa and Michael Sandman, 2017 (2017.1).

FIGURE 7.5. Judaic Art Gallery, 2022. Photo: North Carolina Museum of Art.

was appointed curator of Judaic art. Although the new curator faces the challenge of piloting the gallery through a turbulent social and cultural landscape, the promise of the Judaic Art Gallery has never been brighter.

Fifty years ago the NCMA's Judaic Art Gallery was alone among American art museums. Today a growing number of museums have begun to actively collect and exhibit Jewish ceremonial art. And this is perhaps Abram Kanof's most enduring legacy.

Notes

For a close reading and critique of this text, I am grateful to Gabriel M. Goldstein and Roger M. Berkowitz, my constant advisers in all things Judaic. For assistance in research, I wish to thank Natalia Lonchyna and Erin Rutherford, formerly of the NCMA's Art Reference Library.

1 The sources for this biographical summary are the curriculum vitae of Abram Kanof, Miscellaneous Kanof Papers, North Carolina Museum of Art Archives; Library and Archives of the American Jewish Historical

Society, "Oral History Interviews with Abram Kanof"; and Norden, "Dr. Abram Kanof."
2 Kanof, "Days of Stress," 486.
3 Although not technically the chairman of the Jewish Museum's board of trustees, which was not constituted until 1963, Kanof was chairman of the Museum Committee and Administrative Council as well as a member of the Judaica Acquisitions Committee and the Education Committee.
4 Kanof, *Jewish Ceremonial Art*, 48.
5 The founding director of the Tobe Pascher Workshop was the German Israeli metalsmith Ludwig Y. Wolpert (1900–1981). Wolpert was succeeded in 1981 by his Israeli protégé, Moshe Zabari (b. 1935). The workshop closed in 1988.
6 The Kanofs were also avid collectors of modern American art. Through their friend Edith Halpert of the Downtown Gallery, New York, they acquired Jacob Lawrence's *In the Garden* (1950), a pivotal work in the artist's career, donated to the NCMA in 2020 by the Kanofs' daughter and son-in-law.
7 In addition to Kanof, *Jewish Ceremonial Art*, see Kanof, *Jewish Symbolic Art*.
8 Library and Archives of the American Jewish Historical Society, "Oral History Interviews," 30–33. Later in the interview, Kanof expressed equal pride in his election as the first president of the American Jewish Historical Society who was not a historian (46).
9 A major impetus for expanding the boundaries of the NCMA's collection came from industrialist and philanthropist Gordon Hanes of Winston-Salem. A longtime member of the museum's Board of Trustees, Hanes was chiefly responsible for the NCMA's collections of Egyptian, Classical, African, Ancient American, and Oceanic art by donating objects from his own collection and providing purchase funds. Hanes was a strong supporter of Kanof's project and in 1980 contributed the funds to purchase a Polish Torah crown (80.6.1).
10 Chenkin, "Jewish Population in the United States, 1973," 305. For an excellent historical overview of Jews in North Carolina see Rogoff, *Down Home*.
11 Ruth R. Julian of Winston-Salem and Jeanne G. Rauch, wife of State Senator Marshall Rauch of Gastonia.

12 "Biennial Report," 14.
13 Wood, "Jewish Ceremonial Art Show," V12. Wood's conclusion was seconded by the Greensboro *Daily News*, which ran a story with the headline "Jewish People Do Have Art Tradition" (*Daily News*, June 1, 1975, B12).
14 By comparison, the preceding exhibition of "American Impressionist Painting"—a crowd-pleasing topic—attracted 12,419 visitors (NCMA Archives).
15 Minutes of the Quarterly Meeting of the Art Commission, March 13, 1975, NCMA Archives. Curiously, in his oral history interviews, Kanof credited North Carolina governor James Holshouser with the idea of establishing a permanent collection of Judaica. Impressed by the exhibition, the governor reportedly told Kanof, "This [exhibition] has been a very nice thing for us. Why don't we have a permanent collection?" (Library and Archives of the American Jewish Historical Society, "Oral History Interviews," 47). Given that acquisition funds were raised before the exhibition opened, the gubernatorial suggestion would have only accelerated the project.
16 Kanof also included a miscellaneous category for archeological artifacts and nonceremonial works of art of Jewish subjects.
17 Among the venues were the Fayetteville Art Museum (July 25–August 23, 1975), St. John's Museum of Art, Wilmington (August 31–September 28, 1975), the Gaston County Art and History Museum, Dallas (October 9–November 6, 1978), the Mint Museum of History, Charlotte (April 3–May 20, 1979), and the Mendenhall Student Center, East Carolina University, Greenville (February 1–28, 1980).
18 The number included five minor objects accessioned as a study collection.
19 https://ncartmuseum.org/object/passover-seder-plate-with-four-dishes/. The NCMA's collection now has eight works by Wolpert, sixteen by Zabari, and three by Schor.
20 Kanof, *Guide to the Judaic Art Collection*.
21 At the time of the gallery's opening, Kanof announced that "we're going to add slowly to the collection because pieces added have to be the best, only the best quality" (Burch, "Surprise Gifts," 6A.) In fact, only five objects were added to the collection from the time the gallery opened to Kanof's death in 1999.

22 On more than one occasion, Kanof told me how much he enjoyed giving tours to Baptist church groups because "they know their Bible!"
23 The Friends of Judaic Art also served a valuable advocacy role within and without the NCMA, but its overriding purpose was to underwrite an aggressive acquisitions program. Founding chairs of the Friends were Dr. Elizabeth Kanof Levine, daughter of Abram Kanof, and JoAnn Pizer-Fox, both of Raleigh. Pizer-Fox was later succeeded by Sue R. Finkel, also of Raleigh.
24 The decision to focus on Judaica from the seventeenth century forward was pragmatic: Fine pieces from earlier periods are vanishingly rare and prohibitively expensive.
25 https://ncartmuseum.org/object/standing-hanukkah-lamp/.
26 https://ncartmuseum.org/object/torah-shield-3/.
27 https://ncartmuseum.org/object/torah-case-with-finials-and-pointer/.
28 Segal: https://ncartmuseum.org/object/hanukkah-lamp-3/. Tutnauer: https://ncartmuseum.org/object/passover-seder-plate/; https://ncartmuseum.org/object/spice-container-5/. Srulovitch: https://ncartmuseum.org/object/torah-shield-4/; https://ncartmuseum.org/object/torah-crown-and-pointer/.
29 The North Carolina Torah ornaments—finials, shield, and pointer—were likely made by immigrant silversmiths, probably in New York, for the congregation of Temple Oheb Sholom in Goldsboro. The second oldest synagogue in the state, Oheb Sholom is now inactive.
30 https://ncartmuseum.org/object/standing-hanukkah-lamp-for-a-synagogue/.
31 As with all its collections, the NCMA periodically reviews the existing Judaic art collection. A comprehensive review in 2017 identified fifty-two accessioned items that were deemed inappropriate to the collection for reasons of quality, condition, or authenticity. As a result, fourteen objects were transferred to the Carolina Center for Jewish Studies at the University of North Carolina, Chapel Hill, to be used for teaching purposes. Additional pieces were donated to other North Carolina museums and educational institutions, and one object—a Moroccan *kettubah* with later, spurious additions—was donated for study purposes to the Jewish Theological Seminary in New York. Other objects judged to be inauthentic (i.e., pastiches or forgeries) were permanently sequestered. The remaining objects were sold at public auctions and the proceeds applied to future purchases of Judaic art.

32 https://ncartmuseum.org/object/ceremonial-beaker-of-the-darmstadt-burial-society/.

Bibliography

"Biennial Report, July 1, 1973–June 30, 1975." *North Carolina Museum of Art Bulletin* 13, no. 3 (1976).

Burch, Mary. "Surprise Gifts Enrich Jewish Art Collection in N.C." *News and Observer*, December 17, 1983, p. 6A.

Chenkin, Alvin. "Jewish Population in the United States, 1973." *American Jewish Year Book* 75 (1974–75): 295–313.

Kanof, Abram. "Days of Stress—Days of Progress." *American Jewish History* 71 (1982): 486–92.

———. *A Guide to the Judaic Art Collection of the North Carolina Museum of Art*. Raleigh: North Carolina Museum of Art, 1996.

———. *Jewish Ceremonial Art and Religious Observance*. New York: Abrams, 1970.

———. *Jewish Symbolic Art*. Jerusalem: Gefen, 1990.

Library and Archives of the American Jewish Historical Society, Philadelphia. "Oral History Interviews with Abram Kanof, 1990–1992." Transcript. search.cjh.org/primo-explore/fulldisplay?docid=CJH_ALEPH005519660&context=L&vid=beta&lang=en_US&search_scope=AJHS&adaptor=Local%20Search%20Engine&tab=default_tab&query=any,contains,Kanof&sortby=rank&mode=simple.

Norden, Margaret Kanof. "Dr. Abram Kanof, 1903–1999." *American Jewish History* 87 (March 1999): 95–96.

Rogoff, Leonard. *Down Home: Jewish Life in North Carolina*. Chapel Hill: University of North Carolina Press, 2010.

Wood, Ernie. "Jewish Ceremonial Art Show Opens Today at State Museum." *News and Observer* (Raleigh, NC), April 27, 1975, p. V12.

Part III

JEWISH THINGS UP CLOSE: TWO SOUTHERN STUDIES

8

SANCTIFIED BY WAR

A Tale of Two Silver Bowls

Dale Rosengarten

Wandering objects—the theme of a symposium staged by the North Carolina Museum of Art and the Carolina Center for Jewish Studies in November 2018—provides a perfect frame for the two silver bowls I profile here. As these bowls traveled, their trajectories followed the history of their era: specifically, the upheavals of the American Civil War. One bowl began its career in England, was carried to Charleston, South Carolina, and gifted ceremonially to a synagogue, and then taken to Columbia for safekeeping, where apparently it was looted and transported out of state, showing up a century later in an antiques store in Connecticut. The other bowl was a prized object thrown down a well by an enslaved girl named Rachael when Union general Benjamin Franklin Butler's men were raiding Confederate houses in New Orleans.

Sanctified by war and personal sacrifice, the vessels ascended over time to the status of sacred relics. The stories that spin out from their journeys reveal key aspects of the antebellum Southern Jewish experience: the degree of assimilation of elite (silver-owning) Southern Jews, their complicity in the system of racial slavery, and their steadfast adherence to the Lost Cause, a belief system which holds that the South fought a just fight to save an ethical way of life. The bowls became—at least for a period—shining emblems of this fictional version of the past, without reference to the enslavement and terror that created the region's wealth.

The first bowl went missing sometime after February 17, 1865, the date when Union forces occupied Columbia, South Carolina's state capital.

The small silver object, property of Charleston's historic Kahal Kadosh Beth Elohim, had been sent there along with the congregation's Torah, candelabra, pipe organ, and other valuables. In one of the great miscalculations of the war, many South Carolinians believed that the Yankees would come up the coast and attack Charleston. Instead, General William Tecumseh Sherman and his troops crossed the Savannah River and turned inland toward Columbia. In the conflagration and chaos that ensued, a great deal of real and personal property went up in smoke or was carried off as spoils of war.

The other silver bowl narrowly avoided falling into the hands of the enemy and becoming contraband. An inscribed silver chalice, given by the Louisiana Pilots Association to Edwin Warren Moïse, a prominent Jewish legislator in New Orleans, was thrown down a well by a slave belonging to the family when she saw the Bluecoats coming. Moïse's youngest son, Warren Hubert, declared it "the only piece of silver that escaped the Butler gang,"[1] a reference to General "Beast" Butler, who added the nickname "Spoons Butler" to his moniker after he seized a thirty-eight-piece set of silverware from a woman trying to cross Union lines[2] and perhaps as an allusion to the widespread perception that Butler condoned his troops' looting of household goods from treasonous New Orleanians. Recovered after the Confederate surrender, the slightly dented bowl today occupies a place of pride in the family pantheon.

How many thousands of silver objects have had similar journeys? How many pairs of candlesticks were buried in backyards, how many platters hidden under the hoop skirts of dutiful daughters or faithful servants, how many coins sewn into the hem of a garment or secreted in a hat band?

Many tales of silver hidden from the Yankees are apocryphal, but the destinies of these two bowls can be verified, and because the protagonists were *Jewish* Southerners, they lend themselves to interpretation in the context of that dual identity. Silver has been associated for millennia with things of the spirit. When material wealth symbolized by gold had all but disappeared by the end of the war, silver was a consolation against the loss of real and movable property and social dislocations.

The first bowl might more accurately be described as a basket or pail: a small filigree container, 6 inches tall and 4½ inches in diameter, with a pedestal foot and hinged handle. Fabricated in 1777 by London silversmith David Bell, it was intended for use as a sugar or sweetmeat bowl and was

FIGURE 8.1. Sugar or sweetmeat bowl, David Bell (active 1752–79), inscribed "Presented to the cong: Beth Elohim By Joshua Lazarus, AM 5601"; London, ca. 1777; silver; 6 × 4½ inches. Kahal Kadosh Beth Elohim, College of Charleston.

most likely lined with blue glass. In 1841, in commemoration of a new sanctuary constructed in the aftermath of the Great Fire of 1838 that destroyed the 1794 synagogue, the object was given to Beth Elohim by Joshua Lazarus, chair of the building committee.[3] Lazarus may have bought the bowl on one of his trips abroad, or it may have been passed down by the family of his English wife, Phebe Yates. On the basket's cartouche he had his name and the date of the gift engraved—5601, according to the Hebrew calendar.

Nothing is known about where the sugar bowl was kept or what role it played in the synagogue. The inscription of the Hebrew date marks it as a Jewish object, but the congregation's "Inventory of Silver ware" compiled on May 9, 1862, describes it simply as "One Silver Basket presented by Joshua Lazarus AM 5601," weighing in at 8 ounces. Among the twenty items packed in a "Box marked K.K.BE" were objects of Judaica—a silver *rimonim* and five pairs of bells (two octagonal, two round, and one fancy), "One wine Goblet," "One pointer"—as well as less sacred articles, such as "One Silver Comb," "3 Sets of 5 Needles each," and "2 Tin Tubes, containing Sundry papers."[4]

When the silver basket vanished, the loss was blamed, predictably, on General Sherman. Where it spent the next century is anyone's guess, but in the early 1960s it was purchased from an antiques store in Connecticut by Samuel and Esther Schwartz, collectors from Paterson, New Jersey. Mrs. Schwartz promptly wrote to Beth Elohim's rebbetzin, Jane Lazarus Raisin, asking whether there were records pertaining to Lazarus's gift. In 1964 the Schwartzes visited Charleston to attend a meeting of the American Jewish Historical Society, and there they met Jack Patla, custodian of the Beth Elohim archives, silver expert, and antiques dealer, who confirmed the basket's identification from a photograph. The inscription on the cartouche made it easy.

Two decades later, Patla reminded Beth Elohim's rabbi, William A. Rosenthall—a voracious collector of Judaica himself—to inquire again about the basket. Rosenthall did, "with the happy result that the latter-day owner of the precious antebellum gift . . . has generously and sensitively returned the basket to the congregation."[5] At this point Schwartz, Patla, and Rabbi Rosenthall traded speculations about the possibility that the basket—which Jack now called "the Civil War basket"—could have been used as an *etrog* container, a receptacle for the Sukkot citron, or as "a holder for a lulov."[6] Esther Schwartz sent a picture from a book on Czech

Sanctified by War 223

FIGURE 8.2. *Joshua Lazarus*, Amélie Dautel D'Aubigny (ca. 1796–1861), France, ca. 1840; watercolor on ivory; 5 × 3¾ inches. Gift of Mrs. Edgar M. Lazarus. Carolina Art Association/Gibbes Museum of Art.

Judaic treasures showing a filigree silver *etrog* container, from Vienna, 1807, and underlined the text: "Etrog holders take many forms; some are simple adaptations of preexisting containers. In German lands, silver sugar boxes were often used."[7] This process of adaptive reuse would have been even more pronounced in nineteenth-century North American communities, where locally made Judaica was scarce and secular objects were commonly appropriated for religious purposes. Whether the basket ever had a ritual use or not, it has been worshiped—not too strong a word!—since its return from captivity and occupies a prime spot in the synagogue museum, where visitors can marvel at its travels and near miraculous recovery.

If the idea of return—or of loss averted—accounts for much of the aura surrounding Beth Elohim's basket, it emphatically drives the tale of the second silver bowl under consideration, a simple trophy elevated to the heights of hallowed heirloom. The footed and inscribed silver cup, 5⅞ inches high and 8¾ inches in diameter, was presented by the powerful Louisiana Pilots Association to E. Warren Moïse in appreciation for his legal work, possibly in 1853 when Moïse was speaker of the state's House of Representatives. We do not know what Moïse did to win the Pilots Association's gratitude, but it was sufficient to warrant the purchase of a bowl from Kuchler & Himmel—German-born silversmiths Christopf Christian Küchler (b. 1820) and Adolphe Himmel (1826–77), who formed a short-lived partnership in New Orleans in 1852 and made silver pieces for the retail firm Hyde and Goodrich.[8]

What we can tell from a physical thing is complemented by what we can learn about its context and movements from other sources. Both of our bowls are inscribed, for starters, and because silversmiths mark their wares, we can establish their early history: when they were made, by whom, where, what they were meant to commemorate, and so on. But to glimpse the lived life of the object, we rely on corollary resources, such as letters that Warren Hubert Moïse wrote to his nephew Edwin Warren Moïse (there was an Edwin Warren in every generation), whom he had entrusted with the family's history and lore.

The bowl, in weight "no more, probably, than an ordinary golf cup," was used by the Moïses for fruit or desserts, but it is the story of its rescue that gives it significance. The hero of the hour, Rachael, was a young woman assigned as nurse to baby Warren Hubert, born in 1864. Later in life, Hubert, as he was called, recounted his father's version of events.

> [Rachael] saw the squad of soldiers drive up in the dump cart; she knew they were after the silver. She was frightened & started towards the back of the house & in passing the dining room she saw the bowl on the sideboard. "I just grab[b]ed it & ran in the yard & threw it in the well." On hearing this Papa had the well cleaned out & in the muck at the bottom was found the bowl.

FIGURE 8.3. *Edwin Warren Moïse*, Theodore Sidney Moïse (1808–85), ca. 1856; oil on canvas; 48 × 36 inches. Collection of the Bierwirth family. Photo by David Kelly Crow, courtesy of Princeton University Library.

The story was not over. In fact, for Hubert it was just beginning: "Then it was he gave it to me as my nurse had saved it. Ever since it has been known as my property & no one ever questioned my title to it."[9] Because Rachael was Hubert's nurse, according to the ethics and rules of the peculiar institution, the bounty of her good deed belonged to him!

But why have these particular objects become iconic? What about them makes them *Jewish*? What do they tell us about the nature of *Southern* things?

If Beth Elohim's basket was ever used as an *etrog* container, its claim as Judaica would be affirmed, but at this point that is pure speculation. Rather, its ceremonial importance lies in its association with the 1841 dedication of the new synagogue, a historic occasion at which Rev. Gustavus Poznanski delivered his famous "this happy land" speech marking the ascendency of the Reform faction and proclaiming that Charleston's Jews had reached "our *Palestine*" (no need to look elsewhere) and promising that "their sons" would defend "*this* temple, *this* city, and *this* land."[10] The saga of the basket turns into a tale of redemption, the reversal of loss, appealing to people on both sides of the Mason-Dixon line. Here was a mundane object endowed with reverential importance, stolen as booty in the Civil War, repatriated by a Jewish couple from New Jersey, and returned to its rightful abode in Charleston.

What can we say is Jewish about the Moïse bowl? Descended from a Jewish family that had fled St. Domingue in the West Indies when a slave rebellion broke out in 1791, E. W. Moïse was not religiously observant, as far as we know, once he had settled in New Orleans. However, it can be said that he came from a religiously active family in Charleston. His aunt Penina Moïse and his uncle Abraham Moïse II became leaders of the first movement to reform Judaism in America. Warren and his older brother, the artist Theodore Sidney Moïse, both married Jewish women from Charleston. Both brothers moved away, first to Mississippi and then to New Orleans. Both wives bore children but died young. The brothers married again, this time to devout Catholics who gave birth to many more children. Theodore Sidney's wife, Matilde Vaughn, produced nine offspring in twelve years; Edwin Warren's wife, Louise Hubert, bore ten children and also raised the two who survived from his first marriage, treating them as her own, their youngest sibling, Hubert, remembered, except "they were brought up as jewesses 'as their mother would have wished.'"[11]

I read the inscribed chalice as symbolic of the degree to which Jews from South Carolina had integrated into the social order of Louisiana, reaching high rungs on the ladder of power and prestige. This peculiarity of the state's politics did not go unnoticed at the time. For example, William Howard Russell, a *London Times* correspondent and author of *My Diary*

North and South, remarked on Louisiana's "preponderance and influence of South Carolinian Jews, and Jews generally, such as [Edwin Warren] Moïse, Mordecai, Josephs, and Judah Benjamin, and others. . . . The Governor is supposed to be somewhat under the influence of the Hebrews."[12]

Salomon de Rothschild of the Parisian branch of the renowned banking family, after meeting Benjamin, Moïse, and Louisiana's lieutenant governor Henry Hyams in New Orleans shortly before the Civil War, was surprised not only by their lofty stature but also by the tenacity of their Jewish identity: "What is astonishing here is the high position occupied by our coreligionists, or rather by those who were born into the faith and who, having married Christian women, and without converting, have forgotten the practices of their fathers." Yet he recognized them, and they saw themselves, as Jews: "What is odd, all these men have a Jewish heart and take an interest in me, because I represent the greatest Jewish house in the world."[13]

To Russell and Rothschild, Moïse personified a thoroughly assimilated Jew, an aspiring and ambitious politician, and a Southerner, who merged the elements of his character in a pragmatic balance. Initially a reluctant secessionist, E. Warren Moïse was appointed, in April 1861, a district judge of the Confederate States of America—perhaps President Jefferson Davis's first judicial appointment—with jurisdiction over Mississippi, Louisiana, Arkansas, and Texas.[14] He sold all his securities and invested the proceeds in Confederate bonds, rendered worthless by the South's defeat. He died, broke and broken, just four years after the war. No wonder the trophy Moïse passed on to young Hubert became such a prize—symbolizing everything the family had lost, including its patriarch.[15]

Notes

This chapter is based on an essay that appeared in "Southern Things," a special issue of *Southern Cultures* 23, no. 3 (fall 2017), edited by Bernie Herman (Chapel Hill: University of North Carolina Press for the Center for the Study of the American South), 47–53. Revised for book publication, 2022.

1 Warren Hubert Moïse (1864–1939) to E. W. Moïse (1889–1961), September 7, 1933, Warren Hubert Moïse Letters, Mss. 1132, Gift of Marion Moïse Bierwirth, Special Collections, College of Charleston Library.

Accessible on the Lowcountry Digital Library at Warren Hubert Moise Letters, 1933–1939.
2 Orcutt, "Ben Butler"; Hearn, *When the Devil Came down to Dixie*.
3 For more on Joshua Lazarus, see T. Rosengarten and Rosengarten, *A Portion of the People*, 86–87. For more on the construction and dedication of Beth Elohim's new temple, see Breibart, "Synagogues of Kahal Kadosh Beth Elohim."
4 "Inventory of Silver ware etc. belonging to Beth Elohim Congregation and contained in Box marked K.K.BE," Charleston, May 9, 1862, Special Collections, College of Charleston, Kahal Kadosh Beth Elohim congregational records, Mss. 1047, Box 40, https://lcdl.library.cofc.edu/lcdl/catalog/255033.
5 Rosenthall, "Treasure Returns to Charleston."
6 Correspondence (1964–87) with donor and others re: return of KKBE [Kahal Kadosh Beth Elohim] silver dish looted in Civil War, Special Collections, College of Charleston Library, Kahal Kadosh Beth Elohim congregational records, Mss. 1047, Box 64, Folder 8.
7 Altshuler, *Precious Legacy*, 185.
8 Rainwater and Redfield, *Encyclopedia of American Silver Manufacturers*, 153, 187.
9 W. H. Moïse to E. W. Moïse, September 7, 1933, Warren Hubert Moïse Letters.
10 Dedicatory speech at the consecration of Kahal Kadosh Beth Elohim, "The Rebuilding of the Temple," *Charleston Courier*, March 20, 1841. See also Hagy, *This Happy Land*, 246; and Breibart, "Synagogues of Kahal Kadosh Beth Elohim," 224. Poznanski's words were prophetic: His son, Gustavus Poznanski Jr., at age nineteen, was killed in the Battle of Secessionville on James Island, South Carolina, on June 21, 1862. See Rosengarten and Rosengarten, eds. *A Portion of the People*, 93.
11 W. H. Moïse to E. W. Moïse, October 21, 1933, Warren Hubert Moïse Letters, Mss. 1132, Gift of Marion Moïse Bierwirth, Special Collections, College of Charleston Library. For more on the Moïse family, see D. Rosengarten, "Portrait of Two Painters," 142–61; and Moïse, *Moïse Family of South Carolina*.
12 Russell, *My Diary*, 242, quoted in Rosen, *Jewish Confederates*, 23.
13 Marcus, *Memoirs of American Jews*, 104. See also Evans, *The Provincials*, 61–63.

14 W. H. Moïse to E. W. Moïse, July 12, 1933, Warren Hubert Moïse Letters, Mss. 1132, Gift of Marion Moïse Bierwirth, Special Collections, College of Charleston Library.

15 In recent years many scholars of Jewish history, culture, and literature have turned their attention to exploring the role of objects and spaces as containers and expressions of Jewish life, history, meaning, and culture. Among the most provocative are Diner, *Roads Taken*; Fromm, *Material Culture*; Kirshenblatt-Gimblett, "Objects of Memory"; Leibman, *Art of the Jewish Family*; Rabinowitz, "Reader's Reflections"; and Schwenger, *Tears of Things*.

Bibliography

Altshuler, David, ed., *The Precious Legacy: Judaic Treasures from the Czechoslovak State Collections*. New York: Summit, 1983.

Breibart, Solomon. "The Synagogues of Kahal Kadosh Beth Elohim, Charleston." *South Carolina Historical Magazine* 80, no. 3 (1979): 215–35.

Diner, Hasia R. *Roads Taken: The Great Jewish Migrations to the New World and the Peddlers Who Forged the Way*. New Haven, CT: Yale University Press, 2015.

Evans, Eli N. *The Provincials: A Personal History of Jews in the South*, rev. ed. University of North Carolina Press, 2005 [1973].

Fromm, Ken Kolten. *Material Culture and Jewish Thought in America*. Bloomington: Indiana University Press, 2010.

Hagy, James William Hagy, *This Happy Land: The Jews of Colonial and Antebellum Charleston*. Tuscaloosa: University of Alabama Press, 1993.

Hearn, Chester G. *When the Devil Came down to Dixie: Ben Butler in New Orleans*. Baton Rouge: Louisiana State University Press, 1997.

Kirshenblatt-Gimblett, Barbara. "Objects of Memory: Material Culture as Life Review." In *Folk Groups and Folklore Genres: A Reader*, ed. Elliott Oring, 329–38. Logan: Utah State University Press, 1989.

Leibman, Laura Arnold. *The Art of the Jewish Family: A History of Women in Early New York in Five Objects*. New York: Bard Graduate Center, 2020.

Marcus, Jacob Radar. *Memoirs of American Jews (1775–1865)*, vol. 3. Philadelphia: Jewish Publication Society of America, 1956.

Moïse, Harold. *The Moïse Family of South Carolina*. Columbia, SC: R. L. Bryan, 1961.

Orcutt, William Dana. "Ben Butler and the 'Stolen Spoons.'" *North American Review* 207, no. 746 (January 1918): 66–80.

Rabinowitz, Richard. "A Reader's Reflections." In *Curating America: Journeys through the Storyscapes of the American Past*, by Richard Rabinowitz, 337–60. Chapel Hill: North Carolina University Press, 2016.

Rainwater, Dorothy T., and Judy Redfield. *Encyclopedia of American Silver Manufacturers*. Atglen, PA: Schiffer, 1998.

Rosen, Robert N. *The Jewish Confederates*. Columbia: University of South Carolina Press, 2000.

Rosengarten, Dale. "Portrait of Two Painters: The Work of Theodore Sidney Moïse and Solomon Nunes Carvalho." In *By Dawn's Early Light: Jewish Contributions to American Culture from the Nation's Founding to the Civil War*, ed. Adam D. Mendelsohn, 138–87. Princeton, NJ: Princeton University Library, 2016.

Rosengarten, Theodore, and Dale Rosengarten, eds. *A Portion of the People: Three Hundred Years of Southern Jewish Life*. Columbia: University of South Carolina Press, in association with McKissick Museum, 2002.

Rosenthall, William A. "A Treasure Returns to Charleston." *News and Courier / Evening Post* (Charleston, SC), January 25, 1987.

Russell, William Howard. *My Diary North and South*. Essex, MA: T. O. H. P. Burnham, 1863.

Schwenger, Peter. *The Tears of Things: Melancholy and Physical Objects*. Minneapolis: University of Minnesota Press, 2006.

9

MY GRANDFATHER'S WEST TEXAS SALVAGE STORE

Prophetic Lessons for Twenty-First-Century Museums

Suzanne Seriff

I am a third-generation Jewish Texan. I have a photograph on my desk of myself and my big sister, around three and five years old, standing in matching dresses with my Grandma Honey on the front porch of my grandparents' house at 1010 East Broadway, in Sweetwater, Texas. It's the late 1950s. My mom is sitting behind us on the porch swing, smoking a Kent filtered cigarette and telling stories. My gaze lingers on this photo today as I contemplate my career as a museum curator and academic folklorist. I am one of the lucky ones whose professional and personal lives have coalesced around interlocking passions: my love for the art of a well-crafted story and the stories behind well-crafted arts. I would go further to claim that it is not just the craft behind the story, or the story behind the things, but the ethical lessons embedded within and through them that have fueled my interests all these years. I am convinced that I developed this hunger for uncovering and exhibiting stories, objects, and matters of conscience, at least in part, from those early summer days visiting my grandparents, where my grandfather—Abraham Isaac Berman (A. I. for short)—owned a secondhand salvage store on West First Street in downtown Sweetwater, in the heart of West Texas.

In what follows I try to weave together the lessons I learned from those early years scouting treasures and listening to tales in my grandfather's secondhand store with my career as a museum curator of object-based

FIGURE 9.1. Suzanne Seriff with her sister, mother, and Grandma Honey at 1010 East Broadway, Sweetwater, Texas. Photo by Aaron J. Seriff.

"issues of conscience." I explore four major museum projects that I have directed or guest-curated over the course of my career and try to tease out both the larger meanings and the motivations that guided my work. My grandfather's store—and the lessons for living narrated through the secondhand objects that found their way there—becomes a kind of metaphor for what I have come to see as a particularly Jewish take on object-based storytelling, recycling, questioning, and risk taking, which are recurring themes in my work. I would argue that these same themes also characterize a potentially revolutionary framework for understanding museums as fertile third spaces for civic engagement in the twenty-first century.

In making this perhaps grandiose claim about the prophetic lessons for twenty-first-century museums nestled amid the junk of a first-generation Jewish Texan's salvage store, I draw on the powerful work of a growing number of contemporary scholars who have similarly explored the radical potential behind the Jewishness of such object-based epistemologies.[1] For them—and for me—the materiality of Jewish thought, the almost sacred reverence toward Jewish "trash" and repurposed items, the generational transmission of object-based lessons, and even the biblical roots of Jewish risk taking all point to an approach toward material culture as a logical catalyst for the most profound forms of ethical struggle, engagement, and dialogue about pressing issues of importance in our lives and our world. Even my use of personal memory as a jumping-off point for theoretical reverie owes an intellectual debt of gratitude to several brilliant colleagues in Jewish studies who also fuse personal narrative about their love of things with intellectual explorations on the Jewishness behind the ethical and affective value of things.[2] And the claim about the potential Jewish lessons for twenty-first-century museum practice, as I will attempt to tease out more fully in this essay, directly cycles back to the powerful discussions on Jewish third spaces held during the "Wandering Objects" symposium in the fall of 2018.

So, back to the scene of my intellectual awakening.

From Trash to Treasure: A Granddaughter's Reverie

Early in the twentieth century my grandfather journeyed halfway around the world from revolution-torn Lithuania to the remote West Texas town of Sweetwater, thus ultimately finding freedom in this tumbleweed-tossed haven of fewer than ten thousand people, fueled by cotton, cattle, and oil and gas production. It was here that he made his home, raised a family, and, like so many Jewish immigrant businessmen throughout the American South of that time, opened a retail store where he sold work clothes and school clothes, yard goods and notions, and animal feed and grocery staples to the townspeople and those of the surrounding farm and ranch lands.[3] This was not the secondhand salvage store that I knew as a child but a prosperous business with new merchandise, which he bought on credit from major vendors around the country and sold at a slight profit to his loyal clientele. His was not the only Jewish-owned store in this Bible Belt town, although the Levy Brothers Department Store (formerly known as the Sweetwater Dry Goods Company) across from the Nolan County Courthouse was in a whole different league—selling fancy East Coast women's and men's clothing and luxury goods that catered to the elite of West Texas, where cotton, oil, and cattle provided a level of prosperity for a wealthy few.[4]

After A. I. went bankrupt during the Great Depression, he vowed never again to owe anything to anyone. His days of three-piece suits and profitable downtown retail space were over. By the time his youngest child—my mother—was growing up (she was born in 1929 and poignantly joked that her dad blamed her for the Depression), he had regrouped and opened a secondhand store, A. I. Berman's Salvage Store, which he managed until he retired several decades later. Here he bought and sold—for cash only—used merchandise, old furniture, appliances, household sundries, knick-knacks, and secondhand farm tools and ranching equipment to itinerant cotton pickers, ranch hands, and folks who came in from the neighboring towns and fields.

Although the salvage store was a sore reminder of near financial ruin for my grandfather, and a continued source of embarrassment, if not outright shame, for my mother, I experienced it as a kind of wonderland when we would come to Sweetwater to visit on family holidays. And according to my mother's stories, over time, other young people and small-town regulars in Sweetwater came to think of the store in much the same way. Indeed, she describes how my grandfather's secondhand store ultimately became a favorite gathering place for locals, who would come in to unload a worn-out saddle or to scout out a needed tractor seat or maybe bring home a dusty sack of covered buttons for their wives. Every surface of the interior space—floor, shelves, tables, bureaus, cabinets—was piled high with once-discarded household, farm, and ranch goods just waiting to be excavated from the sedimentary layers, with only two narrow aisles to make your way through the morass.

After a round of exploring and poking around, folks would sometimes pull up a rickety chair or a stool to join my grandparents around the pot-bellied stove toward the back of the shop, to pass the time of day, drink a soda pop, or swap stories about local events, politics, and personalities. A. I. would do most of the visiting and storytelling while Grandma Honey would sit quietly by his side, tending to the teapot boiling on the stove's surface or the fragrant pot roast and potatoes slowly roasting in an iron skillet nestled among its coals. In later years—long after her kids had grown and moved away—she would take out her small set of watercolors to paint a spray of flowers or a landscape scene on discarded scraps of cardboard or the backs of old cards she'd find lying around the store. Her signature touch was to thumbtack the paintings up on the back door of the shop where she'd spray a bit of glitter to make the final piece sparkle in the sunlight.

According to my mother, the salvage store enjoyed a kind of renaissance in the mid-1950s and 1960s. Middle-class housewives would scout for used treasures such as horse collars that they could transform into fashionable "country-chic" bathroom mirrors, and teenage boys would come by on their way home from school or on a lazy Saturday afternoon to hunt for interesting trinkets on either side of the narrow aisles. She recalls, for example, a framed 6-foot-long rattlesnake skin that A. I. had originally acquired from the estate of the solitary old hoarder who lived down the street on Broadway, something that especially appealed to the teenage-boy crowd.

Truth be told, my thickly accented immigrant grandfather had little tolerance for the home décor desires of lady "antique" shoppers, but he took a real interest in the teenage boys, whose impressionable minds he saw potential to mold. Like the Talmudic scholars with whom he had studied as a yeshiva boy back in Vilna, A. I. would weave important life lessons into his explanation of every object the boys might show even a vague interest in, whether it was a piece of braided horsehair rope or a dusty volume or two from a used encyclopedia set. It was not adherence to Jewish faith, religious texts, or observance that guided my grandfather's stories but rather an almost sacred reverence for the history and ethics lessons that could be gleaned from the material world around him. Like many of the first-generation immigrants who escaped the pogroms of Eastern Europe and arrived at the turn of the twentieth century—especially those who settled in small-town American hinterlands—A. I. embodied the classic exodus narrative of the American Jewish experience: "Jews, escapees from persecution" who "came in search of religious freedom and personal survival."[5] But in his case, as with so many of these small-town businessmen, religious freedom meant the freedom to make a religion out of the teachings of his adopted new homeland: freedom, liberty, participatory democracy. My mother recalls one such moment of informal learning when one of the town kids picked up a chalky plaster cast bust of Woodrow Wilson and my grandfather embarked on a twenty-minute lesson about the enduring legacy of our twenty-eighth president, who established the League of Nations and fought to "make the world safe for democracy."[6]

The store awakened a lifelong sense of wonder in one of those curious teenagers, Mondel Rogers, who went on to become a renowned Texas landscape painter, earning the moniker of Texas State Artist in 1990 by the Texas Commission on the Arts. Mondel spent many teenage hours in the disheveled shop, a place he later described as a "storage of all civilization." Once, he asked my grandfather how much he would want for a worn saddle in the corner. A. I. knew the stories behind everything in his store—and he knew that that old worn-out saddle bore the maker's mark of the master leather craftsman S. D. Myres Saddle Company, a favorite of such Hollywood actors as Gene Autry, John Wayne, Tom Mix, and Wallace Berry Jr., and was therefore worth hundreds if not thousands of dollars. Perhaps he recognized in young Mondel Rogers an artist's eye for the beauty of the handmade, the spirit of the American West, or just the freedom to dream. According to my mother, he sold it to Mondel for just a few dollars, knowing that the boy appreciated both the beauty of its craft and the legacy of its story.

By the time my grandfather was ready to retire, the now-adult Mondel had acquired a number of treasures—each accompanied by its own lesson for living—including the aforementioned Woodrow Wilson plaster

FIGURE 9.2. Painting of A. I. Berman's Salvage Store, by Mondel Rogers, Sweetwater, Texas. Photo by Robert Cullick.

bust, the S. D. Myres saddle, and even the salvage shop's back door, where the glittered outlines of Grandma Honey's signature watercolors formed geometric patterns of sparkle in the wood. For Mondel the back door might have represented a modern art study in negative space, or perhaps it reminded him of that unique time and place from his childhood where he was encouraged to explore unbidden, think outside the box, dream the impossible, and see wisdom and beauty where none existed before.

Some years later, Mondel painted a portrait of my grandparents' salvage store—with Grandma Honey standing in the doorway and Granddaddy on the curb in front of the store—a painting that hangs today at the First Financial Bank in downtown Sweetwater. The bank president's son was a friend of Mondel Rogers and one of the teenage boys who used to spend time in Granddaddy's store. On the occasion of the painting's dedication at the bank, Mondel wrote to my mother that Granddaddy's store was "a humble archives full of the past—a place where the poor found necessities, where the rich found antiques, and where an artist boy found adventure, excitement, exploration, and inspiration."

Might Museums Be Our Modern Day "Salvage Stores?"

For the old timers and teenage boys—and impressionable city-slicker grandchildren like myself—who frequented Granddaddy's store, they knew that they could always count on taking home a lesson or two about life and living, whether or not they found the necessity or luxury they were seeking amid the crowded aisles. For them, the afternoon hours were a time to sip coffee and swap stories about the local events and personalities that defined the West Texas landscape, to debate local and national politics, and to take stock of where they had been and where they were headed.

The importance of this tradition of informal learning through a community's stock of stories is one that Jewish storytellers have recognized for a long time. "A people's tales are its memory," says storyteller Ellen Frankel. "Its conscience, the imaginative channel to its place in the world. . . . Such tales teach each generation how to live and what to believe, whom to trust and whom to fear, when to laugh and why to cling fast to hope." "All it takes" says Frankel, "is a teller, a listener, and a moment to catch our breath."[7]

As an adult, I would find myself longing for those moments, that space, to listen to the stories of my elders surrounded by the material treasures of the past. Larry McMurtry, one of Texas's most celebrated fiction writers (*Lonesome Dove*, *The Last Picture Show*, *Terms of Endearment*), wonders whether perhaps our fast-paced, consumer-driven culture has somehow robbed us of those sacred moments in which to catch our breath and those magical spaces to swap stories, engage with history, and find wonder and adventure in the discovered treasures and tales of the past.

In a wonderful memoir titled *Walter Benjamin at the Dairy Queen: Reflections at Sixty and Beyond*, McMurtry examines the small-town way of life in West Texas that big oil and big ranches have nearly destroyed. Walter Benjamin was a German Jewish literary critic whose 1936 essay described what he felt was the growing obsolescence of what might be called "practical memory" in our contemporary lives and the consequent diminution of the power of oral narrative. For Benjamin the cafés of Berlin or Paris held the promise of that passion of practical memory and human connection—"the passion for art, for building a business, . . . for love and self-discovery."[8]

Larry McMurtry, reading Benjamin while nursing a lime Dr. Pepper at his local Dairy Queen in Archer City, used this essay as a springboard to reflect on the fate of storytelling on the rainless, desolate landscape of his West Texas home (just down the way from my grandparents' West Texas home)—and perhaps, more important, on the fate of those places, like Benjamin's coffeehouses or Granddaddy's store, where such exchanges are nurtured and shared. Where in the cities, McMurtry laments, can people ever find the time and the space to learn about their own and each others' history through the practical memories of their ancestors and the objects they leave behind?

In my own "reflections at sixty and beyond," I suggest that part of the answer might be found in those very places where objects and stories still come together to preserve that fleeting history, record precious legacies, and spark those much needed conversations about vital issues of conscience in the present. I am referring here to the modern-day museum, a place in our fast-paced global ethnoscape that is working hard to refashion itself, to be a "democratising, inclusive and polyphonic space for critical dialogue about the pasts and the futures," to quote from a recent mission statement of the International Council of Museums.[9]

What is revolutionary about this statement is not the recognition of the importance of objects to spark stories—or even the place of museums as both archives and exhibitors of those objects. Indeed, scholars have recognized this kind of "object-based epistemology" as the authoritative foundation of public museums since their beginnings in the nineteenth century.[10] Rather, what is important in this statement is what some have described as the recent dialogic impulse in museums—in which objects, artworks, and artifacts are displayed less as static treasures of art, or epistemologies of knowledge, and more as catalysts for conversation and engagement around important issues of conscience in our lives and history. In other words, more, perhaps, like the treasures found and the stories sparked in my grandfather's salvage store in Sweetwater Texas.

It is this civically engaging impulse that has guided my work as an independent museum curator over the last three decades and that is one of the most significant trends in museum curation and display at the dawn of the twenty-first century. As I reflect on my own career in the context of recent scholarship in Jewish studies on the restorative and affective power of material culture, I can't help but notice the Jewish nature of this storytelling impulse in my own exhibitionary work and the lessons this Jewish proclivity in representation might have for contemporary museums more generally.

Lessons from Our Elders: What "Jewish Third Spaces" Can Teach Twenty-First-Century Museums

In developing this line of inquiry, I am indebted to the seminal remarks of a group of Jewish museum curators and scholars who participated in a roundtable on "curatorial dreaming,"[11] which concluded the excellent symposium "Wandering Objects: Collecting and Interpreting Jewish Things," from which this edited volume emanates.[12] As moderator of that session, I borrowed from Erica Lehrer and Shelley Butler's edited volume on curatorial dreaming to invite each of the panel participants—Jewish curators all—to "push the boundaries of museology" to propose a concrete innovative project that reflected their dream exhibition for the twenty-first century. Although some conjectured dream exhibitions on explicitly Jewish topics, in explicitly Jewish museum spaces, others discussed their dreams not so much for a particular content but for a particular process. For them, their commitment and their creative conscience lay in wanting to conceive and participate in a process of engagement in museums—and with museum audiences—that would move beyond traditional static modes of object presentation and label text description and toward a more dialogue-driven mode of engagement, drawing on the power of objects to spark stories about issues of conscience in our lives. All agreed, as well, that there was something very Jewish about this approach to curation and to the idea of museums as sites of civic engagement, whether or not the topic of the exhibition was explicitly Jewish.

Why? Because to them, such public gathering spaces—like my grandfather's store—have become part and parcel of our diasporic patrimony. They are united by three things: the presence of objects and artworks that are the visible and semiotic spark for stories, a place where stories are the catalyst for memories, and a place where memories are the key to conversations of conscience.

Heritage scholar and museum curator Barbara Kirshenblatt-Gimblett—the esteemed respondent on this curatorial panel—agreed, borrowing a term that might be useful in describing the nature of these lively public spaces where beautiful or meaningful or even mundane artifacts spark free-flowing conversations about the world, each other, and the call to action: Jewish third spaces. These spaces can in some ways be described by what they are not: official, authoritarian places (such as synagogues, schools, offices) of didactic learning, prayer, art, commerce, or consumption. Rather, she muses, Jewish third spaces are those informal, affective environments where people—Jews and non-Jews alike—would come to hang out, relax, socialize, debate, barter, and share stories, histories, and memories in the public sphere—stories often sparked by the clatter of dominoes, chess pieces, or mahjongg tiles, the smell of fresh brewed coffee or pickled meats and vegetables, or the evocative signs and material remains of bygone days. They are spaces, she continues, where a distinctly Jewish tradition of informal learning is encouraged to take place through the memories sparked and shared, the artifacts consumed or displayed, the advice proffered and received, the debates waged and worried, and the historical lessons for living passed down from generation to generation.

This notion of third places to describe those public places that are outside work and home but function as vital centers for the creation of civil society is not reserved for Jews or Jewish culture alone. Sociologist Ray Oldenburg first coined the term *third place* in the late 1980s[13] to describe informal public places such as coffeehouses, bookstores, and bars where people could exchange ideas and build communities. Popular historian Robert Putnam, in his national bestseller, *Bowling Alone: The Collapse and Revival of American Community*, elaborates on this idea of the value of civic places such as churches, cafes, clubs, public libraries, and parks, which become "anchors" of community life and vital components for the creation and perpetuation of a modern civil society, democracy, and civic engagement. And postcolonial cultural theorist Homi K. Bhabha explores the notion of the third space in a sociocultural sense, not so much as a physical place but as a hybrid, indeterminate subject position residing between colliding cultures and differing relations of power.[14] For Bhabha, this highly charged liminal space, residing as it must between colonizer and colonized, has the potential to "give rise to something different, something new and unrecognizable, a new area of negotiation of meaning and representation."[15]

It was Shachar Pinsker, Judaic and Middle Eastern studies historian, who originally coined the term *Jewish third spaces* in his work on nineteenth- and early twentieth-century urban European and New York coffeehouses. In his book, *A Rich Brew: How Cafés Created Modern Jewish Culture*, Pinsker argues that these urban coffeehouses in centers such as Vienna, Odessa, Warsaw, Berlin, New York City, and Tel Aviv, though rarely considered Jewish spaces per se, were frequently owned by Jews, patronized by Jews, and embodied a particular kind of Jewish creativity. Like Walter Benjamin and others before him, Pinsker makes the point that such public places sit "on the threshold between Jew and gentile, migrant and 'native,' idleness and productivity, and masculine and feminine."[16] As such, he continues, the café, "as an imaginary and real third space and its perceived Jewishness are fluid, constantly changing expressions of Jewish modernity."[17] Speaking specifically of depictions of such spaces among the Yiddish and Jewish fiction writers of New York City in the first half of the twentieth century, Pinsker notes the particularly American Jewish nature of such cafés, describing them as places "associated with business and gossip, spaces of masculine sociability that were reminiscent of Jewish life in eastern Europe, but they were also a new American urban creation." The Yiddish word "*kibets* (or kibitz), to chat, and *kibitzarnya*, a place associated with chatting and sociability, might have come from German and Hebrew, but they were . . . Yiddish words."[18]

Whether describing nineteenth- or early twentieth-century urban coffeehouses or small-town social hubs like Granddaddy's salvage store, this notion of Jewish third spaces imagines a material and sociospatial dimension to a worldview that pays homage to the intellectual movement of the nineteenth-century Jewish Enlightenment, or Haskalah, from which many modern Ashkenazic Jews like my grandfather descended. As such, Pinsker notes, such spaces introduce a new sense of "playfulness, taste and morality" that he argues are distinctly Jewish.[19]

A number of prophetic lessons are central to this Jewish heritage—and the public third spaces in which they thrive—and I think they have unconsciously guided my own exhibitionary impulses in the exhibits I have curated throughout my career, as well as those of some of the esteemed curatorial colleagues at the "Wandering Objects" symposium. These lessons are (1) the power of informal learning through storytelling, (2) the material sensibility of Jewish thought, (3) the relation between risk taking and freedom, (4) the value of historical humanism, and (5) the lifeline of a kind of playful improvisation as a catalyst for revolutionary change. It is these lessons to which I turn now, as I look back on four of the major exhibitions that have punctuated my career. Guiding this conceit is a larger question of what might be learned from these lessons that could address what some have called a "crisis in museum representation" in the twenty-first century.

Curatorial Lessons 1 and 2: The Stories Objects Tell

In a provocative look at the ways in which Jews think about and work with objects, historian Ken Kolton-Fromm suggests that American Jewish identity and thought is fundamentally rooted in material things. For American Jews, he writes, "objects touched souls in ways that materialized Jewish identity in the accumulation and consumption of objects."[20] "Things do not just enrich our lives," he goes on, "they constitute essential features of personal identity. We experience holiness in and through things, and revivify the sacred by recalling the things intimately associated with it."[21] Indeed, Kolton-Fromm, following the work of twentieth-century

American Jewish theologian and sociologist Mordechai Kaplan, boldly asserts that art—or the aesthetically valuable material object—is itself the functional equivalent of religion for the assimilated American Jew.

> Like traditional religion, the arts unify the emotive experiences of Jewish life. . . . Art reveals the emotional terrain of an engaged self. Artistic creations are material things in which persons invest their "soul, self, or reason." They enliven and give expression to cherished traditions and values, and inspire new experiences and ideals. Material archives compose the stuff of civilizations. Judaism as a civilization is a material archive of self exposure.[22]

Recent scholars exploring the materiality of Jewish tradition might agree. In a 2018 roundtable discussion with the Harry Starr Fellows in Judaica at Harvard's Center for Jewish Studies, the significance of Jewish holy books and their archives—from the Bible to medieval illuminated manuscripts—revolved around a deeper discussion of Jews as a people of learning, a "people of the book," for whom books and other material objects become central to Jewish identity and sense of self.[23]

Other contemporary Jewish studies scholars, novelists, and memoirists have also highlighted the important lessons for living found in the most "unimportant" of material objects—secondhand silverware, discarded shoes, even a wooden-handled bottle opener. It is these otherwise unremarkable and inanimate objects, they suggest, that carry important afterlives in the stories they provide for us in the present. "Stories attach themselves to objects," says museum historian Richard Rabinowitz in his recent memoir, *Objects of Love and Regret: A Brooklyn Story*.[24] And memoirist Edmund de Wall goes further to note the particularly material nature of Jewish stories: "It is not just things that carry stories with them. Stories are a kind of thing, too. Stories and objects share something, a patina. . . . Perhaps patina is a process of rubbing back so that the essential is revealed, the way that a striated stone tumbled in a river feels irreducible."[25] Historian of religion, Laura Levitt amplifies this notion about the affective power of objects when she notes, "Objects hold out the promise of finding something of ourselves. And, if we are lucky, we may find our voices in the narratives of others, making all of us less lonely and the world, perhaps, more beautiful."[26] She even goes so far as to suggest that such everyday objects might be considered sacred. "What are the obstacles," she asks, "that get in the way of our claiming the sacred qualities of everyday life and the objects all around us? Why is it so difficult to embrace them?"[27]

Through these writings on the ethical, nay, sacred lessons bound up in the most simple of everyday objects, I look with new eyes at that jumbled "material archive" of Granddaddy's store that artist Mondel Rogers so aptly recognized as a "storage of civilization." And I reflect anew on my first major exhibition as a newly minted museum curator, which strikes me now as a kind of homage to Granddaddy's salvage shop in Sweetwater. This reflection also provides fertile soil, I think, to explore the first two lessons of Jewish third spaces for modern American museums, more generally: the power of storytelling as a mode of informal learning and the material sensibility of Jewish thought.

"Recycled, Re-Seen: Folk Art from the Global Scrap Heap" was my first nationally traveling exhibition, which I curated for the Museum of International Folk Art in Santa Fe, New Mexico, in 1996.[28] With more than six hundred featured objects from all over the world, the exhibition and accompanying catalog celebrated the art of transforming one person's trash into another's treasure. Whether a Mexican dustpan made from an American license plate or a Moroccan water jug crafted from a discarded tire, each object in that show held within its construction the story of at least two lives, two worlds, two cultures, each with its own material, meaning, makers, and users. Whatever their ultimate design or destination, these recycled artifacts were all, by definition, impure, inauthentic products of past and present, here and there, us and them. They fall into the category of all expressive activities and objects that celebrate, in the words of the famed exiled novelist Salman Rushdie, "hybridity, impurity, intermingling the transformation that comes of new and unexpected combinations of human beings, cultures, identities, politics, movies and songs."[29] It is perhaps not unlike the intermingling of cultures that resulted from my family's immigrant Jewish presence in the largely Christian cowboy culture of West Texas and the dialogues across difference that regularly occurred around the pot-bellied stove in Granddaddy's salvage store on West First Street.

I thought I was taking a huge risk by presenting art made from discarded items of trash—what I called "folk art from the global scrap heap"—in a sophisticated art museum setting. In early negotiations with

FIGURE 9.3. Museum exhibition catalog for "Recycled, Re-Seen: Folk Art from the Global Scrap Heap" at the Museum of International Folk Art in Santa Fe, New Mexico, 2009.

the exhibit design team, I had even proposed that we design the entry to the exhibit as a space where visitors are forced to walk—or perhaps even scavenge—through a messy mound of discarded metals, papers, plastics, and rags—something that would be anathema to the "object lessons" in glass cases formally proffered in the "exhibitionary complexes" of high art museums of the nineteenth and twentieth centuries.[30] I wanted visitors to feel both the thrill and the danger of potentially finding "treasure" amid the piles of discarded trash all around them. Although the living trash heap idea was itself ultimately "scrapped" in the interest of building safety codes, visitors did enter the exhibit through a pulsing, loud, and life-size projected video of scrapyard bulldozers, forklifts, shredders, compactors, and human pickers sorting through mounds of trash for the discarded treasures that might be hidden in their midst.

Little did I know at that time that the risk of scrap recycling and secondhand peddling had been the bread and butter for Jewish immigrants from Eastern Europe who settled in small-town America—including several of my relatives in Texas—for over a hundred years. Indeed, Jewish historian Hasia Diner makes the further point that such trades required a degree of literacy, as did the Jewish tradition itself. For Jews, she notes, "Both their religion and their livelihood pivoted on access to the written word," something that "conjoined them with each other."[31]

One pundit affectionately referred to those who peddle scrap and secondhand goods as "Junkyard Jews":[32] They turned scrap metal into millions, trash into treasure, and secondhand goods into first-world commodities, or even art.[33]

In addition to recent historical scholarship on Jewish peddlers and secondhand shop owners, contemporary Jewish writers have also begun to reflect on the biblically inspired Jewishness behind the practice of repurposing itself. Indeed, some even trace the Jewish value for repurposing—and the holiness of thrift store shopping—to a biblical injunction known as *bal tashchit*, a prohibition against wasting or destroying. As one popular writer in the online blog "Southern & Jewish" writes:

> I don't solely shop secondhand for financial reasons, or even for the fun of it. By being intentional and methodical about spending my money at local resale establishments, I am fulfilling my duty to reduce waste, reuse perfectly good products, and, when I'm done, I

can recycle my own items to keep the wheel turning, *l'dor v'dor* (from generation to generation). For me, shopping secondhand is something holy—it's a family tradition, it reduces waste, and it keeps me feeling great about my clothing choices.[34]

Was it this commandment of *bal tashchit* that guided my grandfather's peddling of secondhand goods and my subsequent career interest in exposing the value of one person's art made from another's trash? In the subsequent quarter-century, dozens of museums would follow this lead in exploring the aesthetics and ethics of recycled arts. In 2019 almost a quarter of a century after the "Recycled, Re-Seen" exhibition debuted around the country, a new exhibition at the Jewish Museum of Maryland[35] made explicit the historic relationship between Jews and repurposed scrap, celebrating the business, the art, and the biblical framing of the junkyard Jews of the last 150 years in American life.[36]

Curatorial Lesson 3: The Importance of Taking Risks

Listening to my curator colleagues at the "Wandering Objects" symposium, I was reminded that, as curator Juliana Ochs Dweck proclaimed, "risk-taking is a particularly Jewish proclivity—one that has long been culturally and historically venerated, codified in Jewish texts and embodied in Jewish practices."[37] In a written draft of her remarks prepared in advance of that symposium roundtable, Dweck went on to highlight the connection between risk taking and objects themselves—something that became a touchstone for all our conversations that day and one that resonated for me on my own narrative with the "Recycled, Re-Seen" exhibit in my debut as a professional museum curator on the national stage. As Dweck notes:

> I think one could argue . . . that this risk-taking proclivity inheres in Jewish objects; it materializes in material culture; it manifests itself in the ways objects are made, the materials that are chosen, the ways objects are used, transported, and stored, and the stories they tell. . . . Jews take risks with these objects—and they take risks for these objects. Risk inheres in their silver, clay and cloth. What forms of

reinterpretation or risk-taking propel the making of objects? What are the risks entailed in re-making or re-using them?

Although most of the objects in the "Recycled, Re-Seen" exhibit were not in themselves Jewish objects, I found myself wondering about my own particularly Jewish proclivity—or patrimony—to recognize and celebrate the transformation of trash into treasure and my own curatorial commitment to taking that risk to display such transformed objects in a fine arts museum setting.

This idea of the risk-taking proclivity of the Jewish curatorial gaze followed me from recycled objects to my next major exhibition project, where I found myself drawn back to the magic of Texas storytelling through the objects of Texas history.

"It Ain't Braggin' If It's True" was the inaugural exhibition in the 6,500-square-foot temporary gallery space of Austin's newly opened Bob Bullock Texas State History Museum in 2001.[38] As the first guest curator of this space, I had been assigned this over-the-top topic and title for the nine-month temporary exhibition, along with the freedom to envision and execute it any way I saw fit. Again, it was the subversive potential of objects and their underlying "lessons for living" that called to me from that particular mix of wit, whimsy, and wisdom inherited from my salvage-store grandfather. Drawing on Carl Sandburg's insight that Texas is "a unique blend of valor and swagger," I divided the exhibit and catalog into six sections, highlighting six "bragging rights" I defined as integral to the Texas character.[39] "Valor" was first, "Swagger" was last and in between were the qualities of "Perseverance," "Vision," "Pride," and "Showmanship." If the exhibit celebrated the many ways in which Texans brag about their state through the stories that objects tell, I was determined to shake up visitor expectations to focus especially on those stories, those objects, and those tellers that are not usually considered worthy of bragging rights in Texas history: Mexican laborers, African American slave descendants, Native American war heroes, female inventors, and small-town Jewish merchants. Again, looking back, I find myself performing that very Jewish sensibility of finding life lessons in objects where, as Kolton-Fromm instructs, "Things do not just enrich our lives; they constitute essential features of personal identity."[40]

If my mission was to subvert those dominant, Anglo-centered, patriarchal, heteronormative narratives of Texas character, my method was to juxtapose alternative narratives—and objects—side by side with the more celebrated stories. And to do so, I intentionally operated right under the nose and within the institution of those very cornerstones of power and privilege in Texas government and history. If I told a story of a known Texas hero like Sam Houston, first president of the new Republic of Texas, I made sure to offer a new spin through an unexpected object—such as the story of the biblical psalm book that kept a bullet from killing his beloved son.[41] And for every known Texas hero or story, I featured a never-before-seen gem that might shed new light on a familiar theme, such as the handmade cactus pear burners that more than once saved the day for starving cattle and desperate ranchers in drought-prone South Texas. I am sure that the object we borrowed to tell that story—which looked like it came straight out of my grandfather's secondhand salvage store—was the last thing then Texas governor George W. Bush imagined would be featured in the inaugural exhibit of his newly opened multimillion dollar flagship state museum. Suffice it to say it was not a thing of beauty or wonder; rather, it was an ugly, rusted, sawed-off length of welded iron pipe that had once been connected to a kerosene container and used by Texas cattle ranchers to burn the sharp thorns off the protein-rich fruit of the native cactus so that hungry cattle wouldn't starve to death in the great drought from 1947 to 1956.

Perhaps I was unconsciously drawing on the spirit of the founder of Jewish Enlightenment philosophy, Moses Mendelssohn, who recast ugliness "as a positive force for moral education and social progress."[42] According to his theory, in which my grandfather was undoubtedly schooled as a young yeshiva *boker* in Vilna, ugly objects cause us to think more and thus exercise—and expand—our mental abilities. That seeming contradiction—an ugly object made beautiful, or at least meaningful—illustrates his theory's possibility: ugliness itself as a positive, even redeeming characteristic of great opportunity.

One of my favorite pieces in that inaugural "Braggin'" exhibit was the hand-appliqued family quilt of African American quilt maker Sherry Byrd.[43] Titled "Homegrown/Handmade/Passed On," Byrd's two-sided masterpiece stitched the story of her ancestor's journey from slavery to freedom in Freestone County, from the patriarch's pre-enslaved life in Africa, to his arrival as an enslaved plantation hand in 1852, to the family's freedom and purchase of a parcel of that former plantation land, to the college education of every subsequent generation of girls down to the present day, five generations later. Sherry Byrd herself appreciated the irony of an African American quilter and a Jewish American curator crafting stories of freedom from slavery in an exhibit on Texas braggin' rights.

An element of risk inhered in both the objects themselves—many of which would never have withstood the registrar's test of "museum quality" time—and the subversive stories I used to tell about triumph over adversity, protest in the face of injustice, and pride of place for those whose place was never officially recognized. It lay in my proclivity to put things together for visitors that they might not expect, that might spark them to think about things differently, focus on something that they otherwise would have passed over, or appreciate an aspect—or a hero—of Texas history whose voice had yet to be heard, or perhaps had been actively silenced.

Some contemporary Jewish writers might even elevate that kind of risk taking to the level of a holy or spiritual endeavor. Indeed, one essayist, in an article titled "Risk and Faith," frames risk taking as an expression of the deepest wellsprings of Jewish faith. Drawing on biblical sources, she notes that, "A vibrant tradition of Jewish risk-taking wends its way through Hebrew Scripture. Essentially spiritual in nature, but always translating itself into courageous action before God, this tradition can be seen as a major component of the belief of ancient Israel."[44] She cites Abraham and Sarah as the first to commit themselves to taking risks before God when they answer his call to "go forth from your father's house, to the land that I will show you" (Genesis 12:1). "Thus, from the outset," she writes, "God steered Abraham to acknowledge that risk-taking would be an essential dynamic of his faith. Exploring Abraham's willingness to embrace risks is to joyfully witness the inception of what was later known as *Z'chut Avot*—merit of our ancestors."[45]

In breaking with the museum standard of what kinds of objects are worthy of museum collection and display, I too took on a certain amount of professional risk. Although I stand by the courage that was required to feature the words and works of those who stood so far outside the canon of official Texas bragging rights, I am not especially proud of what I now might call a kind of curatorial conceit—my own braggadocio bravado—underlying this element of risk, which was so unlike the storytelling style of my soft-spoken immigrant grandfather. Ironically, it was the world-renowned king of Texas Jewish swagger himself—Mr. Stanley Marcus of Neiman-Marcus Department Store fame—who taught me that lesson: to beware of both the power and the hubris that come with trying to break with the "geein' and hawin'" club of the Texas big boys.

It happened within the space of a one-day email exchange in May 2001 when I initially reached out to Mr. Marcus to inquire about featuring the story of his department store's celebrated annual Fortnight tradition in the exhibit's section on swagger. For a particular generation of postwar Texans, Neiman Marcus's extravagant celebration of international culture, cuisine, and fashion was eagerly anticipated each year when the Dallas flagship store was transformed into an architectural stage curated with delicacies and delights from renowned artists, chefs, musicians, designers, and entrepreneurs from around the world. It was these Fortnight celebrations, along with Neiman Marcus's signature Christmas Book catalogs featuring diamond tiaras and rose gold private jets, that catapulted the store to international fame and success. I thought Mr. Marcus would be proud to be celebrated in this way in Texas's brand-new state museum.

Quite the contrary. The twenty-first-century elderly patriarch returned my email inquiry with a curt note declining to participate. By way of explanation, he simply stated that, sadly, he felt that his store's braggadocio extravagance had done far more harm than good in contributing to both an image and a reality of a grossly divided and exploitative Texas. I responded that I hoped to use this platform to subvert this brand of Texas swagger by featuring some of the stories of those very Texans whose voices had been silenced or overlooked, including Neiman Marcus's Fortnight designer himself, a Tony Award–winning set and costume designer from Broadway.

His secretary sent back a note to say that Mr. Marcus had changed his mind, based on my framing of my mission and would now be happy to participate. But the cautionary caveat for me was profound: Be wary about the enterprise of Texas braggin' rights. We Jews may be Texans, but ours is not the patrimony of Texas tall tales. As the highly assimilated German Jews of the twentieth century learned all too well, history, like the Texas weather, can always turn on a dime.

Curatorial Lesson 4: The Importance of Historical Humanism

In 2002 I embarked on another multiyear traveling exhibition project for the Texas State History Museum; the exhibit opened in 2009, after more than five years of original field and archival research. The exhibit, titled "Forgotten Gateway: Coming to America Through Galveston Island," was designed to accomplish two goals: (1) to raise awareness of the role of Galveston Island as one of the top ten transoceanic gateways to America in the nineteenth and early twentieth centuries and (2) to use this little-known piece of American immigration history as a lens through which to explore enduring issues in our nation's struggle over who can be an American and who gets to decide. Both the focus on Galveston as an immigrant port and the use of history to explore contemporary social justice issues fit my sensibilities as a modern American Jewish curator to a T. In the first place this exhibit allowed me to conduct original oral historical research on my own people, Texas Jews, through the little known story of the Galveston Movement: an organized immigration plan that was designed to save ten thousand Jewish immigrants from the Eastern European Pale of Settlement in the early decades of the twentieth century by assisting their safe passage to the Port of Galveston and their ultimate resettlement throughout Texas and the American Midwest. This was only a small part of the overall exhibit, which also included stories of Galveston's early role in the slave trade of our nation, its pioneering experiment to import Chinese laborers after the Civil War to replace freed African Americans in building Texas's railroads, its international aim to lure the "right kind" of fair-haired and blue-eyed immigrants with promises of cheap land, good jobs, and safe passage from Northern Europe, and its early twentieth-century racial profiling of Eastern and Southern European immigrants, including especially Jews and Catholics, as undesirable and unassimilable.

If the Galveston Movement was only a small part of the overall exhibit, it was the story that felt particularly meaningful to me. Although my Granddaddy and my Grandma Honey had not originally entered the United States through Galveston, many of their *landsmen* in West Texas had, including most of the other Jewish peddlers along the railroad routes from Galveston to Amarillo. And their motivations for immigrating to this country in the late nineteenth and early twentieth century—along with three million other Jews from Eastern Europe—matched those arriving at Galveston's gates: They were fleeing the targeted pogroms and economic hardships of their homelands.

Second, and perhaps more significant, my approach to this exhibit, displaying history not as a series of isolated tales from the past but as lessons for living in the present, seemed literally encoded in my Jewish DNA. Indeed, every Jewish immigrant who arrived on America's shores from this part of Europe during this era carried the story of their family's restricted place in history, even sometimes their forced occupations, in their Yiddish/Ashkenazic Jewish name—plowman, baker, tinsmith, tailor, butcher, coppersmith—encoding a history of power, positionality, and persecution in their most nominal identity. My grandfather's surname, Berman, from the Yiddish "bear man," might have derived its meaning from the word for porter—he who carries—but most definitely embodied the symbol of the bear as one of strength, forbearance, and hard work. This seemed somehow poetically fitting for a secondhand store owner who bore the entire history of his diasporic people on his immigrant back.

In addition to encoding the story of their history in their very name, Jews throughout time have kept their history alive through their annual cycle of festivals, none more pertinent than the spring holiday of Passover, when the biblical story of their people's exodus from slavery to freedom is retold around the family's seder table as though the tellers themselves were undergoing the Exodus in real time and exploring its meaning for enslaved or oppressed peoples in the contemporary world. Even my fiercely assimilated grandfather never failed to gather his family and assorted business colleagues or friends to hold an annual Passover seder, the central ritual of which involved the retelling of his people's Exodus story—the very story that would be mirrored in his own journey from extreme poverty and persecution to the *Goldene Medina*—the land of the free—so many generations later.

Thus, as I researched the stories and selected the objects that would form the basis for the "Forgotten Gateway" exhibit, I felt the weight of responsibility of my Texas Jewish patrimony: a responsibility not only to recover this largely untold chapter of my people's immigrant history in Texas but also to use these stories to expose and engage the racial profiling and discrimination tales of those arriving at our nation's gates today. Like my secondhand merchant grandfather, I took seriously my curatorial role as go-between—what my Jewish folklore colleague Richard Kurin referred to as a culture broker—moving between different places, times, and cultures, exposing similarities in stories of power and conceit across time, discovering the valuable lessons in even the most humble and recycled objects, and finding and facilitating common ground along the way.[46]

As a public folklorist, I brought my particular set of tools to this mode of culture brokering that involved sustained and committed engagement with visitors, neighbors, and community members. This commitment to community-based collaboration is one that, in recent years, has significantly affected the ways that exhibits are conceptually framed, the community-driven research and fieldwork behind them, the curation of artifacts and labels, and the community-driven programming that accompanies them—all produced with, by, and for the people.

This explains why the planning and research phase of this exhibit lasted for over half a decade. In the case of the Galveston Movement research alone, my team and I traveled to dozens of cities throughout Texas and in ten states throughout the American Midwest over a period of three years to talk with Jews whose lives had been shaped by their encounters with the Galveston Movement. As we recorded the personal stories of hundreds of Jews who had come to America through Galveston's gates, I was repeatedly struck by the material sensibility through which their stories were remembered and retold. Time and again, the families would bring to our oral history workshops the material mnemonics of their family's immigrant story: silver Shabbat candlesticks, brass menorahs, samovars, Kiddush cups, handwoven prayer shawls, and even sometimes whole Torah scrolls. In my own family, a pair of brass candlesticks and a hand-carved wooden bread bowl—which I still use each week for kneading my Shabbat challah loaves—were the heirlooms that my Grandma Honey brought when she and her mother arrived from Ukraine in the early twentieth century. Each of these largely ceremonial religious artifacts had a story to share, a history to impart, and a cultural patrimony to defend. They were presented to us as prized personal heirlooms—not for the fine craftsmanship or economic value they represented but for the material touchstones they held to the perseverance, the history, and the identity of those who risked their lives to make, and survive, the transoceanic journey almost a century before.

Even though these predominantly ceremonial objects still remained in the hands of the families who brought them, many ultimately ended up on the collection shelves of Jewish museums around the country in the early decades of the twentieth century and, even more recently, on the tables and surfaces of rummage sales, thrift stores, and antique malls across the land—places, in fact, like my grandfather's secondhand store, had there been enough Jewish families in that West Texas landscape to begin to de-accession their estates after a parent's passing.

As Jewish Museum historian David Clark remarks about the underlying message conveyed in the preservation and display of these early collections of Judaica, "Indeed, a narrative that noted the place of Jewish ritual objects within the context of the 'triumphal march of civilisation' also conveyed an important message about the subject positioning of Jews and made a claim for regarding Jews as part of the civilized world."[47] Today, many Jewish museums and exhibitions are drawing on their collections and resources, not just to display the wealth and treasures of our people's past but to explore the most challenging and controversial issues of our collective history and present day. This seemed to be the case with some of the objects that our interviewees from the Galveston Movement showed us—objects that indexed specific stories of the sometimes fraught encounters that their family members had with inspectors or officials upon arrival at Galveston's gates.

Remember that the Jews of Eastern Europe were one of the prime targets of racial profiling in the early twentieth century, and the Galveston port of entry was a prime example of targeted discrimination in action. By the turn of the twentieth century, discriminatory attitudes toward "alien foreigners" were both constituted and reflected in a growing set of gender-, nation-, and race-based legal restrictions on who could enter the country and who could become a citizen. As William Williams, the commissioner of Ellis Island in 1903, summed it up, "The present predominating immigration from southern and eastern Europe is inferior on the whole to the old north European immigration. It contains many undesirable and unintelligent people."[48] One of the areas of increased legal restrictions centered on the physical state of the arriving "aliens." This emphasis reflected the nation's increasing concern with disease and contamination allegedly infecting our nation through the admission of these undesirable foreigners. This was especially true in Texas, where xenophobic and antisemitic medical inspectors were responsible for deporting seven times as many Jews—Hebrews, they were called—from

Galveston as East Coast cities—with physical ailments ranging from the highly contagious trachoma to the significantly less medically justifiable abnormalities as hernias, weak backs, "chicken breasts," prostitution, and other physical manifestations of supposed physical or moral weakness listed as official causes for deportation. Here, the pseudoscientific categories of both public health and eugenics become central to racialization, definitions of citizenship, and the legitimation of violence—or at least forced deportation—during the 1910s and 1920s at the point of entry into the nation.

One of the main grounds for deportation into the United States at the time was a turn-of-the-twentieth-century law targeting "persons afflicted with tuberculosis or with a loathsome or dangerous contagious disease (including trachoma)."[49] If the initial medical exam revealed any of these diseases, the passenger could be quarantined or even sent back to their home country.

This was the case with one of the original Galveston Movement immigrants we interviewed who had arrived with his family on a ship from Bremen, Germany, at the age of three years in 1913. A. I. Schepps was ninety-seven at the time of our interview in Houston. He remembers well the outbreak of measles that ran through the steerage section of the ship during their three-week passage and the telltale rash that appeared on his upper torso and that of his next oldest sister. So fearful was the family that they would be sent back if the medical examiner discovered the spots covering the young boy's torso that A. I.'s oldest sister covered her little brother in a blanket for the whole journey so that no one would detect the signs of the virus on his body. Ultimately, the three-year-old boy and his family were quarantined off the coast of Galveston for a number of weeks upon their arrival on American shores.

It was the faded woolen blanket that Mr. Schepps brought with him to his oral history interview about the Galveston Movement—the one that his sister had kept with her for over a half-century and finally bequeathed to A. I. just months before her passing. It was his most precious heirloom, and the one I selected to tell the tale of increased restrictions at Galveston's gates.

As in the other sections of the "Forgotten Gateway" exhibit, I used Mr. Schepps's and others' stories of racially motivated inspections and increased restrictions as a historic springboard to explore parallel examples in the contemporary landscape. And what felt especially Jewish about this approach to history was my commitment to creating a space where visitors could add their own stories, share their interpretations, wrestle with the ideas, contribute to the national immigration timeline, or engage in a spirited dialogue with each other, with themselves, and with history on issues that are as alive today as they were in our nation's past: Who should be allowed to be an American? And who gets to decide? As Richard Rabinowitz recognizes in his recent memoir about his immigrant family as told through the everyday objects of their lives, "One after another, these objects reveal how we migrated, redefining who were neighbors and who were strangers, what lay close by and what was remote, what was comforting and what was threatening."[50]

Without even realizing it, I think I was trying to recreate a kind of Jewish third space within the museum itself, a space that would function like my grandfather's Sweetwater salvage store where neighbors gathered around the pot-bellied stove and told stories evoked by the objects in their midst. "Tell me the story of an acquisition you cherish," continued Rabinowitz, "and I will plumb the deepest struggles of your heart."[51]

Plumbing the deepest struggles of one's heart lay at the base of my grandfather's training as a young yeshiva *boker* in Vilna before immigrating to the United States. Even in those days, my grandfather's intellectual sensibility and passion were drawn to the radical historical humanism of the Jewish Haskalah as it was manifested in Eastern Europe in the mid- to late nineteenth century rather than the kabbalistic teachings of the more Hasidic yeshivas in Vilna. Among other things, the modern Judaism to which he clung emphasized a notion of the importance of history—and biblical studies—as a fundamentally humanistic discipline, one that sought universal meaning in the events of the past and an obligation to draw from that history necessary lessons for how to leave the world a better place for the future. For him, history encoded a responsibility to learn from the injustices of the past in order to better protect the most vulnerable among us today.[52]

Although I tried mightily to create the feel and effect of a free-flowing salon in the midst of the "Forgotten Gateway" exhibition space, the restrictions of a multimillion dollar state-funded museum—and its authorial mandates for polished design, curation, and presentation—ultimately limited its effectiveness in this regard. Thus, although visitor "talk-back boards" and participatory exercises were woven throughout the exhibit, the professional design elements of lighting, labeling, and display remained firmly in the hands of professionals.

Curatorial Lesson 5: The Importance of Improvisation

In 1927, two years before my Grandma Honey and Granddaddy gave birth to their youngest child—my mother—Hollywood released the first feature-length movie with synchronized dialogue, a "talkie" that revolutionized the American film industry forever. It is perhaps no accident that the film is both a verbal and a visual parable of the American Jewish experience of the early twentieth century. The film, *The Jazz Singer*, follows the story of a young Jewish musician who rejects his father's occupation as synagogue cantor to make a name for himself as a singer of the new Jewish jazz—adapted from African American jazz singers of the early twentieth century and infused with a Yiddish inflection from their synagogue roots. As historian Irv Saposnik notes of the film, "Its story is a paradigm of the Jewish dream in conflict with American reality; its characters exemplify the clash between Old World values and New World ambition; its music is a mix of Black jazz and Yiddish blues, all by way of Jewish Tin Pan Alley."[53]

For my purposes, I wonder about the revolutionary potential of this film and its parabolic message almost a hundred years later, in the first decades of the twenty-first century. In particular, I wonder about the improvisatory pulse of Jewish jazz for a radical reimagining of museums in the twenty-first century. What would it be like if museums truly embraced the flexibility, the possibility, the inquiry, the responsiveness, and the conversationality of jazz's call-and-response foundation? What would it be like if the improvisationality of jazz music could be translated into an improvisationality of museum design?

This was the question I pondered in my most recent major museum stint as the founding curator, and later director, of the Gallery of Conscience at the Museum of International Folk Art (MOIFA) in Santa Fe, New Mexico, from 2010 to 2017. Launched in 2010, MOIFA's Gallery of Conscience was designed to explore timely human rights and social justice issues through the words and works of folk artists from around the world. After several years of successful, curator-driven exhibits in the Gallery of Conscience, addressing such issues as women's empowerment, natural disaster, and internment in times of war, I felt that something was still missing in the fundamentally top-down approach to the exhibit's design and curatorial development. How could we more authentically engage diverse communities and audiences in the conceptualization and development of the exhibits themselves? How could we create a process that was as responsive, responsible, collaborative, and engaged as the social justice work we were trying to present?

In 2012, after an extensive strategic planning process with a broad swath of community and museum stakeholders, we took a major design leap to incubate an improvisatory approach to exhibit development in the Gallery of Conscience with a commitment to ongoing exhibit prototyping at its core. Prototyping is an incremental, inquiry-based mode of exhibition design that allows for an institution to experiment with new ideas—keeping those that work and tossing out or modifying those that don't—in a way that is relatively low risk, low cost, and low maintenance. As internationally recognized exhibit design innovator—and our resident prototyping guru—Kathleen McLean writes, a prototype, drawn from the Greek word meaning "original form," is "a mock-up or a quick and dirty version of an idea; something flexible and changeable; a tool for learning something about the effects of an idea or object on the end user."[54]

As in *The Jazz Singer*, it was an approach built on an equation balancing the exhibitionary equivalent of jazz and prayer, old and new, structure and innovation, call and response. As in *The Jazz Singer*, too, the seduction of this approach was its promise to reach more diverse audiences, engage new ideas, challenge the authority of the past, and forge a path to an exciting and more equitable future.

Looking back on Kirshenblatt-Gimblett's recipe for twenty-first-century museums as Jewish third spaces, it was this project in which all the elements seemed to coalesce: objects telling stories, stories reflecting history, history catalyzing dialogue across difference, dialogue sparking engagement, engagement providing a formula for change. The activating enzyme, it turned out, was that key element of Jewish jazz: improvisation with a *Yiddishkeit* flare. And like all activating agents, this one involved a small yet calculated element of risk—that element of risk that Dweck refers to as "a particularly Jewish proclivity . . . in the sense that it has a deep capacity to weather tension, to withstand pushback, and to embrace disruption in productive ways. In part this is because it is Judaism that wrote the book on reinterpretation—interpretations that are nuanced and multifaceted and relevant in their day and to this day."[55]

In the Gallery of Conscience we started this act of "reinterpretation" by throwing out the more traditional curator/designer/educator model of exhibit expertise in favor of a team approach that sought to be fundamentally collaborative, improvisational, and flexible. This allowed us to focus on community and audience engagement rather than on specialized knowledge. Three staff members plus a prototype consultant, a community engagement coordinator, and a team manager led a prototyping process based on visitor, artist, and community input and exchange. We conceived of the Gallery of Conscience as an experimental space or lab—not as a means to an end but as the end itself.

Like a jazz tune, we sparked the exhibit development process metaphorically with a single melodic line—a pressing issue of conscience (AIDS, immigration, the ethics of the marketplace)—and a public call

FIGURE 9.4. Gallery of Conscience team inviting visitors to help prototype the exhibition "Negotiate, Navigate, Innovate: Choices Folk Artists Make in Today's Global Marketplace."

to respond. Our melodic line was a limited set of artworks, a few artist quotes, and photos taped up on butcher-block paper around the walls and a number of participatory prompts that invite response. We then opened the space to artistic amplification, improvisation, and interrogation. We invited local and international traditional artists, community youth, neighborhood activists, and drop-in visitors to riff on the initial pieces, adding their own stories, comments, signs, poems, artworks, stitches, and songs along the way.

Folk art proved to be a compelling catalyst for this kind of honest conversation about human rights issues sometimes spanning generations, cultures, geographies, and histories. As a Jewish folklorist, I knew the value of traditional, familiar, and hence readily understandable forms of storytelling to reach people and effectively transcend the barriers of language, taboo, religion, or race. Meaningful, heartfelt, and sometimes controversial conversations were effectively sparked by the artworks themselves, the words of their creators, and the invitations for visitors and community members to participate in the conversations.

At any one time, the project might support as many as a dozen collaborative spin-offs both within and outside the museum walls—artist conversations and residencies, poetry slams and graffiti parties, candlelit ceremonies and immigrant food trucks, maker space workshops, and activist marches—which all fed back into the gallery space itself.

During the years when we explored this experimental design technique, the Gallery of Conscience team worked hard to keep the gallery's design intentionally unpolished; everything existing in a rough, prototyped state, ready to be nimbly adjusted, changed, added to, or removed based on visitor response and engagement. Our goal was to constantly break down and challenge the idea of our own authority as curators and designers while ratcheting up the authority of our visitors and our community members as cocreators of the space.

Such a radical revisioning of the role of museums, visitors, staff members, and community members is not for the faint of heart. At every moment, we found our experimental lab precariously balanced on the fault line of institutional or stakeholder controversy. Staff members, administrators, docents, designers, political officials, and some longtime patrons expressed outrage at the process itself, for example, when a "fact" might appear to be wrong, when the artwork seemed "amateurish," when the makeshift labels failed to stick to the walls, when the interactive elements seemed to "overshadow the art," or when individual pieces were deemed just too provocative for a "family" audience. One patron complained that one of the exhibits was "the ugliest exhibit MOIFA has ever done!" and a volunteer quipped that "dealing with social issues is getting too far away from the art!"

But input from visitors, artists, and community members consistently told a different tale. Our audiences commended us time and again for "the brave thing" we were doing in the space. They wrote notes of thanks, exclaiming "I saw myself here for the first time." One visitor commented specifically on the improvisatory nature of the design process, noting, "I love that the gallery is always changing, and is changed by the people who have responded." And another opined, "There should be a place in every museum where you have to commit your own opinions. More museums should get a hold of people emotionally, not just intellectually."

As Dweck so presciently commented in her remarks at our "Wandering Objects" symposium, it is important to distinguish between risk taking and controversy and to evaluate the fundamental question at the heart of this kind of institutional change: "What are the risks worth taking and what are the ones not worth taking? For whom are these risks?" She goes on to provide a partial answer: "I have in mind museum exhibitions or installations that thoughtfully try to encourage audiences to question the state of the world, the role of art, or their own subjectivity in the world. Not ones that have provocation as an end unto itself." Even recognizing this ultimate goal, Dweck recognizes that, when it comes to risk taking in its exhibitions and design, institutions must ultimately decide for themselves what they are comfortable with and what is good institutional practice.

In the case of the Museum of International Folk Art, the institutional needs for structure, beauty, and more-regulated expectations for exhibition design, development, and display ultimately won out over what they deemed as unnecessary risk. In the fall of 2016, under the direction of a new museum director, a hasty strategic planning session was called. The Gallery of Conscience was labeled "unsightly and uninviting" and "a problem that needs fixing." A decision was made to revert back to a more conventional design process and more visually polished exhibitions in the gallery; my position as director of the space was terminated; and the Gallery of Conscience, though still featuring meaningful stories of social justice and conscience, no longer reflects the same improvisatory nature in its process of design or structure of authority.

But for a fleeting moment, this messy, improvisatory experiment in exhibition and engagement became for me the kind of revolutionary third space that one prominent Jewish museum critic called "a model of museum practice for the twenty-first century."[56] And in 2018, long after the Gallery of Conscience no longer held its improvisatory edge, the original director of the museum and I were recognized with the Michael M. Ames Award for innovative exhibitions by the Council of Museum Anthropology.

As Jewish museum curators and directors have recognized for a long time, together, museums and communities have the potential—the responsibility—to create an entirely new and replicable third space for civic engagement in the twenty-first century. Jewish folklorist and social justice activist William Westerman stated that "museums have a leading role to play in becoming cultural centers where multiple narratives can be told, where people can find safe spaces for cultures to mix, and where xenophobia can be overcome." The challenge, he continues, "is how to become inclusive and relevant to the framework of civic democracy at a time when larger societies are grappling with strong exclusionist tendencies and fear."[57]

The answer to that challenge, as Jewish peddlers have known for generations, is a willingness to dialogue across difference, to take risks, to improvise, to dream and to fail—something that jazz musicians and community-based artists have known all along. As Miles Davis, one of the kings of American jazz, once said, "Improvising is live inspiration, something happening at that very moment. Do not fear mistakes. There are none."[58]

A Final Lesson in Democracy

Which brings me back to the West Texas landscape where we began this journey. My immigrant grandfather, who escaped the pogroms of Eastern Europe to find freedom in West Texas, understood the revolutionary potential of such democratizing spaces early on, especially in the wide-open wily world of West Texas, where corporate cronies can be known to play fast and loose with the law, the rules, and those who might dare to cross 'em in or out of a court of law. I'll end with one of my favorite stories about my grandfather's passion for locating justice and human dignity in his adopted homeland, a story that embodies the lessons of history, risk, and voice in those Jewish third spaces of the American public sphere—and their efficacy as catalysts for action in the official sphere of American politics.

It was the year of the "Shivercrats in Texas politics"—1952—the year that the popular war hero General Ike Eisenhower was the Republican candidate for president, running against the Democrat's chosen candidate, Adlai Stevenson. Texas was a dependably Democratic state, although fiercely divided within the party as to whether one was liberal or conservative. But that year Alan Shivers led the conservatives in the state to split the ticket: vote Democratic for local offices, such as his gubernatorial run, but Republican for president and vice president.

There is always a local meeting, a caucus, after the polls close on Election Day where delegates are selected to go to the state primary later in the year. In Sweetwater the meeting was to be held at the Court House on the town square after the polls closed for the night. As the clock started to peal 7:00 p.m. to mark the opening of the meeting, the very conservative chairman, seeing one more elderly man, a member of the traditional FDR liberal Democrats, coming up the walk, exulted, "It's 7:00! We can lock the door!"

As it was reported to my mother, and from her to me, my grandfather, A. I. Berman, another passionate Roosevelt Democrat and a proud naturalized citizen, rose from the courthouse table, and, in a strong, clear voice, still heavily accented after over half a century in the United States, declared, "THIS IS AMERICA! WE ARE NOT LOCKING THE DOOR ON ANYONE!"

Legends have been told—and ballads sung—for less.

Notes

1 See, most recently Rabinowitz, *Objects of Love and Regret*; Leibman, *Art of the Jewish Family*; Levitt, *Objects That Remain*; Schwenger, *The Tears of Things*; and Wall, *The Hare with Amber Eyes*. Levitt, significantly, combines personal memoir with a historical examination of the ways

in which the material remains of violent crimes inform our experience of, and thinking about, trauma and loss. By considering both artifacts in the Unites States Holocaust Memorial Museum and evidence in police storage facilities across the country, Levitt's story moves between intimate trauma, the story of an unsolved race, and genocide. Barbara Kirshenblatt-Gimblett also presaged the discussion in her article, "Objects of Memory."

2 See Stella Suberman's *The Jew Store*, chronicling one such modest establishment common in immigrant Jewish life in the American South. Unlike Suberman, my mother never remembers anyone referring to her father's or any Jewish merchant's store as "the Jew store" and found the term horribly offensive.

3 See Guzman, "West of Neiman's."

4 For an interesting focus on the economic and emotional scars of the Depression on Jewish merchants, see Wasserman, "Good Old Days of Poverty."

5 Diner, *Lower East Side Memories*, 220.

6 On April 2, 1917, President Woodrow Wilson went before a joint session of Congress to seek a Declaration of War against Germany in order that the world "be made safe for democracy." Four days later, Congress voted to declare war, with six senators and fifty House members dissenting (historymatters.gmu.edu/d/4943/).

7 Frankel, *Jewish Spirit*, 7.

8 See Kochlar-Lindgren, "Passion for Waiting."

9 For the proposed alternative statement of the modern-day museum, see the International Council of Museums 2019 statement as crafted during the annual meeting of the International Council of Museums, Kyoto, Japan: icom.museum/en/news/icom-announces-the-alternative-museum-definition-that-will-be-subject-to-a-vote/ (accessed April 29, 2024).

10 For a smart overview of this ample scholarship, see Conn, *Museums and American Intellectual Life*. Conn argues that Americans, endowed with the belief that knowledge resided in objects themselves, built these institutions with the confidence that they could collect, organize, and display the sum of the world's knowledge.

11 The notion of curatorial dreaming comes from Erica Lehrer and Shelley Butler's collection of essays of the same name from fourteen

distinguished museum curators, scholars, and practitioners. See Butler and Lehrer, *Curatorial Dreams*.

12 The "Wandering Objects" symposium, which took place November 11–13, 2018, included collectors, curators, and scholars who explored twenty-first-century perspectives on Judaica and Jewish material culture. The session in question was titled "Curators' Roundtable: New Directions in Community Engagement Within and Beyond the Museum Walls."

13 For an expanded version of Oldenburg's ideas of third places as the public places on neutral ground where people can gather and interact, see Oldenburg, *Celebrating the Third Place*.

14 Bhabha, *Location of Culture*.

15 Bhabha, "Third Space," 211.

16 Pinsker, *Rich Brew*, 10. See also Gopnik, "One More Cup of Coffee."

17 Pinsker, *Rich Brew*, 10.

18 Pinsker, *Rich Brew*, 202.

19 Pinsker, *Rich Brew*, 147.

20 Kolton-Fromm, *Material Culture*, 50.

21 Kolton-Fromm, *Material Culture*, 179.

22 Kolton-Fromm, *Material Culture*, 40.

23 This podcast discussion about the materiality of Jewish culture with Aleksandra Buncic, Nathan Mastnjack, David Sclar, and Jason Lustig can be found on the 2019 episode of Jewish Lives Matter called "The Materiality of Jewish Culture," www.jewishhistory.fm/roundtable-discussion-on-the-materiality-of-jewish-culture-with-aleksandra-buncic-nathan-mastnjack-david-sclar-and-jason-lustig/.

24 Rabinowitz, *Objects of Love and Regret*, 9.

25 Wall, *The Hare with Amber Eyes*, 349.

26 Levitt, *Objects That Remain*, 52.

27 Levitt, *Objects That Remain*, 118.

28 See my introductory article on this exhibit in the exhibition catalogue: Seriff, "Folk Art from the Global Scrap Heap."

29 Rushdie, *Imaginary Homelands*, 394.

30 For a discussion of museums as exhibitionary complexes that reproduced through their displays the idea of civilization's march toward progress and the place of dominant white Anglo-Saxon's position at the helm of this march, see Bennett, "Exhibitionary Complex."

31 Diner, "Editorial Introduction," xvi.

32　Eskenazi, "Junkyard Jews."
33　Zimring, *Cash for Your Trash*.
34　Glazer, "Holiness of Thrift Shopping."
35　"Scrap Yard: Innovators of Recycling," temporary exhibit curated by Zachary Paul Levine, Jewish Museum of Maryland, October 27, 2019–August 1, 2020.
36　It is important to emphasize here that my Sweetwater grandfather would never have considered his secondhand salvage store a "scrap" or industrial recycling shop. If a secondhand store was a source of shame for his family, it was still considered a step up from the dirty, labor-intensive industrial scrap business of other Jewish businessmen in Texas.
37　Unpublished notes submitted November 2, 2018, to me as roundtable chair, in advance of Dweck's participation in the roundtable.
38　The exhibition catalog was edited by me and contained guest essays by such famed Texas writers as Elmer Kolton, Stephen Harrigan, Carolyn Osborn, Anita Buckley, Tom Pilkington and Dagoberto Gilb. See Seriff, *It Ain't Braggin' If It's True*.
39　Barry Popik wrote in his blog *The Big Apple* (November 25, 2007), "Historian/poet Carl Sandburg (1878–1967) is sometimes given credit for saying 'Texas is a blend of valor and swagger.' Texas author Boyce House (1896–1961) is best known for his short, best-selling Texas humor books published during World War II, providing a chuckle to Texans and non-Texans everywhere. House also wrote newspaper columns, had a radio show, and produced a book of poetry titled *Texas Rhythm, and Other Poems* (1950). Carl Sandburg read the book and said that House's poems have 'That peculiar blend of swagger and valor which is Texas.' Sandburg's quotation is usually taken out of context, with no mention given of Boyce House" (www.barrypopik.com/index.php/new_york_city/entry/texas_is_a_blend_of_valor_and_swagger_carl_sandburg, accessed April 28, 2024).
40　Kolton-Fromm, *Material Culture*, 178.
41　At the Battle of Shiloh, Private Sam Houston Jr. not only fought the Union but also his father's pro-Union stand. A bullet headed for his back instead tore into his mother's Bible carried in his knapsack. Ripping through the pages, the ball stopped at the 70th Psalm: "O God: Thou art my help and my deliverer."
42　For more on this idea of ugliness as a positive, even redeeming characteristic of great opportunity, see Hochman, *Ugliness of Moses Mendelssohn*.

43 The first "It Ain't Braggin' If It's True" exhibit opened in 2001 as the inaugural exhibition in the newly opened temporary gallery of the Bob Bullock Texas State History Museum in downtown Austin and was accompanied by a catalog published by the museum. The second exhibit in this extremely well-received series, which I also curated, commemorated the fifth anniversary of the museum's opening and included a new round of objects and stories under the same six headings and was called "It Still Ain't Braggin' If It's True."

44 Ingwer, "Risks and Faith."

45 Ingwer, "Risks and Faith."

46 Kurin, *Reflections of a Culture Broker*.

47 Clark, "Jewish Museums."

48 William Williams Papers, New York Public Library.

49 "Information as to the Immigration Laws and Their Execution," July 15, 1910, Department of Commerce and Labor, US Immigration Service, Office of Commissioner of Immigration, Ellis Island, New York Harbor.

50 Rabinowitz, *Objects of Love and Regret*, 12.

51 Rabinowitz, *Objects of Love and Regret*, 12.

52 For a fuller understanding of the philosophical and practical elements of this tradition, see Stampfer, *Lithuanian Yeshivas*.

53 Saposnik, "Jolson," 433.

54 McLean, *Museum Exhibit Prototyping*, 2.

55 Juliana Ochs Dweck, notes submitted November 2, 2018, in anticipation of her participation in a roundtable at the "Wandering Objects" symposium.

56 Jennings, "Critique," 69.

57 Westerman "Museums," 159.

58 Brian Coney, "Thurston Moore and Charles Hayward: Improvisations," *Drowned in Sound*, December 11, 2017, drownedinsound.com/releases/20164/reviews/4151533 (accessed April 29, 2024).

Bibliography

Bennett, Tony. "The Exhibitionary Complex." *New Formations* 4 (Spring 1988): 73–102.

Bhabha, Homi K. *The Location of Culture*. London: Routledge, 2006 [1994].
——. "The Third Space: Interview with Homi Bhabha." In *Identity: Community, Culture, Difference*, ed. Jonathan Rutehrford, 207–21. London: Lawrence & Wishart, 1990.
Butler, Shelley Ruth, and Erica Lehrer, eds. *Curatorial Dreams: Critics Imagine Exhibitions*. Montreal: McGill-Queen's University Press, 2016.
Cerny, Charlene, and Suzanne Seriff, eds. *Recycled, Re-Seen: Folk Art from the Global Scrap Heap*. New York: Harry N. Abrams Press, 1996.
Clark, David. "Jewish Museums: Jewish Icons to Jewish Narratives." *European Judaism: A Journal for the New Europe* 36, no. 2 (2003): 4–17.
Conn, Steven. *Museums and American Intellectual Life, 1876–1926*. Chicago: University of Chicago Press, 1998.
Diner, Hasia R. "Editorial Introduction." In *Doing Business in America: A Jewish History*, ed. Hasia R. Diner, ix–xxii. West Lafayette, IN: Purdue University Press, 2018.
——. *Lower East Side Memories: A Jewish Place in America*. Princeton, NJ: Princeton University Press, 2002.
——. *Roads Taken: The Great Jewish Migrations to the New World and the Peddlers Who Forged the Way*. New Haven, CT: Yale University Press, 2015.
Eskenazi, Joe. "Junkyard Jews." *Jewish News of Northern California*, August 20, 2004.
Frankel, Ellen. *The Jewish Spirit: A Celebration in Stories and Art*. New York: Abrams, 1997.
Glazer, Rachel Savannah. "The Holiness of Thrift Shopping." *My Jewish Learning*, February 1, 2017. www.myjewishlearning.com/2017/02/01/the-holiness-of-thrift-shopping/ (accessed April 20, 2024).
Gopnik, Adam. "One More Cup of Coffee." *New Yorker Magazine*, December 24 and 31, 2018, p. 82.
Guzman, Jane Bock. "West of Neiman's: Best Little Department Store in Sweetwater." In *Lone Stars of David: The Jews of Texas*, ed. Hollace Weiner, 172–81. Waltham, MA: Brandeis University Press, 2007.
Hochman, Leah. *The Ugliness of Moses Mendelssohn: Aesthetics, Religion, and Morality in the Eighteenth Century*. London: Routledge, 2015.
Ingwer, Carmela. "Risks and Faith." *Jewish Review: A Journal of Torah, Judaism, Philosophy, Life, and Culture* 5, no. 1 (1991) thejewishreview.org/articles/?id=149 (accessed April 25, 2024).

Jennings, Gretchen. "Critique of 'Between Two Worlds.'" *Exhibitionist Journal: American Alliance of Museums* (Spring 2005): 69. www.name-aam.org/exhibition_spring2015 (accessed April 30, 2024).

Kirshenblatt-Gimblett, Barbara. "Objects of Memory: Material Culture as Life Review." In *Folk Groups and Folklore Genres: A Reader*, ed. Elliott Oring, 329–38. Logan: Utah State University Press, 1989.

Kochlar-Lindgren, "A Passion for Waiting: Walter Benjamin in the Cafés." *The Café Irreal* 27 (2008). cafeirreal.alicewhittenburg.com/review10.htm (accessed April 28, 2024).

Kolton-Fromm, Ken. *Material Culture and Jewish Thought in America*. Bloomington: Indiana University Press, 2010.

Kurin, Richard. *Reflections of a Culture Broker: A View from the Smithsonian*. Washington, DC: Smithsonian Institution Press, 1997.

Leibman, Laura Arnold. *The Art of the Jewish Family: A History of Women in Early New York in Five Objects*. New York: Bard Graduate Center, 2020.

Levitt, Laura. *The Objects That Remain*. University Park: Penn State University Press, 2020.

McLean, Kathleen. *Museum Exhibit Prototyping as a Method of Community Conversation and Participation*. Report of the Consultancy and Professional Development Program of the American Folklife Society, 2013. Unpublished.

McMurtry, Larry. *Walter Benjamin at the Dairy Queen: Reflections at Sixty and Beyond*. New York: Simon & Schuster, 2001.

Oldenburg, Ray. *Celebrating the Third Place: Inspiring Stories about the "Great Good Places" at the Heart of Our Communities*. New York: Marlowe, 2001.

Pinsker, Shachar. *A Rich Brew: How Cafés Created Modern Jewish Culture*. New York: New York University Press, 2018.

Putnam, Robert D. *Bowling Alone: The Collapse and Revival of American Community*. New York: Simon & Schuster, 2000.

Rabinowitz, Richard. *Objects of Love and Regret: A Brooklyn Story*. Cambridge, MA: Harvard University Press, 2002.

Rushdie, Salman. *Imaginary Homelands: Essays and Criticism, 1981–1991*. London: Granta, 1991.

Saposnik, Irv. "Jolson, *The Jazz Singer*, and the Jewish Mother: or How My Yiddishe Momme Became My Mammy." *Judaism: A Quarterly Journal of Jewish Life and Thought* 43, no. 4 (1994): 432–42.

Schwenger, Peter. *The Tears of Things: Melancholy and Physical Objects*. Minneapolis: University of Minnesota Press, 2006.

Seriff, Suzanne. "Folk Art from the Global Scrap Heap: The Place of Irony in the Politics of Poverty." In *Recycled, Re-Seen: Folk Art from the Global Scrap Heap*, ed. Charlene Cerny and Suzanne Seriff, 8–29. New York: Abrams, 1996.

———, ed. *It Ain't Braggin' If It's True*. Austin: Bob Bullock Texas State History Museum, 2001.

Seriff, Suzanne, and Marsha C. Bol. "Folk Art and Social Change in an American Museum." In *Folklife and Museums: Twenty-First Century Perspectives*, ed. C. Kurt Dewhurst, Patricia Hall, and Charlie Seeman, 107–30. Lanham: Rowman & Littlefield, 2017.

Stampfer, Shaul. *Lithuanian Yeshivas of the Nineteenth Century: Creating a Tradition of Learning*, trans. Lindsay Taylor-Guthartz. Liverpool, UK: Littman Library of Jewish Civilization, 2012.

Suberman, Stella. *The Jew Store: A Family Memoir*. Chapel Hill, NC: Algonquin Books, 1998.

Wall, Edmund de. *The Hare with Amber Eyes: A Hidden Inheritance*. New York: Picador, 2010.

Wasserman, Suzanne R. "The Good Old Days of Poverty: The Battle over the Fate of New York City's Lower East Side During the Depression." PhD diss., New York University, 1990.

Westerman, William. "Museums, Immigrants, and the Inversion of Xenophobia: Or, the Inclusive Museum in the Exclusive Society." *International Journal of the Inclusive Museum* 1, no. 4 (2008): 157–62.

Zimring, Carl A. *Cash for Your Trash: Scrap Recycling in America*. New Brunswick, NJ: Rutgers University Press, 2005.

AFTERWORD

Barbara Kirshenblatt-Gimblett

This volume arises from the conference organized by the North Carolina Museum of Art, the Carolina Center for Jewish Studies, and the University of North Carolina at Chapel Hill on November 11–13, 2018. Titled "Wandering Objects: Collecting and Interpreting Jewish Things," the conference took as a starting point the latest iteration of the Judaica gallery at the North Carolina Museum of Art. Arranged in three areas, these objects are the most Jewish of things by virtue of their connection to Jewish religious observance. The die was cast by Abraham Kanof, who initiated the Judaica program at the North Carolina Museum of Art in 1973. He set the parameters for what to collect and how to exhibit the collection, namely, according to ceremonies associated with the Jewish life cycle, calendar year, and synagogue. This is the most common way of exhibiting Judaica to this day.

On the Move

The conference and this volume greatly expand the category of Jewish things, untethering it from its secure moorings in Jewish religious life and putting into question what makes a thing Jewish and, indeed, even a thing. At the heart of this project is mobility, whether "Wandering Things," the title of the conference, or "Lives of Jewish Things," the title of this volume. The focus on mobility is intended to capture the movement of things not only from place to place but also from one category to another and from one context to another. With each movement the thing becomes something else—more or less Jewish, valuable, intelligible, or meaningful. The gold ring that was a curiosity in a sixteenth-century Bavarian art cabinet becomes a masterpiece in an exhibition at the Jewish Museum in Munich centuries later. After the Holocaust a Jewish headstone in Poland might become a millstone for sharpening knives. We might therefore distinguish between things "made Jewish," which can be anything; things "born Jewish," such as Jewish ceremonial art; and things "once Jewish." Oyster platters used as seder plates (made Jewish), seder plates created on the model of oyster platters (born Jewish), and seder plates as unclaimed property (post-Jewish) illustrate the fungibility of these distinctions. Similarly, we might distinguish between objects that were born to move (postcards, stamps, coins) and those that were set in motion.

Things are what they are by virtue of their biographies, contexts, and the lens through which we consider them. Is there anything Jewish about a bench? Juliana Ochs Dweck argues that there is. Is there anything Jewish about the material from which Hanukkah lamps are made? Apparently, yes, as evidenced in a recent display at the Jewish Museum in New York of Hanukkah lamps according to material: tin and lead low on the rabbinic ranking of metals, silver and brass higher, ceramic and wood less durable, pewter popular, and tin-plated iron sheets less so (those were called *khanuke-ayzn* [Hanukkah iron] in Western Yiddish).[1] Even though the Nazi documents and architectural elements in *The Evidence Room* are not Jewish things per se, they are the evidence of the means by which Jews were murdered and, at the same time, evidence of the denial of what happened, hence appearing only in white relief. War has a way of both profaning and sanctifying things, whether a lamp is made from a Torah scroll or two silver bowls are sanctified through personal sacrifice during the Civil War.

New Jewish things are constantly emerging and challenge museums to collect them. During the COVID-19 pandemic, American Israeli artist Ken Goldman printed on a face mask a sixteenth-century amulet against the plague, which he found reproduced in a nineteenth-century kabbalistic work printed in Lwów. I asked him to gift this mask to POLIN Museum of the History of Polish Jews in Warsaw, and it is now in the collection. I also collected Holocaust-themed face masks in the hope that POLIN Museum would accept them, but I am waiting for the right moment to broach the subject.

Those masks were created by Tyler Kozdron and sold on his website https://www.holocaust.claims/. He had been working in a gas station in the Upper Midwest and became an essential worker from the start of the pandemic. The elaborate safety precautions at his workplace, which he found onerous and ineffective, inspired him to make and sell Holocaust face masks in 2020. He was twenty-eight at the time. He printed images on the masks: the crematoria in Auschwitz; a colorized black-and-white photograph of a child at gunpoint from the Stroop report documenting the German suppression of the Warsaw Ghetto Uprising in 1942, with the caption "Young Child at Gunpoint. Another bold image that gets the point across without being overly offensive"; and a member of the Waffen-SS shooting a Jew in the head at the edge of a mass grave in Vinnitsa, Ukraine, in July 1941, with the caption "Execution. For those wanting to 'stand out' a bit. May be offensive to some, but hey, this is the art of making people think for themselves." Kozdron's intention was to protest tyranny by protesting the mandate to wear masks, which he interpreted as a violation of individual freedom.

The yellow star that the Germans forced Jews to wear during the Holocaust has also been weaponized to the same end. Although this false analogy distorts the Holocaust and reduces the predicament of its victims to a failure to defend their personal freedom, such objects, like antisemitica more generally, are part of a larger story of Jewish and antisemitic responses to the pandemic.

A new category of things has emerged in Poland since the Holocaust: *pożydowskie*, "post-Jewish," referring to property whose Jewish owners perished during the Holocaust or who survived but cannot be found.[2] Although the term *post-Jewish* has an air of finality about it, as if to say these objects are no longer Jewish, they actually occupy a space of uncertainty and disquietude. They are haunted by the ghosts of their former owners and arouse fear that their rightful owners or their heirs might return. Formerly Jewish things are defined by what they once were but leave open what they now are and might become. Poland is awash in formerly Jewish things—apartments and houses, synagogues and cemeteries, shops and factories, and things of all kinds, whether collected at flea markets, at auctions, or online or unearthed. Far from a settled matter, property, from dishes, clothing, and furniture to real estate, is post-Jewish for as long as it is unclaimed by its rightful Jewish owner.

These objects' biographies, to the extent that they can be recovered, tell a story of dispossession by confiscation, expropriation, theft, pillage, looting, plunder, murder, and grave robbing, as well as stories of safekeeping, restitution, and legitimate transfer of ownership. For some of their current custodians, they are proxies for the Jews who once owned them. Others prefer to deny or forget those to whom their homes and things once belonged. The term *pożydowskie* affirms and negates in one gesture: Jewish no longer. Can these things ever be anything else? Although the term *post-Jewish* can be found in English, it is rare and, when it does turn up, it never refers to property but rather to identity, alongside postethnic and post-Judaism, indicating the point after which "Jewish" or "ethnic" has ceased to be relevant, except as a former state, which is to make post-Jewish, like *pożydowskie*, an example of constitutive negativity. Whereas identity is intangible, objects are not, and their persistent materiality is also an enduring reminder, as is the word *pożydowskie*, of their earlier life as Jewish things.

What do post-Jewish objects become in a museum setting? They appear in the many small museums dedicated to the history of Jews in Poland, often in former synagogues. Were they to appear in American Jewish museums, they would not be considered post-Jewish. In a sense, everything in a history or ethnographic museum is "post" something or it would not be there. Things have had many lives, the last one as a museum object. That said, how does the "museum effect" work on post-Jewish things? Do they become post-post-Jewish in a move that makes them Jewish in a new way—a post-Jewish museum artifact that is valued for its former life as a Jewish thing?

Consider the objects displayed in "Afterlives: Recovering the Lost Stories of Looted Art," a temporary exhibition at the Jewish Museum in New York (August 20, 2021–January 9, 2022). The curators included ceremonial art sent by the Jewish community in Danzig to the Jewish Theological Seminary in 1939 for safekeeping. This treasure is today part of the Jewish Museum's collection. To define these objects as "looted" is to foreground the crime and the prospect of restitution, even if restitution is impossible. In contrast, "post-Jewish" effaces the crime, reduces Judaica to property, and nullifies prior ownership—post-Jewish things are simply unclaimed. The PWN dictionary defines *pożydowski* thus: "post-Jewish: about property—remaining from Jews who died during World War II," as though they simply abandoned their things and relinquished ownership. By definition without heirs, possibly forever, these things are de facto no longer Jewish property.³

Judaica as looted object is one of several ways that the Jewish Museum has found to exhibit Judaica without exhibiting it as Judaica. Note the contrast between how the Danzig treasure was displayed in "Afterlives," carefully ordered on glass shelves in the style of open storage or a warehouse, and how such objects were displayed in the exhibition "Kraków Under Nazi Occupation, 1939–1945" in the former administrative building of Oskar Schindler's Enamel Factory in Kraków, which opened in 2010. There the objects are arranged somewhat haphazardly, as though in an antiquarian shop, a mix of Judaica, silverware, clocks, and the like—in a word, as plunder on its way to becoming post-Jewish. The word *plunder* appears on an adjacent touchscreen.

Throughout Poland today, door frames in dwellings where Jews once lived are marked by the absence of their mezuzah. The mezuzah was ripped off, leaving a raw indentation. Mi Polin, the first design studio in Poland since World War II to create Judaica, has found a way to heal the wound by creating a new kind of object: a mezuzah cast in bronze from a wax imprint of the indentation. Helena Czernek and Aleksander Prugar, who founded Mi Polin in 2014, try to find out as much as possible about those who once lived at that address, which they include in the documentation.

On Display

To the extent that Jewish things are collected by museums other than Jewish ones, the objects either appear in their own gallery or are integrated into the permanent exhibition.⁴ The North Carolina Museum of Art takes the former approach, the Museum of Fine Arts Boston, the latter approach (and recently also the former approach), and in both cases Jewish things fall within the category of decorative art, an unfortunate term, especially today when such hierarchies—fine versus decorative—are in question. When they are shown in their own gallery, the Jewish nature of these things, their meanings and ritual contexts, are at the fore. Integrated into the permanent exhibition, their relationship to the decorative arts of the time and place of their making is paramount—or their presence might also support a message of cultural or religious diversity.

Although some Jewish museums continue to show their Judaica collections in permanent dedicated galleries—such as the recently shuttered Jewish Museum London and the Maltz Museum of Jewish Heritage in a suburb of Cleveland, Ohio—the Jewish Museum in New York City has put this approach on display while putting it into question. In 2018 the Jewish Museum replaced their old permanent exhibition, "Culture and Continuity: The Jewish Journey," by then twenty-five years old, with "Scenes from the Collection," their answer to the question of whether permanent exhibitions are a thing of the past. The new permanent exhibition consists of rotating displays, essentially temporary mini-exhibitions, in seven permanent spaces defined thematically—they too can change. The current themes are Constellations, Taxonomies, Masterpieces and Curiosities, Accumulations, Signs and Symbols, Television and Beyond, and Personas. This approach allows the Jewish Museum to feature objects in the collection that might otherwise never be shown or shown together, a solution consistent with their identity as an art museum and with their contemporary art sensibility, and an opportunity to show their outstanding Judaica collection in a new way.

The old way—all the Judaica together, in a dedicated space, organized according to the calendar year, life cycle, and synagogue life—was not only predictable but also normative. Such displays generally introduce the public to Judaism, regardless of the provenance of the objects and their relation to a particular time, place, and community, as could be seen in the old permanent exhibition at the Jewish Museum Berlin. There was also the feeling that their visitors were not interested in Kiddush cups, seder plates, and Torah crowns, although many people still miss the spectacular display of Hanukkah lamps in the old permanent exhibition; it was an effective way to communicate the diversity and commonality of Jewish communities across time and space—the Jewish Museum's collection, at over a thousand Hanukkah lamps, is the largest of its kind.

Instead, the Jewish Museum has integrated Judaica into several of the thematic spaces: things bearing a Star of David in Signs and Symbols; a hand-carved Hanukkah lamp from Theresienstadt in Masterpieces and Curiosities (an unfortunate rubric for Holocaust objects); Hanukkah lamps in Accumulations, organized according to material; and Judaica among other kinds of things in Taxonomies. According to the Taxonomies text panel, this dazzling display was inspired by the Renaissance cabinet of wonder and is intended to bring together the "rare and curious," show the eclectic nature of the Jewish Museum's collections, and juxtapose objects based on "non-traditional classifications according to activities such as marking time, praying, travel, or by material." A Torah crown, a ship model, and a watch are among the rare and curious objects shown in this red treasure box. Judaica appears here not as Judaica per se but as "rare and curious" things. The curators hope that those tired of conventional exhibitions of Judaica might be surprised and intrigued by seeing Jewish ceremonial art in relation to other rare and curious things.

Tight curation, exquisite installation, and a light interpretive touch are hallmarks of "Scenes from the Collection." Selection, aggregation, juxtaposition, and arrangement in space relate objects to each other in familiar and surprising ways—the juxtaposition of a papercut *mizrah*, a Kehinde Wiley painting, and a Torah ark, based on their visual similarities, for example. By bringing out surprising affinities between objects, the curators could override conventional distinctions between ancient and modern, traditional and avant-garde, mass media and fine art, fine art and decorative art, art and artifact. Visitors are trusted to engage with the objects as art, without the mediation of extensive texts and multimedia interpretive tools. An audioguide, docents, and guided tours serve visitors who want to know more, thus clearing the space of informational clutter for those who prefer a less mediated experience.

Ethnographic museums present different challenges. First and foremost, they are museums of ethnography, of ethnographic knowledge, of ethnography as a disciplinary formation. As such, they reflect the absence or marginalization of Jews as an anthropological subject both in the academy and in museums, whether those dedicated to world cultures or to national or regional folk culture. Their historical collections reflect the project of salvage ethnography, which aims to record a changing if not disappearing way of life. Although there were Jewish ethnographic expeditions, collections, and museums in Europe before the Holocaust, most famously those led by S. An-sky in the Pale of Settlement on the eve of World War I, relatively little of those efforts remains. Today in Warsaw, the State Ethnographic Museum recently created a Jewish corner and filled it with an eclectic collection of things, including a scale model of the Gąbin (Gombin, in Yiddish) wooden synagogue. In Kraków the Seweryn Udziela Ethnographic Museum has neither created a separate area for Jewish things nor integrated Jewish things into its permanent exhibition, although it has mounted temporary exhibitions on topics related to Jews, thanks to the good efforts of Erica Lehrer.

In history museums, things, Jewish or not, are either the basis for telling the story of a Jewish community or they support a multimedia narrative exhibition. At POLIN Museum of the History of Polish Jews, in Warsaw, an eighteenth-century Torah crown anchors the presentation of synagogue life in the early modern period, and the impact of the railway during the nineteenth century is made more vivid by train tickets from the period, copies of which visitors can take away with them.

Among the objects most valued by history museums are those with a story, things that bear witness. One of the most precious things in POLIN Museum's collection is a spoon, the root of a tree having twisted around it, that was found on the site of the former Warsaw ghetto during the archeological excavation preceding the construction of POLIN Museum. Although Holocaust museums are outside the scope of this volume, they are a prime site for thinking about things made Jewish by the stories told by and about them. This is the principle governing the new permanent exhibition at the Museum of Jewish Heritage: A Living Memorial to the Holocaust in Lower Manhattan, where the history of the Holocaust is presented through 1,250 original objects and their stories, supported by survivor testimony and historical documents.

Museums have historically been repositories for the tangible, but it is the intangible, the stories, that makes matter matter. Beit Hatfutsot: Museum of the Diaspora prided itself on its pioneering multimedia narrative exhibition, which as a matter of principle presented the story of the Jewish people without original objects when it opened in 1978 in Tel Aviv, preferring copies even when originals could have been shown. Among the most beloved things in this exhibition are the twenty-one meticulous scale models of synagogues across the Diaspora. Created for the museum, these scale models have become Jewish things in their own right—Jewish "museum things." In 2016 the synagogue models were reinstalled in a gallery of their own, Synagogue Hall, in anticipation of the 2021 opening of ANU Museum of the Jewish People, the renewed and rebranded Beit Hatfutsot. The "Hallelujah! Assemble, Pray, Study: Synagogues Past and

Present" installation departs from the old Beit Hatfutsot in several ways. First, the curators added an original object related to each synagogue, and, second, they shifted the emphasis from the tangible to the intangible, from synagogue architecture to synagogue life, and from the physical models to multimedia.

A centerpiece of POLIN Museum's core exhibition is the painted ceiling and timber-frame roof based on the seventeenth-century wooden synagogue that once stood in Gwoździec, today in Ukraine. That synagogue was destroyed by fire during World War I. The remaining wooden synagogues were destroyed by the Germans during the Holocaust. POLIN Museum had always intended to feature a wooden synagogue in its multimedia narrative core exhibition. According to the original masterplan, a prop maker was to make a wooden synagogue ceiling based on a historical one. A meeting in 2007 with Handshouse Studio, an educational nonprofit in Massachusetts, persuaded the museum to change course.

The mission of Handshouse Studio is to recover lost objects. Although it is not possible to recover the original object, it is possible to recover the knowledge of how to build it by using traditional tools, materials, and techniques. Recovery of that knowledge, which is intangible, is a material practice resulting in a new kind of object. The result is not a reconstruction, copy, facsimile, or other second-order version of the original. It is not virtual. It is actual. It is a new kind of object by virtue of how it was made and the knowledge recovered in the process.

Handshouse proposed the synagogue that once stood in Gwoździec because it is the single best documented of all the great wooden synagogues. Today the exquisite painted ceiling and timber-frame roof created by a team of more than three hundred volunteers and experts anchors the presentation of Jewish everyday life in towns during the early modern period. The value of this new kind of Jewish thing lies in the intangible knowledge recovered during its making.

This volume offers a capacious understanding of Jewish things. Although the starting point was Judaica, those most Jewish of Jewish things, the idea that things move unsettles received categories. As things escape those categories, they acquire new roles and meanings in the world and in the museum.

Notes

1. See, for instance, London, *Koheles Shlomo*, 157.
2. See Waligórska and Sorkina, "Second Life of Jewish Belongings."
3. "Pożydowski: O mieniu: pozostały po Żydach, którzy zginęli w czasie II wojny światowej," *Słownik jędzyk polskiego*, sjp.pwn.pl/poradnia/szukaj/%C5%BCydowska (accessed June 22, 2023). See also Forecki, "Nasze mienie 'pożydowskie.'"
4. I first took up these issues almost fifty years ago; see Kirshenblatt-Gimblett, "American Jewish Life." I elaborated on them a decade later; see Kirshenblatt-Gimblett, *Destination Culture*.

Bibliography

Forecki, Piotr. "Nasze mienie 'pożydowskie.'" *Krytyka polityczna* (December 14, 2014).

Kirshenblatt-Gimblett, Barbara. "American Jewish Life: Ethnographic Approaches to Collection, Presentation, and Interpretation in Museums." *Jewish Folklore and Ethnology Newsletter* 7 (1985): 4–12.

———. *Destination Culture: Tourism, Museums, and Heritage*. Berkeley: University of California Press, 1997.

London, Shlomo Zalman. *Koheles Shlomo*, ed. Shlomo Bloch. Hannover, Germany: Telgener, 1836.

Waligórska, Magdalena, and Ina Sorkina. "The Second Life of Jewish Belongings: Jewish Personal Objects and Their Afterlives in the Polish and Belarusian Post-Holocaust Shtetls." *Holocaust Studies* 29, no. 3 (2023): 341–62. doi.org/10.1080/17504902.2022.2047292 (accessed June 16, 2023).

ACKNOWLEDGMENTS

The Lives of Jewish Things, like the "Wandering Objects" symposium out of which it was born, has been an exhilarating interdisciplinary, transnational, cross-cultural collaboration. Many individuals, organizations, and institutions united to offer inspiration and support as our symposium gathering of 2018 was transformed into text. First and foremost, we thank dedicated scholar, editor, and teacher Dan Ben-Amos, *z"l*, who had the initial vision of this volume as a part of the Raphael Patai Series in Jewish Folklore and Anthropology at Wayne State University Press. Our editor, Sandra Korn, has steadfastly guided us in his absence with patience and care. We thank both Sandra and the anonymous readers for their thoughtful feedback on the manuscript, and we thank Bernie Herman and Catherine Whalen for their valuable suggestions on first drafts. Thanks go as well to Justine Orlovsky-Schnitzler, who helped transcribe the Collectors' Roundtable.

At our home institution, the University of North Carolina at Chapel Hill, we are grateful for the support of our departments, the Department of Germanic and Slavic Languages and Literatures and its Melanie and Frank Spencer Fund, the Department of American Studies, as well as the Ackland Museum of Art. Our greatest thanks go to the Carolina Center for Jewish Studies and the North Carolina Museum of Art (NCMA), the two partners that made our symposium possible and that continue to support our collaborative efforts to bridge public and academic study of Jewish material culture. The success of an institution relies on the people behind it, and Karen Gajewski, the executive director of the Carolina Center for Jewish Studies, was instrumental throughout all stages of this project. At the NCMA, curator emeritus John Coffey, who oversaw the Judaic Art Gallery until 2023 and brought Gabriel Goldstein on board as consulting curator and collaborator, first envisioned the symposium. John's commitment to bringing students into the museum and curators into the classroom has fostered a relationship between UNC–Chapel Hill and the NCMA that continues to enrich our teaching, research, and service.

At the "Wandering Objects" symposium, we were fortunate to welcome an international array of curators, scholars, and collectors to consider the contemporary collection and interpretation of Jewish material culture. We are grateful to all the symposium presenters, moderators, the Jewish Studies Graduate Student Network, and community participants who made the three-day exchange so stimulating and generative, and, in particular, to those participants who carried their work through onto these pages with enduring patience throughout the pandemic years. WenLi Heffner, from the Carolina Center for Jewish Studies, worked closely with the partners from the NCMA. Curator of Judaic art Sean Burrus and Friends of the Judaic Art Gallery at the NCMA and supporters of the Carolina Center for Jewish Studies provided invaluable public and financial support for the symposium and this publication, without which we could not have produced either. We also thank the editors at *Museum Worlds*, *Southern Cultures*, and Penn State University Press, who permitted versions of their previously published works to reappear in this volume. Finally, we owe great gratitude to our families, in particular, Manette and Aron Berlinger and Noam and Nelya Fachtag, for their patient listening, careful reading, insightful dialogue, and creative engagement of all things Jewish over the past many years.

Editing this volume has been a journey as we wandered with wonder through changing landscapes of meaning. En route, the individual objects in this book became a collection, the single voices became a chorus, and the distinct ideas became patterns of thought and practice. To all the caretakers—material, intellectual, and cultural—of the moving pieces in this book and beyond, we thank you for journeying with us in the space between. Neither here nor there, these objects affirm the deep meanings produced on the move and the powerful roles they play in Jewish experience.

APPENDIX

Collectors' Roundtable: Gabriel Goldstein in Conversation with Max N. Berry, Jane Gershon Weitzman, and William L. Gross

The "Wandering Objects: Collecting and Interpreting Jewish Things" symposium (November 11–13, 2018), the first of its kind in the southeastern United States, was interdisciplinary and expansive in its inquiry. The panel presentations, roundtable discussions, and museum tours engaged the insights of art historians, anthropologists, folklorists, religious studies scholars, philosophers, cultural critics, curators, and private collectors into the changing meanings of Jewish material culture today. Participants examined how these materials are displayed and interpreted in museums, used as instruments of inquiry, and drawn on as archives of information. Featured scholars, curators, and collectors traced histories of the struggle to define the identity and purpose of the "Jewish" object and imagined futures of this effort as material things move with increasing ease across the globe today in physical, virtual, and imagined forms.

The Collectors' Roundtable was a key part of the symposium's work—a space where curators and scholars could hear from and pose questions to active collectors of Judaica about shared and valued things. Collectors have been a crucial force in the preservation, connoisseurship, and analysis of these objects over the past several generations, and their activities, outlooks, and priorities have been formative to an understanding of the importance, resonance, and potential of Jewish objects in all contexts—homes, synagogues, private collections, museums, and beyond. This appendix offers an abridged transcript of the conversation between the three collectors featured at the symposium—Max N. Berry, Jane Gershon Weitzman, and William L. Gross—who shared their ideas and insights in conversation with curator Gabriel Goldstein.

GABRIEL GOLDSTEIN: One of the highlights of this project, of this conference, was the bringing together of university scholarship—the world of the academy—and the world of public scholarship and curation from the museum. Both of those are very much entwined and enhanced by the worlds of private collecting. That is true in every area of art and material culture, and I think particularly in this aspect. The idea of the ephemeral—and I think every object truly is ephemeral—relies on someone to make sure that there are survivors.

In so many ways in the world of Judaica, in the world of Jewish material culture, it has been private collectors who have ensured and protected the objects and have seen this as a priority. They have worked hand in hand with museums and with the academy to reach new levels of recognition, which we are seeing today—and which is ongoing.

I'm just thrilled to be joined here today by three prominent and different collectors from across the world who can tell us their own personal narratives about their collections and their own histories. Together, we will discuss repositories of fine or fascinating objects and repositories of thinking, of leadership, and of connoisseurship. We ask why they collect, and they ask themselves why they collect, how they collect, what is the purpose of that collecting, and what happens next. These are questions we should be asking ourselves as institutions and as scholars and as individuals. So, it's my privilege to introduce to you now William Gross, Jane Weitzman, and Max Berry. I've invited each of these three to present one object from their collection as an entry point into talking about their own journeys, their own missions, and priorities in their collecting.

WILLIAM GROSS: A week and a half ago, Gabe sent me an email that said, "Can you pick out an object that you like, you think is important, and send it to me?" Thirty seconds later, he had it on his computer and he immediately wrote back, "I was hoping you would pick that one!" Were we to have the time, I would love to tell you how it came up and how I established what it was. The research I did on the man that it memorializes—there are so many aspects to it—but basically, it is a pair of *atzei chaim*, the tops of Torah staves, with beautiful late Gothic carving and a wonderful inscription memorializing one Netanel Trabo.

If you were to see the "Trabo," [it is carved] with a little what we call a *tshuptshik* at the end of his name, which means there is a letter missing. He didn't have room to carve, and I think it was he who carved these himself, for "Trabot." It turns out, through research, Trabot was a family who in one of the two fifteenth-century expulsions of Jews from the town of Trévoux in France, moved over the border and changed their name in honor of the town to Trabot. For virtually three centuries, until into the eighteenth century, they were a major rabbinical family in Italy. Then, somehow, and I have not been able to discover why, they completely died out. After, there were dozens and dozens and dozens of famous rabbis who worked in Italy, but no family with that name, either Jewish or non-Jewish, exists in Italy today. So, we are looking at a fifteenth-century Jewish ritual object of which there are, I would imagine, a number that you can more or less count on the fingers of both hands, carved in wood, which I adore—and of extreme importance because it turns out that this man was a famous scribe. We know of five manuscripts and other libraries in which he is signed. He was a merchant. He was a renaissance man. He was like rabbis used to be. [*laughter*] Well, we won't get into that. [*laughter*]. So it is absolutely perhaps the most important object that I have in the collection. Is it my favorite? Um, you know, you can ask me, Who is your favorite grandchild? I mean, anybody who has those can absolutely understand—there is no choice.

I like this object. Now, why do I like it? What does it have to do with how I started in this field? I will immediately give you this spoiler. My father-in-law was Maurice Spertus, and his collection—and he was a major Judaica collector in the '60s and '70s—is the Spertus Museum in Chicago. And so Judaically, I grew up at his knees. He was like a second father to me and he was an incredible inspiration in terms of collecting. I've been an obsessive collector of something or everything since I was six years old. I don't know if any of you remember baby

FIGURE 10.1. *Atzei chaim* (Torah staves), Italian or French, ca. 1450; wood; 37.7 × 25.1 × 14.7 cm. Princeton University Art Museum, museum purchase, Fowler McCormick, Class of 1921, Fund. Photo by Joseph Hu.

books that mothers used to keep for their children, but my mother specifically has it that at the age of six, I was collecting playing cards of all different sorts. So at that point in my life, in my early twenties, when I married his daughter—we've been together sixty-two years now—these two streams of my Jewish identity, encouraged by my father-in-law and my own family and my obsessive collecting, came together.

My father-in-law used to have many groups coming to his home to view his collection. He gave me a philosophy that has been the leitmotif of my collecting ever since. He said, Bill, the wonderful thing about Judaica is that I could invite religious people to my house and they could look at these objects and immediately understand their significance within Jewish ritual but basically have no particular relationship to their aesthetics and work that they represent in terms of material art objects within the Jewish people. And, I can invite secular people, and they understand because they have some background and exposure to art, and through them I can explain the Jewish values that are behind them. So they're just great for everybody. That has served me ever since.

I have always viewed my collection as an educational tool, nothing more and nothing less. And that has led me to certain things. If I were to look at the paradigm of what John [Coffey] has incredibly done here [at the North Carolina Museum of Art], and we've talked about it, this is Judaica presented as an art object. The fact that it's organized by life cycle and that they are presented as art objects—I have never, ever looked at a piece of Judaica that I have as an art object! I'm a historian by training. For me, every piece I have, whether it's a piece of paper, silver, etc.—they are documents of Jewish history. When you look at them primarily as art objects, it's perfect for this museum, but for me, they lose something. They lose context, and I love context! I adore context! Without it nothing in our life has meaning, and these objects don't either.

So I, from the very beginning, looked at my collection and looked at arranging my collection in a way that has not been mentioned until now. Yesterday we heard an incredible lecture [by Barbara Kirshenblatt-Gimblett] and she went over a number of different approaches that museums can use. My approach wasn't mentioned, and perhaps it's because I'm a historian. I look at these objects from the point of view of what I would call a geographical cultural perspective. If you were to come to my house and see—and by the way, you are all invited when you come to Israel, John has my details, he's been there, he knows the way, he can tell you about it—you will see the objects displayed in cases and grouped by place of origin, right? I have Austro-Hungarian, which is primarily Vienna, and then I have Eastern Europe, which is a term I don't like, but we have to use it, where the source is 90 percent Ukrainian, and then German, of course, which is a major category, and then France and Holland and then Hungary, Czechia, Ashkenaz.

Over on the other side of the vitrine, Sepharad, and the Mizrahim, which I like more. Why? Because most of those objects were made by Jewish craftsmen. Whenever I think about a Jew writing a manuscript, making an object, I always have this feeling he's investing part of his soul into it, imbuing this object with something more than it is. It creates an aura, as it were, around it that truly gives contextual meaning to it. So, what do I achieve by dividing them this way? Well, I think it's a unique way of looking at Judaica. If I have this vitrine of Vienna items next to a vitrine of German items, it's my hope that people will see the difference between, let's say, the Biedermeier Austrian-ness of this versus the German classical approach to it. And then you get to Eastern Europe, with these wild panoplies of animals and foliage, done in completely different techniques.

To me, this is vitally important because what interests me now in Judaica, is, What does it mean for the Jewish people? What does it tell us about where they live and about how they relate to their surroundings? To look at Judaica in isolation is to lose its meaning. Jews never lived alone, as much as we think they were ghettoized or lived in the *mellah*, or lived in separate Jewish quarters—it just isn't true. They did, but there was a steady social and artistic and cultural intercourse between the Jews and their surrounding cultures that never ended. This is so obvious when you look at the objects in this particular way. I think that if I present Austrian Judaica and I illuminate that with buildings from Vienna, with non-Jewish objects from Vienna, that people begin to understand there is a relationship between these Jewish objects and their surrounding cultures and that there were mutual influences going on materially, culturally, in every way. That creates an incredibly important environment in which people can understand Jewish life and Jewish history.

The other thing is slightly political, because today I live in Israel and the ultra-Orthodox community, which constitutes 15 to 20 percent of Israel, which has an amazing cultural and political influence in the country, are basically isolationist. From the time of Moses Mendelssohn and the rise of the Enlightenment and the rise of the Hasidism and the reaction to it came through, and then, of course, finally, with the Holocaust, which just destroyed everything that was important to this group of people, they have circled their covered wagons and resist everything from the outside. What's even worse—excuse me for getting political—is that they tell the rest of us that they are inheritors of the true tradition of Judaism, whereas Jews, as obviously demonstrated by *tashmishei kedushah*—ritual objects—were more open to their outside surroundings three hundred years ago than Jews are today. So I like very much this geographic cultural approach because I think it tells things about Jewish life that are missed in these kinds of exhibitions. All of these things amplify the life that they represent at that time. So that's my *mi ani* [who am I].

GABRIEL GOLDSTEIN: Thank you, William. Next, we have Jane Weitzman.

JANE WEITZMAN: Hi. I started collecting right after I got out of college, I moved to Boston and a cousin of mine used to go to the Canary Islands every year, and he would bring back Judaica. I said, when I finally had about $150 together, I said, "I want you to buy me something." He said, "So what do you want? How much can you spend?" He brought me back a Kiddush cup that was, of course, fake, but that got me started. I later inherited the *megillah* that a cousin of my father's—a first cousin who lived in a little shtetl called Stepan and was a scribe—used. He sent these things he made to Atlanta, where my grandfather sold them and then sent back money. I hid it somewhere, and I did such a good job that I just couldn't find it for today. Those two things had an impact on me. In those days, I couldn't afford very much. I used to buy ephemera, which seems to be a big thing here today. I came up with some interesting things: I found a pamphlet from the Spanish Portuguese synagogue where the women's, the Ladies Guild, had taken it upon themselves to rehabilitate the Jewish prostitutes in New York, the young Jewish prostitutes. I also can't find that, but I will find all of these things. At any rate, for a while, I had to buy ephemera, and then, you know, I finally had enough money to purchase some things, and I bought a lot of *ketubbot* [marriage contracts]. And somehow I got into women's prayer books from different countries with the pretty bindings.

People say, "How do you decide to buy something?" Usually, I like to buy things that are beautiful, that I feel are beautiful. This piece is neither beautiful nor worth anything, except to me. About thirty years ago, a man named Dr. José Miller, who was the president of the Havana, Cuba, Jewish community, called the American Jewish Joint Distribution Committee [JDC], which I will now refer to as the Joint, and said, "My community needs your help." A couple of years later, I was invited to be on the board of the Joint. I was part of the first Jewish mission, the first JDC mission to Cuba. At that time, the 92nd Street Y wasn't taking people, the synagogues weren't taking people, and it was hard to go there. So the first time I went, we went through Mexico, and the night we arrived, we went to the Patronato, which is the large synagogue there. I couldn't find a place to sit down because the roof was open. It was in such a bad state that there was pigeon stuff all over the pews. It was disgusting, and we really saw what we had to do, to fix things in this community. I had been in Latvia and Lithuania the month before with a friend of mine, Lynn Schusterman—many of you know her—and we said, "Well, there's just as much poverty here, except that it's warm. At least these people weren't freezing!" We didn't have to provide the money for heat for them.

We saw all the things we were taken to see, all aspects of the community, and later in the afternoon, they said, "Would anybody like to see the Sephardic synagogue?" I have been a Sephardophile my entire life. I grew up in Atlanta with a community that was mostly from Rhodes. My father was their attorney, so we were honored guests at every event they had. So I said yes and Lynn said yes, and we went to the Sephardic synagogue, which, of course, was in terrible shape, just like the Patronato was in those days. We saw this poverty and we knew how the people were living. We had cash on us, and we gave it to them—American dollars were very helpful—and an elderly gentleman said there were two *tzedakah* boxes left. There was no need for a *tzedakah* box because there wasn't anybody there who could afford to put even a coin into them. They had to worry about what was going to be on their table. So he said, "I would like each of you to have one of these," and that's what this is, so this was for them to take care of the sick in their community.

Well, pretty soon, you know, we really went back and we all raised money. I remember going to some Cuban Jewish people that I knew, and they wouldn't help. They said, "No, the people who stayed were Communists and they were terrible, and I won't give one dime." When I went back the second time, the tone in the Cuban community had changed and the roof was fixed. The Patronato looked beautiful. I didn't go back to the Sephardic synagogue again, but everything had changed. On the second floor was a computer room donated by the woman—the first woman I called to solicit, to see if she would give something. Someone in her own community probably got to her. So this, to me, really symbolizes helping our fellow Jews. I'm not religious, but I really believe that all Jews are responsible for one another. And if you're Jewish, and I know many of you aren't, and unless you chose to be Jewish, you wouldn't be sitting in this room, nor would I be here, if someone along the way didn't help. Until recent times, this has been a major priority of Jews all over the world.

So now I'd like to disagree with Bill [*laughter*] . . .

WILLIAM GROSS: You, my wife, my children, my grandchildren, most audiences—join the crowd, Jane!

JANE WEITZMAN: I do see the things that I've collected—not this obviously, because it's neither beautiful nor art—but I do see the things, most of the things, or many of the things that I've bought over the years, over my more than fifty years of collecting—as art. First of all, when the Hebrew language is written beautifully as it can be, it's art. Some of us saw this gentleman here—I'm sorry, I don't remember your name—but you contributed a [John Singer] Sargent piece to the museum and some of us saw it last night. And when somebody like Sargent writes Hebrew, it's art. Believe me. And even my cousin, whom I never got to meet because he was murdered in a pogrom, his family never even made it to the Holocaust—but that *megillah*, which unfortunately, I couldn't find—next time—it's, it's art. It's really beautiful. And I display these things as if they're art. Actually, I know you're

FIGURE 10.2. *Tzedakah* box (charity container), Cuba, twentieth century. Weitzman Family Collection.

supposed to do it by theme, but I have so little room in my New York apartment where I've brought some of my better pieces, that I just put them all in together, and they look pretty good. In Greenwich, it's arranged more toward the way it's supposed to be. I have really loved being Jewish, so I've loved collecting the artifacts of who I am and what my past is. I keep falling into wonderful things like today. My husband commuted to Spain for forty years, and he became friendly with the Jews in Madrid. They are building a museum, and I have some records and things from the Inquisition—and, of course, now they will go there. I'm just so lucky that I will get to see all these beautiful things. So, my collection has really led me to many wonderful things. I have been able to travel all over the world, not just to Cuba with the Joint. I've picked up some very interesting things along the way, but this to me, poor as it is, just a piece of paper glued onto some tin, it symbolizes a lot to me.

GABRIEL GOLDSTEIN: Thank you, Jane. And next, Max Berry.

MAX BERRY: Thank you, Gabe. First of all, I thank the sponsors of this symposium, the North Carolina Museum of Art at which John Coffey is the curator and has been the chief curator for many years. While he is not Jewish, he runs perhaps the best museum gallery of Judaica in the country, and it rivals some in Europe. So, I take my hat off to you, you're a real hero and I know you have a staff that does a lot of this work and people are scattered around the room, but you are the quarterback and you've done a great job and it's important. I think that we're on the cusp of Judaica making more inroads than it has in the last fifty years in this country. It's very important. I think we'll look back on this symposium as being one of the kickoffs.

Before I talk about these finials from Ancona, Italy, I want to talk about my philosophy of collecting. I've collected since I was a little boy. Marbles—remember, you used to draw a circle in the sand? Well, I collected those marbles and lost a few agates along the way. I collected baseball cards like a lot of people. I collected minerals because Oklahoma and Arkansas and all those states out southwest have lots of good minerals, and we collected them. They were rarely expensive at the time. I collected stamps and coins and things as I got older, and when I went to Washington, DC, in 1960, I collected American paintings and European paintings and sculpture.

I started collecting Judaica in the '60s, and a little more in the '80s because I went to Israel. I bought some things there and a couple of them weren't right. You learn the hard way, but every collector I know has made a mistake or two. People like Bill Gross, I asked advice from and got it. I'm going to incorporate by reference everything that Bill said and everything that Jane said in my talk, so if I don't say another word, I feel good about that. So, what do I want in my collection? Well, I'm not disciplined. I never have been. So in paintings, I go from the Peales to Hartnett to Calder to Deborah Butterfield and beyond. I'm not a slow collector. When I started collecting Judaica, I studied, I asked people who are curators and collectors and people that have knowledge for advice. I checked things out, even going to some labs to check metals out. I'm a sort of tenacious person, trying not to make a mistake, so you first associate yourself with curators and other people that know a lot more than you, and hopefully it brushes off. But I'm still able to make a mistake, believe me. I had to get a chief curator that really kept me honest, because on details like labels and filing and so forth, I'm not good. So, I found a chief curator, and I married her. It's Pam Berry, right over there. [*laughter, applause*] People come to our home to see the collection, and it's evident that someone else besides me has made it. When we started out, we made a mistake. We put everything by subject—menorahs, Hanukkah lamps, pointers, or *yad*—and it looked right. Then I started reading books on famous collections like Stieglitz and others, and I saw that they all grouped by country. And here, Bill Gross has just said that. So we changed everything, and that was a big job. The labels and everything had to be moved, and it took us several days. Now we do it by country or geographical area, and it does make more sense.

What do I want with this collection? Well, I want to give it away. I want to give it away to either one or more museums. I've learned by a sort of vicarious experience not to favor giving it away to a synagogue. I don't want to get into it, because we have Warren Klein here who has one of the best synagogue museums as a curator, and the world, in Temple Emanu-El, where we are recent members, and I think it's a great congregation. That's the exception, I think, to the rule. I would certainly favor a museum that organized and it's there to stay. The Tulsa Museum where I grew up, the Sherwin Miller Museum is a really good Judaica museum, a separate building in the Jewish community center, and that's going to be there to stay. And, there are others. But many times synagogues have financial troubles and there are new rabbis. The Sherwin Miller has three great Judaica stained glass windows, 20 foot tall panels as you enter in, one of these by Tiffany, that came from a Dallas synagogue.

So what do I want? I want my collection, like Bill and Jane, to be for the diffusion of knowledge, but you can't do that in a home like I have. You can approach doing that by giving it to a museum or museums, but I don't want to do that because when you walk through, all due respect to all the museums, we only have three cases in our country now of museums having separate Judaica galleries and this one was the first over thirty years ago. I coincidentally bumped into it when I was here for a Monet show, and I was startled that it was there. The Met has nineteen galleries for its Islamic galleries. They have no gallery for Judaica. They are buying terrific pieces, and they are spotting them around the museum, like other museums do. That's one way to do it. But I can tell you, talking to the people that have given collections to museums that have done that, they can't find the Judaica in that museum, even when they ask the people who are supposed to tell them where it is. I can't find that Judaica very easily, and I'm on the board of the Met. Some is at the Cloisters.

So, I want a separate Judaica gallery in the museum, and, I don't want just that. I want it connected to an educational institution which has a Jewish studies program or institutions. It could be a synagogue, university, or other kind of group. I have a client in Charlotte who has written a history of the Jewish origins of Charlotte. He gave it to me, and we need more of that. But why do I want that? Because walking through a museum, even if it's a separate Jewish gallery like we have here, people walk through—and that's a Hanukkah lamp, a menorah, a pointer, whatever—but then that's it. If you study why it's important to the history of Jews, to Judaism, why it's important to the future, why are we still here as Jews, what has connected us—the history is not ancient, only. The ancient leads to today, the contemporary. Rembrandt was a contemporary artist at one time, so, things change. Everyone's going into contemporary now, even the Jewish Museum on Fifth Avenue is emphasizing contemporary more than their historical things, and that's caused a little bit of discussion. I want a university study program to make a partnership with, so when I'm talking to the museums, first of all, it looks good to them. I want to give them a lot of things, but it doesn't look good after a while when I say I insist on a separate gallery and I insist on an educational concept of that—for five-year-olds and for ninety-five-year-olds. So, I want to leave you with that now.

The finials now. Ancona, Italy, is where a lot of *ketubbah*s are made. But you don't find a lot of finials. These are quite rare and they're large, about 20 inches tall. And, at the bottom, you can't see it, but there's musical instruments and the design is hallmarked on the bottom. They're made by Paolo Ruzzoli in 1800. I have a lot of finials but I think that these are probably among the most exciting pieces that I have. When I have to pick my favorite object, it changes weekly because I get something new and that's my favorite object. But I picked this over all the others because I think they're quite exciting and I don't have other finials from Ancona.

Gabriel Goldstein: I think I'm going to ask each of you a question, about a particular aspect of your collecting, which I think is different than others. So, in the same order—William, you've been kind of Central Command in this field for quite a long time, as long as I've been at it, which is already a long time. That's unusual, I think, for a private collector to have a distinct role as a catalyst for study, a catalyst for new exhibitions, really the seat of connoisseurship. So how do you see that as being a private collector and working with the academy and museums? Who takes on that role next? I don't see another private, core collection of that scale. . . . How do we build that body of knowledge and the impetus to do more?

William Gross: First of all, I've never completely thought of myself as a collector. I would say that my approach has always been much more museological than collector, and my acquisitions, as much as I could, were always with a view to a particular vision that I had as to, let's say, how I wanted the German section to look. Where there was a gap, I would try to find an object that would fill that gap. But it goes even more back, Gabe, before I get to the last part of your question, to attitude, because as I explained to you, my father-in-law, of blessed memory, raised me on the idea that Judaica is educational. So when

FIGURE 10.3. Torah finials made by Paolo Ruzzoli, Ancona, Italy, ca. 1800. Collection of Max N. Berry.

my objects sit in drawers or on the shelves in my house, they're dead. They're nothing. It's only by getting them out by exposure, and there are a number of different ways that I do this. One is proactive lending to museums. Last week, two weeks ago, a group of objects went out to Vienna for a Kabbalah exhibition, and that was the 170th exhibition that the family collection has been represented at. That gives me joy, not because they look at their label and see it's from the Gross Family Collection. It gives me joy because these objects are being renewed—they're being given a second life and otherwise, they're truly dead.

The second way I do it is by having a fairly good cataloging system and computerization. I would say probably that my collection is the best organized and computerized collection in the world, in Judaica, so it makes it easy for museums to work with me. I'll give you an example. Fifteen years ago, the Israel Museum put on an exhibition about the zodiac. They have eighteen thousand items, but they don't know which ones have the zodiac, and they came to me and I pressed a button because my collection is cataloged not only subject-wise but also by iconography. I pushed "Zodiac" and up come 227 items, and they chose about fifty because it was so easy.

The same thing is true of scholars. I encourage scholars to come. Shalom [Sabar] brings his classes every year. People from Bar-Ilan bring their classes every year. I insist that they take the items out, and I insist that they touch them without gloves. Terrible! I know it's anti-museological, but to me, the very fact of touching an object gives an entirely different understanding of it than just looking at it through glass or it being shown on a slide. I always feel that that's important. Education is just the most important, and that ties in to your last question.

Gabe, I've had a charmed life, literally a charmed life, and my passion for this and for research and writing and lecturing and understanding Judaica was always so great. I made the decision at fifty-two to retire and to devote my entire time, which is a lot of hours a day, just to this subject. I don't see where there's any other collector or curator who will be able to do that. It's a very sad fact. But curators, at one time, were stewards of their collections. That was their job. Their job was to study, to write about, to publicize. Today, curators have to raise funds for their exhibitions. There is no exhibition department. They have to do their own exhibition work. They don't have time to know their own collections, let alone go to another museum or collector and sit for weeks and study that collection. I've had that privilege at virtually every—or most—major collections in the world because I've done evaluations, etc. I've had the privilege of handling item by item, without gloves. So I don't know, because nobody's had the opportunity to examine physically tens of thousands of Judaica items like I have. Nobody can spend ten, twelve hours a day looking at things, cataloging things, researching them, dealing with museums, dealing with scholars. I mean, I was really privileged.

GABRIEL GOLDSTEIN: We've all been privileged because of that. I mean, the field really has been privileged.

WILLIAM GROSS: I love to share. People come to me all the time, every day, there's people visiting me and I adore it, and Lisa, my wife, sometimes goes crazy with that, of course. I tell her, Lisa, there isn't anybody who walks into this house and who sees this collection from whom I don't learn something. He can be the worst of the great unwashed, as my colleague says, who knows nothing about anything—but when he looks at my vitrine and a pair of Biedermeier Vienna *rimonim*, he sees things that I don't see. And if he talks to me, it gives me a whole new perspective on those things and the view—there's no absolute view, there's no absolute knowledge in this field. This is the most relativist field that ever existed. Gabe, you know it very, very well. So it's only by discussion and only by doing that—and, you know, Gabe, I hope you'll be the guy, I really do! I don't even know that it's that important anymore because the field is much more spread out today than it was. And, who knows who is going to come up. I mean, that's a wonderful thing. People come up there, you know, right now, basically, there are no young collectors. I'm sorry, Jane, outside of the way that Shalom [Sabar] does it, it's a relatively expensive hobby. Wealthy young Jews, like everyone wealthy, are in the game of contemporary art. Nothing else means anything. It's a great game, and if you guess well, you can make millions of dollars overnight, but nobody collects—does Sotheby's have old silver sales anymore? Sales of coins? Sales of stamps? Hardly. Sales of antique furniture? Collectibles at this time at this period are dead. Nobody's interested. Objects don't interest young people. And that's why we have to come up with ways of approaching them in a different way, of appealing to some kind of concept that perhaps innately and automatically they can argue with, or at least feel stimulated by.

GABRIEL GOLDSTEIN: Thanks. So, Jane, I was really impressed that you chose this piece, but [also] in talking to you about your passion for how these objects linked to your own personal commitment, your family commitment over generations, to Jewish communal life, to peoplehood, and to philanthropy in a broad and international Jewish world. And, on a much more personal level, there's this feeling, in our personal conversation today, that you're not religious, which is an interesting term, but you told me the story that for many years you bought traditional Eastern European–style Shabbat candlesticks and had them repaired and gave them as wedding gifts. You said there were many, many women whose mothers did not like Shabbat candles and when you gave them, they started to light Shabbat candles. So how does your collecting as a mission fit into that idea of continuity and practice? And you also mentioned that in your practice you tend not to collect synagogue objects, because you think they belong in the synagogue in that traditional ritual use. So there is, I think, something very religious to your collection.

JANE WEITZMAN: Well, you know, I do make exceptions. I have some *rimonim*. If I see something that's so outstanding—I have a pair of *rimonim* that are like hands holding, and a dealer came in to see me, and he said, "Oh my gosh, those are rock stars. If you ever sell them, please call me," but I'll never sell them because I think they're really amazing. Unlike you, I'm not planning for the end; I want to enjoy my collection.

I am as Jewish as anyone, I think. I have always believed in patrilineal descent long before I even knew what it was because when I was a kid growing up in Atlanta and if your father was Jewish, you experienced exactly the same antisemitism that I did. When I went to Emory University, we could go through rush, but it was a joke because the charters of the sororities weren't going to let you in if you were Jewish—there was one Jewish sorority we could all join. And, you know, if your father was Jewish, that was the one you had to join.

I think our heritage is so important. People are Jewish in different ways now. I became president of the Jewish Book Council a few years ago because I saw this small jewel of an organization, and I said, you know, people aren't joining synagogues. We can do something if we can get them to read Jewish books. They'll understand how wonderful it is to be Jewish. We started book clubs three years ago. We now have 1,600 Jewish book clubs, not just in America, some in Israel, some around the world, and I think that number will keep growing because it just happened so quickly. We have to look at new ways of becoming Jewish. These objects will connect people to the past ways of being Jewish. Look, Orthodox Judaism isn't going to change that much. It's going to probably be what it is. But other forms of being Jewish—when 20 percent or less of people join the synagogue in today's communities, that's not a good thing. So even though I'm not religious, I do go four days a year. I do belong.

GABRIEL GOLDSTEIN: Thanks, Jane. So, Max, you commented that your favorite piece changes weekly, because you keep on buying and you've been an inveterate collector with an amazing American painting collection. You built this huge Judaica collection exponentially fast, right? With such an array of material, and being attached to national and international museum and art communities, why Judaica now?

MAX BERRY: Talking about passion and collecting—I didn't really know what passion was in my other collections until I started collecting Judaica. And it sounds a little weird, but when I picked up some of the great pieces—not money-wise but of other significance—I thought, you know, my grandfather or great-grandfather may have picked this piece up or something very similar. In fact, they did, all of my family is Orthodox and half still are. I'm Reform. I'm the only Reform Jew on the Yeshiva University Museum's Board. I love being on the board. What's the future? At my age, eighty-three, I want to keep adding. As long as I live, I will collect for entities that need something. I'm not going to stop just because I'm giving it away, because the passion is still in me. I think to really collect Judaica in the right way—and Bill's remarks are right on—you have to move it beyond just the shelf. You've got to move it into the minds—[Rabbi Norman] Gerstenfeld of Washington Hebrew Congregation said, "Religion is caught, not taught." That's a profound statement in my book. I caught this passion by handling it and then learning more about each item. The more you learn, the more you appreciate it, and then it becomes important.

What do you do with it in the end? Hopefully, collectors will take those objects down the road a little further and hopefully some museums will buy them.

GABRIEL GOLDSTEIN: Your passion in collecting reflects the three of you in every way. I was very excited that Isaac Pollak joined us for this conference because he's a specialized Judaica collector, so I did invite Isaac to explain that and why. Isaac?

ISAAC POLLAK: I collect *hevra kadisha* [burial society] related items—I suppose most you know what that is. I've been collecting them for over forty years and I have over three hundred items in my collection. It got me so turned on that I went to Vivian Mann's program—a master's program at the Jewish Theological Seminary on material culture. I continued my education and two years later, I got a master's in art history from Columbia University and, hopefully, will be very shortly getting a DHL, a Doctor of Hebrew Letters, from JTS.

So, I live on the Upper East Side of Manhattan. We do *taharot* [performing the ritual of purification]—we do it for anybody on the Upper East Side of Manhattan for anyone who is interested in one and wants to make it the prescribed way. I'm Orthodox, I belong to an Orthodox synagogue, but we do it for Reform, Conservative, Reconstructionist. In fact, about four years ago, I gave a seminar to a bunch of the rabbis at Temple Emanu-El—classical Reform—because they were very interested to know about it because some of their members said they want to go back to the original. They wanted to do a *tahara*. But I got fascinated by it because our synagogue was starting their own about forty-one years ago and they needed volunteers. I volunteered, and I started looking in the books, and there's nothing. There's absolutely nothing. In fact, everything we do now amongst Sephardic and Ashkenazic communities comes from a book called *Maavar Yabok* written by Rabbi Aharon Berachia, published in Mantua in 1626. And that's where most traditions derive from today. It's all traditional, and I have, I travel a great deal on business. I participated in fourteen *aharoth*, in Gibraltar, in Hong Kong, Australia, Serbia, Calcutta, you know, all over the world. I started looking for traditions, and I started collecting and the bug caught me. In fact, there's an auction happening very shortly by Jonathan Greenstein. There's a very important *hevra kadisha* cup that I bid on. I'm going to be anxiously getting on my computer very shortly to see if I got my bid. I collect, I speak on it, I give classes to rabbinical students and for university seminars. So anybody who wants to meet their maker or anybody who is interested, I could show my collection. You call me. Last name is Pollak. I live on Park Avenue. I'm the only Pollak on Park Avenue in Manhattan, so you can find me.

GABRIEL GOLDSTEIN: Thank you. A few questions from the audience?

AUDIENCE MEMBER 1: I grew up in Europe and it is amazing to see the kinds of family collections that, actually, I was able to bring over. I had an idea after listening to your panel that if you could just have an exhibit of sacred objects that were inherited and brought over from Europe here—the things, the few things that were not destroyed—I think it would be a wonderful thing. We have a Kiddush cup dating from about 1700. I have prayer books, and these are not very artistic prayer books, dating from late 1700s, 1800s, some bound in ivory. Now, these things will be going to our families, I guess. I wish that this could be actually seen in public and explained.

GABRIEL GOLDSTEIN: I think that the way we think about collectors and their passion and what they bring to the field—the field could also bring the story of collecting itself.

AUDIENCE MEMBER 2: This is a nosy question. What does it feel like to be courted by curators for your collection?

GABRIEL GOLDSTEIN: We wouldn't do that! Right? Who's going first on that one?

JANE WEITZMAN: Well, I'm under the radar, so not that many people know about me. Elka, where are you? I saw you here. You once borrowed something for the Temple Emanu-El for an exhibit there. It came back to me in this huge plexiglass frame. And it just didn't look right, so I took it out of the frame and put it on the floor of my husband's dressing room where he didn't keep any clothes.

GABRIEL GOLDSTEIN: Do curators ever court you Max?

MAX BERRY: A few times, and it usually leads to a fruitful discussion and sharing of views much like we're doing here. I have all kinds of ideas. One of them is more traveling exhibitions on Judaica, and I'm joining Benjamin Zucker because he's such an authority on *ketubbah*s and wedding rings and things. I learned from all these kind of people like Bill and Benjamin and others, but also I'm also a collector of those things. It's because he's seen the collection and [is] helping me collect some things that he's now loaned out to Houston or the Walters in Baltimore and so forth.

My other idealistic idea, which maybe my grandson will see it happen, is doing something internationally. Why not take that exhibition to London, to France, etc., and put that exhibition in international hands and then receive one over there? Why not have international exhibitions on Judaica traveling to a lot of places where other people can see them that would never see anything like this? I think that's important, and I'll end with a lending library concept that I have for Judaica. Bill, maybe you share your things around the world. You're probably the only collector that has that ability and knowledge of how to do it. I don't, but I'm hoping to simulate that through other organizations. I'm an idealistic collector. If I get half of it done before I drop, I'll be satisfied up there.

GABRIEL GOLDSTEIN: Bill, on courting curators and curators courting you?

WILLIAM GROSS: I would make two observations. One, the average age of the three collectors facing you is seventy-nine. That tells you something. It's sad. Number two—go to the CAJM [Council of American Jewish Museums] website and look at what are the currently presented exhibitions and try to find one that has one single object of Judaica being presented in it. You won't find it. So, somewhere we lost it. We haven't done our jobs. None of us, and we may be too old to deal with a younger generation. I mean, I don't want to be so pessimistic because if you look, things go in and out of fashion, etc., but my own belief is that we are the last generation whose connection to Judaica, Jewish objects, is colored by the Holocaust. That emotional element, which is a *vital* part of collectiveness, in my children's generation is a distant memory, what they've heard about. For my grandchildren, it's paragraphs in the textbook. How do we bring the idea and incentivize these people about Judaica? I haven't found the way. I tried to do what I can do. I lend, and I give to scholars and everything I can do. The National Library in Israel has an Institute of Microfilm Manuscripts, a brilliant project founded by David Ben-Gurion in 1950. This man, in the midst of the founding of Israel, had the vision to envision an institute where there would be images of every single Hebrew manuscript in the world. They now have eighty thousand. From the first manuscript that I ever bought, there's been many hundreds since then, the first thing that happens is it goes there, because it's open to people. People can see it. I don't know what it is, but the one thing I do know is that we haven't done it.

GABRIEL GOLDSTEIN: Well, certainly the three of you exemplify passion, attention to the detail, and vision from the past to the present to the future. It's been so wonderful to hear you, and I think really we see that this is a partnership, a partnership between universities and museums and private collectors and our audiences. We've been collectively listening to you, and we have been willing to learn from you. You're passing on the torch, and we will try to run with it. I thank you.

CONTRIBUTORS

GABRIELLE ANNA BERLINGER is an associate professor of American studies and folklore and the Babette S. and Bernard J. Tanenbaum Scholar in Jewish History and Culture at the University of North Carolina at Chapel Hill. Prior, she was an Andrew W. Mellon Postdoctoral Fellow in the Cultures of Conservation initiative at the Bard Graduate Center, where she conducted research at the Lower East Side Tenement Museum. She is the author of *Framing Sukkot: Tradition and Transformation in Jewish Vernacular Architecture* (2017).

RUTH VON BERNUTH is a professor in the Department of Germanic and Slavic Languages and Literatures at the University of North Carolina at Chapel Hill. Her publications include *Wunder, Spott und Prophetie: Natürliche Narrheit in den "Historien von Claus Narren"* (Wonder, Ridicule, and Prophecy: Natural Foolishness in the Stories of Claus Fool; 2009) and *How the Wise Men Got to Chelm: The Life and Times of a Yiddish Folk Tradition* (2016). She directed the Carolina Center for Jewish Studies from 2013 to 2022.

JOHN COFFEY is the retired deputy director of the North Carolina Museum of Art, where he was also the Jim and Betty Becher Curator of American and Modern Art emeritus and Curator of Judaic Art emeritus. Between 1999 and 2021 he oversaw the development of the NCMA's Judaic Art Gallery. Coffey organized numerous exhibitions, including "Louis Rémy Mignot: A Southern Painter Abroad" (1996), "Color, Myth, and Music: Stanton Macdonald-Wright and Synchromism" (2001), and "American Impressionist: Childe Hassam and the Isles of Shoals" (2016). In addition to his work as a curator, Coffey served as director of the Israel/North Carolina Cultural Exchange (1993–96).

Simona Di Nepi is Charles and Lynn Schusterman Curator of Judaica at the Museum of Fine Arts, Boston, where she curated "Intentional Beauty: Jewish Ritual Art from the Collection." From 2002 to 2017 she filled curatorial roles at the Victoria and Albert Museum, the National Gallery, and the Royal Academy of Arts in London, where she cared for permanent collections and curated exhibitions. In Israel she worked as a curator at Anu: The Museum of the Jewish People and as a lecturer at Reichman University, Herzliya.

Juliana Ochs Dweck is chief curator at the Princeton University Art Museum. Her exhibitions include "Surfaces Seen and Unseen: African Art at Princeton" (2016), "Picturing Protest" (2018), "Time Capsule 1970: Rauschenberg's Currents" (2019), and "Miracles on the Border: *Retablos* of Mexican Migrants to the United States" (2019).

Gabriel Goldstein was the interim director and chief curator at Yeshiva University Museum from 2022 to 2024 and since 2002 has been the consulting curator of Judaic art at the North Carolina Museum of Art. He has served in consultant curatorial roles with the Capital Jewish Museum, Washington, DC, the Claims Conference, and the National Archives and previously worked at Yeshiva University Museum for over twenty years as well as at the Jewish Museum and the Royal Ontario Museum.

Barbara Kirshenblatt-Gimblett is professor emerita of performance studies at New York University and chief curator of the "Core Exhibition" at POLIN Museum of the History of Polish Jews. Her books include *Destination Culture: Tourism, Museums, and Heritage*; *Image before My Eyes: A Photographic History of Jewish Life in Poland, 1864–1939* (with Lucjan Dobroszycki); *They Called Me Mayer July: Painted Memories of a Jewish Childhood in Poland before the Holocaust* (with Mayer Kirshenblatt); *The Art of Being Jewish in Modern Times* (with Jonathan Karp); and *Anne Frank Unbound: Media, Imagination, Memory* (with Jeffrey Shandler).

Erica Lehrer is a professor in the Departments of History and Sociology-Anthropology at Concordia University. She is also the founding director of the university's Curating and Public Scholarship Lab (CaPSL). From 2007 to 2017 she held the Canada Research Chair in Museum and Heritage

Studies, and she currently directs the international team project Thinking Through the Museum (TTTM): A Partnership Approach to Curating Difficult Knowledge in Public (2021–28).

LAURA LEVITT is a professor of religion, Jewish studies, and gender at Temple University. Her publications include *The Objects That Remain* (2020), *American Jewish Loss after the Holocaust* (2007), and *Jews and Feminism: The Ambivalent Search for Home* (1997).

MONIKA MURZYN-KUPISZ is a professor at the Institute of Geography and Spatial Management at Jagiellonian University in Kraków, Poland. She is the author, coauthor, or editor of numerous publications in English and Polish, including *The Impact of Artists on Contemporary Urban Development in Europe* (2017), *Reclaiming Memory: Urban Regeneration in the Historic Jewish Quarters of Central European Cities* (2009), and *Kazimierz: The Central European Experience of Urban Regeneration* (2006).

DALE ROSENGARTEN is founding curator of the Jewish Heritage Collection and former director of the Center for Southern Jewish Culture, both at the College of Charleston. She developed the exhibition "A Portion of the People: Three Hundred Years of Southern Jewish Life" (2002–3) with McKissick Museum at the University of South Carolina and coedited a book by the same name. She was also cocurator of the exhibition "By Dawn's Early Light: Jewish Contributions to American Culture from the Nation's Founding to the Civil War" (2015–16).

DIEGO ROTMAN is a senior lecturer and head of the Department of Theater Studies at the Hebrew University in Jerusalem. His publications include *Possession and Dispossession: Performing Jewish Ethnography in Jerusalem* (2022; coedited with Lea Mauas and Michelle MacQueen) and *The Yiddish Stage as Temporary Home* (2021). In 2000 Rotman and Lea Mauas founded the Sala-Manca Group, which is active in contemporary art, performance, curatorial practice, and public art, and in 2009 they founded the Mamuta Art and Research Center in Jerusalem.

SUZANNE SERIFF is a professor of instruction in the Department of Anthropology at the University of Texas at Austin. Seriff directs the Arts and Social Justice Internship Program at UT's Schusterman Center for Jewish Studies and has guest-curated nationally traveling exhibition projects, including "Empowering Women: Artisan Cooperatives That Transform Communities" (2010), "Recycled, Re-Seen: Folk Art from the Global Scrap Heap" (1996–97), and "Forgotten Gateway: Coming to America Through Galveston Island" (2009).

FRANCESCO SPAGNOLO is the curator of The Magnes Collection of Jewish Art and Life and an associate adjunct professor in the Department of Music at the University of California, Berkeley. His publications include the Italian edition of Imre Toth's *Palimpsest* (2003), the audio-anthology *Italian Jewish Musical Traditions* (2006), and *The Jewish World: 100 Objects of Art and Culture* (2014).

INDEX

Note: Page numbers appearing in *italics* refer to figures.

Abrahamin, Isidor, 77
Abram, Simone, 89n65
Absentee's Property Law of 5710/1950 (Israel, 1950), 33–34
Adler, Cyrus, 164–65
"aesthetics of the *gestus*," 50–51
"Afterlives: Recovering the Lost Stories of Looted Art" exhibition, 276
A. I. Berman's Salvage Store, 233–37
Albrecht V, Duke, 1
Aldridge, Edward, 179, 193n75
al-Korshan, Mohammed (Abu Suleiman), 19–20, 22, 23, 24, 30, 33, 34, 35
American Civil War, 219–27
American Jewish Joint Distribution Committee (JDC), 292
Ames, Kenneth, 69, 81, 89n56
Aravatz, Isaac, 194n77
Architectural Biennale (2012), 108
architectural spolia, 21, 40
art(s): collected Judaica as, 293–94; meaning of, to assimilated American Jews, 243
art museums. *See* museums
Attia, Mordecai, 194n77
atzei chaim (Torah staves), 287–89
Auschwitz-Birkenau. *See Evidence Room, The*

bal tashchit, 246–47
Barry, Andrew, 83
Bartlett, Francis, 163
Bartosz, Antoni, 136, 140, 143
Bawadi ecotourism initiative, 36–40, 44n44
beaker, acquired by NCMA, 210
Bedouin hut, 18–19, *23*; and Bawadi ecotourism initiative, 36–40; connection between sukkah and, 41n4; construction of, 20; dismantling and translocation of, 23–24; as negative spolia, 20–22; purchase of, 22; reconstructed in Hansen House gardens, 25–26. *See also Eternal Sukkah, The*
Beit Hatfutsot: Museum of the Diaspora, 280–81
Bell, David, 220, 221
belonging, pews and sense of, 76–77
benches, 65–68, 82–83; versus chairs, 84n15, 86n26; of exclusion, 79–81; introduction of, in parish buildings, 87n36; of learning, 68–71; liturgical, 74–79; as ritual objects, 71–74
benches for prayer, 74–79
Benguiat, Ephraim, 164–65, 185n3
Ben-Gurion, David, 306–7
Benjamin, Walter, 50–51, 238
Ben-Shaul, Daphna, 34–35, 36
Ben-Ur, Aviva, 81, 88n54, 89n59
Berkowitz, Roger M., 206
Berman, Abraham Isaac (A. I.), 231, 233–37, 253, 257, 263–64
Berman, Honey, 231, *232*, 234–35, 254
Berman, meaning of name, 253
Berry, Max N., 295–98, 303–4, 305–6

Berry, Pam, 296
Between Sacred and Not (Paley), 183
Bezalel School of Arts and Crafts, 174, 176
Bhabha, Homi K., 241
Bigelow, William, 163
Binder, Jacob, 167
Bolaffi, Michele, 52–53, 62n8
Boltanski, Christian, 109
Bordeleau, Anne, 106
Bossi, Ferdinando Ildebrando, 191n59
Bottle with Synagogue Tableau, 184
bowls, silver, 219–27
Brandon, Edouard, 176
Brimmer, Martin, 185n1
Brin, Alexander, 166–67, 187n21
Bukowiecki, Łukasz, 120
Burrus, Sean P., 210–12
Butler, "Beast," 220
Butler, Shelley, 239, 265n11
Byrd, Sherry, 249–50

Cambareri, Marietta, 170, 171, 173, 189n29
Camillo, Giulio, 107
Canaan, Tawfiq, 26, 43n24
Canada, 109, 113n35
Canada (Boltanski), 109
cantors, 59–60
Carpentras, 85n19
casting, of relics, 102–5
Cavaillon, 85n19
"Celebration Time in Polish and European Folk Cultures" exhibit, 130–32, 133
Cepelia, 131
"Ceremonial Art in the Judaic Tradition" exhibition, 202
chairs, 84n15, 86n26
Chairs of Elijah, 71–73, 85n19
Cherkassky, Zoya, 182–83
circumcisions, 71, 73
Civil War, 219–27
Clark, David, 255
Clifton, James, 106, 113n26, 113n28
Code of Jewish Law, 82
Coffey, John W., 205, 210, 289, 295
Cohen, Chen, 18
Cohen, Richard I., 4
Cohen-Lifshitz, Alon, 19, 34
Collectors' Roundtable, 285–307

Columbia, South Carolina, 219–20
Comaroff, Jean, 37
Comaroff, John, 37
common usage, 99
community, liturgical music and formation of cultural identity in, 55–56
Conn, Steven, 265n10
context, 290–91
COVID-19 pandemic, 274
Cuba, 292–93
cultural identity, music in formation of, 55–56
"Culture and Continuity: The Jewish Journey" exhibition, 278
culture brokering, 254
curatorial dreaming, 239–40, 265n11
Czernek, Helena, 277
Czyżewski, Adam, 130, 132, 133, 134

Darmstadt Burial Society, 210
Davis, Miles, 263
decorative arts, 277–78
Delftware, 173
democratizing spaces, 263–64
Denial (2016), 96–97, 103, 111n5, 112n18
deportation of Jews, 256
Derrida, Jacques, 99
de Wall, Edmund, 243
Diner, Hasia, 246
Domit, Moussa M., 201–2
dream exhibitions, 239–40, 265n11
Dreyfus, Carl, 187n21
Dweck, Juliana Ochs, 247–48, 259–60, 262

E1 Plan, 39, 44n45
"Early American Jewish Portraits and Silver" exhibit, 167
ecotourism initiative, by Bedouin community, 18
education, benches in infrastructure of Jewish, 68–71
Efrat, Zvi, 31
Ein Chud, 42n20
Ein Hod, 42n20
Elazar ben Azarya, Rabbi, 68
Eldad, Arie, 33
Elijah, Chairs of, 71–73, 85n19
Elior, Rachel, 34

Esch, Arnold, 21
Eternal Sukkah, The, 18–19, *25*; and Bawadi ecotourism initiative, 39–40; current status of, 40, 44n46; interior of, *28*; launch of, 27–29; merchandised as art piece, 29–31; politicization of, 35–36; transported to Israel Museum, 31–33, *32*. *See also* Bedouin hut
ethnographic museology, 118–19, 121, 136. *See also* Polish museums
ethnographic museums: approaches to inclusion of ethnic minorities, 142–43; challenges presented by, 279–80; Jews in Polish, 121–23; National Ethnographic Museum, 122, 130–34; perspectives offered by, 141; Przedbórz Regional Folk Museum, 122, 123–29, 148n25; Seweryn Udziela Ethnographic Museum (MEK), 122, 134–41, 143–44, 151n60, 151n62, 151–52n64, 153n72, 153n74, 153n76; social role in Poland, 122; temporary exhibitions in, 151n59
ethnomusicology, 52–53, 55
etrog containers, 223, 226
Evidence Room, The, 110; and connection between Canada and holding places within camps, 109, 113n35; as holder, 95–100; pieces in, as having talismanic and evidentiary qualities, 100, 274; and reproduction and handling of artifacts, 101–8, 113n34
Evidence Room Foundation, 110
exclusion, benches of, 79–81
Exodus, 253

face masks, Holocaust-themed, 274–75
Fach, Zelig Hendel, 85n21
family, in shaping communal life, 55
Ferris, Marcie Cohen, 66
festivals, 253
FestivALT: New Currents in Contemporary Jewish Art, 144
Fine, Steven, 167
folk art, 261
"Forgotten Gateway: Coming to America Through Galveston Island," 252–58
Frankel, Ellen, 237
Freedom Seder, 210

Friedenthal, Rabbi Ermanno (Ermin Zvi), 50
Furman, Jacobo, 174

Gallery of Conscience, 258–63
Galpin, Francis W., 165
Galveston Island, 252
Galveston Movement, 252–53, 254, 255, 256
Garden of Lights (Threadgill), 184
gathering spaces, public. *See* Jewish third spaces; salvage store(s)
gender, and synagogue seating, 74–75
geographical cultural perspective, 290–91
Gerstenfeld, Rabbi Norman, 303
gesture, 50–52
Gittelson, Rabbi Roland B., 190n35
Godfather Awaits the Child, The (Oppenheim), 85n18
Goldman, Karla, 86n30
Goldman, Ken, 274
Goldschmidt, Selig Meier, 170
Goldstein, Gabriel M., 206, 210, 286, 302, 303, 304, 307
Goren, Hagar, 18
Gottesman, Itzik, 150n46
Gotz, Elly, 102
"Granice" exhibition, 133–34
Gray, Henry, 166
Grier, Katherine, 78, 83n5
Gross, Jan, 119
Gross, Lisa, 301
Gross, William L., 286–91, 293, 296, 298–302, 306–7
Gualdo collection, 106–7
Gurock, Jeffrey, 77
Gwozdziec Synagogue, 88n46

Haggadah(s), acquired by MFA, 182–83
"Hallelujah! Assemble, Pray, Study: Synagogues Past and Present" installation, 280–81
Halpert, Edith, 213n6
Hamavdil (Paley), 183
Handshouse Studio, 281
Hanes, Gordon, 213n9
Hannah (Kaufmann), 174–76, 190n42

Hansen, Gerhard Henrik Armauer, 26–27
Hansen House, 24, 26–27
Hanukkah lamp(s): acquired by MFA, 168–70, 172, 173, 174, 181–82, 187n24, 188–89nn26–28, 195n89; acquired by NCMA, 206; Jewish aspects of materials of, 274
Harvey, Penny, 89n63
Hasson, Nir, 34
Hatchfield, Pamela, 171
Havdalah, 60
Heilman, Samuel, 67, 77, 86n27, 87n43
Herman, Bernie, 2–3
Hillel, 52
Himmel, Adolphe, 224
Hirshhorn Museum and Sculpture Garden, 110, 114n39
Hirshler, Erica, 167
historical humanism, 252–58
history museums, 280
holding(s), 95–100
Holiday Kiddush Cup (Zabari), 184
Holocaust memory, as coloring connections to Judaica, 306–7. See also *Evidence Room, The*; Polish museums
Holocaust-themed face masks, 274
Holshouser, James, 214n15
Hornstein, Shelley, 105, 111nn7–8, 112n21, 113n34
House, Boyce, 267n39
Houston, Sam, 249, 267n41
Hubka, Thomas, 88n46
humanism, historical, 252–58
Hunt, James B., 203
Husserl, Edmund, 52

implication, 117–18
improvisation, in museum curation, 258–63
infrastructure, 82–83, 84n10, 89n63
infrastructure of Judaism, 67–68
in situ curating, 144
Institute of Microfilm Manuscripts, 306–7
intangible, 280–81
In the Garden (Lawrence), 213n6
isolationism, 291
Israel Museum: *The Eternal Sukkah* transported to, 31–33; and merchandising of *The Eternal Sukkah* as art piece, 29–31; and politicization of *The Eternal Sukkah*, 35–36; reconstructed synagogues in, 79–81; as symbolic architectural spolia, 40; "We the People" exhibition, 32–33; zodiac exhibition at, 300
"It Ain't Braggin' If It's True" exhibition, 248–51, 268n43
"It Still Ain't Braggin' If It's True" exhibition, 268n43

Jahalin, 19, 22, 24, 25, 30, 32–33, 36, 39. See also Bedouin hut; *Eternal Sukkah, The*
Jamal, Abu, 33, 34
Jazz Singer, The (1927), 258, 259
"Jesus' Hilfe," 26
Jewish Book Council, 302–3
Jewish Bride, The (Kaufmann), 192n61
"Jewish Festivities in Poland" exhibit (Annex), 132–33, 134
Jewish heritage, Polish museums and preservation of, 128–29
Jewish inn, 126–28, 149n29
Jewish Man Reading (Brandon), 176
Jewish Museum, 200–201, 247, 276, 278–79, 297–98
Jewish names, 253
Jewishness: in "Celebration Time in Polish and European Folk Cultures" exhibit, 133; defining, 117; in Polish museums, 119–23
Jewish studies: marginality of music in, 49; material culture in, 49–50
Jewish things: categorizing, 1–2, 273–76; curation of, 5–6; as decorative arts, 277–78; as looted objects, 276–77; and material culture studies, 2–5, 7; as moving between Jewish and non-Jewish realms, 4–5; multidimensional value of, 6; as parts of greater whole, 5; post-Jewish, 275–77; Southern Jewish objects, 219–27; stories told by, 242–47; viewing, in context, 290–91
Jewish third spaces, 240–42, 257, 263
Jewish wedding ring(s), 1, *2*, 5, 174
"Jews of Wrocław, 1850–1944" exhibit, 146n11

Jones, Rosalind, 101
Joselit, Jenna Weissman, 84n15
Judaica. *See* Jewish things
Judaic Art Gallery: acquisitions for, 202–4, 213n9, 214n15, 214n21; community outreach of, 210; curation of, 215n31; evolution of, 209–10; future of, 210–12; opening of, 204–5; relocation of, 205–7, 210; renewed development of, 205–7; visitor engagement with, 209
Judas effigy, torture of, 134, 140, 152n70

Kafka, Franz, 50–51
Kahal Kadosh Beth Elohim, 220, 222–24, 226
Kanof, Abram: and acquisitions of NCMA's permanent collection of Judaica, 202–4, 214n15, 214n21; background of, 199–201; early involvement with NCMA, 201–2; legacy of, 273; and opening of Judaic Art Gallery, 205; roles held by, 213n3
Kanof, Frances, 200–201
Kaplan, Mordechai, 243
Karolik, Martha, 166
Karolik, Max, 166, 186n17
Katz, Sam, 166
Kaufmann, Isidor, 174–76, 190n42, 192n61
Kaufmann, Marie Pauline, 192n61
Kaufmann, Philipp, 192n61
Kehal Adath Jeshurun, 77
Kersting, Rita, 29, 32, 34
ketubbot, 182, 194n83
Kiddush, 50–52
Kiddush cup, 184
Kirshenblatt-Gimblett, Barbara, 4, 38, 44n41, 120, 144, 240
Kirstein, Louis E., 187n21
Klein, Warren, 296
knowledge, recovery of, 281
Kolton-Fromm, Ken, 242–43, 248
Kozdron, Tyler, 275
Krajewska, Monika, 134
Kraków Ethnographic Museum, 147n19, 153n71
"Kraków Under Nazi Occupation, 1939–1945" exhibition, 277

Küchler, Christopf Christian, 224
Kurin, Richard, 254

Lapidot, Mira, 29–30, 34, 35
Larkin, Brian, 82–83
Larsen, Johanna, 43n24
Lawrence, Jacob, 213n6
Lazarus, Joshua, 222, *223*
learning, benches of, 68–71
Lecker, Moshe, 35
Lehman, Carrie, 166, 186n14
Lehman, Philip, 166, 186n14
Lehman, Robert, 186n14
Lehrer, Erica, 239, 265n11, 280
leprosarium, 26, 43n24
Levin, Shmaryahu, 65–66, 68, 69, 83n3
Levitt, Laura, 243–44, 264n1
"Levy-Franks Family Colonial Portraits, The" exhibit, 167
Liber, Yosef ben Harav, 76–77
Linde, Charles, 171
Linde, Joyce, 171
Lindsey, William, 165–66, 186n11
lion, gilded wood, 166, 186n17
Lipstadt trial (2000), 97, 99, 111n5, 112n18
Livorno synagogue song, 52–53
looted objects, 276–77
Loring, Charles Greely, 164
Louisiana Pilots Association, 224

Maimonides, 43n25
Mann, Vivian B., 172–73, 184
Mann *z"l*, Vivian, 4
Manor, Ktura, 18, 29
Marcus, Stanley, 251
masks: displayed at Seweryn Udziela Ethnographic Museum (MEK) in Kraków, 135–36, *143*, 144, *145*; Holocaust-themed, 274–75
Mason, Leslie Lindsey, 165–66
material culture: American Jewish identity and thought as rooted in, 242–43; approach toward, 232–33; defining Jewish, 117–18; in Jewish studies, 49–50; stories told by objects, 242–47
material culture studies, 2–5, 7
Material Religion, 4

McBee, Richard, 177
McLean, Kathleen, 259
McMurtry, Larry, 238
measles, 256
MEK. *See* Seweryn Udziela Ethnographic Museum
Mendelsohn, Amitai, 29, 34–35, 36
Mendelssohn, Moses, 249
Mendes-Flohr, Itamar, 18
Michalski, Tadeusz, 124, 126, 128, 129, 148n27, 149n29. *See also* Przedbórz Regional Folk Museum
Michie, Thomas, 168
Milgrom, Rabbi, 27–28
Miller, José, 292
Mintz, Sharon Liberman, 171
Mi Polin, 277
Mizmor le-david havu ladonai bene elim (Bolaffi), 52–53, 62n8
mobility, 273–74
Moïse, Abraham, II, 226
Moïse, Edwin Warren, 220, 224, *225*, 226, 227
Moïse, Louise Hubert, 226
Moïse, Matilde Vaughn, 226
Moïse, Penina, 226
Moïse, Theodore Sidney, 226
Moïse, Warren Hubert, 220, 224–25, 226
Moses, Seat of, 85n17
mourning benches, 73–74
multiculturalism, 142
Museum of Fine Arts (MFA, Boston), 163–64; Benguiat's contributions to, 164–65; changes approach to Judaica acquisitions, 167–72; integration of Judaica in, 172–76; Jewish objects haphazardly entered in, 165–67; new momentum and broadened vision for Judaica in, 176–85
Museum of International Folk Art (MOIFA). *See* Gallery of Conscience
museums: improvisationality in design of, 258–63; Jewish Museum, 200–201, 247, 276, 278–79, 297–98; National Ethnographic Museum, 122, 130–34; POLIN Museum of the History of Polish Jews, 119–20, 134, 150n45, 274, 280, 281; Przedbórz Regional Folk Museum, 123–29, 148n25; Seweryn Udziela Ethnographic Museum (MEK), 122, 134–41, 143–44, 151n60, 151n62, 151–52n64, 153n72, 153n74, 153n76, 280; State Ethnographic Museum, 279–80. *See also* ethnographic museology; ethnographic museums; history museums; Israel Museum; Jewish Museum; Museum of Fine Arts (MFA, Boston); North Carolina Museum of Art (NCMA); Polish museums
music: in context of synagogue's soundscape, 57–61; in formation of cultural identity, 55–56; marginality of, in Jewish studies, 49
muzeum rejestrowane, 148n24
Myers, Myer, 167, 170, 172

Nagel, Alexander, 100, 105–7
names, Jewish, 253
National Ethnographic Museum, 122, 130–34
Neiman Marcus, 251
Nicholes, Kate, 111n8
Noily, Rabbi Dev, 69
noisemaking, 59
North Carolina Bicentennial Commission, 203
North Carolina Museum of Art (NCMA), 199–212; acquisition of permanent collection of Judaica, 202–4, 213n9, 214n15, 214n21; "Ceremonial Art in the Judaic Tradition" exhibition, 202; community outreach of Judaic Art Gallery, 210; curation of Judaic Art Gallery, 215n31; evolution of Judaic Art Gallery, 209–10; future of Judaic Art Gallery, 210–12; Kanof's early involvement with, 201–2, 213n3; and Kanof's legacy, 273; opening of Judaic Art Gallery, 204–5; relocation of Judaic Art Gallery, 205–7, 210; renewed development of Judaic Art Gallery, 205–7; visitor engagement with Judaic Art Gallery, 209
Noy, Orly, 41n4

Oldenburg, Ray, 241
Olin, Laurie, 66
Oppenheim, Moritz Daniel, 85n18

Paige, James William, 165
Palestinian Authority (PA), 41n9
Paley, Tamar, 183
"Passages and Repassages" exhibit, 139
Passover, 253
Passover Seder Plate (Schor), 204
Passover Seder Set with Plates, Dishes, and Wine Cup (Wolpert), 204
Patla, Jack, 222
Patronato, 292, 293
"Performing Texts: Music, Liturgy and Jewish Life" seminar, 57
pews, 74–81, 87n43, 87n45, 88n46, 88n51
Phillips, Jetskalina H., 163, 170, 190n35
Philpott, A. J., 187n21
Pinsker, Shachar, 241, 242
Piwocki, Ksawery, 130
POLIN Museum of the History of Polish Jews, 119–20, 134, 150n45, 274, 280, 281
Polish culture, 142
"Polish Jews" exhibition, 146n11
Polish Museum Law of November 21, 1996, 148n24
Polish museums, 117–20, 141–45; integration of Jewish themes in, 120; Jews in ethnographic, 121–23; National Ethnographic Museum, 122, 130–34; organizational structure of, 147n16; POLIN Museum of the History of Polish Jews, 119–20, 134, 150n45, 274, 280, 281; Przedbórz Regional Folk Museum, 122, 123–29, 148n25; Seweryn Udziela Ethnographic Museum (MEK), 122, 134–41, 143–44, 151n60, 151n62, 151–52n64, 153n72, 153n74, 153n76, 280; State Ethnographic Museum, 279–80
Pollak, Isaac, 304–5
Pollard, Annie, 87n45
post-Jewish (*pożydowskie*), 275–77
Poznanski, Gustavus, 226, 228n10
pożydowskie (post-Jewish), 275–77

practical memory, 238
prayer: orientation of synagogue, 87n39; seated, 75
Prell, Riv-Ellen, 85n16
private collectors, 286. *See also* Collectors' Roundtable
prototyping, 259, 260
proxemics, 86n24
Prugar, Aleksander, 277
Przedbórz, 123–24
Przedbórz Regional Folk Museum, 122, 123–29, 148n25
public gathering spaces. *See* Jewish third spaces; salvage store(s)
Purim, 59
Putnam, Robert, 241

Quiccheberg, Samuel, 1

Raban, Ze'ev, 71, 174, 206
Rabinowitz, Richard, 243, 257
Rabinowitz, Yeshaiau, 18
Rachael (Moïse family nurse), 224–25
Raisin, Jane Lazarus, 222
Rathbone, Perry T., 191n59
Ratshesky, A. C., 187n21
Rau, Max, 77–78
"Recycled, Re-Seen: Folk Art from the Global Scrap Heap" exhibition, 244–46, 248
refugees, 18
Regis, Hatfield, 186n11
reinterpretation, 260
"Re-Jewing Polish Folk Culture," 144
relics/reliquary: as having talismanic and evidentiary qualities, 100–101; reproduction and handling of, 101–8, 113n34. *See also Evidence Room, The*
"Re-newal" project, 136
repetition, 50–51
Ressel, Ida, 43n24
Reymont, Władysław, 149n29
Richels, Jurgen, 177–79
Richetti, Rabbi Elia, 50–51
rimonim, 179, 302. *See also* Torah finial(s)
risk-taking, 247–51, 262
ritual, 50–51

ritual identity of community, 55
ritual noise, 59
ritual objects, benches as, 71–74
ritual sound objects, 57–61
Rogers, Malcom, 170, 171
Rogers, Mondel, 235–37
Rohrer, Grace, 203
Roma people, 153n76
Rosenthall, William A., 222
Rosier, Willem Hendrik, 207
Ross, Denman Waldo, 166
Rothberg, Michael, 117–18
Rothschild, Salomon de, 227
Royal Ontario Museum, 108, 110
Rushdie, Salman, 244
Russell, William Howard, 226–27
Ruzzoli, Paolo, 298, 299

Sabar, Shalom, 4, 71, 72
Sabbath laws, regarding using and fixing broken things, 82
Sala-Manca Artists Group, 17–18, 42n23, 44n46
Salomons, Philip, 179, 193nn71–72
salvage store(s): museums as modern-day, 237–39; owned by A. I. Berman, 233–37; versus "scrap" or industrial recycling shops, 267n36; and waste reduction, 246–47
Sandburg, Carl, 248, 267n39
sandek, 71–72
Saposnik, Irv, 258
Sargent, John Singer, 167, 293
Sarna, Jonathan, 173
Sassoon, Isaac, 182
"Scenes from the Collection" exhibition, 278–79
Schepps, A. I., 256
Schor, Ilya, 204, 208
Schuessler, Jennifer, 113n24
Schusterman, Charles, 171–72
Schusterman, Lynn, 163, 171–72, 292
Schwab, Mrs. Noah, 78
Schwartz, Esther, 222–23
Schwartz, Samuel, 222
scrap recycling, 246–47. *See also* "Recycled, Re-Seen: Folk Art from the Global Scrap Heap" exhibition; salvage store(s)

S. D. Myres Saddle Company, 236
seated prayer, 75
Seat of Moses, 85n17
secondhand stores. *See* salvage store(s)
Seroussi, Edwin, 49
700 Benches initiative, 69
Seweryn, Tadeusz, 137
Seweryn Udziela Ethnographic Museum (MEK), 122, 134–41, 143–44, 151n60, 151n62, 151–52n64, 153n72, 153n74, 153n76, 280
Shabbat candlesticks, 302
Shabbat cloth, 182
Shackelford, George, 168
Shahn, Ben, 183
Shammai, 52
Shandler, Jeffrey, 4
Sherman, William Tecumseh, 220
shiva benches, 73–74
shofar, 58–59, 166
Sign upon Your Hand, A (Paley), 183
silver, 220
silver bowls, 219–27
Simone, AbdouMaliq, 84n10
Six Day War (1967), 43n33
skansen, 125, 149n32
Small, Zachary, 114n39
Snyder, James, 33
social class, and synagogue seating, 77, 87n43
Society for the Protection of Nature in Israel, 38
"Sound Objects" exhibition, 57, 60–61
sound study: methodological entryways for, of synagogue, 50–54; music in context of synagogue's soundscape, 57–61
Southern Jewish objects, 219–27
Spertus, Maurice, 287–89
spice towers, 173, 174
Spigel, Chad S., 84n12
spolia, 21
Srulovitch, Sari, 208
Stallybrass, Peter, 101
Star, Susan Leigh, 67
State Ethnographic Museum, 279–80
Stewart, Susan, 11n17
stories, told by objects, 242–47
sugar bowl, 219–24, 226

sukkah: Bedouin hut reconstructed as, 24, 25–26; connection between Bedouin home and, 41n4; as refugee home, 17–19. See also *Eternal Sukkah, The*
Suleiman, Abu (Mohammed al-Korshan), 19–20, 22, 23, 24, 30, 33, 34, 35
Suriname, 79–81, 88n54
SVARA, 69
synagogue(s): ceiling of, at POLIN Museum, 281; Chairs of Elijah in, 85n19; in Cuba, 292–93; freestanding stone chairs in ancient, 85n17; as intersection of music and material culture, 49–50; Jewish identity and architecture of, 86n28; methodological entryways for sound study of, 50–54; music in context of soundscape of, 57–61; occupation of space in, 67; orientation of prayer, 87n39; pews in, 74–79, 87n43, 87–88nn45–46, 88n51; reconstructed, in Israel Museum, 79–81; seating capacity of, 84n12; Tzedek v'Shalom Synagogue, 79–81
Synagogue Hall, 280–81
synagogue models, 280–81
synagogue songs, 52–54

taharot, 304
Talmud, and benches in infrastructure of Jewish education, 68
Talmudist, The (Binder), 167
Tamari, Salim, 43n24
Temple Beth-El, 78
Temple Emanu-El, 77–78, 79, 88n51
Ten Commandments Flanked by Lions, 184
"Terribly Close: Polish Vernacular Artists Face the Holocaust" exhibition, 151n62
Texas: deportation of Jews from, 255–56; "Forgotten Gateway: Coming to America Through Galveston Island," 252–58; Galveston Movement, 252–53, 254, 255, 256; "It Ain't Braggin' If It's True" exhibition, 248–51, 268n43; "It Still Ain't Braggin' If It's True" exhibition, 268n43. *See also* salvage store(s)
Theatre of Memory, 107
third spaces, Jewish, 240–42, 257, 263

Threadgill, Linda, 184
Tobe Pascher Workshop, 200, 201, 203, 204, 213n5
Tokarska-Bakir, Joanna, 148n27
Torah, sounds of, 60–61
Torah binder, 184, 186n17
Torah crown, 210, *211*
Torah finial(s): acquired by MFA, 170–71, 172, 177–80, *180*, *181*, 192n68, 193nn73–74; acquired by NCMA, 206, *207*; in Max Berry's collection, 298, *299*
Torah shield(s), 177, *178*, 180, 182, 192n64, 193n76
Torah staves (*atzei chaim*), 287–89
Trabo, Netanel, 287
"Treasures of Heaven" exhibition, 105–6
Tree of Life synagogue, 209
Triumph of Religion murals (Sargent), 167
tsara'at, 27, 43n25
Tsror, Rino, 35
Twelfth Baptist Church (Boston), 76
Tzahal, Galey, 35
tzedakah boxes, 292–93, *295*
Tzedek v'Shalom Synagogue, 79–81
Tzoref, Elimelekh, 177, 178, 192n64

Udziela, Seweryn, 143
ugliness, 249
Ujma, Magdalena, 143–44
University of Waterloo, 95. See also *Evidence Room, The*

van Alphen, Ernst, 109, 113n35
van Pelt, Robert Jan, 95, 107. See also *Evidence Room, The*
Venice, 103, 106–7
vernacular religion, 2–3
Vilna Shul, 76
Völkerkunde, 142

Walters Art Museum, 190n45
Wambel, Guglielmo, 107
wandering Jewish musical objects, 54
wandering melodies, 52–54
"Wandering Objects: Collecting and Interpreting Jewish Things" symposium, 6, 11–12nn18–19

Wasilewska-Prędki, Kamila, 153n72
waste, prohibition against, 246–47
wedding ring(s), 1, 2, 5, 174
Weitzman, Jane Gershon, 291–95, 302–3, 305
West Bank, division of, 41n9
Westerman, William, 263
Weszkalnys, Gisa, 89n65
"We the People" exhibition, 32–33, 40
Williams, William, 255
Wilson, Woodrow, 235, 236–37, 265n6

Woleńska, Maria, 147n19
Wolpert, Ludwig Y., 184, 204, 213n5

Yaacovi, Haim, 27
Yates, Dame Frances, 107
Yemini, Yehia, 174

Zabari, Moshe, 184, 204, 213n5
Zafran, Eric, 184
Zarrow, Sarah, 150n46
Zilber, Emily, 171
Zucker, Benjamin, 190n45, 305–6

Printed and bound by CPI Group (UK) Ltd, Croydon, CR0 4YY
22/04/2026